Negative Ecstasies

John D. Caputo, *series editor*

PERSPECTIVES IN
CONTINENTAL
PHILOSOPHY

Edited by JEREMY BILES
and KENT L. BRINTNALL

Negative Ecstasies

Georges Bataille and the Study of Religion

FORDHAM UNIVERSITY PRESS
New York ■ 2015

Fordham University Press has no responsibility for the persistence or accuracy of URLs
for external or third-party Internet websites referred to in this publication and does not
guarantee that any content on such websites is, or will remain, accurate or appropriate.

Fordham University Press also publishes its books in a variety of electronic formats. Some
content that appears in print may not be available in electronic books.

Visit us online at www.fordhampress.com.

Library of Congress Cataloging-in-Publication Data

Negative ecstasies : Georges Bataille and the study of religion / edited by Jeremy Biles and
Kent L. Brintnall.
        pages cm. — (Perspectives in Continental philosophy)
    Includes bibliographical references and index.
    ISBN 978-0-8232-6519-0 (cloth : alk. paper) — ISBN 978-0-8232-6520-6
(pbk. : alk. paper)
    1. Bataille, Georges, 1897–1962.   2. Religion.   3. Religions.   I. Biles, Jeremy,
editor.
    B2430.B33954N44 2015
    200.92—dc23
                                                                        2014047800

Printed in the United States of America

17 16 15   5 4 3 2 1

First edition

For Helen Tartar,
1951–2014,
who gifted us exuberantly with so many glorious words

Contents

Acknowledgments   *xi*

Introduction: Sacred with a Vengeance   *1*
    Jeremy Biles and Kent L. Brintnall

Movements of Luxurious Exuberance: Georges Bataille
and Fat Politics   *19*
    Lynne Gerber

Sovereignty and Cruelty: Self-Affirmation, Self-Dissolution,
and the Bataillean Subject   *38*
    Stephen S. Bush

Erotic Ruination: Embracing the "Savage Spirituality"
of Barebacking   *51*
    Kent L. Brintnall

Desire, Blood, and Power: Georges Bataille and the Study
of Hindu Tantra in Northeastern India   *68*
    Hugh B. Urban

The Religion of Football: Sacrifice, Festival, and Sovereignty
at the 2010 FIFA World Cup in South Africa   *81*
    David Chidester

Violent Silence: Noise and Bataille's "Method of Meditation"   *95*
    Paul Hegarty

Georges Bataille and the Religion of Capitalism   *106*
Jean-Joseph Goux

Sacrifice as Ethics: The Strange Religiosity of Neoliberalism   *123*
Shannon Winnubst

**Bataille's Contestation of Interpretive Anthropology
and the Sociology of Religion**   *138*
Alphonso Lingis

**The Traumatic Secret: Bataille and the Comparative
Erotics of Mystical Literature**   *153*
Jeffrey J. Kripal

Foucault's Sacred Sociology   *169*
Mark D. Jordan

Bataille and Kristeva on Religion   *182*
Zeynep Direk

Bataille, Teilhard de Chardin, and the Death of God   *202*
Allan Stoekl

Does the Acéphale Dream of Headless Sheep?   *217*
Jeremy Biles

Afterword   *239*
Amy Hollywood

Notes   *245*

Works Cited   *285*

List of Contributors   *303*

Index   *307*

Acknowledgments

Negative Ecstasies had its genesis over a breakfast at an annual meeting of the American Academy of Religion, more years ago than the editors are comfortable remembering or admitting. We were strangers then, and the risk we took in working together produced not only this collection of essays but, as important, camaraderie and friendship. One of the losses of this project's coming to fruition will be fewer excuses for laughter-filled phone conversations, for e-mail exchanges littered with movie and novel recommendations. For many reasons, production of this volume has been a source of much joy.

We are exceptionally grateful that our contributors decided to take this risk with us. The quality of their work speaks for itself, but we want to speak to their patience in sticking it out across many fits, starts, and delays. We are particularly pleased that so many established scholars—many known for their work on Bataille—have contributed, but we are also pleased we could provide a forum for emerging voices.

We express thanks to the University of California Press for permission to reprint David Chidester's essay from *Wild Religion: Tracking the Sacred in South Africa* (2012) and to Stanford University Press for permission to reprint those portions of Mark Jordan's essay that appear in *Convulsing Bodies: Religion and Resistance in Foucault* (2014). We also thank the André Masson estate and the Artists Rights Society for permissions to reprint images that adorn the cover and interior of this book.

After deciding upon the title for the present volume, the editors were reminded that a similar phrase—"negative ecstasy"—appears in Jean Baudrillard's essay "The Ecstasy of Communication." In light of Baudrillard's engagements with Bataille, this echo is not surprising, but neither is it intentional, nor should it signal any particular connection to Baudrillard.

It has been both easy and a pleasure—or, perhaps, it has been a pleasure because it has been so easy—to work with Fordham University Press. Much of the credit for this goes to Tom Lay and Eric Newman. We thank John Caputo for making a home for *Negative Ecstasies* in his Perspectives on Continental Philosophy series.

When we initially submitted the manuscript to Fordham, we entrusted it to the capable hands of the inimitable Helen Tartar, who shepherded it through the review and approval process. During the production phase, Helen died in a car accident. Her death was a shock to everyone connected with this volume and a huge loss to the world of academic publishing generally. It is to her memory that we dedicate this volume.

Negative Ecstasies

Introduction
Sacred with a Vengeance

JEREMY BILES AND KENT L. BRINTNALL

Only negative experience is worthy of our attention.

—**Georges Bataille**

A Ferociously Religious Biography

Negative Ecstasies. The title of this volume is excessive, pleonastic—for according to Georges Bataille (1897–1962), *all* genuine ecstasy is necessarily, and violently, negative. Bataille characterizes ecstasy as a laceration of the ego, a rupture that for a time dissolves the self-contained character of the individual as she exists in her everyday life. It is in the varieties of ecstatic experience—erotic fulminations, poetic effervescence, wrenching laughter, wracking sobs, and other excessive moments—that the self as defined and conditioned by the structures and strictures, the prohibitions and taboos, of profane, workaday life, is lost. Bataille's writings are dramatic evidence of his relentless pursuit of the self-dissolving negative experience of ecstasy. They repeatedly reveal the sacrificial violence, the profound negativity, that haunts the always excessive moments that he deemed sacred. The essays collected here treat, in sundry ways, the category of the sacred as conceived by Bataille. They pay heed to Bataille's own focus on the "negative" heart of religion. And they take seriously Bataille as a profoundly religious thinker—a figure possessed by religion in both his writings and his life.

To be sure, Bataille's life, like his writings, evidenced the work of the negative. Though Bataille remains best known to most American readers as the author of a classic of pornographic fiction, *Story of the Eye*, throughout his life he was interested, indeed obsessed, with the many manifestations of the "radical, subversive negativity which he called the sacred."[1] Bataille was born in 1897, in Billom, France, to a blind, partially paralyzed, and syphilitic father, Josephe-Aristide, and a debauched mother, Marie-Antoinette Tournadre.[2] Though raised "with no religious instruction," Georges Bataille became interested in Catholicism as a child and converted in 1914.[3] When threat of bombardment from the German forces compelled him and his mother to flee Billom, they left behind the blind Joseph-Aristide, who had by this time "gone mad."[4] During a brief stint in the service, Bataille's piety intensified. Upon discharge, he "consider[ed] becoming a priest, or rather a monk," but after residing for a time with Benedictine monks at Quarr Abbey, he enrolled in the School of Paleography and Library Science in 1918. Then, in 1920, Bataille abruptly lost his faith; his Catholicism had "caused a woman he . . . loved to shed tears."[5]

This loss of faith did not, however, entail a loss of a sense of the sacred. On the contrary, Bataille's idiosyncratic religious sensibilities, defined by experiences of explosive affective ambivalence—horror and bliss, anguish and delight—intensified through a range of encounters that underscored the connections between violence, death, and excess—all keyed to negativity—that Bataille saw at the heart of the sacred. In the early 1920s, he developed an "enthusiasm" for bullfights, witnessing the death of the famed matador Granero, whose eye was enucleated by a bull's horn—an event that for Bataille amounted to a spectacular and horrific sacrificial ritual.[6] In 1923, Bataille read Nietzsche, an event he described as "decisive."[7] The reading was not strictly philosophical; it exceeded philosophy in its Dionysian explosion of the Hegelian dialectic, an explosion instigating a wounding religious experience, a *sparagmos* of the self. In Nietzsche, Bataille had found a weapon for destroying Hegel's idealist philosophy and its aspirations to synthetic resolution. Transvaluing the Hegelian concept of negativity, Bataille characterized his own life as an "open wound"[8] of "unemployed negativity" with no specific aim or point of future resolution. Bataille would go on to develop a quasi-mystical identification with the "mad" Nietzsche, "repeating" his ecstatic vision of the eternal return near the pyramidal rock at Surlei.[9] Nietzsche's proclamation of the death of God, far from diminishing Bataille's religious intensity, became a point of meditation stimulating his "negative inner experience."[10]

It was also in the 1920s that Bataille began his lifelong engagement with surrealism, which he admired for its spirit of rebellion and its investigation of the powers of the unconscious, even as he remained outside the "official" surrealist circle centering on André Breton, whom Bataille accused of an impotent poetic idealism animated by a Hegelian "spirit of 'synthesis.'"[11] But like the surrealists, Bataille displayed a deep interest in psycho-analysis. In the mid-1920s, as an aspiring writer suffering from paralyzing inhibitions, Bataille entered into treatment under the heterodox analyst Dr. Adrien Borel. It was Dr. Borel, by all accounts a most affable individual, who gifted Bataille with the now iconic photos of a Chinese man undergoing the *lingchi* method of torture and execution, in which flesh, organs, and limbs are slowly sliced from the still-living victim until he succumbs—"death by a thousand cuts." Bataille meditated upon this "insane" and "shocking" image of "pain, at once ecstatic(?) and intolerable," with the fervency of a monk contemplating the crucified body of Christ. The meditation elicited an ambivalent spiritual convulsion whose reverberations carried into Bataille's final days. And like the Christian mystics with whose spiritual literature he was so well versed, Bataille found in his meditation a path to a sinister rapture and a dark insight. He closes his last book, *The Tears of Eros*, with a commentary on the photo: "What I suddenly saw was the identity of these perfect contraries, divine ecstasy and its opposite, extreme horror."[12] Bataille's highly unusual, indeed harrowing, course of analysis was "decisive"—liberating in its "brutal efficacity,"[13] putting "an end to the series of dreary mishaps and failures in which [he] had been floundering, but not to the state of [his] intellectual intensity," which remained undiminished.[14]

Bataille's peculiar psychological dispositions helped shape the influential journal *Documents*. In 1929, Bataille took over editorship of the journal, publishing, along with his own work, articles by a number of ex-surrealists, many condemned by Breton in his *Second Manifesto of Surrealism*;[15] Michel Leiris, André Masson, Jacques-André Boiffard, Jacques Prévert, Raymond Queneau, and Roger Vitrac were among the contributors. Conceived as a "war machine against received ideas,"[16] *Documents* became a venue for Bataille to rage against Breton's idealist brand of surrealism, publishing articles exemplifying Bataille's interest in things lowly, abject, and monstrous—so many aspects of what he called "base materialism": the erotic aspect of the big toe, the horror of the eye, the absurd appearance of crustaceans, the pretenses of architecture, the ridiculousness of the human face, the sacrilegious nature of spittle.[17] In such articles one finds a Nietzschean will to destruction coupled with a psychoanalytically informed interest in the symbolics of excretion, together forming the basis of an aggressive counter-surrealism indicative of Bataille's evolving conception of the sacred as tied to transgressive heterogeneity: "The notion of the (heterogeneous) *foreign body* permits one to note the elementary *subjective* identity between types of excrement . . . and everything that can be seen as sacred, divine, or marvelous."[18]

Nietzsche, surrealism, psychoanalysis: this triad of "decisive" encounters forms a background for Bataille's investigations of the limits of human experience, or what he will variously call ecstasy, inner experience, and the impossible—so many aspects of the negative, the loss of self that he took to be crucial. But however personal, solitary, and idiosyncratic his experiences, Bataille remained resolutely turned *outward*, toward others, toward the other. His obsession with the sacred was inseparable from his desire for *intimacy*, for a mode of *communication* that demanded the wounding of self-enclosed individuals. "'Communication' cannot proceed from one full and intact individual to another," writes Bataille. "It requires individuals whose separate existence in themselves is *risked*, placed at the limit of death and nothingness."[19]

This longing for a wounding intimacy, a negative ecstasy, impelled Bataille, in 1936, to convene a secret society known as Acéphale ("headless"), which "would pursue goals that would be solely religious (but anti-Christian, essentially Nietzschean)."[20] Carrying out its secret sacrificial rituals in the dead of night by a lightning-blasted tree, this "FEROCIOUSLY RELIGIOUS" group sought to reactivate a primitive, chthonic form of the sacred through a "rapturous escape from the self."[21] Five issues of a journal sharing the secret society's name were published under the editorship of Bataille, Pierre Klossowski, and Georges Ambrosino. In their pages, Bataille and his fellow contributors presented articles on sacrifice, Heraclitus, the Dionysian mysteries, monstrosity, and, above all, Nietzsche—the *insane* Nietzsche, whose madness was interpreted as a sacrifice and whose furious spirit was the journal's main inspiration. André Masson, one of the cadre of "dissident" surrealists in Bataille's orbit, executed the images of the Acéphale—a monstrous "Nietzsche-Dionysus," a headless, self-mutilated god emblematizing the will to sacrificial ecstasy that defined the group—that appeared throughout the journal's pages.

Although both the journal and the community of thinkers who converged in the name of the Acéphale soon disbanded, Bataille had meanwhile established, with Roger Caillois and Michel Leiris, the Collège de Sociologie, a group of intellectuals, convening from 1937 to 1939, dedicated to investigating the role of the sacred in modern life. The Collège derived its basic principles from Émile Durkheim, adapting his sociological studies toward its own particular goals. Following Durkheim, the collegians saw the sacred both as radically opposed to the profane or everyday as well as acutely ambivalent, internally divided between pure and impure, beneficent and dangerous, right and left aspects. A sinister counterpart to the mainline French sociological school, the Collège took the sacred to be a dangerous but preeminently social phenomenon—in Bataille's words, a "privileged moment of communal unity, a moment of the convulsive communication of what is ordinarily stifled," especially unconscious forces, transgressive erotic desires, and excessive affects.[22] It is thus the communal, social nature of even the most solitary and private moments that interested the group. Through critical engagement with Nietzsche, Sade, and Freud, as well as investigations of Christian brotherhoods, secret societies, shamanism, festival, and the like, Bataille and his cohort sought not only to understand but also, one might surmise, to *activate* the sacred, particularly its subversive, left-handed aspects in their full negativity.[23]

For Bataille, the Collège's pursuits, though dedicated to scrupulous analysis of these forms of the sacred, were not exercises in academic abstraction. Rather, the Collège was, at least in part, a politically motivated community of intellectuals interested in discerning the workings of fascism and also *countering* fascism through a deployment of the forces of the sinister side of the sacred. To be sure, Bataille's politics were inseparable from his religious sensibilities.[24] His involvement with the Democratic Communist Circle in the early 1930s and his initiation, in 1935, of Counter-Attack, a political group gathering "former members of the Communist Circle and, following a definite reconciliation with André Breton, the whole of the surrealist group,"[25] already announced a strong resonance in Bataille's thought and life between certain leftist political commitments and the left sacred. With his "headless" secret society, Bataille pursued a religious antipolitics, a principled refusal of conventional political activism through the attempted creation of community convening around the Acéphalic myth.[26] For Bataille, the political exigencies corresponding to the rise of fascism, the affiliation of the surrealists with the Communist Party, and his intensifying interest in the psychological and sociological dimensions of group movements were all so many indications of the eminently collective dimensions of the sacred.

Thus, with the onset of war in 1939, Bataille's sudden turn to near-total reclusiveness may be surprising. But disillusioned with the prospects of political engagement and "torn apart" by the death of his lover, Laure (Colette Peignot), Bataille withdrew from the political scene and undertook a mystical counterpolitics carried out in solitude.[27] He had begun practicing a heterodoxical form of yoga "in considerable chaos and in a state of mental turmoil pushed to the extreme."[28] In solitude, but with an unrelinquished desire for "communication," Bataille underwent a violent mystical experience, pursuing a method of meditation geared toward self-rupture and culminating in an ecstatic, impossible, and "totally negative" experience.[29] He recounts—in fragments, aphorisms, and highly personal, diaristic writing—the vicissitudes of this mystical itinerary in his book

Inner Experience. During this time, he also composed the wartime journal that would appear under the title *Guilty.* A third book from this period, *On Nietzsche,* is a dense meshwork of quotes from the German visionary with commentary by Bataille. The commentary is not, as noted above, precisely of a philosophical nature—though Bataille does philosophize—but rather an exacerbated rewriting of Nietzsche in an attempt to identify with him and his experience. These three books are together comprised under the rubric *La somme athéologique.*[30] A parody of the integral architecture of Thomas Aquinas's *Summa,* Bataille's atheological triumvirate—with cries of laughter and tears, agony and ecstasy, erupting from the wound created by the death of God—is fragmentary, sporadic, and incomplete, fraught with emotional excruciations. In his attempts to write of *experience* at the limits, Bataille tortures and contorts language and writerly forms, seeking to communicate his mystical agnosia, an apophatic aporia that he called "the impossible." These books are anti- or transgeneric, monstrously hybrid, at once or by turns spiritual handbook, autobiography, dream journal, fiction, fantasy, and quasi-philosophical exposition.

Subsequent to this emotionally turbulent outpouring, following the war, Bataille's writing turned more systematic but no less intensely oriented toward investigation of negative ecstatic experience. Bataille's three-volume treatise on economics, *The Accursed Share,* elaborates a theory of a "general economy" that takes excess and expenditure, rather than lack and the need for accumulation, as its starting point. Bataille links the solar "superabundance of energy on the surface of the globe" to the need for sacrifice, which, under various guises, eliminates the dangerous energetic surplus that threatens to annihilate those who hoard it.[31] *Erotism* is a distinctive account of the sacrificial dimensions of physical and religious eroticism, linking eroticism to an experience "at the level of death"[32] that "jerks us out of a tenacious obsession with the lastingness of our discontinuous," individual being.[33] And in *Lascaux* and *Tears of Eros,* Bataille links the history and practice of art to the history and practice of religious sacrifice and erotic bliss. Whether through economics, erotics, or aesthetics, Bataille seeks to overcome concern with the lastingness of the individual self through negative operations—sacrifice, orgiastic festivals, art, and the like. Generosity, expenditure, waste, and sacrifice are imperative.

It is, ultimately, sacrifice as a means of contact with, or activation of, the sacred that Bataille sees as the central question of his work and indeed of human existence. And it is in sacrifice, in whatever form—mysticism, eroticism, art, poetry, gambling, and other "deficit operations"—that Bataille finds a key to the "sovereign" existence he pursued in his life and writings, an "existence free of all limitations of interest."[34] According to Bataille (who again extends and modifies Durkheim), the profane world is the sphere of useful activity, goal-oriented thought, instrumental reason, and concern for the discontinuous, individual self. It is the workaday world of utility, lasting order, and the accumulation of goods against the threat of death. The sacred, in stark opposition, includes those moods, moments, and operations that undo, always and only for a fleeting time, the usefulness of mere things, the pretenses to accomplishment, the claims of our future-oriented projects, the limits of mere reason. Sacrifice is a transgression of those prohibitions that constrict and restrict human experience, soldering the individual into a hermetic shell of self-protection defined by pecuniary interest, individual concern, and fear of death.

The profane world, the world of discontinuity, can never be definitively erased; Bataille knew this all too well. Yet what he desired to the very end of his life was "to bring into a world founded on discontinuity all the continuity such a world can sustain."[35] Continuity, intimacy, sovereignty: these demand the ceaseless counteroperation of negativity, the risk of transgression, the relentless unworking of the work of instrumental reason.[36] Sovereignty is thus achieved by turning the tools of reason and project against themselves.[37] "The issue," Bataille writes, "is not that of attainment of a goal, but rather of escape from those traps which goals represent."[38] Ecstasy is the "negative miracle" of self-annihilation, the quintessence of the sacred—with a vengeance.[39]

The Return of Religion: Toward a General Economy of Religious Studies

> The world of understanding is to religion as the clarity of day is to the horror of the night.
>
> Georges Bataille

Given the religious biography sketched above as well as Bataille's lifelong engagement with the sacred in its sundry forms, it is perplexing that Bataille has received so little attention in the field of religious studies (and indeed is often regarded as antireligious), even as his astonishingly multifarious writings have afforded him posthumous recognition across a variety of other disciplines. A precursor to poststructuralist thought who broke the "French path to postmodernity,"[40] Bataille has exercised influence in art criticism, critical and literary theory, philosophy, psychoanalysis, sociology, and anthropology.[41] Many of the twentieth century's leading intellectuals—Michel Foucault, Roland Barthes, Jacques Derrida, and Julia Kristeva, among others—cite Bataille as a major figure in the development of their own thought.[42]

Bataille's impact in the areas of art criticism and theory has been significant, but probably nowhere more so than in the critique of modernism and the rereading of surrealism over the past three decades. Theorists affiliated with the avant-garde art journal *October* have long championed Bataille, taking up his work to elaborate a sinister counterpart to André Breton's sunnier brand of surrealism. In this connection, Bataille's minuscule essay "*Informe*" ("Formless") has exercised a wildly disproportionate influence. In this six-sentence article, Bataille provocatively claims that "a dictionary begins when it no longer gives the meaning of words, but their tasks. Thus *formless* is not only an adjective having a given meaning, but a term that serves to bring things down in the world, generally requiring that each thing have its form."[43] Prominent critics and theorists including Rosalind Krauss, Yve-Alain Bois, Denis Hollier, and Hal Foster have found in this formulation an incitement for developing provocative readings of surrealist and other modern and contemporary art in the registers of lowness, baseness, horizontality, and the death drive.[44] In the present volume, Paul Hegarty extends this conversation to the province of aural art forms—namely, the formal experiment of noise music. Exploring Bataille's longstanding fascination with silence—as well as his understanding of the paradox of writing about silence—Hegarty thinks about the ways that noise, when assembled in certain ways, functions like silence by way of contrast to what is commonly understood as music, just as silence pierces and hinders discursive speech. In this way, noise music fosters access to the sacred. Moving beyond the realm of aesthetic artifacts, Jeremy Biles's contribution to this collection extends his prior elaboration of Bataille's engagement with surrealism by examining the place of dreams and dream interpretation in Bataille's writings. Examining Bataille's references to dreams, Biles's essay not only furthers understanding of Bataille's relationship to Breton but provides a rich picture of Bataille's engagement with Freud.[45]

Many prominent thinkers have embraced Bataille as a poststructuralist avant la lettre as well as a critic of the self-contained, autonomous subject. In the pages of the avant-garde literary journal *Tel Quel*, whose ethos was strongly shaped by Bataille's writings, Foucault, Kristeva, and others take up Bataille in forwarding their critiques of the modern subject.[46] But Bataille's influence extended well beyond this venue. For example, in a special issue of *Critique* dedicated to Bataille, Foucault published his famous essay "A Preface to Transgression," in which he cites Bataille's formulation of transgression as crucial to the explosion of dialectical language and, with it, self-contained subjectivity. In her influential book *Powers of Horror*, Kristeva turns to Bataille in conceptualizing abjection and the limits of subjectivity within a broadly psychoanalytic framework. While Foucault and Kristeva name and demonstrate their indebtedness to Bataille, very little work has traced their specific engagements with and reliances on Bataille. Zeynep Direk's and Mark Jordan's contributions to this volume begin to address this gap. Starting with the most obvious connections between Bataille and Kristeva related to the latter's examination of the abject, Direk expands her gaze to consider Kristeva's later work and explain how it represents a critical distancing from an earlier investment in Bataille's ideas. Jordan's consideration of Foucault's romance with Bataille not only sheds light on Foucault's "Preface"; it also finesses both Foucault's and Bataille's understanding of the "death of God" and its significance. Jordan uses his examination of Foucault's relation to Bataille to sketch a clearer picture of Foucault's relation to Christianity and theology more generally. In his contribution to this volume, Allan Stoekl also nuances and clarifies what the "death of God" means for Bataille. Stoekl complicates Bataille's relation to Catholicism and Catholic theology by showing points of contact between his notion of expenditure and Teilhard de Chardin's cosmology. Stoekl's unexpected comparison shows there are virtually innumerable examples that could be adduced to support the notion that Bataille is perhaps *the* thinker for instigating the overcoming of the "autonomous subject of modernity."[47]

This postmodern interrogation of subjectivity has been advanced on multiple fronts and by many thinkers. One of the most prominent has been Jacques Derrida, whose reading of Bataille in his essay "From Restricted to General Economy: A Hegelianism Without Reserve" shaped the reception of Bataille in literary theory and philosophy, where Bataille has been seen as a forerunner of deconstruction and a pathbreaking exemplar of an antidialectical mode of philosophy. But Derrida is not, of course, alone among philosophers who have found in Bataille a way to exceed (Hegelian) dialectics. As noted above, Foucault embraces and elaborates Bataille's concept of transgression. Jean-Luc Nancy takes Bataille as the starting point for his innovative account of "the inoperative community," and Giorgio Agamben turns to Bataille in formulating his well-known concept of *homo sacer*, "sacred man." Bataille is also a prominent, if mostly implicit, presence in Gilles Deleuze and Félix Guattari's lucidly delirious exposition of schizoanalysis and their critique of capitalism in *Anti-Oedipus* and *A Thousand Plateaus*. And, by way of Deleuze and Guattari, Bataille makes an appearance—textually and thematically—in Guy Hocquenghem's *Homosexual Desire*, a queer theory treatise avant la lettre.

Although not relying on Deleuze and Guattari, Jean-Joseph Goux's essay for this collection turns to Bataille to examine the ways that capitalism and its model of consumption function as a religion, posing as an access point to the sacred, in our historical moment. At the same time, Goux challenges Bataille's understanding of the connections between religion and economy by turning to what Bataille missed by overlooking the role of Catholicism in the relevant historical transformations. Moving beyond capitalism and the narrow frame of economics in the classic sense, Shannon Winnubst's contribution to this volume shows the relevance of Bataille's work for thinking about neoliberalism's construction of the consumptive, utilitarian, instrumental subject. Developing the analysis found in her book *Queering Freedom*, Winnubst demonstrates the ongoing relevance of Bataille's work to contemporary historical, cultural, political, and economic conditions, gesturing toward the way his conception of sacrificial expenditure highlights possibilities for interrupting and subverting neoliberal logics. As part of this exploration, Winnubst sketches an account of the difference between Bataille's and Lacan's understandings of desire. Fully consistent with Winnubst's proposed intervention, Alphonso Lingis's recent writings in books like *Dangerous Emotions* might be seen in part as Bataillean meditations on eroticism, expenditure, intimacy, and carnal encounters. In the present collection, Lingis examines how Bataille engages major themes from the anthropology and sociology of religion, offering alternative understandings and interpretations of topics and texts familiar to those engaged with the academic study of religion.[48] Like Winnubst, Allan Stoekl develops themes from his recent publication, *Bataille's Peak*, in his essay for this volume. Turning to virtual reality as a site where the self can be lost, spent, and sundered, Stoekl develops his insights about the ethical possibilities of ecstatic self-loss and demonstrates Bataille's continuing relevance for interpreting the conditions of life in this new millennium. And in placing Bataille into conversation with Leo Bersani and Tim Dean, Kent Brintnall's contribution to this collection furthers the slowly developing conversation between Bataille and queer theory, which, necessarily, must become a conversation between queer theory and the study of religion.[49]

Notwithstanding his strong and in many cases crucial influence on major philosophical thinkers, Bataille nonetheless represents the less traveled of two paths in (post)modern continental philosophy, each claiming the "impossible heritage of Nietzsche" and the death of God. The dominant path runs through Heidegger. As Jürgen Habermas demonstrates, however, Bataille "gave the philosophical discourse of modernity a direction similar to Heidegger's; but for his departure from modernity he chose a completely different path."[50] Both Heidegger and Bataille seek to "break out of the prison of modernity, out of an Occidental rationalism that has been victorious on the scale of world history. Both want to overcome subjectivism, which covers the world with its reifying violence and lets it harden into a totality of technically manipulable and economically realizable goods."[51] Both wage a "relentless attack on the pre-eminence of the philosophical subject."[52] But it has been Heidegger's critique of "reason at the foundations of *cognitive* rationalization or at the *ontological* presuppositions of objectifying science and technology"[53] that has predominated the "postmodern overcoming of metaphysics or onto-theo-logy."[54]

The philosophical theologian Jean-Luc Marion exemplifies this point concerning Heidegger's predominance. Deconstructing ontotheology and metaphysics in thinking a "God without being," Marion engages the phenomenological tradition via Heidegger in his well-known treatments of eroticism, sacrifice, the gift, excess, ecstasy, and the impossible. Though contemporary debates around these ideas have Bataille at their roots, he goes virtually unacknowledged in Marion's writings. Other thinkers in the postmodern "turn to religion" also eschew Bataille. John Caputo, a disciple of Derrida and "one of the leading readers of continental philosophy's turn to religion,"[55] cites Heidegger and the legacy of "death of God" theology— particularly through the writings of Thomas J. J. Altizer—as key confrontations. But curiously, neither Caputo nor Gianni Vattimo—another important theorist of post-death-of-God religion—attend to Bataille, despite the profound implications Bataille's singular writings hold for readings of Nietzsche, the absence of God, mysticism, negative theology, the impossible, and other major concerns such thinkers incessantly engage.[56] As noted above, Jordan's and Stoekl's essays in this volume offer extended, nuanced accounts of Bataille's understanding of the "death of God." Their contributions serve as a corrective to the neglect of Bataille in other quarters. Similarly, by staging a conversation among Bataille, Bersani, and Dean, Brintnall's essay introduces Bataille to a stream of intellectual inquiry where his absence is notable and puzzling.

When Caputo and Vattimo ask, "How do we get from the post-Christian, post-Holocaust, and largely secular death of God theologies of the 1960s to the postmodern return of religion?" the responses offered extend Heideggerian thought through Derrida's deconstruction of ontotheology and articulation of messianic desire, but Bataille again goes unmentioned.[57] This absence is surprising on at least two counts. First, when addressing the historical events that shaped the theologies Caputo and Vattimo have in mind, Bataille turns to the sacred, thus presaging the "return" that Caputo and Vattimo seek to explain. As Amy Hollywood persuasively argues in *Sensible Ecstasy*, Bataille's writings during and after the war sought to practice a sacrificial form of writing and an antisacrificial form of witnessing that could substantially respond to the historical traumas of World War II without repeating the instrumental violences that were their cause. Similarly, Michèle Richman's *Sacred Revolutions* shows how the Collège de Sociologie sought to revivify the sacred as a means of combating fascism. Richman suggests that more recent political fulgurations, like the events of May '68, can be understood as distant cousins of this experiment. Finally, as Alexander Irwin carefully explains in *Saints of the Impossible*, Bataille's practices of ecstatic self-loss were pursued and presented as an alternative to the cataclysmic violence constituting his historical moment. For Bataille, the traumatic violence that followed and comprised the death of God demanded that the sacred be conjured in some Godless form.

Second, and as important, Bataille's intellectual commitments are remarkably similar to those articulated by Caputo and Vattimo. As Jeffrey Kosky has written, Caputo's postmodern "religion without religion" is, like Bataille's, "impassioned by the impossible, by the impossible experience toward which sovereign moments of ecstasy and rapture gesture."[58] Kosky's commentary on the situation is worth citing at length. Even more than Marion, Levinas, and Derrida, Kosky argues,

> Bataille was willing to abandon the name "God" and the identity of the tradition left behind by the ecstasy of inner experience, sovereign moments, and nonknowledge. Bataille's overcoming of the modern (metaphysical) subject involves an interpretation of human experience in the wake of modernity as an experience of the death of God and demise of religious tradition—a death of God that opens the religious experience of the sacred. Caputo and the recent turn to religion, by contrast, interpret the postmodern, postmetaphysical horizon in terms of the desire for God, a God who continues with the eschatological God of the Judeo-Christian tradition. And yet, Bataille's "hermeneutic of the death of God" is just as surely impassioned by the impossible as is Caputo's "hermeneutic of the desire for God," and his mystical anthropology's desire for the impossible is articulated in a discourse that is at least as religious, without religion, as is Caputo's Derrida. Wouldn't this justify at the very least considering Bataille's relation to the canon of continental philosophers belonging to the turn to religion?[59]

But as Kosky notes, "Bataille has been omitted from the tradition that defines postmodernism as it is considered by the latest wave of scholars of the turn to religion."[60] Why this should be the case is not entirely clear, though one suspects that Bataille's violent, excessive, sexually charged—often obscene—writings, along with his insistence that our hope is to be found in opening wide our eyes to the most troubling aspects of human existence, are simply at odds with the aesthetico-moral sensibilities of many scholars of religion. In this sense, Bataille remains a kind of repressed element in the field of religious studies. But as Freud has made clear, the repressed tends to return with a vengeance, and to be sure, Bataille's value as a religious thinker—that is, as someone who not only thinks *about* religion but thinks *in terms of* religion—is increasingly undeniable. Musing on the connection between his major works and Bataille's key ideas, Jeffrey Kripal's essay in this collection treats Bataille as the repressed undercurrent of his career—the traumatic secret that helps him, finally, articulate the significance of the traumatic secret to the interpretation of religious experience. Biles's consideration of dreams in Bataille's writing provides another angle on Bataille's relation to—or suspicion of—the repressed.

The a/theologian and critic Mark C. Taylor was among the first to recognize Bataille's work for its importance in religious studies, introducing students of religion to Bataille in a "pioneering chapter" on Bataille entitled "Ecstasy."[61] Placing Bataille in a current of post-Hegelian responses to the ethical and political problem of difference, Taylor examines how Bataille's obsession with the transgressive, catastrophic dimension of the sacred generates a jouissance that exceeds the self-other binary by exploding it.[62] Taylor's insistence on the ethical and political significance of Bataille's obsession with ecstatic self-loss as a definitive feature of the sacred has been taken up by scholars who focus their attention on Bataille's fascination with mysticism. In *Sensible Ecstasy*, Hollywood places Bataille alongside Jacques Lacan, Simone de Beauvoir, and Luce Irigaray as one of a constellation of French intellectuals who identify explicitly as atheist yet remain fascinated with female Christian mystics. Although she ultimately finds Bataille's approach to ecstatic self-loss wanting for the way it conceptualizes the gendered dimension of the encounter with the other, Hollywood provides a rich, nuanced account of the political seriousness of Bataille's turn to mysticism, inner experience, and self-sundering.[63] In her afterword to this volume, Hollywood revisits these questions and offers a slightly different account of her relationship to Bataille, one grounded in autobiographical reflections on her earliest encounters with his work.

Published in the same year as *Sensible Ecstasy*, Peter Connor's and Andrew Hussey's respective studies of Bataille's mysticism go to great lengths to show its similarity to its religious counterparts and its departure from them—namely, its absence of any theistic commitments and its insistence on the experiential power of literary expression as a mode of mystical encounter.[64] Like Hollywood, though absent the feminist critique, Connor and Hussey also insist on the ethical and political import of Bataille's method of meditation. In *Saints of the Impossible*, his comparative study of Bataille and Simone Weil, Alexander Irwin examines the political and ethical insight—as counterintuitive as it might be—in Bataille's insistence on sacrificial annihilation of the self as a response to the tragedy and trauma of fascism and war. While not giving as much attention to Bataille's fascination with mysticism, Allan Stoekl's recent work explores the ethical dimensions of Bataille's understanding of expenditure, consumption, and self-loss, especially for the way it provides a response to the various forms of violence—including religious fundamentalisms—that constitute our contemporary historical moment.[65]

Engaging and extending this body of work, several essays in this volume interrogate the ethical and political dimension of Bataille's understanding of the sacred, sacrifice, and ecstatic loss of self. Building on Hussey's reminder that Bataille was familiar not only with Christian but also Hindu forms of mystical practice, Hugh Urban provides a detailed analysis of the worship of the goddess Kamakhya in northeastern India. His analysis shows both how Bataille can be a generative guide in the study of mysticism and, relying on Hollywood's critique, how Bataille's understanding of gender and its possible limitations must be grappled with when relying on his ideas. Stephen Bush's essay also explores potential limitations in Bataille's approach to violence. Like Hollywood and Irwin, Bush investigates Bataille's fascination with certain kinds of violence as responses to other forms of violence. Following an exceptionally nuanced and sympathetic reading of Bataille's thinking on these questions, Bush expresses concerns that Bataille's approach may run too great a risk of fostering dispositions of sadism and cruelty. Brintnall's essay, which addresses the questions posed by Bush, Hollywood, and Irwin in slightly different terms, comes to almost the exactly opposite conclusion, contending that it is Bataille's insistence that commitment to the self and its sustenance be abandoned that makes him a profound ethical thinker. Taking up ideas from Stoekl and Hollywood, Lynne Gerber's contribution to this volume takes as its field of investigation the fat body: its excessiveness; its capacity to generate anxiety; its proximity to death, fantasized and actual. Gerber stakes out the territory between Bush's and Brintnall's accounts, explaining the ways that Bataille's notion of sacrificial expenditure can fund a fat politics, which recognizes the fat body as the corporealization of the sacred, as well as the ways in which Bataille's insistence on the ecstasy accompanying sacrificial violence fails to take seriously the way in which such violence and the "bearing of death" is not equally distributed among social actors.

As the work summarized in this introduction demonstrates, Bataille has far-reaching implications for the academic study of religion, even as he represents a still repressed element within it. One aim of the present volume is to join in the spirit of such work to instigate further a turn to—or return of—Bataille, in and beyond academic departments of religion. As the essays collected here demonstrate, Bataille offers generative frames for considering the questions and materials that comprise the heart of the academic study of religion. Urban's essay, for example, continues his work of bringing Bataille into contact with the study of Tantric ritual. With his examination of the sacrificial expenditure related to the construction of arenas for the World Cup in South Africa as well as the performance of actual sacrifices in those arenas prior to the commencement of the games, David Chidester's essay explores a case study that reveals the ways religion bleeds across the putatively secular. And, as noted above, Lingis gives an account of Bataille's engagement with and challenges to the texts and themes that comprise the field named as religious studies. The contributions by Jordan and Direk also show how Bataille compels us to rethink our understanding and interpretation of figures central to the religious studies canon.

But, to be clear, this volume's purpose is not to promote the canonization of Bataille or anyone else—nor is it precisely to (re)integrate him into the debates that his work, even if indirectly, has done so much to shape. Rather, taking inspiration from Bataille's economic theory, this collection strives to break open the field of religious studies; taken as a whole, it adumbrates a general economy of religious studies and in so doing suggests new paths into, and approaches for, the study of religion.[66] Long before the debates about secularism that currently occupy so much scholarly attention, Bataille saw the sacred as, in turn, opposed to, lurking within, and constituting the ostensibly secular, which he often called the profane. He recognized that the sacred may appear and be experienced in unexpected forms. And he recognized that the sacred is, like Marcel Mauss's "gift," a "total social fact" circulating throughout human culture—indeed, making genuinely human culture possible.[67]

This recognition, and the general economy of religious studies that corresponds to it, means that following Bataille's intuitions may lead the scholar of religion to consider a variety of phenomena not typically taken to be within the purview of religious studies. For example, attending to the emphasis Bataille places on sacrifice, transgression, and ecstatic self-loss, Brintnall turns to barebacking, Gerber considers the fat body, Hegarty listens to walls of sound, and Biles moves across the dreamscape. Although none of these should surprise anyone familiar with the expansive definitions of religion that operate in the academy, the persistence of disruption, fracture, transgression, and excess in these examples gives the study of religion a different flavor and resonance.

Bataille's work also commends a transdisciplinary attitude toward the study of religion. The editors have therefore solicited work from thinkers beyond academic departments of religion. It is here that one locates contributions from philosophers like Alphonso Lingis, whose own work exceeds disciplinary boundaries. Similarly, here one finds Goux's reliance on economic theory and history, Winnubst's consideration of governmentality and sovereignty, Bush's turn to ethics, and Stoekl's exploration of virtual realities.

The essays collected here engage queer theory, feminist theory, and psychoanalysis; they draw insights from anthropology, philosophy, and theology. Their authors investigate the paranormal and the oneiric; they traverse political, sexual, and economic realms. This volume coheres through the animating spirit of Bataille—but in that same spirit, it is decidedly, enthusiastically heterogeneous. It not only does the necessary work of further exegeting Bataille; it *activates* Bataille, applying his insights to the interpretation of facets of religious and ostensibly secular culture that might otherwise go unnoticed or underappreciated by scholars of religion. To apprehend the full amplitude and dynamics of religion requires that students of religion keep in mind that religion "is often most interesting where it is least obvious,"[68] especially, as Bataille would say, in the "horror of night."

Some may fear that Bataille's radicality will be neutralized through further appropriation into the academy. While this is always a risk, the editors have something else in mind. The point is not to integrate Bataille into the discourse of religion in the academy; rather, the accent is placed on injecting Bataille into that discourse and thereby altering it. Thus the primary "use-value" of Bataille lies not only in the insights the application of his work produces; more radically, it promotes an alteration of an attitude within the "academic imagination of religion," a will to open the field of religious studies.[69] It commends an experimental, risk-taking attitude, a willingness to confront the negative, to attend to even the most perverse expressions of the human passions, and to find religion at work in places where it is most hidden. As David Chidester would suggest, Bataille calls into question what *counts* as religion.[70]

In this sense, the present volume enacts the sort of negative operation to which Bataille himself was dedicated; it seeks less to define religious studies than to disrupt it, less to support disciplinary boundaries than to see them as so many occasions for transgression. A general economy of religious studies is realized in such gestures. Discussing Bataille's theory of general economics, Lingis notes that "in today's industrialized countries, the problem is not production but distribution."[71] Similarly, a general economy of religious studies recognizes that increasing specialization and ever more rigorously defined disciplines—notwithstanding increasing lip service to academic "interdisciplinarity"—may produce knowledge, but in a manner that also narrows the scope and distribution of knowledge. A willed transgression of disciplinary boundaries is the cornerstone of a Bataillean attitude toward the study of religion.

This attitude works in the other direction as well—which is to say that disciplines beyond religious studies should recognize that so much of what they deal with is, or has to do with, religion. Opening the field of religious studies also means realizing that other disciplines are already "doing" religious studies, even if not in a readily recognizable, self-conscious, or well-informed way. Mark C. Taylor has suggested that art criticism from the likes of Yve-Alain Bois and Rosalind Krauss, who engage Bataillean ideas of the sacred, sacrifice, and transgression, nonetheless suffers from "the failure . . . to appreciate the importance of religion" in the art they examine.[72] But the basic insight of Taylor's critique reaches far beyond the domain of art theory. Thinkers from across the academy would do well to cultivate greater awareness of how religion informs, animates, and otherwise inf(l)ects the subject matter of their areas of study.

In attempting to instigate such recognitions, *Negative Ecstasies* represents an intervention into the politics of religious studies, affirming that the basic attitude taken toward imagining and theorizing about religion will largely determine the amplitude of insight available to the scholar. Among many other things, what this collection of essays proposes—often implicitly, but in its entirety—is that scholars of religion must consider, through Bataille, human passions and negativity both *in* and *as* religion. But it also suggests that the study of religion might itself take on the character of an ecstatic pursuit, unsettling disciplinary boundaries, unworking scholarly categories, and undoing comforting discontinuities by opening, rather than by more rigorously defining, the field of religious studies, by creating rapturous, disturbing, continuous intimacies among and between scholars and scholarly fields. Just as Bataille's seeming turn away from political engagement for the private realm of inner experience and mysticism has been analyzed as politics from another location and in a different key, this volume's attempt to transform the politics of the academic study of religion should be understood as politics per se, as an attempt to render more viable, by rendering more visible, the excessive, explosive power of the sacred, with its creative, cataclysmic affects and desires.

One need not worry that adopting such an attitude and enacting such counteroperations will hasten the academy's demise. Like the world of the profane about which Bataille wrote, reason and order are destined to pre-vail, particularly as the academy's ethos is increasingly shaped by a neolib-eral worldview. But it is in gestures that echo the negative work of sacrifice that the study of religion might take on, in however minor a key, however subtle a manner, the disruptive, transgressive character of the Bataillean sacred.

Movements of Luxurious Exuberance
Georges Bataille and Fat Politics

LYNNE GERBER

> We lie to ourselves when we dream of escaping the movement of luxurious exuberance of which we are only the most intense form.
> —**Georges Bataille**, *The Accursed Share*, **vol. 1**

> Our refusal to acknowledge that we are limited beings has devastating and often fatal consequences for others.
> —**Kaja Silverman**, *Flesh of My Flesh*

America's fascination with body size, weight loss, and fatness has decidedly religious overtones.[1] The development of dieting as a cultural imperative has been marked by a moral intensity that, in the view of some historians, grew in direct proportion to the decline of religious authority in American life.[2] By the early twentieth century, "fat," writes the historian Peter Stearns, "became a secular sin, and an obvious one at that."[3] By the mid-twentieth century, the weight loss–religion connection was being expressed in the popular media. A 1960 *Vogue* article opined: "Weight control is emerging as the new morality; fat one of the deadlier sins. The bathroom scales are a shrine to which believers turn daily. Converts are marked by their usual unctuous zeal. Doctors become father confessors to whom grievous sins are whispered."[4] In the early twenty-first century, those sins are no longer whispered. Approximately ten million viewers tune in each week to watch fat people go through the stations of the weight-loss cross as established by the producers of the popular moral drama/television show *The Biggest Loser.*

This sacred aura that permeates weight-loss struggles, dramas, and spectacles is difficult to pin down. Religious language in the United States tends to be reserved for what we most value, what we most strive for, what we hope to be. While the argument can certainly be made that thinness is all of those things, that line of analysis and that kind of religious language fail to touch the elements of dread and disgust that bind us to the dramas of weight loss, the sacred repulsion that gives the pursuit its power, that highly charged, almost holy revulsion at its center: the potent fear and hatred the culture reserves for fat, fatness, and fat people.

That a certain revulsion stands at the center of what has become, in many ways, a secular sacred in American culture would be of no surprise to Georges Bataille. "It is obviously the combination of abhorrence and desire," he wrote, "that gives the sacred world a paradoxical character, holding the one who considers it without cheating in a state of anxious fascination"—an apt description, perhaps, of the state of *The Biggest Loser*'s audience.[5] Indeed there is much in Bataille's thought and language that can help us think through the many contradictions, problems, and possibilities of fatness, fat subjectivity, and fat politics in the age of the loudly trumpeted "obesity epidemic" and its increasingly powerful prerogatives.

Fatness and fat people are associated with a variety of excesses. Fat bodies are considered "bodies out of bounds,"[6] bodies that traverse the boundaries of standard clothing sizes, public seating, and recognized aesthetic forms. "The obese," Jean Baudrillard famously wrote, "is not only large, of a size opposed to normal morphology: he is larger than large. He no longer makes sense in some distinctive opposition, but in his excess, his redundancy."[7] Fatness on bodies is also associated with excessive eating. People are presumed to get fat because they eat far more than is necessary for their energetic needs, and bodily fatness is widely perceived as tangible evidence that the person who carries it consumes food in immodest, excessive ways. In part because of this perception, and the associated presumption that weight and body size are largely under an individual's direct control, fat people are also popularly depicted as social excesses. In a time of heated debate over scarce social resources such as jobs and health care, fat people are depicted as a drain on the economy; they are presumed to be less productive workers and greater consumers of health care, evoking popular resentment at the alleged price the rest of society pays for such excessive needs.

Fatness is also associated with the excesses of consumer capitalism. According to Stearns, concern over fatness and the regulation of body size developed in the United States in tandem with industrialization, the modernization of production, and the concomitant economic and increasingly social demand that Americans consume more goods more freely and more excessively. This demand came into conflict with older, religion-based concerns about indulgence and calls for moral comportment and restraint. The loosening of restraints regarding consumer consumption was accompanied by an increase in those regarding eating and body size.[8] Fat also became a symbol of a rising middle class that was perceived to be unable to conduct themselves properly amid newfound excess.[9] This tension between demands for indulgence and for restraint has continued to shape advanced capitalist societies, the practices of those who live in them, and their bodies. The neoliberal demand for continuous, ongoing consumption, according to the sociologists Julie Guthman and Melanie Dupuis, has shaped both the food market and food consumption, "both produc[ing] obesity and produc[ing] it as a problem."[10] For critics of American overconsumption, fatness has become "a tribal stigma," a symbol of its excesses and horrors.[11]

Resistance to this cultural dread of fat and the depiction of fatness as excess has taken different forms. Most are rooted in efforts to sever the association between fat people and excess and to redeem fat subjectivity from the personal and social ravages of spoiled identity. Perhaps the most popular has been the call for size acceptance, articulated most unequivocally by the advocacy group the National Association for the Advancement of Fat Acceptance (NAAFA). For over forty years, NAAFA has challenged the social denigration of fat people, contested the practices that cultivate it, and provided a social harbor for fat people from the storms of fat hatred.[12] Fatness, in their view, is a natural human variant and the connection between fat and excess an ugly stereotype that needs to be dispelled if fat people are to achieve acceptance and inclusion. A related and increasingly visible site of resistance is the Health at Every Size (HAES) movement. This effort addresses the issue of body size and health by trying to uncouple the two. By encouraging healthy behaviors independently of weight loss or weight gain, this movement makes space for the possibility of health for fat people *as* fat people and cultivates that space by maintaining neutrality regarding weight per se and relying on other measures to evaluate health. The emerging academic field of critical fat studies has also taken up the call to disrupt discursive connections between fat and excess[13] and position "an inhabitable subjectivity for fat people,"[14] even if there is some ambivalence about the kinds of subjectivities some fat activists are trying rehabilitate.[15] All of these efforts share the underlying aim of forming a socially legible and legitimized fat subjectivity, one that can take fat people out of the realm of the excessive and make a place for them in the world of the respectable.[16]

Bataille provides us with another way to think about fat politics and practice, a way explored in some arenas of fat culture and analyzed by some fat studies thinkers, a way of, in the words of the writer Dorothy Allison, "embracing the scary, embracing being unacceptable."[17] Bataille's work revolves around a vocabulary of words, ideas, meditative practices, and religious sensibilities that are often used in relation to fat—indeed is the vocabulary that many fat people despise—but that is refigured within his broader mystical and social vision. Excess, dread, monstrosity, filth, disgust, and death are words that saturate his writings in a way that embraces, rather than expels, the kind of personal and social dissolution each connotes. They point to the way in which fat and fatness have become sources of the sacred in American culture: prohibited and therefore powerful, dangerous yet strangely alluring, a source of disgust but also of desire. Bataille's work can be extremely generative in analyzing fat hatred, understanding practices that seek to expel fat and their necessary limitations, and formulating a fat politics that goes beyond the demand for a legitimized fat subjectivity within our deeply flawed liberal capitalist culture and points us toward possibilities simultaneously greater and humbler. His understanding of excess, and related notions of expenditure, and sacrifice can be used to understand the religiosity that infuses American discourse on fat and dieting, critique the project of weight loss and its dominance in our culture, and fund a fat politics of excess, monstrosity, and generosity.

Bataille's work is not without its problems in relation to fat, though, and this chapter will discuss those as well. Some of those problems raise questions that are critical for fat politics to explore. Specifically, his discussion—some might say valorization—of death and the kind of religious and human possibilities that come from representational, if not literal, proximity to it has both possibilities and problems related to fat politics. The case of fatness, its hyperassociation with death, and the varying death threats, real and rhetorical, that fat people face as a result highlight how experiences like dread and disgust can be generated not just by the existential contingency of human life but by powerful social forces, social hatreds, and social interests that shape our responses to that contingency. In overlooking the social production and allocation of disgust, Bataille's work can obscure the disproportionate price paid by those who evoke those experiences as a result of their social designations. His valorization of inner experiences generated by "com[ing] *as close as possible* to death" becomes problematic in a social context where particular groups, fat people among them, are consigned to carry the dread of death for a culture that prefers to deny it.[18] Bataille's continual return to death and the problems with that return underscore the importance of developing a critical understanding of death as part of fat politics.

The chapter begins with a discussion of some of Bataille's central concepts and how they might be applied to an analysis of fat phobia, a critique of dieting in American culture, and the possibilities of a monstrous fat politics. I then look at some examples of monstrous fat politics at work in publications and performances by fat artists, writers, and activists, namely in the work of Divine, the novelist Susan Stinson and the 1990s zine *FaT GiRL*. In the last section I turn to the question of fat and death. I look at Bataille's discussion of death in conversation with the dominant discursive connection between fatness and death in order to point to some political problems with his analysis. I conclude with a call for fat activists to use Bataille and his work to develop an analysis of death and generosity as part of fat politics.

Fat, Excess, and the Project of Dieting

Bataille's work offers fat scholars and activists ways to resignify fat's excesses. In his three-volume work *The Accursed Share*, Bataille takes on questions of economy, religion, and eroticism. In his view, the central problem of human economy is not scarcity, as posed by classical liberal economic theory, but abundance.[19] Energy is abundant in the world, life is profligate in its effusion, and wealth is marked by its excess. The sun is Bataille's exemplar of this exuberance, throwing off energy with no sense of purpose and no need for return. "The sun," he writes, "gives without ever receiving."[20] Social systems, once they have used the energy they need to grow, must address the issue of excess. "If the excess cannot be completely absorbed in its growth," according to Bataille, "it must necessarily be lost without profit; it must be spent, willingly or not, gloriously or catastrophically."[21] Excess will be dispersed somehow; in his view it must be. The question is how it will be dispersed: more specifically, whether it will be spent in gloriously nonproductive ways, what he calls expenditure, or whether a society will try to make use of its excess by redeploying it for productive ends. Bataille makes the case for the former, that this excess needs to be expended splendidly, burnt out, given of itself until it is exhausted, with no reason, no end, and no purpose in view. This kind of expenditure can be seen in transgressive, nonreproductive sexuality, festivals of indulgence and abundance, transgressive violence, and sacrifice.

Expenditure and sacrifice, in Bataille's view, are contrasted to utility and project. In rational models of economic development, excess is deployed back into the system for useful purposes. Profits are not squandered in bacchanalia that undo the logic of productivity that generated them; they are put back into the machinery of production to garner even greater profits. Excess is used toward planned, measured ends, encouraging belief in the possibility of a system of production based wholly upon reason and that can eventually encompass and make use of all energy. Systems based on such notions of utility, in Bataille's view, do not recognize or validate the expenditure of excess except in limited or grudging ways: "humanity recognizes the right to acquire, to conserve, and to consume rationally, but it excludes in principle *nonproductive expenditure*."[22] But despite the fantasy of utility, he notes that no society can avoid useless expenditure, pointing to the insistent presence of factors in economic life that exceed the principles of utilitarian thought, such as honor, duty, and altruism.

The kinds of expenditures Bataille favors involve the transgression of the world of work, of things, of rational planning for useful ends, and entrance into a world of intimacy, where wealth is expended with no productive end in view and where the illusions of human separation and discontinuous selfhood are shattered in a sometimes violent excessive exuberance. This can be seen in his discussion of sacrifice. In his view, sacrifice is about transforming the object to be sacrificed from its status as an object and returning it to a place where it is beyond use, a sacred, if accursed, place, one that he identifies as intimacy. Sacrifice does not need to destroy the thing sacrificed, but it destroys its utility, its function as a thing related to the world of work, productivity, and labor.[23] Human intimacy, the sense of continuity between people and the world, is generated through the destruction of utility. "Sacrifice," he writes, "is the heat in which the intimacy of those who make up the system of common works is rediscovered."[24] Expenditure and the generation of this kind of intimacy have, in his view, been a central function of religious rites, rituals, and festivals.[25]

But in contemporary society, Bataille argues, these forms of expenditure no longer exist.[26] This is because of the pervasiveness of economic models, capitalist or Marxist, that insist on channeling all excess back into systems of productivity. These models, as any reader of social theory might guess, are aided and abetted by Protestantism, a religious system that expels all excess from the worldly sphere, deploying wealth only for productivity, never for transgressive splendor.[27] This does not result, as these models might posit, in a lack of excess, with all extra wealth efficiently producing further wealth; it merely results in ways of dispersing excess that are, in his view, highly undesirable and ungenerous, ways that refuse to recognize the limitations of utility, of reason, and of planning and that, in that refusal, run even greater risks. "In trying to maintain sterility in regard to expenditure in conformity with a reasoning that balances *accounts*," he writes, "bourgeois society has only managed to develop a universal meanness,"[28] rather than the generosity of expenditure.

For Bataille, excess happens—thus expenditure must. What we get to decide is how excess is expended: the kind of squander we can live with. "Excess energy," he writes, "if it cannot be used for growth, is lost. Moreover, in no way can this inevitable loss be accounted useful. It is only a matter of an acceptable loss, preferable to another that is regarded as unacceptable: a question of *acceptability*, not utility. Its consequences are decisive, however."[29] For him, acceptable means of expenditure generate intimacy by taking people out of the logic of productivity and into the intimacy with the world that they crave. Social structures founded on utility will disperse their excess too, but those dispersions may run much higher risks than the dispersions he prefers. In the first volume of *The Accursed Share*, he illustrates the contrast with two historical cases: the Marshall Plan and Hiroshima. The former expended excess through a radical redistribution that confounded the logic of national self-interest and the illusion of separateness; the latter reflected a denial of limitation and an insistence on the usefulness of excess that ultimately exploded, annihilating life itself.

Bataille's notion of expenditure can be used in at least two ways in thinking about fatness. From the perspective of critics of modern industrial capitalism, of fatness, and of the connection between the two, there is a reading of Bataille that supports their view. For those with a certain critique of consumption and consumer capitalism, fat could be seen as yet another way contemporary society and its economic structure denies excess and refuses its useless expenditure, channeling it instead into the bodies of fat people who then become living sacrifices of a sort to a society that has reached but will not recognize its productive limits. In our denial, we will deal with our excess by having a nonproductive segment of the population that, presumably because ill health will kill fat people before reproductive age, will eventually deplete it. We see a version of this view in Allan Stoekl's application of Bataille to the crisis of energy, energy production, and energy consumption, a crisis that threatens to undo energy-dependent societies. Using Heidegger as a guide, Stoekl argues that Bataille made a critical error in failing to distinguish between energy that can be quantified, measured, and reserved for future use versus "heterogeneous" energy, a bodily energy that can only be dispersed.[30] In applying this distinction to contemporary life, he contrasts stockpiled energy, such as oil, gas, and electricity, with "muscle power." The latter, exemplified in bike riding and walking, is an expenditure in ideal Bataillean fashion because it forces us to be intimate with our energy, our bodies, our sweat, and our smells, whereas the former is seen in driving and its denial of the limitation and depletion of resources. In discussing driving, he writes: "In the car we do not need a body, we have no thought for energy flows and expenditures. Cursed flesh is miraculously transformed into an idea. The body's energy is stored as immense amounts of fat, it can barely move on its own, barely breathe; fewer and fewer people notice."[31] In this view, fat is simply stockpiled energy that, rather than being gloriously expended in excessive fat lives, is simply inert, waiting for the application of muscle power to dissipate it. This view overlooks the kind of charge with which fat has become invested in American culture, the charge of disgust and desire that marks Bataille's notion of the sacred. Bataille's work helps us recognize that sacred quality of fat and fatness, opening the possibility of a fat-positive application of his work. Because he addresses so many things that are central to the construction of fatness in American culture, because fatness is a symbol of excess, a source of social dread, and holds such discursive proximity to death, it becomes even more important that fat studies scholars and thinkers interrogate Bataille for new fat possibilities.

His understanding of excess and expenditure, utility and project can also be used to understand and formulate a critique of dieting and other weight-loss practices. In our world, food and the desire for it is supposed to be regulated by highly rationalized programs balancing intake and expenditure. Food should exist for fuel only and any excess eliminated. Diets are practices of measurement and planning; dieted bodies are efficient bodies, productive bodies, bodies governed by reason and control. But dieting can also be viewed as an utterly nonproductive expenditure. It does not actually do what it purports to do, and frequently it does nothing at all.[32] The pursuit of weight loss is most often an exercise in futility, with weight lost regained and time, energy, and money squandered toward an end never reached. The level of squander is excessive, with an estimated $58 billion dollars spent on weight loss per year in the United States.[33] Thus weight-loss culture can be seen as a way of dispersing excess even when it purports to be primarily about its elimination.

Weight loss is also an activity that can be seen in sacred contexts. Taboos about food, eating, and consumption frequently originate in religious beliefs and practices. In American culture, food practices have long been intertwined with Protestant Christianity. Movements touting healthy eating and restrictive practices ranging from fasting to vegetarianism had their origins in religious movements, and the two have frequently been intertwined.[34] Contemporary weight-loss practices, observers have noted, frequently take religious forms, including ritualized behavior, the generation of feelings of virtue and vice, and of temptation, transgression, and redemption.[35] In a more recent turn, religious groups have taken up weight loss in explicitly religious contexts, with groups like First Place offering weight-loss programs in churches around the country.[36]

The excess and dispersion of weight loss, however, is caught up in the logic of utility. It may provide the opportunity to touch the sacred, accursed share of fat, fatness, and the excesses of eating that are associated with it, but in a way that tries to recuperate it within its own utilitarian scheme. War, Bataille suggests, contains and thereby destroys the mystical possibilities that its proximity to death and violence generate by using a logic of utility and an investment in project to overcome its inherent horror.[37] In a similar way, dieting sanitizes the left-hand sacredness of fatness through the logic of productivity that structures the encounter. But its utility is belied by the excesses it generates. Its lack of efficacy only stimulates the generation of more and more unproductive dieting programs, weight-loss schemes, and the like. And there is reason to believe that dieting itself produces the excessive bodies it despises; weight loss often leads to greater weight gain, and yo-yo dieting raises the body's original set point to a higher one. Highly regulated eating systems cannot consider fat as exuberant excess, seeing it only as more fuel for its nonproductive system. Dieting, then, can be seen as a dispersion of excess that, in its interest in efficiency, utility, and rational calculation, destroys rather than sacrifices: Hiroshima rather than the Marshall Plan. These failures of dieting would not have surprised Bataille. "The extreme limit," he wrote, in opposition to asceticism, "is accessible through excess, not through want."[38]

Fat Monsters: Turning Toward Excess

In addition to providing a new way of understanding dieting, its relationship to capitalist culture, and its ambivalent relationship to fatness and excessive eating practices, Bataille's work provides the possibility of resignifying the excess with which fat is so closely identified. By doing so, it can provide some language, analysis, and support for the impulse in some strands of fat politics that unflinchingly moves toward fat, the monstrosity it represents, the dread it evokes, seeing in its excessiveness an opportunity for generosity and intimacy. It also makes space for an ambivalence toward fatness that can turn toward fat without insisting that fat subjectivity be fully redeemed in the culture's terms. I will sketch these possibilities first by discussing Bataille's notion of the left-hand sacred. I will then discuss the possibilities he sees in turning toward, rather than away from, the left-hand sacred as a means of generating inner experience, communication, and intimacy. Finally, I will discuss how some of these themes are played out in three different sites in fat culture: the film partnership of John Waters and Divine, the writings of the novelist and fat activist Susan Stinson, and the 1990s zine *FaT GiRL*.

Bataille's understanding of sacrifice is deeply connected to what is called, following Durkheim, the left-hand sacred. According to both, the sacred has two dimensions. The right-hand sacred is connected to wholeness, recuperation, cohesion, order, and stability; the left-hand sacred is connected to filth, brokenness, dissolution, and that which we dread: our monsters. Christianity, Bataille argues, made a crucial mistake by recognizing only the right-hand sacred as sacred and relegating the left-hand sacred to the realm of the profane.[39] Bataille's view of expenditure and sacrifice are based on a turn toward the left-hand sacred as a resource for inner experience, his atheological, atheistic mysticism. Turning toward the left-hand sacred means turning toward our monsters and the strange combination of anguish and ecstasy they provoke. This is most evidently accomplished through the Bataillean mystical position of "joy before death."[40] This notion of turning toward the left-hand sacred, toward what is most monstrous, and toward death gives Bataillean mystics an opportunity to challenge much that is problematic in the social order, starting with fantasies of coherence, wholeness, and order itself.

For those associated with dread, with filth and defilement, with uselessness, excess, and the anxiety of death, Bataille's work points to the particular possibilities in their position of effecting sacrifice and the inner experience associated with it. "Through the 'throwing out of their own parts,'" writes Alexander Irwin, "Bataillean mystics explode the myth of social organicity, perform their refusal to function as docile members of the social body. Their sacrifice is an expulsive rupture for which Bataille had offered a crude but apposite metaphor . . . : vomiting."[41] Bataille's writing gives those associated with the accursed share, by designation or identification, a vision for how a turn toward excess might generate new artistic and political possibilities. Fat artists and activists attempt this "throwing out of their own parts" in various ways: through explorations of the excessive fat body, excessive eating practices, and resisting the move toward a restored fat subjectivity based on the fantasy of individual coherence and completeness.

Jeremy Biles writes that one important possibility that Bataille points to is the power of the monster in evoking inner experience. He writes: "The presentation of monstrosity—the showing of the monster—*provokes* a sacrificial experience. Beholding the monster incites affective contradictions, a rupturing experience of both life and death, joy and anguish."[42] The move toward excesses of the body can be seen in the ways that fat artists and writers play with fat monstrosity, endowing fat characters with excessive size and excessive powers, some of which are monstrous, some that appear monstrous, and some of which are simply superhuman in their imagined powers, but all of which have the potential to generate the kind of rupturing experience Biles and Bataille discuss. At the end of the film *Multiple Maniacs*, for example, the fat drag queen Divine sings of how she has become a monster: " You're finally there, Divine . . . You can stamp out shopping centers with one stub of your foot! You can wipe out entire cities with a single blast of your fiery breath! You're a *monster* now, and only a monster can feel the fulfillment I'm capable of feeling now!"[43] In Susan Stinson's novel *Martha Moody* the title character, a fat shopkeeper in a small town in the nineteenth-century West, is imagined by her lover as endowed with excessive powers: "She flew. She spoke with angels. She played Jesus in the Bible. She carved a canyon with her tireless hands. She shook and brought forth waters. She sang whales into the ocean. She ploughed the ground with her knee while she rode a ridge and stroked her hands along the surfaces of grasses in the field."[44]

But perhaps the most intentional deployment of the fat body as image of both fear and comfort, desire and repulsion is the image of Fat Girl, emblem, totem, and guardian protector of the zine *FaT GiRL*. Her image graced the cover of its initial publication: a fat woman with spiky hair and multiple piercings dressed and posed in superhero style. She charges out of the logo with an outstretched, leather-gloved fist, revealing a wildly hairy armpit. She wears a skimpy bikini, with an F and G printed on each breast, and her fat belly hangs over the bottom. She is both the frightful embodiment of the fat lesbian stereotype and a desirable and desirous fat supergirl. By way of introduction, a piece in the zine addresses readers:

Who is Fat Girl? If you need to ask this question, I think it's time we sat down and had a little chat. Sit back and relax. Think back, think back just a few minutes to the moment you picked up this 'zine. What made you do it? Are you fat? Remember back a few minutes further to the last time you didn't fit into a chair and had to ask for a different one. Who kept you above your shame and humiliation? Remember the last time some creepy guy hurled insults at you and you told him to fuck off and die. Who was that moving your mouth for you, keeping you from sinking into deep depression and self-hate? Remember the last time your great belly shook with the thunderous roar of an orgasm. Who helped you get rid of that brainwashing bullshit about fat women having no sexuality? Who? Come on, say it! Who? Fat Girl that's who.[45]

By turning toward fat, these artists are able to channel some of the power of the left-hand sacred in their work, creating characters and stories that force the reader to face some of the dizzying contradictions of fat and fatness, its excesses, its monstrosities, and its potential generosity.

Fat art also plays with excesses in relation to eating, provoking anxiety and dread and also a sense of celebration and communication that goes past what eating is supposed to do within the logic of utility. Michael Moon and Eve Sedgwick write about how John Waters and Divine disrupt the recuperative impulse of size acceptance by insisting on, rather than decoupling, the association between fat bodies, excessive eating, and waste.[46] Perhaps the most iconic image of this connection is the infamous final scene of *Pink Flamingos*, where Divine follows a small dog along a city street and eats a pile of shit it leaves. Fat bodies, eating excesses, and waste are all fused in this image, which has left viewers perennially wondering if the scene was "real."[47] Readers of the novelist Susan Stinson's short piece "Drink" have asked her similar questions about the "reality" of her tale. The story depicts an annual ritual in which fat women gather in a low-budget hotel and collectively drink the contents of a swimming pool.

> When it happens, the swimmers howl and swallow. The rest of us reach into the water, motioning it toward us with great wet swoops of our arms. We lower our faces and open our mouths. Then we drink. As the water level drops, we lean farther out. Women go on falling into the water. Some slide in, or, carefully, jump. We float, slurping like thirsty animals. Some of us lick each other's skin. We stay away from the suits, which are, in general, conservatively cut. Some of us stand in the shallow end and bend to drink. When the water is low, some kneel. We lap until our faces are pressed to the damp blue bottom. Then we turn on our backs and stare at the ceiling, sated.[48]

In this strange rite of excessive bodies and excessive consumption, drinking an entire swimming pool is an opportunity for intimacy, communication between fat women. Excessive eating is intertwined with excessive bodies and excessive sexuality throughout *FaT GiRL*, which is as well known for its images of fat women eating as it is for its images of fat lesbian S/M sex. In one of many examples, the Kitchen Slut column contains images of a woman licking icing and cake off of naked women's bodies. In a moment exemplary of Bataillean excess, the subtitle reads, "Dinner has ended and you are stuffed with good food and sparkling conversation. Perhaps you think you are sated . . . but wait! Your presence is requested in the next room."[49] Dessert awaits.

Images of fat women eating have become powerful sites of allure and disgust: they have such a transgressive charge that they support an industry of fat food pornography centering exclusively around fat women eating.[50] Images made by fat women themselves that highlight not just eating but excessive eating, mysterious eating, repulsive eating have, like images of the monstrous, the capacity to provoke sacrificial experiences in those acculturated to its emotional contradictions. Using those contradictions to effect change in how fatness is perceived is a particular possibility posed by fat art and the turn toward fat that a Bataillean view suggests.

But perhaps one of the most striking Bataillean aspects of *FaT GiRL* in relation to other fat political strategies is the resistance to positing a fat subject that is healed and made whole as a result of accepting her size. In contrast to both size-acceptance and fat-liberationist strains of fat politics, the jumble of fat politics that was *FaT GiRL* made space for the profound ambivalence regarding fat, fatness, and living as a fat person that often marks the fat experience but tends to be squeezed out of or squeezed into recuperative narratives in other fat political projects.[51] The collective member, artist, and *FaT GiRL* visionary Max Airborne expresses her own ambivalence, confusion, and struggle in relation to fat beginning in the first issue, where she says, "I think of myself as fat; ever since I came out as a dyke I've called myself a fat dyke and tried to be proud about it, whether I actually felt that way or not."[52] This acknowledgment that the position of fat pride is a difficult one to keep up in the face of the struggle of living in a fat-hating society was a radical move in the context of a fat politics that is, at times, insistent on fat pride and fat positivity. *FaT GiRL*'s willingness to linger in the confusion, pain, and difficulty of fat identity in the midst of a fat-phobic society that insists on the conflation of fat with death was, in my view, intimately related to its stance of turning toward fat in all its "infinitely ruined splendor" in order not necessarily to resolidify a positive fat identity but to explore the possibilities of the left-hand sacred of fatness.[53]

Fat Death Threats and the Distribution of Dread

The ambivalence expressed in *FaT GiRL* is in part a reflection of the psychic difficulties of living under a perpetual death sentence. Fat people in American culture face death threats from all sides: real and imaginary, physical and discursive, biological and social.[54] In a society that both fears and denies death, the fear of death is frequently projected onto fat and fat people, and dieting and exercise are infused with the fantastical ability to ward off death for the deserving. It is difficult to read anything in the popular media regarding fat and weight loss that does not underscore the threats to life that fat is supposed to pose. The discursive oversignification of fatness with death creates a powerful, dread-filled cultural context that fat people continually must navigate in order to live their daily lives. To do so successfully, they must work to tease apart the actual risks of death from those merely threatened.

Physically, body size is correlated with some conditions that can shorten life. But the actual number of excess deaths in the United States directly attributable to larger body sizes is considerably lower than once thought (although the higher numbers are still frequently bandied about) and are roughly the same as those that result from below average body sizes.[55] The insistence of the fat/death connection, some postulate, could contribute to a "nocebo" effect, where negative health messages result in negative health outcomes.[56] In a context where body size may be correlated with some, but not many, excess deaths, fat people need to take care to distinguish real mortal threat from purported threats that are continually and loudly directed toward them.

This need becomes more acute when the potential medical and health costs of this discursive threat are taken into account. Fat people face risks of literal death through this rhetorical association, risks rarely accounted for and thus difficult to judge and avoid. Because of this association, and the correlation between BMI and some medical conditions, for example, fat people have more difficulty gaining access to health insurance. As a result, existing health problems are less likely to be treated, particularly in a timely fashion, and more likely to have highly problematic, and perhaps lethal, effects. In some cases, fat people are denied health care, even when they have insurance, by doctors reluctant to take them on as patients.[57] When health care can be accessed, fat people face another set of death threats. The use of body size as a proxy for health leads to an overemphasis on fat as causal in a range of health concerns and a concomitant reluctance on the part of many medical practitioners to investigate other possible causal issues. Stories of fat patients who have had grave medical problems overlooked with blithe advice to lose weight are evident both anecdotally and in documented research on anti-fat bias on the part of health care workers.[58] When fat people heed weight-loss advice, they face further potentially lethal risks that are often drowned out by the insistence on the deadliness of fat itself. Weight-loss drugs like phen-fen at times lead to lethal complications.[59] Weight-loss surgery has high levels of mortality associated with it.[60] And the health risks of dieting are hinted at in the literature on weight loss but are left largely unexamined; the deaths of fat people who engage in extreme dieting practices or who have histories of weight cycling are often considered death by fat rather than death by weight loss.[61] The insistence on the lethality of fat itself obfuscates the real threats to life and health that are faced by fat people either by the lack of access to health care, inadequate health care, or by the most common treatments prescribed to fat people.

In addition to threats to physical health, fat people also face the threat of what the sociologist Orlando Patterson termed "social death."[62] As highly stigmatized persons, fat people face the ongoing possibility of being disconnected from a range of social institutions and cultural contexts that make human life livable. The pervasiveness of anti-fat stigma is well documented. Fat people face difficulties finding and keeping employment and are often economically penalized for their body size.[63] They find extensive difficulty in their romantic pursuits and are continually informed by the culture that they are undesirable, a poor choice of mate, and destined for perpetual social isolation. All fat people are susceptible to public and private acts of fat hatred, ranging from verbal street-level assaults, to criticism and shame in the family, to fat-specific acts of social hatred such as hogging.[64] Recent media speculation on fat as socially contagious both reflects and encourages the marginalization of fat people from social life and social connectivity.[65] The death threats faced by fat people are social as well as physical.

These various, pervasive, and disproportionate death threats are important to consider when thinking about the application of Bataille's work to fat politics. Death is central to Bataille's thought and to his insights into the possibilities of sacrifice, the left-hand sacred, and the accursed share. His mysticism relies on the contemplation of death and the full experience of its anguish and desire, without the safety net of a redemptive theology or a restored subjectivity. In order to experience the realm Bataille points us toward, he writes, "You have to come *as close as possible* to death. Without flinching. And even, if necessary, flinching."[66] The depths of inner experience are achieved when we are willing to encounter death, dissolution, the dirt and disorder to which we are destined, and to find the anguish/ecstasy there. "The extreme limit of the 'possible,'" he writes, "assumes laughter, ecstasy, terrified approach towards death; assumes terror, nausea, unceasing agitation of the 'possible' and the impossible and, to conclude—broken, nevertheless, by degrees, slowly desired—the state of supplication, its absorption into despair."[67] Encountering death in this way allows for intimacy, for communication, for the kind of human connection that is possible only when brokenness, vulnerability, contingency are the shared basis for it. This encounter with death need not be literal; indeed, subjectivity must remain sufficiently intact for the experience to be experienced.[68] But it does need to be visceral, experiential, evocative of the dread, laughter, ecstasy, nausea, "unceasing agitation of the 'possible' and the impossible" that is the core of inner experience.[69] Because death is a fate we all share, this inner experience has the potential to be accessible to all: death ultimately makes no distinctions and neither need inner experience, Bataillean mysticism, or its turn toward excess, expenditure, and anguish/ecstasy.

But what Bataille does not adequately acknowledge is that, in a society that fears death, persists in fantasies of overcoming its limit, and is enthralled to the logic of project and utility, not all members share that dread equally. Managing the fear of death is a social project, one that is most often effected by assigning certain groups of people with its discursive (and at times literal) burden and allowing the rest of society to pursue the project/fantasy of longevity—not by a collective Bataillean experiment with the horrors and ecstasies of inner experience. While death is a fate we all physically share, we are socially able, and more than willing, to manage that threat by projecting it onto particular groups that are called upon to carry a disproportionate share of its dread. Those consigned to carry the cultural burden of death are consigned to live in super-fear, super-dread, super-anguish. Those lines of social management become charged with the power of the sacred, and those conflated with death become charged with its disgust and revulsion. Sacrifice in this context becomes less about restoring subjectivity to that which has been rendered a thing than about making tools for the management of the fear of death out of the subjects socially assigned to carry that burden.

There are Bataillean possibilities in this discursive, if not always—although sometimes—literal proximity to death. Some fat activists and artists have played with this proximity to provoke the dread and fascination that fat has come to represent. The fourth issue of *FaT GiRL*, for example, takes death as a theme, with an editorial about the losses recently faced by Barbarism, one of the collective members; an article in memory of Joanna, a young, fat heroin addict; and a photo spread of Barbarism in a cemetery, naked, eating, masturbating. Lesley Kinzel and other fat activists have started using the term "death fat" as a self-designation, in part to counter the terror of being continually designated "morbidly obese" by others, especially those with power over their health and medical treatment, by injecting much-needed humor.[70] The possibilities in a politics of death have been suggested by some queer writers, perhaps most famously by Leo Bersani when he writes, "if the rectum is the grave in which the masculine ideal (an ideal shared—differently—by men *and* women) of proud subjectivity is buried, then it should be celebrated for its very potential for death."[71] But in the next sentence he points to the problem of this proximity when discursive death threats become literal, as they have with AIDS.

This is the problem that fat politics faces in relation to Bataille and to death. The possibilities of communication, intimacy, interhuman connection on the basis of shared vulnerability, and incompleteness in the face of death are powerful. And those who are discursively associated with death may be in a particularly powerful position to effect these possibilities through art, activism, and radical fat expenditure. But the death threats that fat people continually face—literal and discursive, social and biological, evident and confusing—often put them in a state of super-anguish, super-despair, super-dread in relation to death. The Bataillean balance between dread and desire becomes, as Bataille himself suggests, more difficult to achieve when dread is disproportionately assigned and continually re-evoked:

> I will take for granted the assertion that every horror conceals a possibility of enticement. I can then assume the operation of a relatively simple mechanism. An object that is repugnant presents a force of repulsion more or less great. I will add that, following my hypothesis, it should also present a force of attraction: like the force of repulsion, its opposite, the force of attraction will be more or less great. But I didn't say that the repulsion and attraction were always directly proportional to one another. Things are far from being so simple. Indeed, instead of increasing desire, *excessive* horror paralyzes it, shuts it off.[72]

This kind of paralysis in the face of the continual assignment of death dread can be seen in Max Airborne's ruminations on fat and exercise: "I tell myself that I'm out of breath for lack of exercise, but the truth is I don't exercise because I am afraid to find out. . . . My fears take over, and as I get older and fatter, my fears grow. The longer I go, the harder it gets. I'm only 28. I am terrified of my future."[73] People who are culturally assigned a disproportionate share of the dread of death touch that dread continually, often under circumstances they do not choose and cannot always opt out of. Asking them to take up the possibilities that discursive proximity to death allows may well be asking too much, may be too paralyzing for people who are already continually being frightened to death. Turning toward fat, its excess, its simultaneous attraction and repulsion may offer sublime Bataillean opportunities. But turning toward vulnerability, dread, dissolution, and death may be too high a price to pay for people and groups already burdened with discursive associations with death and the actual death threats that often accompany them.[74]

Fat Generosity and Redistributing Dread

In thinking through the relation between Bataille's work and feminist politics, Amy Hollywood writes: "Just as there are two conceptions of history standing alongside each other in Bataille's text, perhaps we should distinguish two conceptions of political action: one that would contest power and injustice through narrativizations, and one that would contest those very narrativizations themselves in the name of that which is unassimilable to redemptive political projects—the bodies of those who can never again be made whole."[75] Fat politics has generated numerous projects that attempt to challenge fat hatred and social stigma by telling new stories about the meaning of fatness and the lives of fat people. Fat people, these projects tell us, can be whole, beautiful, healthy, and productive, all virtues in our project-driven culture. Their subjectivity can be restored and their personhood legitimated. And these stories are true, or at least possible, as far as they go.

Bataille's work, however, as I have argued, points to the possibilities for fat politics in taking the second path. By resisting redemptive resignifications of fatness and turning toward fat excesses, fat culture and fat politics has the potential to be a critical site for the kind of disruptive, generous politics that Bataille imagines. Not flinching from the dread, disgust, and desires generated by the left-hand sacred provides opportunity for communication, human intimacy, and forging new possibilities based not on the limitations of scarcity but the abundance of excess. "I wanted experience to lead where it would," Bataille writes, "not lead it to some end point given in advance. And I say at once that it leads to no harbor (but to a place of bewilderment, of nonsense)."[76] A fat politics that offers no harbor either in the promises of future scientific knowledge or the comforts of a reconsolidated fat subjectivity has the potential to generate transgressive possibilities that could take us to places we can not yet imagine. But, as I have also argued, it is problematic to eliminate the possibility of a harbor for those who are so often deprived of shelter from dread. The dominant discursive association between fat and death, along with the actual death threats fat people continually need to navigate, make the necessity of a harbor perhaps more pressing. And leave me ambivalent about Bataille and his work in relation to fat.

This ambivalence, I suggest, points to the need for fat politics to take the question of death more seriously. Not by taking exaggerated claims about the morbidity of fat more seriously and getting to the project of weight loss but by more fearlessly approaching the tangle of death threats fat people face, the ceaseless dread they generate, and potential strategies for resistance and change: "a thinking that does not fall apart in the face of horror, a self-consciousness that does not steal away when it is time to explore possibility to the limit."[77] Addressing that question in conversation with Bataille may help us see possibilities in a politics of death that might be otherwise invisible when we are in thrall to its fear.[78] It may help us develop a fat politics that has space for insufficiency, for ambivalence, for the kind of brokenness that comes from carrying more than one's share of the fear of death without becoming a maudlin celebration of a victim status. With his help, we may find ways of calling on our excess, expending the abundance we represent, in ways that redistribute the dread of death more equally, that allow others to face it, touch its dread and desire, without the need to recoup their wholeness at our expense. Thinking fat and death with Bataille may help us generate the kind of generosity that excess, brokenness, and dancing with death facilitates, one that resists the unproductive excess of weight loss and its fantasy of utility by turning toward our excesses and, rather than trying to make them useful, expends them gloriously. A Bataille-informed fat generosity might resist the lie that death can be overcome by projects like weight loss by using our proximity to death to insist that everyone face its possibilities with the kind of glorious expenditure that our bodies represent. "One might say," or one might hope, "that the lie destines life's exuberance to revolt."[79]

Sovereignty and Cruelty
*Self-Affirmation, Self-Dissolution,
and the Bataillean Subject*

STEPHEN S. BUSH

Georges Bataille populates his writings with the imagery of torture and murder. His fiction revels in sexual assault. He speaks of evil as having a sovereign value for humanity. He speaks of there being intimacy between the sacrificers and the victims in human sacrificial rituals. He compares sex to human sacrifice. He describes himself meditating on photos of a man being dismembered and recounts his ecstatic experiences of joy and anguish in doing so, going so far as to call the wounded victim beautiful. He holds forth violation and transgression as things that reveal our true nature.

In light of these considerations, it might seem that Bataille is the last person that ethicists, or anyone for that matter, should consult on moral matters. Or perhaps, if we do consult him, it would only be in a negative way: that is to say, we can learn lessons about what is wrong with humanity but not lessons about how to make things right. This is how Simone de Beauvoir suggests we read the Marquis de Sade. "Must we burn de Sade?" Beauvoir asks. She concludes, "no." She does not think he has a constructive ethical vision, but she admits he can teach us important facts about human nature. We learn from Sade, for example, the extent to which human beings are violent and cruel, and we learn that violence is a pervasive, ineradicable feature of social relationships. We are ill served, Beauvoir says, by ethical proposals that are idealistic about human nature, that assume that in the proper conditions, people will not be violent. But as to how best to respond to violence, as to what we should do about it, Sade has nothing to say.[1]

We can pose the same question about Bataille. Must we burn Bataille? Perhaps we could think of Bataille like Beauvoir thinks of Sade, as someone who helps us diagnose ethical problems, even if he has no prescriptive advice for them. In fact, Bataille has the same diagnostic lessons to teach as Sade, as we would expect, since he was a devout reader of Sade. Like the marquis, Bataille sees cruelty and violence as ineradicable features of human life. Our social theories, then, should take account of this fact. So Bataille, like Sade, diagnoses important features of the human condition. But is Bataille's significance limited to negative lessons?

An important group of contemporary scholars thinks that we can learn positive lessons from Bataille, not just negative ones. They claim that Bataille has a constructive ethical vision that we should take seriously. These ethicists focus on one or both of two features of Bataille's philosophy. First, there is the fact that Bataille is critical of the way in which we instrumentalize people. He is sensitive to the violence that results from treating people as a means to an end. Bataille refers to our ordinary way of conducting our affairs as "project." In the realm of project, we engage in future-oriented, means-end activity. Bataille recognizes that in doing so, we treat our fellow humans as things that we can employ for the sake of some end. This dehumanizes people, for one thing, but for another thing, treating people in this way is highly conducive to violating people in various ways; such violation comes specifically as a result of regarding the people as means to ends. The second feature of Bataille's philosophy that holds ethical promise is his promotion of a special form of relationship between the self and others that he calls "communication." Bataillean communication is ecstatic; it is a break from the normal sense of oneself as a distinct subject, a self-contained entity that is discrete and separate from all the other entities with which one interacts. In Bataillean communication, the subject's normal sense of him- or herself is disrupted, and he or she experiences him- or herself as one with some other particular person or object or with the universe as a whole.

Amy Hollywood is one of these contemporary scholars who finds potential in Bataille's ethics, although not without reservations. For Hollywood, what is important in Bataille is that in challenging our ordinary sense of our self as a discrete entity, he renounces the desire for totality and wholeness, a desire that keeps one from properly recognizing and encountering others.[2] She says that in his encounter with suffering individuals, he prioritizes an important type of compassion that should take precedence over goal-directed activities to end suffering.[3] Kent Brintnall proposes that Bataillean experiences of self-laceration undo our illusions of autonomy and self-sufficiency and foster intimacy and generosity.[4] Alexander Irwin suggests that the psychological violence that one inflicts upon oneself in inner experience serves as an alternative to and contestation of the violence of warfare.[5] Jeremy Biles speaks of the "relinquishment of power" in Bataillean ecstasy.[6]

All of these studies, and others as well, are full of important insights. They individually and cumulatively present powerful considerations in favor of the idea that Bataille is a constructive ethical thinker. However, Bataille and those who would want to appropriate him for ethical purposes are open to two significant challenges. The first concerns the primacy of self-negation in his writings. In writing of ecstasy and communication, Bataille emphasizes that these are states of self-dissolution. To achieve ecstatic communication, one must lacerate the boundaries of oneself. In doing so, one participates in death, the ultimate self-dissolution, to the degree possible. We can agree with Bataille that self-negation is ethically important. It mitigates our tendency to assert ourselves at the expense of others. Typically, it takes a centered self to dominate and control others, so the ethical payoff from Bataille's ecstatic self-dissolution is that in renouncing the urge to be a total, self-contained entity, one renounces various associated urges, like the need to control others and indeed to control history. These are the sorts of urges that are responsible for the worst evils people commit against one another, and so Bataille has important answers to urgent questions.

The problem, however, is that whereas a good dose of self-negation could be just what is needed for individuals at the top of the social hierarchy, whose agency needs to be restrained, it could be precisely the wrong thing for those who are already marginalized or oppressed. In religious ethics, Barbara Andolsen has raised these issues forcefully. In a 1981 essay, Andolsen writes about the tendency among Christian theologians to view pride as the preeminent sin. By pride, the theologians mean excessive self-regard. The proper antidote to pride, they say, is self-sacrifice. This is all well and good for men, Andolsen says. Men have been culturally conditioned into a self-affirming identity and a corresponding tendency to exercise excessive self-regard. Women, however, are more likely to be already living self-sacrificially. They are living for the sake of others, sacrificing their own goals and ambitions to the welfare of their husbands and children. So while it makes sense to tell men that they need to embrace self-sacrifice, women need to hear precisely the opposite, Andolsen says. What women need is more self-regard. They need to attend to their own development, ambitions, and needs and to stop subordinating their goals to others' needs all the time. So the charge to be more self-sacrificial affects women differently than men. Women are already self-negating and need to develop themselves into a centered self.[7]

Andolsen's essay is dated in certain regards, and today we would want to emphasize that self-affirmation and self-negation do not fall neatly along gender lines but are distributed across a matrix of multiple intersecting lines: gender, class, ethnicity, and race, among others. Nevertheless, there is still a lesson to be learned from Andolsen, which is that an ethic of self-negation is appropriate for those agents who are so well formed as autonomous, centered selves that they make their way through the world with their elbows out. But an ethic of self-negation is highly problematic for those who have been socialized into positions of subordination. Those who are devoted to caring for others to the exclusion of themselves or who are exploited or abused by others to an extent that they have lost "the ability to be a centered self"[8] need a proper dose of self-assertiveness and self-regard. So there is a significant problem here if Bataille has only an ethics of self-negation to offer.

The second objection to Bataille and those who would appropriate him is the problem of cruelty in Bataille's work. Ethical interpretations of Bataille have done well in grappling with Bataille's ambiguous treatment of violence.[9] Why does Bataille emphasize violence so much? For one thing, Bataille thinks that it takes a jolt to get us out of our normal experience of ourselves as discrete, individuated things. And for another thing, Bataille sees the rupture of psychological integrity in ecstasy as a violence of sorts that is similar to the rupture of fleshly integrity in physical violence. In both cases, the boundary of the individual is disrupted, and what is usually inside is exposed to what is usually outside; the outer and inner mingle. But why is Bataille relatively uninterested in forms of violence that do not involve cruelty, like violence in self-defense perhaps, in natural disasters or accidents, or even in surgery?

It is easier to see that violence could have beneficial effects than it is to see that cruelty could. After all, everyone except the devoted pacifist sees physical violence as morally justified in some circumstances, such as self-defense, defense of the innocent, or just war. But it is harder to make a plausible case for cruelty. Indeed, according to some political theorists, cruelty is the *summum malum*, the greatest evil. Judith Shklar is famous for making this case: she sees the highest priority of the state as to protect its citizens against cruelty.[10] Violence may be ethically ambiguous, justifiable in some cases but not others, but surely cruelty deserves our condemnation across the board.

This is not what we find in Bataille's work. Cruelty is a persistent theme throughout his fictional and nonfictional writings. Sometimes he uses the term explicitly, but more often he writes about behavior that can only be described as cruel, such as human sacrifice, sexual assault, torture, and murder. His repeated engagements with Sade, too, are occasions for him to reflect on cruelty. The cruel actions Bataille discusses so frequently are not merely violent; they combine violence with callous disregard for the victims' suffering. The troubling thing about Bataille is that he thinks these sorts of cruel actions can have some sort of positive ethical significance.

In the remainder of this essay, I will argue that these two issues, the problem of self-negation and the problem of cruelty, are closely related. I will propose that Bataille's ethics is not just an ethics of self-negation but that it is simultaneously an ethics of self-affirmation, and I will explain how cruelty plays a key role in his ethics of self-affirmation.

To work toward an understanding of the significance of cruelty in Bataille's work, we need to take a closer look at important instances in Bataille's corpus where he is discussing cruelty or deploying cruel imagery. First, though, it will help to take a brief look at how others in Bataille's intellectual context were thinking about cruelty, especially Antonin Artaud and Maurice Blanchot. Artaud (1896–1948) is famous for his promotion of a "theater of cruelty," a notion that he exposits in a series of essays written in the 1930s. Artaud wants theater to forego its reliance on linguistic communication and reach its audience on more visceral levels, through intense, transgressive, anarchic spectacles that would question the reigning "social and moral system."[11] Such productions would employ depictions of violence, but the cruelty of Artaud's theater is not to be reduced to bloodiness.[12] The cruelty "will be bloody when necessary but not systematically so."[13] What Artaud primarily means by cruelty is "rigor, implacable intention and decision, irreversible and absolute determination." Such determination is in service of a "blind appetite for life capable of overriding everything" in its aim to wake people up—jolt them out of complacency—and put them in touch with vital forces of creativity that cannot but upend settled patterns of thought and conduct.[14]

Maurice Blanchot's (1907–2003) ideas on cruelty and sadism directly shaped Bataille's own, as Bataille refers repeatedly and appreciatively to Blanchot's essay "Sade's Reason" (originally published in 1947) in his important chapters on Sade in *Erotism*.[15] One of the principal points about Sadean cruelty that Blanchot wants to make is that whereas in Sade cruelty finds its initial expression in the actions and impulses of people who gratify their own desires with total disregard for the suffering they inflict on others, the ultimate goal is to become so committed to cruelty and crime that one acts not for self-gratification but for the sake of cruelty as an end in itself. This is the height of cruelty, cruelty for the sake of cruelty, even when it destroys not just the victim but the perpetrator too. So Blanchot can say,

"Cruelty is only the negation of the self, carried so far that it is transformed into a destructive explosion."[16]

Bataille's usage of the term "cruelty" (*cruauté*) resembles in important ways both Artaud's and Blanchot's.[17] In a general sense, Bataille links cruelty with—indeed comes close to defining it as—a "desire to destroy" and "the desire to hurt and to kill."[18] Like Artaud, for Bataille cruelty may very well involve scenes of bloodshed, but it is not exclusively that. It can refer more generally to any force that disrupts us from our settled patterns of conduct, thought, and emotion. So Bataille can refer to modern art, specifically surrealism and cubism, as cruel in its effects on its viewers' consciousness. The destruction of conventional ways of representing objects in modern art breaks down the viewers' sense of their own subjectivity, similar to the way Artaud's theater of cruelty breaks from conventional dramatic forms to unsettle the audience's consciousness.[19]

As important for my purposes as Bataille's explicit use of the words "cruel" and "cruelty" are, just as significant are the repeated depictions of cruel actions that populate his texts, oftentimes very much employing scenery of bloodshed. I will give some representative examples. In the first volume of *The Accursed Share*, he has a chapter on Aztec sacrifices, describing the "apex of horror in the cruel chain of religious rites": "The priests killed their victims on top of the pyramids. They would stretch them over a stone altar and strike them in the chest with an obsidian knife. They would tear out the still-beating heart and raise it thus to the sun."[20] *Story of the Eye* follows the wild exploits, sexual and violent, of Simone and the narrator. They have orgies, rape people, urinate on each other, and have sex in the company of the corpse of a girl who has just committed suicide because of the insanity that Simone and the narrator have brought upon her. Toward the end of the story, they capture a priest, and Simone rapes him as the narrator strangles him to death. Then Simone has their accomplice, Sir Edmond, remove the priest's eyeball so she can insert it in her vagina and urinate over it.[21] In *Erotism*, Bataille brings to our attention sacrificial rites that were "extravagantly cruel": "children were offered to monsters of red-hot metal, gigantic wicker figures crammed with human beings were set alight, priests flayed living women and clad themselves in the streaming spoils."[22] He rewrites an account of torture to render it from the perspective of the torturer: "I flung myself upon him with insults and as he could not retaliate with his hands tied behind his back, I rammed my flailing fists into his face; he fell down and my heel finished off the work; disgusted, I spat into a swollen face. I could not help bursting into loud laughter: I had just insulted a dead man!"[23] In *Inner Experience*, Bataille writes of a series of photographs of a Chinese man in the process of being executed by dismemberment that he would use in his meditational practices: "I would gaze at the photographic image—or sometimes the memory which I have of it—of a Chinese man who must have been tortured in my lifetime. . . . In the end, the patient writhed, his chest flayed, arms and legs cut off at the elbows and at the knees. His hair standing on end, hideous, haggard, striped with blood, beautiful as a wasp."[24] In *The Trial of Gilles de Rais*, he details the heinous serial murders that Rais, a contemporary of Joan of Arc, committed. Rais would sexually stimulate himself on the bellies of children as he killed them, slitting their throats and then decapitating them.[25]

What initially strikes one as especially problematic about these cruel spectacles is that Bataille seems to attribute ethical benefits to them. In describing rituals of human sacrifice, Bataille says, "The victim dies and the spectators share in what his death reveals."[26] Similar considerations apply in the case of the photographs of the Chinese victim. Bataille thinks his death too revealed something for those who would properly apprehend the photographs. When Bataille meditated on the photographs of the man, he would experience ecstatic anguish and loving compassion. What this execution victim and the victims of human sacrifice reveal is the dissolution of the self that transpires at death, and the effect on the spectators is for them to undergo a related dissolution in ecstasy. In his discussions of both human sacrifice and the execution photographs, we see a troubling link between victimization and ethical insight for the spectators. Bataille's ambiguous relation to cruelty is a much bigger problem for his interpreters than his ambiguous relation to violence more generally. How are we to make sense of the recurrence of cruel horrors in his work?

The key to the ethical significance of cruelty for Bataille has to do with the centrality of the notion of sovereignty in his work. He explores sovereignty most extensively in *Sovereignty* (volume 3 of *The Accursed Share*), but the theme is prominent throughout his corpus. Bataille understands sovereignty to be a condition in which one is subject to no external authority: neither the authority of persons, institutions, texts, norms, or laws. In *Inner Experience*, he describes the mystical-like experiences that are so important for breaking out of self-contained subjectivity in such terms:

> Inner experience . . . cannot have any other concern nor other goal than itself. Henceforth I can have no other value, no other authority . . . I call this experience a voyage to the end of the possible of man. Anyone may not embark on this voyage, but if he does embark on it, this supposes the negation of the authorities, the existing val-

ues which limit the possible. By virtue of the fact that it is negation of other values, other authorities, experience, having a positive existence, becomes itself positively value *and authority*.[27]

In *Sovereignty*, Bataille explicates the concept in these terms: it is that which is "opposed to the servile and the subordinate."[28] The sovereign "does not depend on anything."[29] The sovereign is the one who refuses to submit.[30] Sovereignty is "the negation of prohibition."[31] Above all else, to be sovereign is to be in a state in which one is not a means to an end. Not to others' ends and not to one's own future ends. To be sovereign is to be in the present moment, subject to nothing and no one else.

The movement toward sovereignty, then, involves self-affirmation. In rejecting all authority that is external to oneself, one is regarding oneself as radically independent, and one is assigning the supreme value to one's own desires, satisfactions, and experiences. This is autonomy in the most extreme form. Bataille's avowal of sovereignty throughout his work indicates that his ethics is not one purely of self-negation. Sovereign individuals stand above every claim and demand placed upon them from conventional morality or other people. Sovereignty denies all that is not the self and, in doing so, affirms the self.

There is a paradoxical aspect to this, in that at the extreme, sovereignty denies even the self. The sovereign moments that Bataille prizes are those moments in which the self disregards even its own future, its own ambitions, and its own resources. Our normal tendency is to look out for our future self. Indeed, such care for our future is constitutive of our present self. We accumulate and conserve resources out of concern for our future well-being and comfort. This, for Bataille, is a form of subordination. When we subordinate the present moment to the future, we are making our present selves servile to something other than our present selves. The sovereign moment, then, in its purest form cannot count straightforwardly as self-affirmation, because there is no longer a self to affirm in the ecstatic sovereign moment.[32] At its end point, sovereignty disregards our sense of self as much as it disregards everything external to ourselves. The sovereign moment is then "NOTHING," Bataille says.[33] So I must admit that in the end, self-denial overcomes self-affirmation. But I would point out that sovereignty occurs along a continuum, and not all sovereignty transpires at the extreme limit. Furthermore, even at the extreme moment of ecstatic dissolution, this side of death, the self is not altogether entirely eradicated.[34]

Paradoxically, then, sovereignty encompasses both self-affirmation and self-denial. It affirms the self in that it values the subject's desires and impulses at the moment. It denies the self in that it permits those desires and impulses to take the subject into ecstasy and so dissolve the self. In his account of sovereignty, Bataille is proposing a subjectivity that neither errs in the extreme of self-negation nor in the extreme of excessive self-regard, but a subjectivity that incorporates both of these impulses.

What cruelty has to do with all this is that the cruel person exemplifies in the most striking ways the qualities of sovereignty. Bataille is quite explicit about this:

> The solitary man for whom [Sade] speaks pays not the slightest heed to his fellows; in his loneliness he is a sovereign being, never called to account, never needing to justify himself to anyone. He never pauses at the fear that the wrongs he inflicts on others will recoil upon himself; he is alone and never subject to the bounds that a common feeling of weakness imposes on other people. All this calls for enormous moral energy.[35]

Cruel actions, more than any other kind, are acts of self-affirmation. Cruel acts affirm the self because in cruelty, one is concerned with nothing but one's own desires. Bataille describes sadism as the "desire to hurt and to kill,"[36] and when this desire is given license to express itself, the sadist is not restrained by empathy, sympathy, compassion, or any such thing. The cruel person is not concerned about the feelings and sufferings of the victim. Those sufferings may even be a source of pleasure. Furthermore, the cruel person is not concerned with moral norms or legal prohibitions. Acts of cruelty are morally wrong, by conventional standards, yet the cruel agent trammels over the prohibition. Acts of cruelty in many cases are illegal, yet the cruel agent defies both the statute and its penalties. Cruel people are radically independent from all that would limit or restrain them and from anything that would oppose their desires. Parallel to the way sovereignty undoes the self in the end, cruelty for Bataille undoes the cruel person in the end. This is the point discussed above in Blanchot's reading of Sade, where the perpetrator is finally to act for the sake of cruelty itself, not for self-gratification. Bataille endorses this reading of Sade. The ultimate cruelty is to act cruelly even to the destruction of the self.

Bataille's insistence that we repeatedly attend to cruelty does not mean that he condones cruel acts or prescribes them. He quite clearly does not. His point in discussing cruelty is not to encourage his readers to be cruel. In "L'art, exercise de la cruauté," he insists that his attention to cruelty is not a defense of or a call for horrible actions.[37] In *Erotism*, after voicing the opinion that Sade's characters are pathological, Bataille says he has no quarrel with this point of view. Short of a paradoxical capacity to defend the indefensible, no one would suggest that the cruelty of the heroes of *Justine* and *Juliette* should not be wholeheartedly abominated. It is a denial of the principles on which humanity is founded. We are bound to reject something that would end in the ruin of all our works. If instinct urges us to destroy the very thing we are building we must condemn those instincts and defend ourselves from them.[38]

If Bataille is not recommending cruelty, what is his point in exposing us to cruel agents and actions? For one thing, it is certainly the case that he wants us to acknowledge that humans by and large possess cruel tendencies and that these are ineliminable. Cruel violence is "the deep truth at the heart of man."[39] Moreover, he wants to insist that this is a fact about human nature that we typically deny and suppress. Our violent tendencies—and the pleasure humans take in viewing and committing acts of cruelty—are something "we have almost completely turned our backs on."[40] These are important points, but they are merely diagnostic, whereas our question is whether Bataille has constructive, prescriptive things to say.

The case I am trying to make is that Bataille's constructive ethics has to do with both self-negation and self-affirmation. It is somewhat strange to put forth Bataille as a proponent of self-affirmation because he is best known, especially among ethicists, for his relentless pursuit of self-negation, as we have seen. Indeed, Bataille's emphasis on self-negation is so prominent that many interpreters have read his explorations of cruelty as nothing but a means toward self-dissolution. The shock of cruelty ruptures one's psyche, leading to the ecstatic dissolution of self-negation.[41] This is correct, to be sure. However, there is just as importantly the precisely opposite dynamic. The shock of cruelty is also the shock of beholding individuals who are subject to no constraints, who obey no norms, no conventions, and no authorities other than themselves.

The implications of Bataille's views of subjectivity are relevant not just to the concerns that Andolsen has but also to contemporary debates about the nature of agency. Feminists and others are working now to correct notions of agency that idealize the autonomous, independent subject. Judith Butler, for example, argues for the importance of a conception of subjectivity that acknowledges vulnerability and interdependence. She warns that denial of this vulnerability will result in fantasies of mastery that lead to violence. Yet Butler acknowledges that there is a proper place for a sort of autonomy. We should want a politics, for example, that protects the freedom of lesbian, gay, and transgender people, she says.[42] Here Butler is grappling with just the sorts of issues we see in Bataille and Andolsen: how to strike a proper balance between autonomy and dependency in our normative conception of agency.

Bataille, like Butler and Andolsen, construes subjectivity as a proper mix of self-negation and self-affirmation. To be sure, he isn't precise on these matters. He idealizes two extremes. The extreme of self-negation: the ecstatic subject dissipated to the extent that there is no longer a self. And the extreme of self-affirmation: the cruel sadist who cares nothing for the welfare of others or for society's norms. The Bataillean subject is situated square in the middle of these two forces as they come at it from both directions at full speed. An ethicist might want more subtlety and more precision. The ethicist might want to hear specifics about the sorts of circumstances and the sorts of ways in which we should be more self-affirming. And specifics about the sorts of circumstances and the sorts of ways in which we should be more self-negating.

But Bataille's aim is not to offer specific instructions on how to live. His aim is to shape the subject for and through ecstatic experiences. These experiences are ends in themselves for Bataille, but in my reading, the ecstatic experiences shape people's character for their social lives when they have exited ecstasy. And for that process, he thinks what is called for is exposure to the extremes. Bataille wants ecstasy to expose the subject to extreme forces of absolute self-denial and absolute self-affirmation. The result is to bring about lasting changes in the subject so formed. We emerge from ecstasy with "new knowledge," Bataille says.[43] Further, he speaks of the possibility of change, "awakening," that occurs as a result of encounters with cruelty.[44] And it is important to note that whereas he presents sovereignty in its purest form as transpiring in ecstatic moments, he does see continuities between ecstatic sovereignty and forms of political and economic sovereignty that transpire in the realm of project, as his repeated references to political sovereignty indicate in *Sovereignty*.[45] The primary continuity is the refusal to be subordinated to others. This is an important political ideal, a democratic ideal, even. At its extreme it gives rise to the ideal of the invulnerable agent that Butler is worried about. But if the self-negating aspects of Bataillean ecstasy exercise lasting influence in one's character and lead to dispositions toward nonmastery, then we have a form of subjectivity that is important for not erring on the side of self-affirmation or self-negation.

We can state the lessons that Bataille would have us learn from cruelty as follows. First, in the spectacle of cruelty, what we are supposed to recognize is that the cruel action is an expression of the cruel person's refusal to be subservient to anyone or anything. Second, we are supposed to recognize that we ourselves, at least many of us, also have a drive that refuses subservience and that this drive is a commonality between the cruel person and us. We are supposed to identify with the cruel person, not to think of ourselves as innocent of impulses that lead to cruelty. When we consider a scene of execution, we must not just sympathize with the victims but identify with the executioners, who are "our fellow-creatures." "We must ask ourselves: is there anything in our nature that renders such horror impossible? And we would be correct in answering: no, nothing."[46] If we view cruel monsters as categorically different from ourselves, and if we view the impulse toward violence and cruelty as something that we do not have or that we can easily eradicate, through ascetic self-denial in ourselves and through punishment in others, we fall prey to "a certain form of moral condemnation" that is in fact "escapist denial," Bataille warns.[47] If we do not see in ourselves the insubordinate drive that so easily turns to cruelty, we will not be in a position to grapple with cruelty adequately. Third, though we should be wary of the way in which our drive against subservience can lead to cruel victimization, we should recognize something of value in this drive. We must acknowledge that the impulse against subservience is not unfortunate and regrettable, but rather it is a "vital," "divine," and "sacred" aspect of ourselves. If we were to stifle our insubordinate, sovereign urges, we would "languish" in passivity.[48] Fourth, we must find ways to express our sovereign desires without victimizing others. It is necessary for "the normal man of today to become aware of himself and to know clearly what his sovereign aspirations are in order to limit their possibly disastrous consequences; to accept these if it suits him but not to push them any further than he needs, and resolutely to oppose them if his self awareness cannot tolerate them."[49] Bataille calls this "awakening," and in this state we prevail over the "negation" of cruel violence not in a "decisive victory" but only by retaining a "relentless consciousness of . . . possible horror."[50]

Bataille provides numerous examples of the sort of actions that he thinks give appropriate expression to our sovereign impulses, for example: reading and writing certain types of literature, especially poetry, certain sexual practices, and certain meditational practices. The goal in all of these practices is the achievement of ecstatic communication with others and with the world in total. These practices combine the self-assertion that consists in rejecting our subordination to other people, to laws, and to rules with the self-negation of dissolving our self-contained subjectivity and its tendencies toward controlling and dominating others.

Questions remain as to whether these practices can give a proper place to the desires in us that so easily can give rise to cruel victimization without allowing them actually to do so. I have voiced my concerns and reservations on this matter elsewhere, worrying that Bataille's rejection of all external authority in the ecstatic moment is so thoroughgoing that it leaves us with no protection against the entrenchment of cruelty in our character.[51] We also might wonder whether the precarious and paradoxical combination of self-affirmation and self-negation can shape us in ways that Andolsen or others like her could endorse. My aim in this essay is not to answer these questions decisively, either in defense or refutation of Bataille. Whatever we might want to say in response to these questions, though, we must view Bataille as a thinker whose ethical position includes self-affirmation, not just self-effacement. And we must acknowledge that his ethical insights on such matters are wrought from the most unlikely places, reflection on the most monstrous forms of cruelty.[52]

Erotic Ruination
Embracing the "Savage Spirituality" of Barebacking

KENT L. BRINTNALL

> The meaning of eroticism escapes anyone who cannot see its religious meaning! Reciprocally, the meaning of religion in its totality escapes anyone who disregards the link it has with eroticism.
>   Religion is the moving force behind the breaking of taboos.
>   —**Georges Bataille**, *Erotism*

"Eroticism," according to Georges Bataille, "unlike simple sexual activity, is a psychological quest." And while it "is in the first place an exuberance of life, [its] object . . . is not alien to death."[1] In this quest, "the being loses himself deliberately."[2] Like religion, eroticism is a "search for lost intimacy."[3] To regain intimacy, eroticism—and religion—"destroy the self-contained character of the participators as they are in their normal lives," "breaking down . . . the regulated social order."[4] For this reason, both the sacred and the erotic are experienced as "domain[s] of violence, of violation."[5] Disrupting and disturbing participants' sense of corporeal and psychic integrity, of social and moral order, eroticism produces pleasure and terror, providing access to ecstasy.

As Tim Dean observes in *Unlimited Intimacy*, his important, provocative, and aptly titled study of the barebacking subculture, "barebacking concerns an experience of unfettered intimacy, of overcoming the boundaries between persons."[6] According to Dean, barebacking deserves attention because it "gives physical form" to an encounter with alterity that "may be regarded as ethically exemplary."[7] Rather than seeking to protect and preserve the discrete, bounded self from the various dangers that comprise life, the subculture's participants embrace and eroticize risk, recognizing it as a "permanent condition of existence," in profound tension with a social order that seeks to discipline its members in the pursuit of health and life.[8] Barebacking, then, transgresses a variety of cultural norms, dispenses with the value traditionally assigned to the self, and confronts its practitioners with the violence that attends erotic desire.

But Dean draws a distinction between barebacking's ethical dispositions, which he finds laudatory, and the practice itself, which he is unwilling to advocate.[9] For Dean, "it is imperative to distinguish what's *psychically* dangerous from what's *physically* dangerous."[10] In his essay "Shame on You," Leo Bersani denounces barebacking for similar reasons.[11] For Bersani, the practice must be rejected because it "literaliz[es] . . . the [self-rupturing] ontology of the sexual . . . , destroy[ing] the crucial psychoanalytic distinction between fantasy and reality."[12] Restating Dean's and Bersani's distinctions in Bataille's terminology, eroticism not only is but must always remain a psychological quest, else it becomes too risky, too dangerous, too violent, *too great a challenge to the physical survival of the individual who seeks to lose himself psychically.*

Dean's reticence, like Bersani's repulsion, is likely applauded by most readers—indeed, it seems utterly rational and sane—but it is not merely a cautionary limitation on the championed disposition; it is its eradication. By insisting that some voluntarily assumed risks are simply too risky, that some threats to the preservation of (physical) life are too great, individual survival becomes the foundational principle of the ethical (cultural, psychical) order, and the radical embrace of alterity transforms into a reasonable openness to some (most?) forms of nonthreatening otherness. The ideology of safety rears its head, and protection of the self, with its suspicion of and hostility toward the other, cannot be far behind. To secure the commonsense and seemingly worthwhile goal of sustaining the self requires a critique of practices that are self-destructive in ethically problematic ways: this entails, at least implicitly, a repudiation of those desires and of those desiring subjects, who are too threatening to the coherence, stability, and security of other subjects. Contrary to Dean's and Bersani's insistence, this is not, in the final analysis, a new vision of relationality but only a slightly modified one, fully consistent with the racist, sexist, classist, and nationalist anxieties about dangerous others that comprise our contemporary cultural order. To avoid replicating the oppositional violence that attends an imaginary built on protection of the self, we must be willing to conceive the pleasures of (erotic) self-dissolution without reserve. While recognizing the inevitable oscillation between the temporary loss of self in ecstatic abandon and its reconstitution in ordinary experience, Bataille relishes, without Bersani's and Dean's cautionary insistence, the former experience. Fantasies and dispositions subtending barebacking do as well.

Taking Dean's and Bersani's treatments of barebacking as its lodestar, this essay traces the ethical implications and insights of Bataille's conception of eroticism. Bataille compels us to ask whether our desire to retain a coherent, recognizable sense of self—perhaps even our very desire to survive—is, in and of itself, ethically and politically suspect. More importantly, he helps us understand why abandoning—or, at the very least, resisting—such desires could generate an entirely new ethical and political imaginary.

When discussing barebacking, Bersani compares it to the "pure love" mysticism of Fénelon and Guyon. "Both can be thought of as disciplines in which the subject allows himself to be penetrated, even replaced, by an unknowable otherness."[13] Although Bataille would undoubtedly endorse this comparison between a transgressive sexual act and a mystical practice, as well as the characterization of both as mechanisms for dislodging the subject,[14] he would likely part company with Bersani's denunciation of the "savage spirituality" represented by these disciplines.[15]

Bersani's rejection of masochistic pleasure may surprise readers familiar only with his essay "Is the Rectum a Grave?" As he memorably—and astutely—observes in the essay's opening sentence, "There is a big secret about sex: most people don't like it."[16] According to Bersani, this aversion to sex is directly proportional to affection for the coherent self. Following Freud and Laplanche, Bersani notes that "sexual pleasure occurs whenever a certain threshold of intensity is reached, when the organization of the self is momentarily disturbed by sensation or affective processes somehow 'beyond' those connected with psychic organization."[17] He therefore concludes: "Sexuality, at least in the mode in which it is constituted, may be a tautology for masochism."[18]

Although masochistic jouissance shatters the coherent self, Bersani insists that it also serves life. On the one hand, by making pleasurable the overwhelming sensations that come upon the human infant too early to be fully processed and assimilated, masochism represents "an evolutionary conquest . . . that partially defeats a biologically dysfunctional process of maturation."[19] On this understanding, masochism helps the infant endure excessive stimulation, transforming it into pleasure, until the child develops "resistant or defensive ego structures."[20] On the other hand, by conjuring fantasies that threaten "psychic wholeness" and stability, masochism "destroy[s] the structures and centers which lock the individual within a few repeatable patterns."[21] On this understanding, masochism releases and circulates exuberant, generative, stimulating energy that ego defenses seek to discipline and control.[22] The "life" served by masochism is quite different in these two accounts: in the former, masochism serves life by sustaining the ego; in the latter, by shattering it.

Because Western conceptions of autonomy and dignity generate strong affection for the coherent self, sexuality is condemned, in our cultural order, "to becoming a struggle for power."[23] Precisely because the protection and maintenance of a coherent self becomes, both explicitly and unwittingly, a sanction for aggression toward and mastery over the other, Bersani decries "pastoral" projects that seek to purify and redeem sexuality by disentangling it from power. Instead, he embraces indictments of sexuality's relation to power—"refusal[s] to prettify it, to romanticize it"—because they "lucidly lay[ ] out for us, the inestimable value of sex as . . . anticommunal, antiegalitarian, antinurturing, antiloving."[24] These are the features that make sexuality a threat to the self. And, as Bersani concludes, "the self is a practical convenience; promoted to the status of an ethical ideal, it is a sanction for violence. If sexuality is socially dysfunctional in that it brings people together only to plunge them into a self-shattering and solipsistic *jouissance* that drives them apart, it could also be thought of as our primary hygienic practice of nonviolence."[25]

In "Is the Rectum a Grave?" Bersani recognizes the marked similarities between his understanding of masochism and Bataille's conception of eroticism. Both entail an experience in which "the self is exuberantly discarded."[26] Similar to Bersani's insistence that masochism serves life, Bataille "defines" eroticism as "assenting to life up to the point of death," noting that it includes both "exuberance of life" and dissolution of self.[27] Bataille's eroticism, like Bersani's masochism, "entails a breaking down of established patterns . . . basic to our . . . existence as defined and separate individuals."[28] For Bataille, eroticism is opposed to work and production, to human endeavors to control and master the world, to sustain and preserve life, to guarantee the future.[29] These endeavors, albeit essential to human survival, foster alienation, aggression, and violence and must, therefore, be countered and interrupted by play, expenditure, and consumption. Exuberance will inevitably have its say; the only choice is what kind of violence will be unleashed.[30] Eroticism replaces aggressive, appropriative violence directed toward the other with a shared experience of violence that disturbs participants' sense of isolated existence.[31] As Bataille explains in his wartime journal, *Guilty*,

> Here's something to express forcefully, to keep clearly in mind—that there's no truth when people look at each other as if they're separate

individuals. Truth starts with conversations, shared laughter, friendship and sex, and it only happens *going from one person to another.* I hate the thought of a person being connected to isolation. . . . As I picture it, the world doesn't resemble a separate or circumscribed being but *what goes from one person to another* when we laugh or make love. When I think this is the way things are, immensity opens and I'm lost. How little *self* matters then![32]

Bataille and Bersani both explore erotic experience for its ethical aftermath. Moving away from his celebration of self-shattering jouissance, Bersani has more recently emphasized the ego's self-divestiture and self-dissemination in "impersonal narcissism."[33] This divestiture and dispersal forestalls the ego's violently appropriative gestures in a manner similar to masochistic shattering, but it also includes "the pleasure of finding multiple parts of ourselves inaccurately replicated everywhere in the world."[34] These replications, while inaccurate because not identical to us, provide a sense of security, by revealing "our already established at-homeness in the world."[35]

Bersani's analysis of how certain works of art can help us see the world as a reassuring, homey environment echoes Bataille's description of the nostalgic yearning for a lost continuity, characterized as an intimate connection to the world. According to Bataille, eroticism's capacity to "rend the seamless garment of . . . separate individuality," to "call[ ] into question . . . the subjective consciousness [of] the feeling of self . . . and . . . the limits of isolated being," violently disturbs, through the self's negation, the typical experience of discontinuous existence, thereby restoring "the possibility of continuity."[36] Continuity—an experience of being "lost in the world like water is lost in water"[37]—is, according to Bataille, something for which we yearn obsessively, a state of affairs we desperately long to restore.[38]

The similar affective resonance of their respective language masks a profound conceptual distinction between Bersani's impersonal narcissism and Bataille's continuity. Bataille does not emphasize relational presence but rather "the passion of an absence of individuality."[39] For Bataille, "intimacy is violence, and it is destruction, because it is not compatible with the positing of the separate individual."[40] It does not reassure; it generates anxiety by disturbing the familiar coordinates of day-to-day experience. "In the trembling of the individual, [intimacy] is . . . suffused with anguish."[41] Similarly, continuity "strike[s] to the inmost core of the living being, so that the heart stands still"; it requires "a partial dissolution of the person as he exists in the realm of discontinuity."[42] When experiencing orgasm—the objective foundation for the subjective experience of eroticism—Bataille contends that "each being contributes to the self-negation of the other, yet the negation is not by any means a recognition of the other. . . . The violence of one goes out to meet the violence of the other. . . . [T]here is no real union. . . . Both creatures are simultaneously open to continuity."[43] In Bataille's usage, continuity and intimacy describe disruptive, unsettling forces that defy expression and understanding, not reassuring states of being, relation, or recognition.

Meditating on the subject's nonsuicidal disappearance, striving to dissociate masochism from the death drive,[44] Bersani has repudiated "Rectum" as "naïve and dangerous,"[45] as "a rather facile, even irresponsible celebration of 'self-defeat.'"[46] Bersani now rejects the necessity, or advisability, of the ego's sacrificial, psychic death that self-shattering masochistic jouissance entails but looks instead to works of art and literature that facilitate self-disruption and self-dissemination while still allowing a refinding of the self, inaccurately replicated, in the world. Bataille, on the other hand, explicitly analogizes witnessing the sacrificial victim's immolation, encountering the literary hero's risk, and arousing the erotic partner's desire in order to identify various means by which the self can undergo psychic death.[47] These profound, terrifying, alluring, ecstatic self-dissolutions rupture the distinction between subject and object that fosters instrumental, alienating, violent relations to the world. Because impersonal narcissism allows the subject to see itself reflected in the world, reassuring the self that it has always belonged to a world that it incorrectly perceived as threatening and overwhelming, Bersani contends it will also prevent such violent appropriations. But to maintain the distinction between ego disruptions that lead to psychic death and those that allow for psychic replication, Bersani must identify threats to the ego's coherence and stability that go too far, that are too extreme, too excessive. In other words, he must promote the self—in some form, to some extent, after some fashion—as an ethical norm. While impersonal narcissism may reduce—perhaps even eliminate—relations of appropriation and mastery, because the world is now perceived as a reflection of, rather than opposed to, the self, some aspects of the world, some of its features, some of its experiences, must necessarily be repudiated, rejected, defended against, held at bay—because they carry with them the risk of self-shattering jouissance, "biological or psychic death."[48]

In repudiating his earlier celebration of self-loss, Bersani may also mean to disclaim his observation that the self's promotion to an ethical ideal can become a sanction for violence. Given his movement away from psychoanalysis—because it conceives the relation between self and world as opposition, where defense against the world's overwhelming presence is the primary developmental goal—he seems committed to his important insight about the risks inherent in promoting the self's coherence as an ethical ideal. But impersonal narcissism, in the final analysis, requires just such an ethically problematic promotional endeavor. Bersani has moved away from self-shattering jouissance because he wants to retain the self in some form, in some space. With the self, however, comes self-defensive violence. Because Bataille valorizes the capacity to *experience* the violence that is intimacy and the conflagration that is continuity, he also seeks a nonsuicidal disappearance of the subject. Unlike Bersani, however, Bataille's "retention" of the self is an incidental precondition to having the experience of self-loss rather than a structural limitation that seeks to replace loss of self with another set of pleasures. Bataille understands that as long as self-recognition—even displaced and distorted—remains a constitutive dimension of the system, then some form of self-protection, which is only ever thinly disguised self-aggrandizement—which, as a practical matter, is only ever aggressive, appropriative violence—is inevitable.

In a recent essay on gay male pornographic literature, Dean observes that barebacking porn fits "squarely in the domain of eroticism as defined by Bataille."[49] In *Unlimited Intimacy*, Dean examines barebacking culture's complex, multifaceted imaginary, tracing the ethical dispositions that accompany the respective practices. As Dean's thoughtful exploration reveals, not all the dispositions line up on the same side of the ethical and political divide. For example, noting that bug chasers describe their practices in terms of kinship and reproduction, Dean intriguingly suggests that they be understood as an alternative relational system, one opposed to both normative heterosexuality and same-sex marriage.[50] At the same time, highlighting barebackers' erotic investment in masculine strength and power, he cautions, "bareback subculture may be ethically troubling less for its radical departure from mainstream values than for its perpetuation of them."[51] However we describe and assess the ethical dispositions that arise from these practices, reviewing Dean's discussion with Bataille in mind generates importantly different insights than Dean's assessments.[52]

"According to subcultural nomenclature, the partner for whom a bug chaser searches is known as a gift giver or 'gifter.'"[53] Acknowledging that this characterization of HIV infection "seems utterly perverse," Dean examines "gift giving . . . as an elementary mode of relating to others."[54] Because Dean and Bataille derive their understanding of gift giving from Marcel Mauss, they recognize that a gift imposes an obligation on, establishes power over, and secures prestige in relation to the recipient.[55] For Dean, the gift's capacity to rank erotic partners, its marking the gift giver as more important than the bug chaser, is in tension with barebacking's equalizing embrace of alterity. For Bataille, the gift's capacity to secure something useful, its role in establishing social privilege, is in tension with the meaningless expenditure gift giving seemingly embodies. For both Bataille and Dean, then, the gift, which appears to figure and embody ideals they endorse, represents, on closer inspection, values they reject.

While Dean does not spell out all the relevant implications, his analysis reveals that gift giving has a different logic within barebacking communities. For example, "bug chaser" and "gift giver" are not fixed identities but fungible roles.[56] While the gifter is pursued, and therefore valorized, by the bug chaser, prestige attaches to the role, not the person; it affixes to any body that occupies the relevant structural position.[57] Thus, insofar as possession of the gift generates prestige, this prestige circulates much more easily than material wealth. Moreover, given that barebackers often refuse to test to determine whether they are infected with HIV, they do not necessarily prove their possession of the relevant wealth in the same way as a tribal chieftain would in potlatch.[58] Participants in a given bareback encounter may very well have no guarantee that they are gifters, that they are having sex with gift givers, or that the sex being had has bestowed the sought-after gift. The encounter's structure and attendant fantasies—rather than the participants' properties—are the principal coin of the realm: this currency is available to anyone.

When discussing Jacques Derrida's notion that a true gift "would be given freely, without expectation of return," Dean emphasizes the unique logic of barebackers' gift giving. While "the subcultural gift of seroconversion appears to fulfill [Derrida's] criterion for ethical exemplarity insofar as it cannot be returned to the donor," it also *exceeds* the terms of Mauss's and Derrida's understanding of exchange.[59] Mauss and Derrida conceptualize gift giving dyadically, but "the subculture's gift economy always exceeds the couple."[60] As Dean observes, "bug chasers and gift givers are having sex with a virus as well as with each other. They have opened their bodies to intimate relations with nonhuman life."[61] Viral "exchange," then, is not constrained by the usual terms of gift giving.[62] The relevant circuit of exchange for the virus extends beyond "particular operations with limited ends" to encompass "the play of *living matter in general.*"[63]

If I receive the virus, I ostensibly cannot return it, because—unlike wealth squandered in potlatch—I retain it as I give it away. Of course, as a technical matter, I *can* return the virus: reinfection is a physiological possibility. More importantly, whether or not I am infected, whether or not I know I am infected, I can still harbor fantasies of giving and receiving the virus; my serostatus and my ability to pursue the pleasures that comprise bug chasing and gift giving are completely independent from each other.[64] From at least one perspective, however, I am unable to make a gift of the virus: once I have obtained it, I am unable to rid myself of it, given the present state of medical knowledge. Of course, as safe-sex educators and bug chasers alike know, I can "give" the virus profligately: viral transmission, unlike potlatch's squandering, distributes without depleting; it is an expenditure that increases rather than diminishes the circulating resource. The viral gift, then, bears a striking similarity to the solar energy that Bataille valorizes: a seemingly limitless resource with the capacity to expand exponentially.[65] It is an ever-circulating, always-replenishing, never-receding resource.[66]

Dean recognizes this unique character of barebacking's gift giving: "the virus as gift circulates within bareback subculture as in a *general economy* of exchange."[67] When making this statement, Dean fails to acknowledge Bataille's significant contribution to examining human society from the perspective of general, rather than restrictive, economy.[68] Barebacking's gift giving is an almost perfect illustration of Bataille's understanding of general economy. This gift is an "extravagant" form of wealth: it can be both possessed and given away; it can be spent without loss.[69] In addition, as Dean articulates so powerfully, dispositions related to barebacking, like perspectives related to general economy, have the capacity to "accomplish[ ] a Copernican transformation . . . of ethics."[70] Insofar as barebacking's dispositions challenge participants' relation to alterity, intimacy, and risk, attending to barebacking—as an exemplification of the principles of general economy—reveals the political and ethical significance of erotic practices.[71] Given that *Unlimited Intimacy* arrives at Bataillean conclusions about barebacking's logic of gift giving while failing to engage Bataille's texts, focusing on the lack of a citation to *The Accursed Share* might seem like unwarranted fussiness about bibliographic comprehensiveness. But the consequences of Dean's omission reveal themselves when considering his critique of bug chasers' self-sacrificial rhetoric.

Dean contends that the bareback subculture perpetuates rather than resists mainstream values by celebrating "barebacking as a heroic sacrifice on behalf of the gay community."[72] To illustrate this perspective, Dean quotes at length Paul Morris, a well-known "documentary pornographer" who produces bareback and fetish films:

> "Unsafe sex" is not only insane, it is also essential. For a subculture to
> be sustained, there must be those who engage in central and defining
> activities with little regard for anything else, including life itself. In

a sense, not only the nature but also the coherence of the subculture is determined and maintained by passionate devotees who serve a contextually heroic purpose in their relationship with danger, death and communion.

. . . The individual becomes an agent through which a darker and more fragile tradition is enabled to continue. Irresponsibility to the everyday persona and to the general culture is necessary for allegiance to the sexual subculture, and this allegiance takes the gay male directly to the hot and central point where what is at stake isn't the survival of the individual, but the survival of the practices and patterns which are discoveries and properties of the subculture. . . .

In such a situation, how does one balance the struggle between the needs of the survival of the body and the needs within the body for the survival of traditions, truths and practices?[73]

According to Dean, Morris's argument "promotes an ethic homologous with that of patriotism": "barebackers sacrifice themselves on behalf of gay culture in the same way that . . . soldiers sacrifice themselves on behalf of their country during war."[74] Laying aside both that Morris's rhetoric seems more descriptive than hortatory, markedly distinguishing it from most appeals to civic pride, and that he never uses the word "sacrifice" to describe allegiance to subcultural traditions and practices, Dean's comparison still falters because the patriotic commitment he renounces is qualitatively different than the subcultural allegiance Morris envisions.

When citizens sacrifice time, energy, resources, and life for their homeland, it more easily, more quickly, more efficiently accomplishes its goals. What exactly is accomplished, acquired, or attained through the allegiance Morris describes? Bug chasing, as both Morris and Dean describe it, is a passionate embrace of danger, an exciting acceptance of risk, an uninhibited encounter with the other, an energizing confrontation with death.[75] Although such an exercise may have value, it has no *lasting* value: for this very reason, the traditions, beliefs, and practices Morris describes are radically contrary to the machinations of the modern nation-state.[76] In this context, Bataille's distinction between warrior societies and military societies is helpful. Although both rely on rhetorics of sacrifice to justify members' risking their lives in violent combat,

a truly *military* society is a venture society, for which war means a development of power, an orderly progression of empire. It is a relatively mild society; it makes a custom of the rational principles of enterprise, whose purpose is given in the future, and it excludes the madness of sacrifice.[77]

A warrior society's sacrificial violence, on the other hand, is wasteful expenditure rather than calculated pursuit.

For Bataille, sacrifice is, at its core, the consumption of useful things, sometimes through utter destruction, sometimes through lesser means. It never has a goal or purpose beyond itself, beyond the moment of conflagration. Sacrificial ritual, on Bataille's account, restores the thing to the status of a subject, removes it from the profane order of instrumentality, and returns it to the sacred order of intimacy.

> It does not have to destroy as fire does; only the tie that connected the offering to the world of profitable activity is severed, but this separation has the sense of a definitive consumption; the consecrated offering cannot be restored to the *real* order. . . . The world of *intimacy* is as antithetical to the *real* world as immoderation is to moderation, madness to reason, drunkenness to lucidity.[78]

The subcultural ethos Morris describes bears a much closer resemblance to Bataille's immoderate, consumptive madness than to the rational, goal-oriented patriotic values "invoked so persistently in the United States at present."[79] While Morris's argument rhetorically privileges group ethos over individual survival in a way that mirrors some nationalistic discourses, the "group" is an experience or attitude, not an assemblage of persons with interests.[80] While Morris uses the language of survival, the survival he has in mind necessarily incorporates loss and death. Moreover, Morris makes no demand that anyone submit to the subcultural ethos he describes. Most significantly, this ethos—far from being identified with conquest, power or aggrandizement—is typified by a desire for communion forged in the shared risk of uninhibited intimacy.

Near the end of *Unlimited Intimacy*, Dean contrasts an ethics of pleasure, which he advocates, with an ethics of self-sacrifice, which he abjures. The pleasure he has in mind entails an "openness to contact with the other."[81] Characterizing the relevant other as the unconscious, Dean admits that it "requires the mediation—we might say, the *provocation*—of another person who may or may not be a stranger and who may or may not inhabit a different social register from oneself."[82] Similarly, Bataille contends that the key feature of erotic activity is a mutual provocation that dissolves "the separate beings that participate in it."[83] "There is an inner compulsion to get out of the limits of individual discontinuity. There is a meeting between two beings projected beyond their limits by the sexual orgasm. . . . Two individuals in the grip of violence brought together by the preordained reflexes of sexual intercourse share in a state of crisis in which both are beside themselves."[84] Unlike Dean, Bataille does not distinguish this self-rupturing experience from sacrifice but parallels eroticism and sacrifice to better understand the dynamics of each.[85] Moreover, unlike Dean, who distinguishes disruption of the self from pleasure,[86] Bataille recognizes that suspension of the everyday experience of discontinuous, separate existence is, while anxiety provoking and terrifying, deeply satisfying and sought after.

At the same time, recognizing that the openness to alterity entails anxiety, Dean insists that a distinct, and arguably superior, "quality of pleasure [is] achieved through risk taking."[87] Why would this be true?[88] Encountering risk could generate greater and better pleasure than guaranteeing safety only if self-endangerment is pleasurable. But if self-endangerment is pleasurable, then why consistently deny the pleasures—and ethical value—of self-sacrifice? What else could be risked in an encounter with the other than the viability, integrity, survival of the self? If "engagement with otherness is never completely safe; [if] contact with the unfamiliar, the strange, always entails risk," why not acknowledge that endorsing radical openness to alterity as a commendable ethical stance demands, at least, a recognition that self-sacrifice could be ethically viable?[89] The only meaning that can be assigned to Dean's distinction between an ethics of pleasure and an ethics of self-sacrifice is that it is unethical to pursue risks so great that they will most likely overcome and eradicate the self. If risk and danger are an essential part of an ethic of pleasure *that must always remain distinct from an ethic of self-sacrifice*, the distinguishing feature of an ethic of pleasure is its concern for the self and the self's survival. Despite his celebration of bug chasers' openness to alterity and their critique of the ideology of safety, Dean has built a wall along the self's border, without explicitly acknowledging he has done so, to keep certain risks from migrating too far into the self's territory.

In the closing chapter of *Unlimited Intimacy*, Dean argues that cruising, like barebacking, "involves intimacy with strangers" not predicated "on knowledge or understanding of the other—that is, without the subtle violence that usually accompanies epistemological relations."[90] Bersani also contends that cruising allows for encounters with an otherness that cannot be named, defined, known, understood, controlled, or domesticated.[91] Grounded in an "impersonal intimacy," cruising challenges prevailing conceptions of self, desire, intersubjectivity, and relationality.[92] Its most significant feature, according to Dean and Bersani, is its capacity to prevent the self's acquisitive, appropriative, aggressive relation to the world by short-circuiting desire's longing to understand and possess the other. Cruising—in the ideal form Bersani and Dean endorse—promotes contact with the other that impedes the self's instrumental, purpose-driven, goal-oriented relation to the world, contacts resulting from happy accidents with unknown objects of desire. Requiring an openness to the other and a willingness to entertain certain risks, making it similar to the admirable dimensions of barebacking, cruising represents an alternative model for encountering alterity that does not pose significant threats to its practitioners' survival.

In the final sentences of *Unlimited Intimacy*, Dean contrasts his cruising ethic of loving the stranger with the Christian ethic of loving one's neighbor *as oneself*, claiming the latter "annihiliate[s] . . . the other's strangeness" and, through a relation of identification that assumes knowledge of the stranger, molds the other in the form of one's self.[93] Although Bataille recognizes the Christian imaginary's potential to foster an "obsession with a *self*," he identifies another dimension of Christianity that helps expose the shortcomings of Dean's and Bersani's accounts of cruising.[94] In the crucifixion, the "Son of God's ignominious" death, we observe—and are implicated in—a great murder, a sacrifice of the very foundation of being, a transgressive act that enables communication, intimacy, continuity.[95] Without this connection to self-rupturing violence, Bataille argues, Christianity loses its religious character.[96] Similarly, because cruising—even in its ideal form—fails genuinely to risk the self, it fails adequately to displace the appropriative, instrumentalizing, goal-oriented relation to the world that Dean and Bersani (and Bataille) decry.

The first question to be posed to Bersani's and Dean's accounts of cruising, of course, concerns the frequency—nay, the existence—of its ideal form. In "Sociability and Cruising," Bersani writes, "The gay bathhouse is especially favorable to ideal cruising because . . . the common bathhouse uniform—a towel—communicates very little (although there are of course ways of wearing a towel . . .) about our social personality (economic privilege, class status, taste)."[97] In making this observation, he forgets his equally astute observation in "Rectum":

Anyone who has ever spent one night in a gay bathhouse knows that it is (or was) one of the most ruthlessly ranked, hierarchized, and competitive environments imaginable. Your looks, muscles, hair distribution, size of cock, and shape of ass determined exactly how happy you were going to be during those few hours, and rejection, generally accompanied by two or three words at most, could be swift and brutal, with none of the civilizing hypocrisies with which we get rid of undesirables in the outside world.[98]

Although the characteristics connected to bathhouse ruthlessness may seem irrelevant to one's "social personality," they are certainly as amenable to enumeration as race and class—and can be purposefully sought out. And, of course, as Bersani's parenthetical remark reminds, even complete nakedness does not require that a person shed bodily markers of racial, ethnic, class, religious, and national identity. One can know what one wants when ambling through a bathhouse; one can also feel quite possessive once one has found it.[99]

Dean relates a story meant to illustrate the ethic of cruising he commends.[100] During a research trip in San Francisco, he got lost while on his way to the gym. As he wandered, a homeless man came to his aid both by retrieving his baseball cap from traffic after it had blown off his head and by taking him on a shortcut that allowed him to arrive on time for his appointment. At the end of their half-hour journey, while talking outside the gym, the homeless man asked Dean for spare change.

> Had he asked for money when we first met, I probably would have refused, but after such a pleasant encounter and such generous assistance on his part, I was happy to help. To my surprise, the homeless stranger then showered me with kisses and offered to fuck me right outside the gym (earlier, as he rhapsodized about his "girlfriend's pussy," I had taken him for straight). An experience that, for me, began in trepidation ended in delight.
>
> Although we parted ways at the entrance to Gold's [Gym], I suspect that both the homeless stranger and I benefited from the encounter more than either of us could have anticipated.[101]

Although this encounter was unplanned, the stranger's value is measured almost completely by how well he accords with Dean's established goals—retrieving his hat, negotiating the city, arriving on time (and, perhaps, reinforcing Dean's sense of sexual attractiveness). In addition, far from establishing an intimacy that does not require an understanding of the other, Dean presumes to know all kinds of things about this stranger: first, identifying it as the correction of an earlier assumption, he assumes the offer to fuck evinces the man's (true?) identity; second, he freely characterizes the *stranger's* experience of their encounter.

As he goes on to classify the different kinds of spaces in which cruising may occur, Dean opines,

> My homeless acquaintance knew that he could not set foot in Gold's for a quick shower and some time in the sauna without paying an exorbitant fee. Given the history of gay politics in a city as ostensibly

progressive as San Francisco, it is worth considering why such a large, welcoming gay gym seems unable to accommodate such a simple physical desire.[102]

Is it worth considering why a gay man as ostensibly progressive as Dean did not offer to purchase his homeless acquaintance a day pass—instead of, or in addition to, giving him spare change? Would welcoming this stranger into the space of the gym have embarrassed Dean? Made him—and other patrons—uncomfortable? Interfered with the appointment he needed to keep? Prevented effective cruising of the space?

I focus on these details not to malign Dean or his intentions—I doubt I would have acted differently, or even as generously, in a similar situation. Rather, his story highlights a second, more serious difficulty with "proposing" cruising as a "model . . . for a new relationality."[103] Bersani contends that cruising "illuminates" a "*jouissance* of otherness" distinct from masochistic jouissance, a jouissance that "owes nothing to the death drive."[104] Although this jouissance "has as its precondition the stripping away of the self" and can be described as an "ascetic . . . practice," Bersani insists that it is not masochistic and, in fact, requires, as an additional precondition, "a loss of all that gives us pleasure and pain in our negotiable exchanges with the world."[105] Insofar as it requires a loss of all that gives pain, this distinguishes it from masochism, but insofar as it requires a loss of all that gives *pleasure*, it is difficult to understand its relation to cruising, which, even in its ideal form, seems connected, in some fashion, to enjoying an other's bodily presence. More important for the distinction Bersani wants to draw is the way otherness recuperates the lost self: "The otherness I refer to is one that cannot be erased or even reduced by the inaccurate replications that, by inviting multiple and diverse self-recognitions, make of the world a hospitable space in which the subject ceaselessly, and always partially, reoccurs."[106]

For Dean, the most "interesting" feature of "certain practices of cruising is their aimlessness, their encouraging a centrifugal openness to the other without the necessity of having a particular object of seduction in mind. This would be cruising in the Kantian mode of 'purposiveness without purpose.'"[107] In *Inner Experience*, Bataille sketches a set of practices that foster aimlessness by developing a particular kind of relationship to an unknown—but desirable—object.[108] Bataille wants a project that will undo project, a program with the intention of dissolving intentionality, for the purpose of destroying purposiveness.[109] As he notes, however, such a practice uses the object of desire to disturb the subject. As he writes in *Inner Experience*'s preface, "To ask oneself before another: by what means does he calm within himself the desire to be everything"?[110] This desire to be everything—to be powerful, autonomous, capable of achieving one's goals, of knowing and understanding the world, acquiring and possessing the desirable other—is a "hazy illusion[ ] . . . , a narcotic necessary to bear life. But what happens to us when, disintoxicated, we learn what we are?"[111]

For Bataille, inner experience is characterized by perpetual contestation, contestation that will, eventually, undo the subject of the experience itself.[112] The subject's dissolution is, in fact, the goal of those activities undertaken with the purpose of quelling purposiveness. With their advocacy of cruising as the model for impersonal intimacy, Dean and Bersani suggest that reconfiguring the subject's relation to the object will be sufficient to transform the subject's aggressive, appropriative relation to the world. To my mind, such a reconfiguration is insufficient; the subject's relation to itself, to its sense of its power and prerogatives, must be more radically challenged. Dean admires cruising's aimless subject, and Bersani champions its ascetic self, but this merely reforms rather than revolutionizes existing relational forms. Insofar as the desiring subject, the autonomous self, the goal-oriented agent, the individual with individualized predilections is the source of the problems we name as violence, objectification, and instrumentalization, then it must be targeted by a practice that seeks to disrupt, displace—destroy—it, if we truly want to remake our most fundamental conceptions of what it means to relate to the world.

As practices, both cruising and barebacking entail risk. On the one hand, very real risks to life and health accompany bug chasing. On the other, cruising risks perpetuating appropriative, acquisitive, instrumental relations to the object of desire. Bersani and Dean conclude that the former are too great; I suggest the reverse. Do we need to worry more about the subject's tendency to act inhumanely toward that which it longs to possess or about its tendency to protect itself against threats to its existence? Does the self-preservative instinct's strength need reinforcement? Might it wane without constant encouragement and vigilant attention? Our cultural order valorizes individual autonomy. Our prevailing political and ethical frameworks identify a wide array of "others" who embody danger while promising these excluded ones that some day soon they too can occupy the position of subject. Virtually all social, political, ethical, or cultural programs are judged on the extent to which they respect and enhance the rights, privileges, and capacities of the individual. Is there a genuine risk that we will err too far on the side of *not* respecting the self and its value? Or, when we consider the rampant horrors perpetuated in the name of protecting individual dignity, liberty, and autonomy, do we think that something might be gained by adopting practices that allow us to experience—if even for a moment—the pleasures that accompany the rupture of the self and the demeaning of its value? Practices that will "ruin in [us] that which is opposed to ruin"?[113]

The subject attains its worth only by having an other against which it is defined and to which it can be compared. As Bersani so eloquently and brilliantly demonstrates when critiquing psychoanalytic discourses that figure the other solely as an endangering, threatening presence, imaginaries that conceive anything beyond the self as invasive, threatening, and disturbing only reinforce its aggressive, violent tendencies. Rather than assuming the importance of the individual's survival, rather than insisting on the value of attaining selfhood, rather than trying only to frustrate the self's goal-oriented activities, rather than promoting practices that remove the self only to replicate it elsewhere, what if we embraced dispositions that risked "self-dismissal," that promoted the habit of "*losing sight* of the self"?[114] What if, as a means of preventing the violence and cruelty of which subjects are so evidently capable, we fostered habits that, instead of attempting merely to reconfigure the subject's relation to the object, sought to erase the subject's very coherence, stability, and presence?

Desire, Blood, and Power
Georges Bataille and the Study of Hindu Tantra in Northeastern India

HUGH B. URBAN

> But the embrace restores us, not to nature . . . but rather to the totality in which man has his share by *losing himself*. For an embrace is not just a fall into the animal muck, but the anticipation of death. . . . The point is that the totality reached . . . is reached only at the price of a sacrifice: eroticism reaches it precisely inasmuch as love is a kind of immolation.
>
> **—Georges Bataille, *The Accursed Share***

> Merely by worshiping the female sexual organ [*yoni*] the worship of the Goddess as Power [Shakti] is performed. The adept should worship with the blood flowing from the sacrifices of birds, etc. and with the words "*yoni, yoni*," while reciting his prayers.
>
> **—*The Yoni Tantra* (sixteenth century)**

Although he described his own work as a kind of "atheology," more concerned with God's death than with God's existence, Georges Bataille must be counted as one of the twentieth century's most important theorists of religion. From his own *Theory of Religion* to his work on mysticism, sacrifice, and erotic spirituality, Bataille has influenced a wide range of theorists, from philosophers such as Michel Foucault and Gilles Deleuze to anthropologists and historians of religions such as Michael Taussig and Amy Hollywood.[1]

To date, however, most of the work on Bataille and religion has focused on his implications for the study of Christianity, particularly Christian mysticism, a subject that interested Bataille himself intensely. With a few exceptions, there has been little effort to explore the implications of Bataille's work for the study of Hinduism, Buddhism, or any other Asian tradition.[2] This is ironic and unfortunate, given Bataille's own interest in Tibetan Buddhism and in Hindu traditions such as yoga and Tantra. As Andrew Hussey notes in his study of Bataille's mysticism, "although Bataille disparaged any appropriation of Eastern methods which recognized any form of cephalic 'sommet' as the 'point seul' of meditation, and although the vocabulary he uses to describe the movement of inner experience belongs largely to the Western tradition, Bataille was well-read in Classical Hinduism and Buddhism."[3] Bataille was quite familiar with the works of Alexandra David-Néel on Tibetan Buddhism, Mircea Eliade's work on yoga, and Romain Roland's biographies of the Hindu saints Shri Ramakrishna and Swami Vivekananda. He was particularly interested, for example, in the Hindu goddess Kali, dark mother of time and death, whom he described as the goddess of "terror, of destruction, of night and of chaos."[4] Moreover, in late 1938 and 1939, Bataille also began to practice yoga and meditation himself, a practice that, he recalls, helped him realize the "fundamental connection between religious ecstasy and eroticism" and the "infinite capacity for reversal" that characterizes his own atheological form of mystical "inner experience."[5] In short, Bataille's own work on religion was significantly influenced by his encounter with Hinduism and Buddhism, and, in turn, his insights into religious experience have the potential to shed some useful light on non-Western traditions.

In this chapter, I will focus on the tradition of Hindu Tantra and goddess worship in northeastern India, employing but also critically rethinking several of Bataille's key insights into the relations between eroticism, sacrifice, and transgression.[6] Specifically, I will examine the worship of the goddess Kamakhya and her temple in Assam, which is revered as one of the oldest, most important "power centers" or seats of the goddess in South Asia and, indeed, as the locus of the goddess's *yoni* or sexual organ.[7] As the very embodiment of divine desire (*kama*), Kamakhya temple is also the site of the goddess's annual menstruation, which takes place for three days each summer and is the occasion of her most important festival. At the same time, Assam is also often identified as the original homeland of Hindu Tantra and particularly of Tantric sexual rituals, which involve explicit transgressions of conventional social boundaries and the oral consumption of menstrual and other sexual fluids as the ultimate source of spiritual power.[8]

In my analysis, I will by no means attempt to apply simplistically Bataille's work to this South Asian example. Instead, I want to use but also *critically modify* some of Bataille's basic ideas of erotism; the link between sensuality, death, and mystical experience; and his analysis of sexual and religious transgression. Bataille, I will suggest, is extremely useful for understanding the logic of transgression and the systematic use of impurity in Hindu Tantra. Whereas the Tantric traditions have long been misunderstood by modern scholars—both Indian and Western—Bataille gives us some key insights into the role of ritual transgression in Tantric practice. Drawing on Bataille, I will suggest that Tantric practice involves a kind of "unlimited transgression" that aims to shatter not just conventional social norms but the very boundaries of the finite self in intense union with the divine. However, as various feminist authors have pointed out, Bataille's work reflects a consistent masculine and phallic bias, with a general lack of attention to female sexuality or to women as active agents.[9] In the case of Hindu Tantra in Assam, I will argue, female sexuality holds a central place and plays an integral role in the larger phenomena of transgression, expenditure, and ecstatic religious experience. As such, we can also use this South Asian example and Hindu concepts of desire and power to reimagine critically Bataille's work for the contemporary study of religion, as well.

Matrix of Power: Kamakhya and the *Shakta Pithas* in South Asian History

Since at least the eighth century, the temple of the mother goddess Kamakhya has been revered as one of the oldest, most important, and most powerful seats of goddess worship and Hindu Tantra in South Asia. As the locus of the goddess's own sexual organ (*yoni*), Kamakhya temple is literally the "mother of all seats of power." In this sense, Kamakhya temple can be called the "matrix of power," as both the maternal womb (*matr*, etymologically related to Latin mater and English matrix) that gives birth to the universe and all its elements (*matrkas*).[10]

From its origins, however, this temple is intimately tied to the dual themes of sacrificial violence and sexual transgression. Indeed, it is a stunning illustration of what Bataille calls the "similarity between the act of love and sacrifice" and the ways in which the *petit mort* of sexual union often mirrors the larger death of ritual killing.[11] According to a widespread series of myths that appears in the Hindu epics and mythological literature, the origin of Kamakhya goes as follows: Once upon a time Lord Shiva (the cosmic destroyer in the Hindu pantheon) was married to the goddess Sati. However, Sati's father, Daksha, very much disliked Shiva, who is a frightening, wild, outsider deity, so when Daksha threw a huge sacrificial feast and invited all the other gods, he intentionally did not invite Shiva. This snub was such a profound insult that Sati threw herself onto the sacrificial fire, making herself the tragic victim of the ritual. Shiva then went into a rage, destroyed the entire ritual, and beheaded Daksha, thus making his father-in-law the ironic victim of his own sacrifice. Shiva then carried the corpse of Sati away on his shoulder, and his anger was so intense that it threatened to destroy the entire universe. To defuse the situation, the other gods dismembered Sati's body, and the various pieces of her corpse fell in different holy places of India, which then became the "seats of power," or *shakta pithas*. Among the holiest of these became the seat of her *yoni*, which fell in Assam, and it is here that Shiva and Sati eternally reside in secret sexual union. As Lord Shiva declares in one eleventh-century text from Assam, "in this most sacred *pitha* . . . the goddess is secretly joined with Me. Sati's sexual organ, which was severed and fell there, became a stone; and there Kamakhya is present."[12]

Since at least the eleventh or twelfth century, Kamakhya temple has been famous not simply as the primary seat of the goddess's sexual organ but also as the locus of her annual menstruation. To this day, the most important festival here is Ambuvaci Mela, which celebrates the goddess's menstruation during the summer month of Asadha (June-July). Occurring at the beginning of the monsoon season, with the coming of the rains after the heat of summer, Ambuvaci marks the flow of the goddess's life-giving blood to the earth. But it is also a celebration that reflects the profound ambivalence of the goddess's blood and the power it embodies, a power that is tied to impurity and to the dangerous potency of sexual fluids.[13]

To understand the deeper significance of this festival, therefore, we need to understand the place of menstruation and menstrual blood in the Hindu imagination. Like all bodily fluids, and particularly sexual fluids, menstrual blood is considered to be an extremely powerful but ambivalent substance. It is, on the one hand, the sacred power of life and procreation itself. But it is also, on the other hand, extremely impure and polluting. As David Gordon White observes, "Indian traditions have always viewed sexual fluids, and most particularly menstrual blood, as polluting, powerful and therefore dangerous substances."[14] And the act of menstruation is likewise regarded as a powerful and creative but also dangerous and polluting event. As Madhu Khanha notes, "A woman during menstruation is compared to a fallen woman. . . . [The] temporary untouchability attributed to women and the overwhelming number of menstrual taboos imposed on them go to show that the first three days of menstruation were looked upon as dangerous and threatening."[15]

Thus, when Kamakhya menstruates for three days each year, she is considered to be in a state of "impurity, just like the impurity of woman due to her menstruation," and her temple must be closed to all visitors during these days.[16] But it is this very same impure, dangerous, and potentially destructive blood of the goddess that is believed to bring life and creative energy to the earth and to her devotees. Thus on the fourth day after her menstruation, the temple doors are opened up again, and red cloths representing the bloody menstrual flow are distributed to the thousands of pilgrims who thereby receive the power and grace of the goddess. As one cotemporary priest explains, the red cloth represents the *nirmali* of the goddess's menstrual flow—that is, the sacred "remains" of an offering or sacrifice. It is this bloody remnant of her powerful impurity that brings grace and life to the pilgrims' homes: "as the sacred remains of this festival, the goddess' red garments (the cloth she was wearing while in her menstrual period) are very fruitful, and the pilgrims wear them as amulets, considering them to be very holy."[17]

As such, the powerful but impure blood of the goddess is a striking illustration of Bataille's key insight into the dual nature of the sacred—a sacred that is not simply pure but rather contains both "pure and impure," both light and dark, both "right-" and "left-hand" aspects. "The realm of sacred things is composed of the pure and of the impure," Bataille suggests. "Pure or favourable sacredness has been dominant since pagan antiquity. But . . . impure or ill-omened sacredness was there underneath."[18] As David Shulman likewise comments in his discussion of goddess worship and sacrifice in South India: "in a religion that ultimately asserts the divine nature of terrestrial existence, power—however dark its workings, however terrible its effects—never loses its sacred character."[19]

This dynamic of purity and impurity, sacrality and power is also reflected in the primary forms of public worship of the goddess Kamakhya. Since at least the tenth century, the most important public ritual offered to the goddess has been blood sacrifice, the regular performance of which is represented in numerous royal copper plate inscriptions and in rigorous detail in Assamese texts such as the *Kalika Purana*.[20] And sacrifice is in turn part of a larger ritual complex and circulating flow of blood and power. Just as the goddess menstruates each year, offering her fertile, life-giving blood to the earth, so too, blood is returned to her periodically in the form of animal (and at one time human) victims.[21]

The form of sacrifice we see at Kamakhya, however, is quite different from the traditional forms of sacrifice described in the Vedas, the priestly scriptures that lie at the foundation of all later Hindu traditions. Indeed, sacrifices offered to the goddess are in many ways based on explicit inversions and deliberate transgressions of traditional Vedic rites. Whereas the Vedic sacrifice allows only pure, that is, domestic animals, such as horses, cows, sheep and goats, Assamese texts such as the *Kalika Purana* recommend the sacrifice of everything from buffaloes, boars, alligators, and lizards to rhinos, lions, and even elephants. Later Assamese texts such as the *Yogini Tantra* (seventeenth century) also recommend offerings of rabbits, tortoises, and a range of other wild animals. As various scholars have noted, this motley assortment of victims probably reflects not any traditional Vedic rite but rather the sacrificial practices of the many non-Hindu indigenous traditions of the northeastern hills, traditions that have long offered sacrifices of boars, fowl, and other non-Vedic animals.[22]

Even today, Kamakhya's most prized victim is the buffalo—a highly non-Vedic offering, which is killed in a clearly non-Vedic manner by beheading. Whereas victims in the Vedic rite were dispatched by an unbloody act of suffocation, the buffalo is killed in a quite bloody act of beheading, and the focal point of the entire rite is the presentation of the blood and the severed head to the goddess. Again, this is a practice that is much closer to local tribal rites of northeastern India than to any Vedic practice.[23] As Madeleine Biardeau points out in her discussion of sacrifice and goddess worship, the impure and non-Vedic offering of the buffalo is, paradoxically, perhaps the most fitting offering for the goddess as destroyer of evil: "the buffalo is a savage beast, a stranger to the sacrificial world. Vedic literature does not count it among its permitted animals. But it is apt by this fact, to play the role of the principle that is antithetical to the goddess, the incarnation of total evil."[24] As such, the buffalo is very much a "victim, sacred and cursed" in Bataille's sense—that is, "the accursed share" that is withdrawn from the mundane order of things in order to be "utterly destroyed" in sacrifice.[25]

In short, the public ritual performances at Kamakhya represent a cyclical flow of power, embodied in the physical form of blood: the impure but life-giving blood of the goddess flows to the earth each year during her divine menstruation, and blood is regularly given back to her in the form of animal offerings—and particularly offerings of non-Vedic, impure animals such as buffaloes. But this circulation is also intimately linked to impurity and to the "left-handed" or "dark" side of the sacred in Bataille's sense; indeed, it is precisely through the systematic manipulation of impurity—in the form of menstruation and the offering of impure animals by bloody beheading—that one can tap into and unleash the tremendous energy of the goddess that lies within the cosmos and the social order.[26]

The Sacrifice of Desire: Sexual Rites and the Secret Sacrifice

In addition to the public performance of animal sacrifice, however, Kamakhya has also long been worshiped in esoteric Tantric rites that, again, focus primarily on the circulation of blood and power. According to a key tenth-century text called the *Kaulajnana Nirnaya*, it was in Assam that the great sage Matsyendranath first learned esoteric sexual rites from the many female *yoginis* dwelling there, and these techniques then became the basis for one of the oldest schools of Tantric practice, the Yogini Kaula tradition.[27] And here we see the links between death and sensuality, between "bloody sacrifice and sexual rites, eros and thanatos," articulated more explicitly than even Bataille himself might have imagined.[28]

In many of the Tantric texts from this region, the sexual rite is explicitly compared to a sacrificial ritual and is really the esoteric counterpart to the public ritual performance. Following a very old metaphor dating back to the Upanishads (seventh to fourth centuries BCE), the sexual rite is described as the "lineage sacrifice" or "primordial sacrifice" (the *kula yaga* or *adi yaga*), with the shedding of semen likened to the offering poured onto the sacrificial fire of the *yoni*.[29] The focus of the rite is the oral consumption of sexual fluids, particularly menstrual blood, as a sacramental meal. While considered highly impure outside of the ritual context, these fluids become the ultimate source of both worldly and otherworldly power in Tantric practice. As described in the *Kaulajnana Nirnaya*, these rites center primarily on the oral consumption of menstrual blood, semen, and other bodily fluids, which are first emitted, then collected and eaten as a sacramental meal. Thus, "One should fill a vessel with blood together with an equal amount of semen. Menstrual blood, a woman's nectar, and semen are mixed with alcohol by the Brahmin. . . . Together with a prostitute or a maiden, the preceptor should place the sexual fluid into the mouth of the initiate. Thereafter he becomes a yogin."[30]

One of the most explicit descriptions of Tantric sexual rites occurs in the *Yoni Tantra*, a sixteenth-century text from Cooch Behar, immediately adjacent to Assam, which is closely connected to Kamakhya's worship. Here the body of the female partner or *shakti* is imagined as the female embodiment of the goddess herself. Her *yoni* is said to be identical with the great *yoni pitha* itself, and, by entering it, one is entering the *pitha* and worshiping the goddess in her secret form. In this account, the sexual rite is both *compared to* and *accompanied by* the offering of animal sacrifice. The sexual rite is a sacrificial offering (*bali*) that involves the oral consumption of semen and menstrual blood as a food offering (*naivedyam*), and it is accompanied by the offering (*bali*) of various kinds of animal flesh. Sexual union here should also ideally take place while the female is menstruating—normally a highly impure and inauspicious time for intercourse[31]—and in the inverse position—with the woman on top—and the focus is primarily on her menstrual fluids as a sacramental offering:

He should make a sacrificial offering [*bali*] with his own semen and the menstrual blood. . . . At the beginning of the night he should make an offering [*bali*] of cooked fish, a fowl's egg, mouse flesh, buffalo flesh, human flesh, wine, meat and flour cakes. . . . With great effort, he should penetrate the *yoni*, having first caressed her breasts. The goddess herself is in the form of the *shakti* [female partner], if the intercourse is performed in the inverse position [*viparitarata*]. Meditating on the goddess, he should worship the goddess, which is in the form of the *shakti.* . . . With the vulva and penis, with the washing of the vulva . . . and with the nectar of the vulva and penis, the best of adepts should make a food offering [*naivedyam*].[32]

As J. A. Schoterman points out in his discussion of the *Yoni Tantra*, the offering and consumption of the sexual fluid (the *yonitattva*) is in many ways a Tantric analogue of the consumption of the soma beverage in the Vedic sacrificial rite: "Just as the pure soma juice is mixed with milk or water," Schoterman notes, "likewise the *sadhaka* mixes the yonitattva with wine or water. . . . The Vedic drinking of the Soma has been transformed into a yogic practice connected with the *yonitattva.*"[33]

In sum, the esoteric or Tantric ritual cycle again forms a circuit or cyclical flow of power that is parallel to the public ritual cycle of blood sacrifice. Here the power of the goddess flows through the menstrual blood and semen of her human embodiments, the male and female *tantrikas*, and it culminates in the *yonitattva*, the combined male and female sexual fluids, which are first offered to the goddess, then consumed orally by the initiates. At the same, however, this is also a highly transgressive and even inverted sort of sacrifice that focuses primarily on the impure, dangerous, but also creative power inherent in the sexual fluids. Again, the Tantric rite or sexual sacrifice also represents a profound inversion of the Vedic model, by deliberately using substances that are profoundly impure and polluting by mainstream Hindu social standards. Not only should the sexual rite should be performed when the female is menstruating—normally an extremely impure sort of thing to do—but the intercourse explicitly violates normal laws of class and caste, and its final aim is not the normal mingling of sexual fluids to conceive a child but rather the oral consumption of the sexual fluids as a source of esoteric power. But again, it is this very impurity that releases the tremendous power of the goddess, which flows through the bodies and sexual fluids of her devotees.

Yet this explicit use of impurity and transgression in Tantric ritual is by no means a matter of pure chaos or sexual anarchy. As Bataille suggests, the power of transgression does not lie simply in mere hedonism and sexual license; rather, it involves the careful dialectic or play (*le jeu*) between taboo and transgression, prohibition and the violation, through which one constructs and then systematically overturns the law. Indeed, "often the transgression of a taboo is no less subject to rules than the taboo itself."[34] One must first carefully construct and even *exaggerate* the laws of purity before one can violate them, for it is precisely this dialectic of purity and impurity, law and violation, that unleashes the "explosive surge of transgression" and breaks down the boundaries of the isolated self:

> The regularity of transgressions do not affect the intangible stability of the prohibition since they are its expected complement—just as the diastolic movement completes a systolic pone, or just as explosion follows upon compression. The compression is not subservient to the explosion . . . it gives it increased force.[35]

Tantric ritual, we might say, functions like a kind of spiritual slingshot, which is first stretched as tightly as possible and then suddenly released in order to propel the adept into ecstatic liberation. Or to use a more apt metaphor, it works like a kind of socionuclear fission: it first exaggerates and then shatters the laws that make up the social organism at the most fundamental, atomic level, releasing an explosive burst of energy. As Alexis Sanderson suggests, the Tantric "path of power" sets itself up in deliberate contrast to the orthodox path of purity. Whereas the path of purity seeks to eliminate the dangerous pollution of marginal and unclean forces, the Tantric path seeks precisely to "unleash all the awesome power of impurity" and so achieve a kind of "unlimited power through a visionary art of impurity," for "the absolute of the impure is absolute Power."[36]

Transgression Without Limits

Like most Tantric literature, the Tantric texts from Assam discuss in great detail the sorts of powers and supernatural abilities (*siddhis*) that belong to the one who is able to unleash this tremendous energy of the goddess. He becomes indomitable in battle; he can control princes, kings, and women; he can conquer the threefold universe, and so on.[37] Ultimately, however, the final aim of transgression goes far beyond the mere overstepping of social taboos or the acquisition of worldly power.

Here I would argue that Bataille's work sheds some extremely useful light on the larger role of transgression in Tantric practice. As Bataille suggests, the phenomena of blood sacrifice, ritual violence, and sexual transgression do all share certain common links; they each involve the breaking down of normal boundaries, overflowing the limits of both the social order and the physical self through the emission of blood and fluids: "The external violence of the sacrifice reveals the internal violence of the creature, seen as loss of blood and ejaculations."[38] For they each work by breaking down the walls of isolation that separate individual beings, bursting though the limits of the finite, discontinuous ego and opening the self up to the limitless expanse of the infinite: "The embrace restores us," Bataille writes, "not to nature . . . but rather to the totality in which man has his share by *losing himself*. For an embrace is not just a fall into the animal muck, but the anticipation of death. . . . The point is that the totality reached . . . is reached only at the price of a sacrifice: eroticism reaches it precisely inasmuch as love is a kind of immolation."[39] Thus the ultimate or "infinite transgression," for Bataille, is not simply the release of power through bloodshed or sexual union; rather it is the transgression of the very boundaries of the self through mystical experience, the complete dissolution of the finite ego into a state of "divine continuity":

> In the region where the autonomy of the subject breaks away from all restraints, where the categories of good and evil, of pleasure and pain are finitely surpassed, where nothing is connected with anything any more, where there is no longer any form or mode that means anything but the instantaneous annihilation of whatever might claim to be a form or model, so great a spiritual energy is needed that it is all but inconceivable. On this scale, the chain releases of atomic energy are nothing. . . . The universe is the only limit of our revolt . . . an unlimited energy engages one in a limitless revolt.[40]

While surely not identical, Bataille's description of radical and unlimited transgression does shed some useful light onto the nature of transgression in Tantric practice. As Alexis Sanderson concludes, the goal of Tantric transgression goes far beyond the overstepping of mere social or moral boundaries; rather its ultimate aim is nothing short of a radical overstepping of ordinary human consciousness and conventional reality itself:

> This inhibition, which preserves the path of purity and barred his entrance into the path of power, was to be obliterated through the experience of a violent, duality-devouring expansion of consciousness beyond the narrow confines of orthodox control into the domain of excluded possibilities, by gratifying with wine, meat and . . . caste-free intercourse.[41]

Thus the liberated *tantrika* has shattered not just the boundaries of social class and purity but ultimately the limits of the human condition itself. Such a being has transcended any sense of disgust or fear; to him semen and menstrual blood, excrement and urine are pure; he can eat any animal flesh and drink any wine without fear of pollution.[42] Thus the key Tantric text, the *Kaulajnana Nirnaya*, describes the state of ultimate liberation as one in which all dualities between and impure, merit and sin, sacred ritual and defiling pollution have been radically dissolved: "[the yogi] always perceives sweet smells and bad smells without duality. . . . The sin of killing a Brahmin and the result of a horse sacrifice, bathing in all the sacred waters and contact with barbarians—the yogi surely does not perceive any [distinction] between these actions."[43] Having exploded all the dualities of the limited human world, the yogi has thus become equal to the gods themselves. According to the *Akulavira Tantra*, a text also said to have been revealed to Matsyendranath in Assam,

> He is Shiva, he is the Supreme Deity. . . . He is an Arhant and even Buddha. He is himself the goddess and the god; he is the disciple and the guru. He is himself meditation and the one who meditates, and he is himself everywhere the deity [meditated upon].[44]

Here we see that the ultimate transgression is the overstepping of the very boundary between human and divine. Neither mere hedonistic debauchery nor monistic abstraction, this is a far more radical experience that shatters the very boundaries of reality itself—an experience much closer to Bataille's transgression without limits.

Conclusions: Gender, Power, and Sexual Difference

To conclude, I would like to suggest that the example of Tantra in northeastern India not only illustrates the ways in which Bataille's work can be used to shed light on South Asian traditions; more important, I want to suggest we can also use the South Asian materials to critique and rethink certain aspects of Bataille. The best use of Bataille—or of any modern theoretical approach, I would argue—is not just a simplistic application of his work to other historical and cultural examples but rather a more critical dialogue in which both sides are transformed by the encounter.

Perhaps most significantly, the case of Assamese Tantra highlights an important tension and ambivalence in Bataille's otherwise very useful insights into the dynamics of sexuality, violence, and transgression. On the one hand, Bataille clearly emphasizes the radical, orgiastic nature of sexuality and transgression, the power of erotism to dissolve and shatter fixed individual identities. Yet on the other hand, as various feminist critics have observed, Bataille's work is also largely focused on male and phallic sexuality, to the general exclusion of female, nonphallic eroticism. Not only does

Bataille share with other French theorists such as Michel Foucault a certain "gender blindness" and a lack of attention to the ways in which male and female erotic experience is constructed differently in different historical and cultural contexts; more fundamentally, many critics have argued, he reflects a clear masculine bias and a general tendency to treat women as passive objects and victims. As Ladelle McWhorter observes, most feminists find Bataille

> disturbing and, to varying degrees, anti-feminist if not misogynist. A cursory reading of almost any of his texts at any stage of his career gives ample reason for this assessment. . . . Bataille's perspective on the world was that of a heterosexual male, and all too often that perspective valorizes itself, seemingly to the exclusion of all others, so that Bataille begins to sound like a heterosexist masculine supremacist.[45]

This phallic bias can be seen throughout Bataille's work, most notably in texts such as *Erotism*, which consistently emphasizes the primary, dominant, active, and even violently destructive role of the male over the female:

> The male partner has generally an active role, while the female partner is passive. The passive female side is essentially one that is dissolved as a separate entity. But for the male partner the dissolution of the passive partner means one thing only: it is paving the way for a fusion where both are mingled.[46]
>
> I must emphasize that the female partner in eroticism was seen as the victim, the male as the sacrificer, both during the consummation losing themselves in the continuity established by the first destructive act.[47]

Yet despite this masculine bias and general absence of women as agents with perspectives or voices, some feminist authors such as McWhorter also argue that there is room for a radical theorization of difference and nonphallic sexuality in Bataille's work. Using the feminist approach of Luce Irigaray, McWhorter argues that Bataille "resists the primacy of . . . phallic subjectivity. . . . He resists the voracious incorporation of the other that marks so much of our masculinist, heterosexist culture; he refuses to reinstall the primal one in the void left by the individuated phallic subject. . . . Bataille attempts to think difference set free from its servitude to the same."[48]

As such, the example of the Tantric goddess Kamakhya can be very fruitfully put into dialogue with Bataille and his ambivalent attitude toward gender. While Bataille remains torn between an ideal of radically transgressive sexuality and a lingering masculine bias, the example of Kamakhya offers an ideal of sexuality and erotic power that is rooted primarily in the *yoni* rather than simply in the *lingam*, or phallus. The concept of power (*shakti*) in Sanskrit is itself a feminine noun, imagined as the divine female energy that circulates through the cosmos, the body, and human society alike, and its *dépense* or expenditure flows not just through semen but also through the menstrual blood of the goddess and the sexual fluids of the female partner. In the words of the *Yoni Tantra*, "without the vulva . . . everything would be futile. Simply by the worship of the *yoni*, one can obtain the fruit of all religious practices."[49] "Hari, Hara, and all the gods, the agents of the creation, maintenance and destruction of the universe are all born from the *yoni*."[50]

This is not to say, of course, that Hindu Tantra is "feminist" in any modern Western sense of the term; it certainly is not, and it contains many heteronormative and essentialist assumptions of its own.[51] But it *does* contain a model of sexuality that is both centered on the radical logic of transgression *and* rooted in the nonphallic power the *yoni*. It embodies a powerful vision of "transgression without limits" that depends as much on the flowing energy of the female sexual fluids as on the virile expenditure of semen. As such, it provides a very instructive counterpart to Bataille's work and thus an extremely useful way to think about sexual difference in contemporary discourse.

The Religion of Football
Sacrifice, Festival, and Sovereignty at the 2010 FIFA World Cup in South Africa

DAVID CHIDESTER

Football, the world's game, the beautiful game, the sacred game, has often been characterized as a religion. In the advent of the 2010 Fédération Internationale de Football Association (FIFA) World Cup in South Africa, many commentators observed that football is a religion because it looks like religion and acts like religion.

Adopting a morphological analysis of religion by attending to characteristically religious forms, CNN National Editor Dave Schechter declared his devotion to the "religion of football." Schechter identified forms of religion operating in football: prayers, curses, hymns, vestments, transcendent gods, and sacrificial rituals. "Deities will be implored," he noted. "Sacrifices will be pledged, some even offered." All of this religious activity, according to Schechter, must revolve around a sacred center, "a shrine that must be visited at least once in a lifetime."[1] For the "football worshipper," this sacred center, the holy of holies, is the FIFA World Cup, moving to a different location every four years but retaining its structural role as the central shrine of the religion of football. In these terms, football is a religion because it looks like religion.

Adopting a functional analysis of religion, the *Guardian* commentator Theo Hobson argued that football was a religion that was better than any institutionalized religion because it provided the world with a genuine ritual of social solidarity. In his article "The World Cup: A Ritual That Works," Hobson implicitly drew on Durkheim's definition of religion as beliefs and practices in relation to the sacred that draw people into a unified community.[2] In this respect, football is a religion because it acts like a religion, making us "feel that we are participating in something huge and communal." In British society, Christmas or royal events might achieve that religiously ritualized social solidarity, according to Hobson, but conventional religions, which form communities around churches, mosques, or temples, do not generate "a sense of solidarity with society in general." Accordingly, in functional terms, Hobson can conclude that recognized religions are less "religious" than the religion of football in forming social solidarity. Given the diversity of organized religions, "religion divides rather than unites," as religious festivities disguise the demands of authoritarian religious leaders, although Hobson acknowledges that conventional religious institutions can sometimes approach the pure religion of football, noting that he is "impressed by Catholic cultures in which holy days resemble big football events." Nevertheless, if we recognize the essential function of religion as creating a sacred sense of social solidarity, then football religion is more religious than any conventional religion. "The desire for society to be united in common ritual expression, or worship, is basic to religion, and perhaps politics too, but all actual realisations of this ideal should be viewed with suspicion." Hobson concluded, "We should be grateful for a harmless version of this deep-rooted instinct."[3] In these terms, football is a religion, better than most, because it acts like religion.

None of the commentaries on football religion that were framed outside South Africa, the sacred site of the 2010 FIFA World Cup, tried to relate religion to economics. Within South Africa, where hosting the World Cup required enormous capital investment in stadiums and infrastructure, neglecting pressing needs for addressing poverty, crime, housing, health care, and education while ensuring record-breaking profits for FIFA, the intersection between religion and economics, between rituals of solidarity and financial calculations, could not be avoided. Accordingly, when one of South Africa's leading social anthropologists, Steven Robins, defended the religion of football, his article in the popular press was entitled "World Cup Ritual Worth Every Cent."

How should we understand this intersection between football religion and economics? As I will propose, the World Cup was an instance of what Georges Bataille called *expenditure*, nonproductive expenditure evident in sacrifice, destruction of resources, and the "construction of sumptuary monuments, games, [and] spectacles," certifying "a *loss* that must be as great as possible in order for that activity to take on its true meaning."[4] As ritualized expenditure, the World Cup demonstrated the power of what Bataille identified as the general economy of excess, ostentatious loss, and exuberant destruction of resources that can never be contained within capitalist calculations of profit, wealth, and accumulation in the restricted economy. The 2010 FIFA World Cup in South Africa ritualized the relations between religion and economics in ways that cannot be contained by either morphological or functional analysis. Here Bataille might help us understand religion and economics in terms of the sacred dynamics of sacrifice, festival, and competing claims on sovereignty.

Religion, including the religion of football, is not merely forms and functions but also the dynamics, energetics, and political economy of the sacred. Following Durkheim, I define the sacred as "that which is set apart," but set apart at the center of personal subjectivities, social formations, economic exchanges, and political power.[5] By "political economy of the sacred" I refer to the social field of meaning and power in which the sacred is produced, exchanged, owned, operated, and contested. Specifically, I understand that field to be constituted by three overlapping, intersecting activities: the production of the sacred through the labor of intensive interpretation and formal ritualization; the transformation of scarce resources, especially material objects, space, and time, into sacred surplus; and the contestation over legitimate ownership of that sacred surplus.[6] By taking Georges Bataille to the World Cup, I hope to show how the political economy of the sacred was at play in the religion of football in South Africa.

Sacrifice

In December 2009, Zolani Mkiva, speaking on behalf of the Makhonya Royal Trust, which was coordinating cultural events for the 2010 FIFA World Cup, announced the plan to perform ritual sacrifices of cattle at each of the ten stadiums that had been prepared for the tournament. "We must have a cultural ceremony of some sort, where we are going to slaughter a beast," Mkiva explained. "We sacrifice the cow for this great achievement and we call on our ancestors to bless, to grace, to ensure that all goes well."[7] In support of this proposal to perform ten sacrificial rituals, South African Minister of Cooperative Governance and Traditional Affairs Sicelo Shiceka argued that these ceremonies would not only sanctify but also Africanize the international event. "The World Cup will be on the African continent," Minister Shiceka observed, "and we will make sure that African values and cultures are felt by the visitors."[8] Although the term "sacrifice" is often used metaphorically in the religion of football, here was a proposal to perform actual blood sacrifices, rituals that required the killing of an animal, as an integral part of the cultural, spiritual, and religious significance of the World Cup. An international outcry erupted in the media, and animal rights organizations mobilized petition campaigns against the ritual. FIFA remained silent about its policy regarding the sacrifice of animals. As the *Guardian* correspondent Matt Scott reported, "The plan, which apparently involves slicing the throat of a cow with a knife or an assegai, reportedly has the support of South Africa's traditional affairs minister, Sicelo Shiceka." Despite attempts to get a response from FIFA President Joseph "Sepp" Blatter, Scott found that FIFA was not prepared to say "whether it will allow the slaughter rituals to go ahead."[9]

During the previous month, ritual sacrifice had become the focus of controversy in South Africa, as Animal Rights Africa went to court to stop the killing of a bull that forms part of the annual observance of Ukweshwama, the first fruits ceremony presided over by the Zulu king. Besides Zulu King Goodwill Zwelithini, respondents included Minister Shiceka, Minister of Police Nathi Mthethwa, KwaZulu-Natal Premier Zweli Mkhize, and the provincial minister for local government, housing, and traditional affairs, Nomusa Dube. By naming these respondents, Animal Rights Africa was challenging both hereditary traditional leadership and elected democratic leadership in South Africa to prevent the ritual sacrifice of a bull at an annual celebration of Zulu royalty. In this ceremony, young men catch and kill a bull with their bare hands. Characterizations of this ritual differed dramatically. "During the Ukweshwama ritual," according to Animal Rights Africa, "men pulled out the bull's tongue, stuffed sand in its mouth and also attempted to tie its penis in a knot." By stark contrast to this visceral account, defenders of the ritual consistently rendered it as religious symbolism, observing that "Ukweshwama is a symbolic way of thanking God for the first crops of the season."[10] Accepting the argument that the ritual killing was religious symbolism, the judge in this case observed that "the activity was as important to the Zulu tradition as the Holy Communion was to Catholics."[11] Furthermore, acknowledging the royal symbolism of the ceremony, the judge found that the bull was killed by Zulu warriors in order to transfer "symbolic powers" to the Zulu king. "If this is stopped, the symbolic powers would be stopped," he said. "In effect, you are killing the king."[12] Accordingly, religious freedom, guaranteed by the South African Constitution, allowed for the ritual killing of a bull that symbolized thanksgiving to God and the sovereignty of the Zulu king.

On the eve of the 2010 FIFA World Cup, a sacrificial ritual was performed at one stadium, Soccer City, where the opening and closing ceremonies of the World Cup were scheduled. Organized by Zolani Mkiva, the ceremony was officiated by three hundred traditional diviners and healers, *sangomas* and *inyangas*, with about two thousand people in attendance. The ceremony began at six o'clock in the morning with the ritual killing of an ox by a seventy-year-old "Xhosa warrior" who speared the animal at the back of its neck, between its horns, according to tradition. Burning the traditional herb *impepho*, the ritual specialists invoked the ancestors, as Mkiva explained, calling on "the spirits of our African ancestors to usher in their wisdom and energy in setting the scene of what was to follow."[13] Phepsile Maseko, the national coordinator for the Traditional Healers' Organisation, described the ceremony as having three effects—unifying people, welcoming visitors, and appeasing ancestors. "We burnt incense and other medicines and we slaughtered a cow near the stadium," Maseko recounted. "The cow symbolizes strength. . . . It is a unifying cow." Dealing with foreign fans and indigenous ancestors, the ritual was the way "we bless the stadium as a symbol of welcome to the nations that are coming" but also a way to alert the ancestors of the arrival of football fans from all over the world, because "we don't want our spirits to be scared of all the different languages."[14] Spiritually, the energy of this ritual was transmitted to all of the other stadiums throughout the country. As a result, despite abandoning the plan to perform sacrificial rituals at ten stadiums, Zolani Mkiva could conclude, "Our stadiums are now officially blessed according to our culture, for the tournament."[15]

Here we find different understandings of sacrifice not merely in the rift between defenders of cultural traditions and defenders of animal rights but in the contrasting interpretations of sacrifice by participants in the Zulu royal sacrifice and the World Cup sacrifice. On the one hand, the Zulu royal sacrifice during the annual observance of Ukweshwama was interpreted as a ritual of transcendence, invoking a transcendent deity, empowering the sovereign king, which reinforced the legitimacy of a traditional polity. As a ritual symbolizing the supreme power of God and king, this royal sacrifice was interpreted as reestablishing hierarchical relations of domination and subordination in Zulu society. Sacrifice, in this case, was understood as a religious ritual of political sovereignty. On the other hand, the World Cup sacrifice was understood by its officiants as a sacred event that generated a shared spiritual energy that effectively mediated relations among participants, strangers, and ancestors. Not a symbolic invocation of vertical transcendence, this sacrifice was understood to operate on a horizontal plane, extending spiritual energy to the ancestors in the earth, the stadiums throughout the country, and football fans all over the world. By contrast to the Zulu royal offering to the centralized, hierarchical power of God and king, the World Cup sacrifice radiated centrifugal force by transmitting spiritual energy everywhere and centripetal force by drawing everyone into the sacrificial space. Accordingly, this sacrifice was rendered as an act of ritual inclusion in a blessed community.

This distinction between transcendence and the sacred can be illuminated by Georges Bataille's theory of sacrifice. According to Bataille, the sacred is the opposite of transcendence. While transcendence introduces hierarchy and alienation, a "religious" profanation of the sacred, the sacred transforms the profane world of utility into the sacred world of animality, intimacy, immediacy, and immanence. As the primary way of effecting this transformation, sacrifice removes both the victim and the sacrificer from the profane world of useful things, practical projects, economic calculations, and transcendental legitimations. As Bataille argued, "The first fruits of the harvest or a head of livestock are sacrificed in order to remove the plant and the animal, along with the farmer and the stock raiser, from the world of things."[16] In the religious symbolism of Christian Holy Communion and Zulu royal ritual, sacrifice is profaned by being turned back into a useful thing to the extent that it is deployed to legitimate the centralized authority of an ecclesiastical or political hierarchy. In the case of the World Cup ritual, we seem to have an instance of what Bataille regarded as sacrificial immediacy. "In sacrifice," he observed, "it is in the act itself that value is concentrated. Nothing in sacrifice is put off until later—it has the power to contest everything at the instant that it takes place, to summon everything, to render everything present."[17] Certainly, as understood by its organizers, the World Cup sacrifice was an act that brought everyone— foreigners, South Africans, and ancestral spirits—together in the moment of its enactment.

"In his strange myths, in his cruel rites," Bataille observed, "man is in search of a lost intimacy."[18] That intimacy, immediacy, and immanence of the sacred is achieved in the moment of sacrificial destruction and loss, in the sacrificial act of unconditional giving that relinquishes any expectation of return. In that moment of intimacy between sacrificer and victim, which removes both from the profane world of useful things, Bataille hears the sacrificer declare, "*Intimately*, I belong to the sovereign world of gods and myths, to the world of violent and uncalculated generosity."[19] By surrendering to the immanent presence of gods and myths, the sacrificer recovers what Bataille, in his specific definition of the term, identifies as "sovereignty," a momentary redemption of a sovereign self from its *thingification* in the profane world. Rupturing the world of useful things, sacrifice signifies sovereignty, because in sacrifice both offering and offerer are "rescued from all utility."[20] Clearly, Bataille's notion of sovereignty is not the political sovereignty advanced in the renderings of Zulu royal ritual as a celebration of a transcendent God and king. Rather, this sovereignty, the recovery of free subjectivity from the world of things, is a breakthrough of the sacred, an interruption, disruption, or transgression of the profane world, in which a society might be transformed into a community. Although he often seemed to regard sovereignty as individual, as sovereign subjectivity, Bataille also focused on the dynamics of community, noting that "the sacred is only a privileged moment of communal unity, a moment of convulsive communication of what is ordinarily stifled."[21] Festival, carnival, and the display, giving, and destruction of wealth in rituals of potlatch, for Bataille, were instances of such convulsive communication of the sacred that transgressed the stifling order of economic rationality. They rescued human beings from the world of things, the organization of projects, and the calculations of utility. Festivals, as free spaces and times of the sacred, can make anyone and everyone gods or kings. In festivals, sovereignty is not the political authority of royalty, state, or government but the ecstasy of being lost in the sacred.

Festival

On June 11, 2010, Zolani Mkiva, the Poet of Africa,[22] began the opening ceremony of the 2010 FIFA World Cup at Soccer City with a performance of traditional African praise singing. Anticipating his appearance on the global stage, Mkiva said, "I am thrilled. It's a dream come true. I will be watched by more than three billion people from across world." Dedicating his performance to his late father, to the late monarch King Xolilizwe Sigcawu, and to the ninety-two-year-old former president Nelson Mandela, Mkiva called upon all South Africans to come together, in prayer, in support of their national team. "We must keep on praying for our boys, Bafana Bafana," Mkiva urged. "We must see them going to the finals. We must create a vibrant team spirit. They are patriots who have the entire world on their shoulders."[23] Like the sacrificial ritual he officiated at Soccer City before the World Cup, Mkiva's performance in the opening ceremony was intended to radiate sacred energy in larger and larger concentric circles of ancestral spirits, traditional royalty, national leadership, patriotic citizens, and a vast global community. Sixteen years earlier, Mkiva had been on a comparable stage, acting as the *imbongi*, the praise singer, at the inauguration of Nelson Mandela, the first democratically elected president of a new South Africa. His performance on that occasion had also mediated between local tradition, tracing Mandela back through heroic founders of the African National Congress, and a global audience, with special attention to singing the praises of Fidel Castro, Yasser Arafat, and Muammar Gaddafi.[24] Now he was opening the festival of the 2010 FIFA World Cup in South Africa.

According to Bataille, festival is "the place and the time of a spectacular letting loose."[25] In his defense of the World Cup, the anthropologist Steven Robins emphasized the spectacularization of sports as festival, as carnival, as an "ecstatic experience of solidarity and belonging." Individuals, in ecstasy, found themselves "losing one's self in the collective spirit of the carnival." As in Bataille's notion of sovereignty, which has nothing to do with normal politics, economics, or social order, the World Cup provided an occasion for individuals to find their ecstatic sovereignty by abandoning the world of things, utility, projects, and economic calculations. During the World Cup, as the everyday, ordinary, and mundane world was "temporarily cordoned off," South African society was transformed into a community. As Robins concluded, we should appreciate the World Cup for the "benign social solidarity that occurred during this hyper-transient, yet wondrous, collective ritual."[26] Ecstasy and solidarity, as other analysts have observed, were the essence of the religion of football presented at the 2010 FIFA World Cup. For example, according to the political philosopher Achille Mbembe, football at the World Cup was "an act of communion that offers its members the opportunity to share, with countless pilgrims from around the world, the moments of a unique intensity."[27] Durkheim's notions of ecstasy and solidarity—collective effervescence, unified moral community—provided the template for these analyses of the World Cup festival.

However, as Georges Bataille argued, the "spectacular letting loose" of the festival takes place in tension with the profane world of utility, economic calculation, and political authority that it can only temporarily disrupt. The festival's scope for personal ecstasy and social solidarity is "limited by a countervailing prudence that regulates and limits it." Although festival, with all of its sacrificial and celebratory giving, loss, waste, and destruction, might break through the limits of profane regularity into sacred immediacy, it is inevitably limited by the demands of the profane. Given the ongoing struggles between social taboos and their transgressions, "The festival is tolerated to the extent that it reserves the necessities of the profane world."[28] Although festivals are occasions for entering the sacred, for transgressing and disrupting the profane ordering of society, they are negotiated in the face of countervailing demands for restoring profane law and order. As a result, Bataille concluded, "The festival is not a true return to immanence but rather an amicable reconciliation, full of anguish, between the incompatible necessities."[29] Incompatible yet entangled, the sacred excess of festival will inevitably be held to account by the standards of the profane world.

Take the vuvuzela, the central aural icon of the 2010 FIFA World Cup in South Africa, a plastic horn that produced noise that was compared to the buzzing of swarming bees, the moaning of distressed elephants, and the droning of airplanes, all at deafening volume. Certainly, this festive horn, celebrating football, transgressed conventional standards of the profane world by breaking the rules of music and producing senseless noise. Although it was frequently defended as a necessary part of African football culture, even by Sepp Blatter on behalf of FIFA, the vuvuzela was entangled in the profane world of property when its manufacturer was sued by the Nazareth Baptist Church. Founded in 1910 by the Zulu prophet Isaiah Shembe, the church had used such a horn in its worship services to invoke the Holy Spirit. As one follower of Shembe complained, the appropriation of their sacred horn by football meant that their Holy Spirit, rather than the spirit of the game, was being showered over the stadiums. As this dispute was settled out of court, the Nazareth Baptist Church secured a percentage of profits from the sale of vuvuzelas.[30] But profane claims on the sacred horn extended further. Moving from the local to the global, the president of the South African Council of Churches, Tinyiko Maluleke, described the vuvuzela as a "missile-shaped weapon" that was loud enough to awaken the rest of the world to Africa. Against the background of European colonization of Africa, Maluleke argued, the vuvuzela was an African rejoinder to imperial oppression, dispossession, and neglect. "Now," he asserted, "we have created the vuvuzela, which is one of the most obnoxious instruments: very noisy, very annoying. It will dominate the FIFA World Cup. I see the vuvuzela as a symbol, as a symbol of Africa's cry for acknowledgement."[31] Even the festive noise of the vuvuzela, therefore, could become property in legal disputes and a weapon in global politics during the World Cup.

The reconciliation of sacred and profane, the negotiation between festival and cost-accounting, was difficult to adjudicate when dealing with the World Cup in South Africa. Acknowledging the ecstatic enthusiasm and social solidarity generated by football, the South African political philosopher and social activist Richard Pithouse ultimately found that the World Cup festival was an indictment of the African National Congress government that had abandoned the needs of the poor to offer "a mix of empty spectacle, participation in empty rituals like 'Football Friday,' and the fantasy of belonging in a society that is increasingly predicated on active and at times violent exclusion."[32] By any rational cost-accounting, the festival of the World Cup represented a substantial financial loss to South Africa.

Although the precise numbers remain in dispute, South Africa's investment of R24 billion ($3 billion) for six new and four upgraded stadiums and untold costs for new infrastructure, such as R8 billion ($1 billion) for the arguably unnecessary Shaka International Airport and R25 billion ($3.1 billion) for an elite train service between Johannesburg and Pretoria, suggest that enormous local resources were directed into expenditure for the World Cup. Although the anticipated financial benefits to South Africa in the form of tourism and job creation turned out to be negligible, the profit to FIFA, estimated at R24 billion ($3 billion), was substantial.[33] Clearly, FIFA was the winner of the 2010 FIFA World Cup in South Africa.

In his analysis of sacrificial expenditure, Bataille briefly considered competitive games. Like sacrificial rituals, games can be occasions for loss, waste, and destruction of resources that unleash the sacred. "In various competitive games," he observed, "loss in general is produced," confounding the presumption that games are all about winning. Instead, like sacrificial rituals of expenditure, competitive games waste money and energy. In these sports, such as the World Cup, "As much energy as possible is squandered in order to produce a feeling of stupefaction—in any case with an intensity infinitely greater than in productive enterprises."[34] While South African citizens might have been stupefied by this exorbitant expenditure of resources and energy, their political leaders seemed to be engaging in a ritualized expenditure of resources similar to a potlatch, the sacrificial giving and sometimes destroying of wealth, which Bataille focused upon as the model of a general economy. Necessarily connected to festival, according to Bataille, the ritual of potlatch entailed giving, receiving, and returning under obligation, but in its purest form it was pure giving, without any expectation of return, especially when it was enacted "to defy rivals through the spectacular destruction of wealth."[35] In South Africa, the festival of football seemed to inspire rivalry among politicians in the destruction of wealth as long as it could be linked to the spectacle of the World Cup. The entire proceedings, from this perspective, were devoted to sacrificial expenditure. The sacrificial ritual preceding the World Cup signaled this dedication to expenditure, a destruction of wealth like the potlatch, in which "what is destroyed is theoretically offered to the mythical ancestors."[36] The World Cup festival was a ritualized occasion for destroying resources and making myths.

Sovereignty

On November 5, 2009, Zolani Mkiva, the president and director general of the Institute of African Royalty, convened a gathering of dignitaries at

South Africa's Freedom Park, the central shrine of the nation, to bestow the first African Royal Award upon Nelson Mandela, who was praised as the Lion, the "king of the jungle," the icon of the nation. On the eve of the 2010 FIFA World Cup in South Africa, Zolani Mkiva presided over the second ceremony of the Institute of African Royalty, held in a Johannesburg hotel, at which the African Royal Award was presented to FIFA President Sepp Blatter.[37] Ironically, South African critics and cartoonists were fond of representing Blatter as a king, as in Jabulani Sikhakhane's indictment of the World Cup, "The Shame of Being Colonised by King Sepp,"[38] or as a pope, the head of "an organization that seems a bizarre cross between the Vatican and the IMF."[39] During the World Cup, FIFA enjoyed sovereignty over all the stadiums and their precincts, tax-exempt status, freedom from exchange controls, police escorts and security, enforcement of brands and trademarks, restrictions on media reports bringing FIFA into disrepute, and indemnity from any legal proceedings. As Sophie Nakueria, a researcher at the Centre of Criminology of the University of Cape Town, observed, "The traditional notion of national sovereignty is irrelevant when bodies like Fifa . . . use governments to advance their own objects, which in Fifa's case is to further its profits."[40] During the World Cup, FIFA was sovereign and Sepp Blatter a king, honored with the African Royal Award by the Institute of African Royalty.

While celebrating the global sovereignty of FIFA, African traditionalists took the opportunity of the World Cup to revitalize their own royal claims on political sovereignty. Since 1994, South Africa has been a unified, nonracial democracy under the sovereignty of one of the most progressive constitutions in the world, but governance has been shared with over 2,400 kings, queens, chiefs, and headmen presiding over 774 chiefdoms that have maintained the same boundaries that were established under apartheid. Approximately 30 percent of the population lives under the authority of a chief. Responsible for security, dispute resolution, and allocation of land, these traditional leaders are also custodians of ancestral rituals, especially sacrifices, which link traditional sovereignty with the spiritual realm of myths, gods, and ancestors.[41] During the World Cup, the AmaGcaleka Xhosa King Zwelonke Sigcawu, whose predecessor had died in 2005, was installed in a traditional ceremony. Anticipating the coronation, Prince Xhanti Sigcawu asserted, "The build-up towards the coronation of the next Xhosa King will be an exciting activity that presents an opportunity to educate the general public about customs, rituals, norms, values, traditions and protocols of the cultural dynamics of our African Royalty." Besides educating the South African public, the organizers of the coronation also hoped to attract foreign dignitaries, journalists, and tourists who would be in the country for the World Cup. In a statement issued by the chief executive officer of the Xhosa Royal Trust, Zolani Mkiva, the link between royal ritual and World Cup was important. "This event will take place at a time when the eyes of the entire world will be focused in South Africa given the 2010 Fifa World Cup," Mkiva declared. "Surely the coronation of His Majesty, King Zwelonke, will not only attract the local viewership and listenership but the whole world."[42] Asked about the costs of the coronation, which journalists estimated at around R10 million, Zolani Mkiva refused to answer any questions about money because "heritage is priceless."[43]

Although traditional heritage might be priceless, it nevertheless operates in a market economy. Accordingly, Makhonya Investments, on behalf of the Congress of Traditional Leaders of South Africa (CONTRALESA), was formed as a broad-based black empowerment company designed to advance the financial interests of traditional leaders. Under the leadership of its chairman, Zolani Mkiva, the national executive director of CONTRALESA, Makhonya Investments was committed to providing financial support for South African royalty. In its mission statement, Makhonya Investments declared, "We take pride in having ensured that Kings and Queens together with senior Royals of our country are also direct beneficiaries of this investment initiative."[44] This initiative secured lucrative tenders from government, such as a five-year R3 billion contract to manage the vehicle fleet of the Eastern Cape Province, which caused critics to wonder how a poet such as Zolani Mkiva could have the necessary experience to run such an operation.[45] However, as we have seen, Zolani Mkiva has had extraordinary experience in the sacred as Poet of Africa and praise singer to Nelson Mandela, as officiator of the World Cup sacrifice and performer in the World Cup opening ceremony, as chairman of the Makhanya Royal Trust, president of the Institute of African Royalty, chief executive of the Xhosa Royal Trust, executive director of CONTRALESA, and chairman of Makhanya Investments, which presents him on its website as "HRH Zolani Mkiva," His Royal Highness, royalty in his own right.

In the ongoing transactions between sacred and profane, Georges Bataille observed, "sacred things are constituted by an operation of loss."[46] During the 2010 FIFA World Cup, the sacred was generated by sacrifices, festivals, and royal ceremonials, by stadium construction, infrastructural projects, and contractual obligations, all operating at a considerable financial loss to the people of South Africa. In all of these ways, the dynamics of the sacred was driven by sacrifice. The World Cup created a sacred time of sacrificial loss and waste, of destruction of resources and squandering of wealth, which transformed South Africa into a sacred space. As the traditionalist sacrificers of the cow at Soccer City on the eve of the World

Cup observed, sacred space has centrifugal force, radiating everywhere, and centripetal force, drawing everyone inside, recalling Bataille's insight into the power of sacrificial ritual to "summon everything, to render everything present."[47] Harnessing the sacrificial dynamics of the sacred, the World Cup rendered everything and everyone present for the most important festival in the world. The spirit of the World Cup, which was explicitly identified as "spiritual" not only by praise singers and traditional healers but also by FIFA officials, the Local Organising Committee, advertising, and public relations, revealed an energetics of the sacred. Adapting insights from Bataille, we can say that the energetics of the sacred enables individuals to be sovereign and societies to be communities. For individuals, the event was spiritual. In promotions for the World Cup, the Afrikaans word for "spirit"—*gees*—was used for the spirit of the games. Individuals were urged to feel the *gees*, to catch the *gees*, to capture the *gees*, recapturing, in Bataille's peculiar sense, a personal sovereignty by being lost in the sacred. At the same time, the spirit of the games was communal, a Durkheimian "collective effervescence," which promised to transform society—local, national, and international—into community, a sacred solidarity in which personal subjectivity was absorbed into a spiritual collectivity. The World Cup, therefore, mobilized the dynamics and energetics of the sacred.

The sacred, however, is also constituted by the operations of political economy. As I have proposed elsewhere, the sacred is produced through interpretive and ritual labor that generates surplus, immediately available for contested appropriations, in a political economy of the sacred.[48] Even in a market economy, with its economic rationality, calculations of profit, and practices of accumulation, the sacred persists because, as Bataille observed, "ostentatious loss remains universally linked to wealth, as its ultimate function."[49] Social rank, honor, glory, and even royalty in a capitalist economy are linked to an accumulation of wealth, but "only on the condition," as Bataille insisted, "that the fortune be partially sacrificed in unproductive expenditures such as festivals, spectacles, and games."[50] In the dialectic of sacred and profane, the extraordinary festival of the World Cup, during which individuals momentarily recovered personal sovereignty by losing themselves in the sacred, ultimately reinforced the sovereignty of capital in the political economy of the sacred in South Africa.

Beyond formal resemblance or functional equivalence, therefore, the religion of football at the World Cup in South Africa was religion because it demonstrated the dynamics, energetics, and political economy of the sacred. In the aftermath of the 2010 FIFA World Cup, South Africans struggled to figure out what to do with the stadiums, the "white elephants," that entailed massive maintenance costs in perpetuity with no hope of recouping losses or turning a profit. What would Bataille do? Although stadiums built for the 2002 World Cup in Japan and Korea were destroyed for sound fiscal reasons, Bataille might have advanced a different rationale, one based on sacrificial loss, waste, and destruction, for blowing them up. Attended by sacrifices, festivals, and celebrations, blowing up the stadiums might provide new occasions for revitalizing the sacred but also for asserting competing claims on sovereignty in South Africa.

Violent Silence
Noise and Bataille's "Method of Meditation"

PAUL HEGARTY

For close to forty years, Bataille compulsively documented and railed at the loss of the sacred in his contemporary world. The capitalist world he saw was nothing more than the diminishing of human existence, its entire miserable character defined by the progressive removal of the sacred. Bataille was not the first to notice the vital (or morbid) connection between reformed Christianity and capitalism, but, unlike Tawney, Weber, or simple traditionalists, he was not bemoaning the loss of true religion, because religion largely is the thing that stands against the sacred. This can happen in more or less interesting or excessive ways, but organized religion must be other than transgression—at best it can frame it, as in the case of the Aztecs' positioning of sacrifice at the heart of their cosmology, but at worst it can impose strict morality, punish thought, restrict freedom, and close off the sacred. In fact, Christianity had been even more successful in this mission than capitalism would ever need to be. Nonetheless, Christianity is not capable of more than staving off the real sacred realm of excess, waste, eroticism, loss of control, death, and sacrifice, and vestiges remain within it that can never quite be closed off. The blood and wood that epitomizes the sacred in this religion, borrowed as it may be, can never be adequately closed off. For Bataille, though, this is a religion that has only ever restricted the access to the sacred it might have held open as a prospect.

Bataille scratched at modern life to find the lost tributaries of the sacred. In *The Accursed Share* sequence and its predecessor texts from 1929 on, this took the form of perverse anthropology; in *Erotism*, the threat and promise of loss in the sacred crossed many disciplines in a working through of a heterological model of the sacred in the physical encounter with others that threatened the self; in the *Somme athéologique* sequence of the wartime years, Bataille offers a rogue theology, even a rogue phenomenology, that seeks to empty the sacred of religiosity perversely to restore religiousness to its initial mission, which, Bataille can never cease to tell us, is to mediate between us as individuals and us as epiphenomena of the universal wasting of matter amid nothingness. It is this last series of texts, *Inner Experience*, "Method of Meditation," and *Guilty*, that interest me here. Their serious yet risibly doomed purpose cannot be doubted: this is Bataille trying to locate the subject in such a way that being becomes aware of itself as loss of being—and then loses that awareness. On returning, the individual subject will carry the trace of that loss even as the mundane closes in once more.

In *La somme*, Bataille uses resources from within religion itself, most notably the idea of meditation, and it would even be feasible to say that for all its claims otherwise, this meditation is not that different from religious models in its form and that only the content or aim is different. I do not believe that, though, and prefer to begin with this meditation being the thought of a perpetual emptying that cannot bring a reward, however minimal. Readers of Bataille will of course be aware of his visceral hatred of becoming a better person through accessing the sacred, and early on in *Inner Experience* he establishes that he is "against ascesis"[1] and that we should not look for "enriching" states of being.[2] Instead, we should look for a project that undoes itself as project, and this is what he describes as "inner experience."[3] At the time of writing, Bataille was already writing as an antiexistentialist—the idea of realizing oneself or attaining a moral goal is a lie. Yet humans seem to be stuck with the notion that we must in some way develop, grow, build a persona, so, to reach something else, something Bataille believes to be both better and worse, we must begin with a "project" or mission.

The stranger end of Christian mysticism offers him clues, as does anything that challenges physical integrity and control through excess. Art is also a way in, a means that can attain the end of not being an end and retrospectively will no longer have been a means to an end. He explicitly notes that it is not only modern society that has lost or diminished the sacred but also modern art.[4] Poetry occupies a privileged, if difficult, position: "We have become distanced from poetry, its cold violence [*ses violences glacées*] disturbs us."[5] Bataille tried (with mixed results) to restore poetry to its sacrificial, world-altering mission. He also looked to visual art as a location of the sacred, as a place where the operation of destruction could be seen in a way that exceeded visual appraisal (from "Formless" [1929] to *Manet* [1955]). Art could work as both perverse anthropology and as rogue access to subjectivity beyond the limits of the individual.

Slowly, Bataille reveals the importance to him of a set of pictures of a seemingly ecstatic execution victim whose limbs are being removed, which features in *Inner Experience*[6] and acts as the concluding focusing device of his last book, *The Tears of Eros*. Images and words can both move in and out of the aesthetic, and it would seem feasible that music could do the same. Experimental music of the late 1970s, particularly industrial music, took the physical part of performance art and made it part of its attack on an over-controlling moralistic capitalism that offered false freedoms in place of full realization of the self. Although Bataille was never shy of the literal in art, it is not so much these performers that interest me, as they are too directly part of a lineage inspired by writers like Bataille. Instead, I would suggest, we can look to noise music, or noise as music, or noise in the place of music, as something that matches Bataille's approach in form rather than in content. Specifically, the more that music approaches complete noise, the closer it is to being something like a Bataillean sacred and, more relevantly, the more it offers a means to approach something like inner experience. The following piece looks first at the importance of silence in *La somme* and the usability of art in aporetic meditation. It then goes on to look at how the work of the Japanese noise artist Merzbow (Masami Akita) works as Bataillean inner experience.

Meditation, inner experience, silence, the sacred—this list seems far removed from the more transgressive set of actions and experiences Bataille lusted for throughout his life and works, but the difference is less than might seem to be the case, and the beauty of the 1940s writing lies in its corruption of the ascetic. Where the hermit or mystic looks into the self to find truth or empties the self to join with the universe, Bataille is going to drink, fuck, and stumble, braying into a pit that the self cannot withstand. To get to the inner experience that is the loss of subjectivity, extremes must be sought, as only extreme situations and reactions can jolt controlling morality and/or rationality out of place. Where Heidegger sees authentic experience as living in the knowledge of death and in the deconstruction death operates on being, Bataille sees that there is no life without "the extreme."[7] This extreme can be found through a variant of ascesis, where what we need to do is live ascetically in extreme behavior.[8] He paradigmatically refutes tantric sex as it is simply part of the religious and rational closing-off of the sacred, writing of the "calculated tediousness of tantrism."[9] His church will be a brothel where sex is removed from any possible moralizing about love, harmony, respect, reproduction.[10] Instead, all there will be is shame at being in the world where all those things have been removed. The brothel also figures here to illustrate that the absence of moral consideration removes possible barriers to what may or may not be done between bodies. The consent is in the form of a business contract, although arguably Bataille should at least theoretically go further and remove that last concession to economic exchange. But for all the talk of transgressing, Bataille is not advocating breaking free from all consent nor resorting to real violence, as he makes clear on many occasions, the most relevant being the many references to Sade in *The History of Eroticism*, volume 2 of *The Accursed Share*. Here, he argues that literature can inspire the dread, the thrill, the horror that should not occur in the real world. As we will see, this means that despite his initial intentions, Bataille's access to inner experience will be a mediated one, where material, whether physical, sensory, or philosophical, will be needed.

In fact, access to the sacred cannot happen for the isolated individual, removed from stimulus, as what takes over is the "homogeneous" world of rules, limits, linear thinking, and use value (so for example, masturbating over a stored mental image would be much the same as praying, whereas external stimulus can have an effect that exceeds the mental or the secure somatic body). To get to the ecstatic realm of the sacred requires "dramatization,"[11] an acknowledgment that the thinking moral self cannot just be switched off but needs lowering, perversion, undoing. Neither would we want to switch it off entirely, as the rational part of one's being should be somewhere there, losing itself in the sensation of death, coming, and then reemerging in shame.[12] The dramatization will require others or, at least, some thing that is other to yourself. Others provide the means of communication: a community that fails, that as it hits its heights in the exchange of bodily fluids, for example, it shows the impossibility of full communion, and then, whatever was there, fades or, more accurately, lingers as a lost possibility. A lost impossibility.

We are far from the library or chapel, yet silence is the code here. For the Bataille of *La somme*, the goal (that undoes itself) is silence. The connection can be tracked through the importance of apathy Bataille attributes to Sade in volumes 2 and 3 of *The Accursed Share*[13] and read back to *Inner Experience*, where we should not look for "enriching states [of being]"[14]— in other words, you are not going to get ecstatic because you like getting ecstatic or because you like the person you intend getting ecstatic with. Not only must morality and rationality fall away; so must desire. Everything, every attitude or reflection, needs to become nothing. This is the key to the code of silence.

On many occasions, the silence sought by Bataille is very much in line with the mystical search for stillness, but these are accompanied by equally forceful statements about how this silence is a process, not an end, and how it is actually entwined with its privileged other, "noise." What we need to do, he writes, is to block "*discours*"—the organized, structured thinking, speaking, writing, encoding.[15] In so doing, we notice that the most important part of silence is precisely this loss of words, the imposition of order from conscious human interaction with the world.[16] This silence will only ever be fleeting, an interruption ("the sovereign silence that interrupts articulate language"[17]), "accessible only for an instant."[18] There are two parts to this. First, silence is not the end, not an attained state of wisdom. Second, silence is only an act of violence or the result of such an act, and so is an opening, not an access to another reality. Nonetheless, there is a philosophical truth to silence, as the brief dwelling in silence reveals that "I am nothing but silence, the universe is silence."[19] For all Bataille's attempts to escape systematizing thought, this is a philosophical view, a nihilism that brings together Nietzsche and something quite close to Zen Buddhism. Where Bataille differs from both of those is that knowing this changes nothing, as the knowledge of it is also the betrayal of it as truth. It is the failure to master the idea of everything really being nothing that is at work in his idea of silence (or transgression, sacrifice, eroticism, excess . . .). In addition, this is a failure that must be forgotten as we try to attain the sacred (and fail) through our attack on the profane world (which includes organized religion). Even awareness of this spiral of failure is not a gain, as all we get is the haunting sense that somewhere in the attempt to get to the sacred, and failing, was somehow a true failing that approximated the nothingness of the universe.

Once on this path that only leads to a point of not finding the path, the fear of the silence at the heart of everything can come out. This fear leads us to displace complete nothingness into objects of disgust, eroticism, danger, and dispersal of the self, setting up a complex, recursive loop where eroticism is the way into something we are already connected with, and the way out, and the way along. Code, information, and noise all at once, folded in. This circuit which is not one is revealed by Bataille at the end of *Guilty*, where silence becomes part of embodied excess. Silence and nudity appear together, in a premonitory perversion of Levinas's thought of ethics emerging through an encounter with the other:

> Silent and naked, isn't the intimacy of the universe to which you open yourself an intolerable dizziness? And isn't the universe that yawns between your legs unfinished? A question without a response. But you, naked, open to the infinite laughter of the stars, could you

doubt that the distant void would be at the moment heavier than the unavowable intimacy concealed within you?[20]

The body revealed in servile nudity is the exposing of subjectivity such that the subject loses their upstanding nature. All values lose their grounding in the presence of beings lowered in physicality and subjectivity, such that the sacred is on offer: "when offered, your beautiful nudity—silence and the presentiment of a depthless sky—is similar to the horror of the night, whose infinity it designates."[21] Or, as Bataille puts it a few moments later, "your ass is the mouth of a god,"[22] opening up a waiting that is complete silence. For a moment, we need to get very literal here: first, Bataille is addressing someone female, and this raises the problem of who or what might constitute an object for contemplation or loss of the self, a problem that, perhaps oddly, almost never occurs in his fiction. So the nudity being exposed seems to be a "meditational method" for the viewer, not the nude. Maybe it is both, especially as being naked by yourself is not really going to be much of a transgression, unless you are blessed with an astonishingly low transgression threshold. Also, this is not about nudity but nudity as part or prelude to eroticism. A few pages earlier, Bataille talked about shit (*ordure*) as standing in for the void as well as signaling death. Its abjection lies in this opening onto nothingness rather than its mundanely abject condition as something we find unpleasant and have regulated accordingly. So, we have to return to the silent nudity of the bared ass. Silence occurs in the waiting in the face of the "mouth of god." It is not the shit that comes out that will provide ecstasy but the reflective and probably breathless waiting that is the moment of ecstatic silence. Achievement or production of this godly discourse is necessary for the silence to fail ecstatically, but the completion is only an outcome; the sovereign moment lies in the prospect.

Silence is there where the self slips away, but to take silence into the pantheon of transgressive activities is still to underestimate it, because it is in a permanent struggle with noise and, on occasion, in a deconstructive opposition to excess and extreme. Even "the word silence is still a noise" that gets in the way of the potential interruption that silence enacts on discourse, indicating, first, that any definitional category will close off the functioning of an idea and, second, that the reasonable, mundane world is the noise that silence as process must make silent.[23] In the early stages of *La somme* noise is the interruption of the interruption, that is, the restoration of order. This in turn means that silence is the noise of noise, the breakdown of the feedback loops of information and structure. As well as that, silence is the opening into noise that is yet another level (or embedding) of the true and empty universe. At a simple level, Bataille says, writing of himself, that silence heightens his sense of listening to the point where tiny sounds are heard at an excessive level, made both strange and newly available at the same time.[24] In approaching death and the void, we become receptive to them while also feeling anguish, he says, and at the moment we are in the silence of that void (*not* silent contemplation of it), it rushes into us, full with noise:

> Something immense, exorbitant, is liberated in all directions with the noise of catastrophe; it rises up from a void that is unreal, infinite, and at the same time is lost, in the blast of a blinding flash.

> *Quelque chose d'immense, d'exorbitant, se libère en tous sens avec le bruit de catastrophe; cela surgit d'un vide irréel, infini, en même temps s'y perd, dans un choc d'éclat aveuglant.*[25]

Such is the nature of the silence Bataille offers us, and that leads to the infiltration of the void, so that it takes over from the silence.[26] I maintain that silence is noise and that Bataille only seems to suggest that silence in some way unleashes noise, or allows it to be, in order to bring silence and noise into a much closer relation. Silence is where noise happens, not after. And noise is still not the same as silence, even if it can be part of silencing. But still. He does write that on reaching a point of silence, death and volcanoes surge into him, suggesting a causal or at least sequential relation.[27] That there is an element of silence being a first step in a project (that undoes itself) is undeniable, but once we understand silence as part of excess rather than as a standard meditational tool, the simple sequencing has to give way to a more circuitous routing.

Noise itself now seems to be double: it is both what silence allays (the world) and what it opens into (the world as nothing). It is double but always potentially present in its excessive form: "the vast ruin that is humanity drifts endlessly along a river that is deaf to the noise of our discourse, and all of a sudden, it becomes part of the noise of a massive waterfall" ("*jamais la vaste épave humaine ne cesse de dériver le long d'un fleuve sourd au bruit de nos discours: soudain elle entre dans un bruit de cataracte*").[28] The explosion and fall will come, and it is the task of the one seeking inner experience to speed that moment. This speeding-up is in the "dramatization" provided by something outside the self, which can range from the contemplation of a picture until reflective control fades away (like the Chinese torture pictures) to the lowering of the self in eroticism.

Although it is one hundred years since Russolo's *Art of Noises*, there would have been precious little in the way of music attempting to become noise prior to Bataille's death in 1962. In fact, we really have to get past the explicitness of performance art in the 1960s and 1970s, and through industrial music, before we really encounter low forms of noise. Noise music reached a zenith in Japan in the 1980s and 1990s, and the central figure is Merzbow (Masami Akita), who has brought out well over two hundred releases over the last twenty-five years.[29] There is an obvious connection between noise and Bataille's meditation, insofar as both seem excessive, both are beyond the realm of controlling discourse. The connection through silence might seem less blatant, but once we see that silence is one side of double-headed noise, then we can use noise music to explore how silencing might come about in a Bataillean way.

Bataille's own choices in where excess could be found in art are, to be polite, direct. He is always interested in content that is excessive, and only on occasion does he consider the excess of form (this was of note to him in his early writings and to some extent in the late *Manet*). There is something interesting in taking visibly transgressive art and then letting it fall into a Bataillean deconstruction of that same visibility such that its transgression occurs not in the display of transgressive acts but in the crossing of thresholds both within the art and between art and viewer. Noise comes from a very similar place, with Masami Akita's early releases combining harsh noise with BDSM imagery. But there is much more than this superficial connection, as Merzbow can help us read Bataille's meditation even while Bataille provides us with a means of conceiving why noise music exists.

Noise is an interruption of music and a statement about the infinite potential of music itself. Music is an ordering or organization of sound, and noise ostensibly undoes this, but in so doing, it expands the realm of what can occur in the place of music. As noise moves from the more academic avant-garde experimentations into a refusal of the mere incorporation of noise into music, it reaches a point of emptying and becomes a clearing in which music may or may not occur as the residue of a more primordial (if only ever reconceived retrospectively) and potentially endless noise—the cataract that wells inside the flow of the river and shuts out logical and moral orders of meaning. Merzbow's sound is not one where noise is added to music as additional instrumentation or alteration. This is noise all the way down, with the sound built entirely from feedback, white noise, overdriven instruments, relentless change, and it is almost entirely inexplicable from the standpoint of music. Nonetheless, where it happens is on recordings, or in concert, just like music. So it does not fall into the trap of being a simple refusal. This is a refusal from within, a destructuring and not an avoidance. Order is not rejected but dismantled over and over.

White noise can be relaxing, maybe even a meditative aid. One extreme form of recent noise music is the genre of "harsh noise wall," which, in the hands of its leading practitioner Vomir (Romain Perrot) is an unbending mass of noises layered together to become almost static. This has the purpose of stilling the world, an excessive take on the idea of "noise cancellation" available in certain types of headphones, but it does not do as much stilling as Merzbow. It performs one moment of silencing and stays there. Merzbow fractures his own noise, even resorting to bursts of more tangible musical elements, particularly rhythms, to keep noise in play. This is a location of the silence through excess that Bataille goes looking for, its breaking down of form even as it takes form (for example, as a track on a CD), an exact rendering of the project that undoes the idea of project. In Bataille's view, a rendering is not enough—it is a failure to capture the sovereign silence, but, as noted above, this failure is an essential part of the feedback loop that is Bataille's attempt to attain the sacred. The same can be said of the genre of noise music—it would seem to bring order to something that is about deformation, but this failure or, more accurately, pathetic betrayal is almost what allows the possibility of an authentic if fleeting moment where it can escape. It escapes within the series of failures that define it.

The duration of Merzbow's works is also important. It is very hard to predict when a piece will end or why it would end after twenty minutes rather than ten. Merzbow heightens this by releasing very long albums but also mostly rejecting the possibility of one track filling a CD. This length, along with the unpredictability (at least on first listen, one of the reasons for the massive proliferation of his releases) allows the possibility of coming to dwell in his world, but this is a dwelling that cannot settle, a dwelling that lives in the impossibility of fully dwelling. To give an idea of how this works at a pragmatic level, I will turn to the 6 CD album *Houjoue* (released in 2006). The scale of the project alone causes one to pause, even if one has some forewarning of the kind of soundworld encoded in the discs. It was all recorded within a year, from late 2004 on (and is not the only recording Merzbow released in 2006), but each CD section offers a different approach to noise, sometimes drifting close to musicality, as in the arrhythmias of CD 2, or the (loud) ambient build of CD 3. Nonetheless, there is a connection, and this is made through a shared level, style, and quality of recording and mastering. One of the many layers of variation between Merzbow releases is precisely in the engineering phases, so the unity across *Houjoue* makes this a genuine album. The length, in combination with the changes, makes this an excursion into self-aware duration—one that, as it refuses to settle, knocks us out of Bergsonian considerations, out of time, and into silence, away from the river into a cataract of time, where reference points are lost in downward explosiveness.

This is nowhere more the case than in the opening track "Action for Green 1." This opens with instant white noise (no attack), bringing in electronic howls, whistling, and guitarlike feedback squeals. After four and a half minutes it cuts into huge pulses over a seething beelike noise. Harsh bursts drop in and out, over and under. Not only is this impossible for the listener to master, but it tries to undo itself too, with every layer shifting up and down, so that there is no base layer. This is not noise over some kind of steadiness (or vice versa) but an endless crossing from hook to held. Attention is lured in by the dual promise of continual change but also areas of stability, and attention is resisted. The approach and the type of noisiness both alter over the course of different tracks, as well as from CD to CD, but needing to track that all the way through, we can pause on CD 4, track 1, "Frog Variation 0505" (via the chicken sounds of "Houjoue 1" on CD 3), which reveals a different, ostensibly smoother noise. Here, the first seven minutes combine strident alarm bursts with awkward percussiveness, flowing into white noise shunted up and down the frequency levels (that is, dewhitened). It is the middle section of the thirty-eight-minute track that shows a different angle: here it is about repetition and stasis to the point of anguish. For thirteen minutes, rounded and deep pulsing sounds repeat over what sounds like the shuffling of bits of metal. This directionless section sucks out any possibility of imposing narration through listening. This occurs with "pure" noise, but here it is more troubling, less open to contemplation, as it keeps altering, minutely and without ever seeming to resolve. After this "break," the last few minutes fill with competing distortions, feedback squalls, and the like, a parody of resolution, pretending that the middle section in some way paved the way to the end.

There is nothing wrong with "betraying" this noise by reducing it, bringing it to language—it draws sustenance by not being the thing it is not (that is, not being its own description), and betrayal, loss, and failure are all parts of the Bataillean loop of lost subjectivity. But the question remains whether Merzbow is just an illustration, rather than a "method" or location, of the sacred. I think it is all of those, and less, always less. It does illustrate, in a very direct, simplistic manner, how silence comes not at the end of noise but in the positing of a noise that counters the noise of the everyday. It is a presentation of noise that can affect the listener to the point of loss of controlled subjectivity. It is easy to *not* have that, and either imposing musicality or the sense that it is just noise would save you the trouble of getting lost and keep you secure as a listener. Many fans of Merzbow are this type of reasonably contented and conscious listener, and this too is inevitable. As Bataille himself notes, "deliverance eventually sickens."[30] The performance of noise is also a moment that comes close to inner experience (and coming close is the best failure available), despite the need for often very disciplined manipulation of machinery, particularly at the beginning of performances. For the listener, live noise is being caught in excess, loss of control. Listening gives way to mere hearing, maybe even less than that, and imagining a structure for what you hear abuts the un-contained time of noise.

So, noise sets up a circuit that includes content, form, performance, playing, receiving. None of these is the place noise as inner experience happens. It happens in the crossing of one part to another, and the sequence of failures that take place in a piece, for the listener, and in the ultimate grasping onto sense, direction, purpose. This shows the failure of noise to remain noise and also the failure of the listener to let go. Somewhere in the interchange of those failings lies the momentary burst of inner experience. The noise of the cataract that humanity can always fall into is also the end of all sound, the filling of ears, of thought, of the body to the point of somatic failure. This is the silence that even John Cage could not master—the silence of all sound, as if every star was equally visible, and there would be only light, and nothing would be seen. This is noise not only as silencing (of the world, the self, morals, reason) but noise as silence itself, the two in almost quantum relation, only here it is not the observation but the moment of loss of observation that the two potentials become one, and "the scream I let out is silence without end."[31] Or, maybe it the laughter of attaining the height of existence in low abjection (or failing so to do)—in which case we would hear "the ecstatic laugh [that] does *not laugh*."[32] All this. For nothing.

Georges Bataille and the Religion of Capitalism

JEAN-JOSEPH GOUX

Bataille does not cease to interrogate the advent of a society, ours, that totally liberated the production of things from its archaic finality, which was the unproductive destruction of the surplus, a destruction mostly realized in religious sacrifices. These sacrifices had a fundamental function: they operated, according to Bataille, as a return to intimacy, a reaffirmation of the immanence between man and the world, through the death of the sacrificed animal.[1] It is this return to intimacy, to the immanence where the opposition between world and mankind, life and death, the subject and the object, was cancelled during the time of sacrifice, that does not take place anymore in the societies that favor industrial growth over all other goals. Taking into account industrial development and its tendency to separate completely the "divine intimacy" and the "order of the real," Bataille tries to think of the place, the state, and the residual role of religion in an industrial and productive society that pushed to the limits "the reign of things" and radically renounced the quest of intimacy and of immanence, an immemorial quest that, through the always returning sacrificial cult, has produced the meaning of all the religions of the past. From that time onward, what has become of the religious situation for the individual and for society? What has become of religion? Did religion disappear, or did it undergo a transformation that renders it unrecognizable? Have we been freed of religious beliefs and constraints, resulting in a new, more emancipated morality, one in search of purely earthly satisfactions, or have the religious imperatives transposed into imperatives of economic production, imperatives as constraining as the religious devotions of the past?

The problem, as presented, refers to the question of *secularization*. Bataille does not question it in these terms, even though he relies in great part on Weber's analyses, which give a decisive meaning to the idea of secularization. My approach to Bataille's religious theory, which is inseparable from his conception of economy, will be elaborated in this essay, in relation to the notion of secularization. This notion contrasts an enlightening of the spirit of capitalism in regard to the first capitalism, which was ascetic, and the new capitalism, which is dominated by the unleashing of consumption. This notion will also help us comprehend the exceptional status acquired today by economic life, by the economic sciences (or what pretend to be as such), and by economists themselves, with their different and conflicting theoretical and political tendencies.

I

At the end of Jean-Sébastien Mercier's *The Year 2440, a Dream If Ever There Was One*, written in 1771, eighteen years before the French Revolution, which he amazingly anticipated, a strange and pathetic scene precedes the brutal awakening of the narrator, who is deep in his thoughts of a better society: a man crying on the shapeless debris of Versailles, the monument to the unbounded pride of a king, this superb palace now in ruins, a wilted image of its noble and magnificent past. This man is Louis XIV himself or, rather, his ghost, which the justice of God has brought back to life, so that he may contemplate his deplorable piece of work . . .

This final reminiscence gives Mercier the opportunity to mention in an important footnote a more general thought on the uselessness of great sumptuary expenditure (lavish entertainment, theaters, and tombs), the offspring of despotism, which he places in contrast to the usefulness of the erections of the republicans:

> We praise these magnificent and spectacular scenes that were offered to the Roman people. We want to infer from that, the greatness of this people. The Roman people were saddened as soon as they saw these pompous feasts, where the fruit of their victories were lavished. Who built the circuses, the theaters, the thermal baths? Who engineered these artificial lakes where an entire fleet maneuvered as in the great sea? It was these crowded monsters for which the tyrannical pride crushed half of the people, to entertain the eyes of the other half. Egypt prides itself on the huge pyramids that were the monu-

ments of despotism. Republicans build aqueducts, channels, roads, public places, markets, but every palace erected by a monarch is the seed of an impending calamity.[2]

George Bataille would have been intrigued by this footnote. It contrasts with clarity two distinct modes of spending, two political economies that the author of *The Accursed Share* repeatedly interrogated. On the one hand, the unproductive, ostentatious spending, whether it be the Roman circus, the Egyptian pyramids, or the palace of Versailles. On the other hand, the channels, the roads, the public places, the markets, constructions lacking magnificence but useful, constructions facilitating movement and exchange of commodities; in a word, commercial life. For Mercier the contrast between these two orientations of expenditure is clearly political: on the one hand, the tyranny of monarchs, despots, crowned monsters; on the other, the choice of the republicans.

This text is all the more enlightening in that it is inscribed into what will become a deep historical rift: the feudal regime on one side, with its religious expenditures (cathedrals, sumptuous liturgies, contemplations, prayers, ongoing feasts in honor of saints), its seigniorial ostentations (castles, tournaments, extravagant and costly costumes, prestige wars), and on the other side the reign of the bourgeois, with its principle of utility, of productive spending, its commercial, financial, and industrial development. Here is that change in the mode of economy, which fascinates Bataille. He will not only see one historical rupture as like another one, as an enigmatic mutation that puts into play an entire conception of the divine in relation to economy. The theological background and the religious implications of this change will never cease to nourish his thought.

It is not only a new society that rises but a society different from all others that preceded it. This society appeared as an anthropological anomaly, especially on the religious level. It is a society that seems to be able to put aside the sacrifice made to the gods, this expenditure dedicated to the divine, which all societies have manifested in different degrees and various shapes. There are numerous kinds of sacrifices: human sacrifices, animal sacrifices, real or symbolic sacrifices, sacrifices honoring ancestors, the dead, multiple gods, or one god. Sacrifice for expiation, propitiation, reparation. There does not seem to be one human society in the past that has ignored the principle of this gift, this offering, this loss, which is made for the benefit of the divine and which maintains the link between man and the sacred.

However, Western modern societies introduce a novelty: a society that seems to have separated completely the religious and civic spheres, the sacred and political spheres, thus pushing to its extreme the distinction between the temporal and the spiritual, ultimately conferring power, value, only on the temporal sphere. This historical fact gave rise to the thesis of secularization. This thesis

> pinpoints a phenomenon or a process both massive and inescapable for all eyes that look without prejudice (and that are "nonphilosophical") on European history: the withdrawal of religion as a dominant sphere of social life, the swing toward a society structured on a secular basis and with rational claims, with, as corollary, a massive problem: the one of transformations and disappearance of religious representations.[3]

Bataille, following the classical analyses of Max Weber and R. H. Tawney, attributes a decisive place to the influence of the Reformation and especially Calvinism in this important historical transition. The Reformation is the great religious movement that, during the sixteenth and seventeenth centuries, enables the transition (itself a source of great conflicts) from a profligate religion to a spendthrift one. The Roman Catholic religion is strongly associated with glorious and unproductive expenditure, expenses *here below* that are supposed to assure the salvation of the soul *hereafter:* imposing architectural construction, enriched by the sumptuousness of works of art, donations for the contemplative religious orders, an ecclesiastical hierarchy supporting at great cost the princes of the church. By contrast Protestantism is an austere religion, even ascetic, that negates the value of works made for the sake of Heaven and that proclaims the great religious and ethical signification of work here below: the daily tasks, the profession as vocation, including commerce and handling of money.

There are two or three possible interpretations of the meaning and effect of the secularization of Christian religion operating since the Reformation and during the following centuries. It is around these different interpretations that I shall articulate the understanding that one may have of Bataille today and the evaluation of his contribution to the question of religion in Western capitalist societies.

According to a first interpretation, secularization carried out by Protestantism *transposes* Christian values and themes into the practical and terrestrial world of economic activities. This transposition maintains the Christian (and thus religious) meaning. There is a persistence of a religious content (faith, fervor, hope of salvation, expectation of grace) underlying daily activities and interests that at first glance may seem entirely profane.

In a second mode, the secularization ends up *liquidating* all effective religion, and it results in a combination of atheism and productive dynamism. The split between heaven and earth, the hereafter and here below is so deep, so complete, so nonreversible, that heaven is forgotten and, further on, negated, and the only remaining concerns are for earthly life, its goals, its projects, its satisfactions, its hopes. This is Nietzsche's solution. It is also, though derived from other ethical and political postulates, Marx's tendency. On this difference between transposition and liquidation the work of Jean-Claude Monod is enlightening.

With this second mode of secularization, which seeks to liquidate the religious demands and not to transpose them (even though we still may clearly detect this transposition in both Marx and Nietzsche), other tendencies emerged (and they emerged before Marx and Nietzsche) that impatiently freed themselves from the interdictions of Christian ethics, from its asceticism, from its tendency to renounce earthly satisfactions. These are the ethics of not only atheistic, intellectual libertinism (Gassendi, Cyrano de Bergerac in the seventeenth century) but also the "immoral" tendencies of the libertine novels (Crébillon fils, Boyer d'Agens, Diderot, Sade, Casanova) as well as the hedonistic philosophies (as the writing of Helvétius, the father of utilitarianism), which express themselves in an openly transgressive, sometimes blasphemous and strongly anticlerical manner. (Voltaire would probably be the best-known representative of this antireligious criticism.)

It is in Catholicism rather than in Protestantism that we find this third tendency, a tendency hardly analyzed by Monod, who focused on Protestantism and its philosophical effects. This third tendency is heavily accentuated in the works of French writers of the Enlightenment. The need to shake the oppressive domination of the church, to attack its hierarchical institutions, to mock its power and the visibility of the representatives of the ecclesiastic authority and their hypocrisy, to transgress its institutionalized interdictions: all this could explain the difference between secularization in Catholic societies and in Protestant ones. We can also state the contrast between religious interdictions that are extremely strict for the clergy (celibacy of the priests, vow of chastity and poverty for monks and nuns) and a certain aesthetical sensuality in the representation of religious scenes. Liberties taken with the ecclesiastical rules would add a peculiar component that Protestantism has not experienced and that could have repercussions for challenging (or subversive) literary or pictorial works, be they libertine, symbolist, or, later on, surrealist. This third form of secularization that I add to the two forms distinguished by Monod (transposition and liquidation) is historically located in the second position, after the Protestant secularization but before the complete atheistic liquidation by Marx and Nietzsche, a liquidation for which it lays the groundwork.

It is this double or triple orientation of the secularization of Christianity that we must question. It is no less than the meaning that we must attribute today to capitalism and the economic theories that vouch for it that are at stake. Starting from the second part of the twentieth century, capitalism becomes subjected to a tug-of-war between these different and contradictory tendencies of secularization, tendencies Weber was unable to predict and that Bataille anticipated only partially. At first, the various modes of secularization neither opposed themselves to nor distinguished themselves from one another. But given some historical distance, it appears that they succeeded one after the other and even that they fused, changing deeply the nature of the first capitalism and facilitating the passage from the Calvinist capitalism, as Weber and Bataille describe it, to a different capitalism, the one that reigns today, the one with a strong hedonistic and transgressive component and where the ethical model of the artist or, in more banal terms, of the consumer in search of satisfactions plays a central role.[4]

The strong interest that Bataille presents for us today is that he takes into account, through a series of literary, philosophical, and economic works, the different components of the movement of the secularization of Christianity, even though he does not formally distinguish among them. It is clear that Bataille belongs primarily, especially through his literary works, which associate him with the libertine French tradition, to the third mode of secularization, the anti-Christian mode stemming from Catholic cultures. But, in a much more ambiguous and enigmatic way, in reconnecting with the experiences of Christian mystics—and at the same time being under the influence of Hegel and Nietzsche—he chooses a path that will distinguish him from the liquidators of religious experience and that will make him, as Sartre wrote, "a new mystic," a new Pascal, who continues to explore, through the detours of "atheology," the abyss of transcendence. Even more, with his taking into account of Weber and the anthropological contributions of Mauss, Bataille situates in a more general economy the secularization-transposition out of which the spirit of modern capitalism is born. It is probably this multiplicity of sources and his effort to coordinate them into a coherent vision that gives Bataille's interpretation of religious phenomena relevance today.

II

In times of economic, financial, and stock-market crisis, the technical and ideological supremacy of the economists is evident. Instead of the political, religious, ethical, and cultural discourses, it is the economic one that seems continually to be asked to assuage uncertainty, ignorance, and anxiety. Economy seems to be the all-powerful point of view that reigns over all other aspects of life. Unemployment rates, the consumer confidence index, stock quotes, interest rates, the gross national product, the verdicts of credit rating agencies. Has economic discourse become the new decalogue or new gospel of a religion of earthly salvation? Has capitalism become a religion, of which economists have become the priests? Is this religion in line with Bataille's analysis, or is it in contradiction?

If we take seriously Weber's analysis of capitalistic activity favored by a transposition of Christian dogmas operating under the Protestant influence (Lutheran but mostly Calvinist), it is not absurd to consider capitalism itself as a religion. The secularization of Christian values and beliefs is not their liquidation but rather their fulfillment in the economic field. The main Christian beliefs, values, and dogmas continue to be vivid, but instead of expressing themselves in the luxuriance of the holy deeds, in the profound and idle contemplation that separates the hereafter from the here below in lavish ceremonies, they instead realize themselves through daily professional activities; they prove themselves through commercial success and individual profit. The acquired wealth, by an imperceptible but nearly inevitable diversion of the doctrine of predestination, becomes the obvious sign of individual election conferred by the grace of God.

Admittedly! But can we still speak of religion in this case? Doesn't religion first of all imply ceremonies, liturgies—in brief, a worship practiced in common? It is significant that Kant, educated in a strict and rigorous Protestant pietism, has answered this question in introducing the idea of a religion contained within the limits of reason. According to him, a true religion is a purely moral religion. Religious ceremonies, liturgies, masses, and sermons heard in common in a religious building are not necessary to define a religion. The pure moral legislation by which the will of God is originally inscribed in our hearts is not only the indispensable condition of every true religion but is what constitutes it. So the best way to serve God is not through worship but rather through the fulfillment of duties toward others and self. Kant opposes religions based on worship, which correspond to several possible beliefs (Judaism, Catholicism, Islam, Lutheranism), to the true religion, which is purely moral.

So, strictly speaking, the respect of pure moral legislation, which follows the will of God, is a religion. Worship is thus not necessary. It even betrays an incapacity of humankind to conceive religion more purely as the carrying out of duties toward humankind and oneself. Thus Kant accomplishes the ideals of an economical religion, where right action is sufficient and where nothing is squandered on emotional and sensual satisfaction. Religion coincides with a rigorous secular ethic.

It is to this position that Bataille refers in the second part of *Theory of Religion:* religion within the limits of reason (from military order to industrial development). It is only an allusion and not a direct confrontation with Kant's philosophy. For Bataille, the purpose is not to enter into the details of a discussion but to consider the Kantian position as one of a succession of significant figures, or moments, of Western religious development. This figure of religion will be analyzed not via Hegel's dialectic but within Bataille's social and historical framework: the emergence of the industrial world and the development of capitalism.

But Bataille does not explicitly state his conclusions. As soon as capitalist activity is conceived as the successful secularized transposition of Christian morals, and as soon as we consider that a pure morality is a true religion (even *the* true religion, which does not require the trappings of worship), then it is not absurd to conclude that practical capitalism is accompanied by an ethical requirement that satisfies religious principles and that that renders it sufficient as a true and whole religion within the limits of the reason. Capitalism may satisfy religious principles not as a practice equivalent to worship but—as it includes, or is compatible with, the accomplishment of a moral duty toward others and one's self—with the complete and successful transposition into the sphere of economic and professional actions the requirements of the Christian ethic as reinterpreted by Calvinism.

A close but different affirmation of this thesis has been put forth, on another basis, by Walter Benjamin, in a few pages of unpublished and obscure notes that Michael Löwy commented on a few years ago.[5] According to Benjamin, who reaffirms Weber's thesis, though radicalizing it a little, Christianity at the time of the Reformation was not only favorable to the advent of capitalism but transformed itself into capitalism, thereby giving it its religious nature.

Nevertheless, it is not the idea of a religion within the limits of reason that led Benjamin to sustain this argument. On the contrary, he sees in capitalism the most worship-oriented religion that has ever occurred. Though devoid of dogma and theology, the utilitarian practices of capitalism (production, selling and buying, investment, financial operations) are equivalent to worship—or, better, *are* a form of worship. The stock exchange and factory rituals, carried out for the gods of Profit and Wealth, would be the permanent, fevered manifestation of a profound and total devotion to the religion of economy.

This is a terrifying religion because its worship produces a feeling of guilt, not a sense of expiation, unlike all other religions. The poor are guilty and excluded from grace. But not only the poor live with guilt. The threat of running into debt, of insolvency, bankruptcy, hangs over everyone. The universal guilt of insolvency, thus of the possible loss of grace, the permanent threat of damnation, make this religion one of despair. Everyone is on the brink of the abyss, possibly sliding at any moment from the position of the elect to that of the reprobate, in a fall that repeats original sin, this time following both the inscrutable ways of chance and the results of hard work.

The result of Benjamin's thesis, if we adopt it, would be that it is useless in the capitalist world to search for religious phenomena of great weight and great scope because capitalism in itself, in its practices, its beliefs, its aims, individual or collective, would be the dominant religion, the only significant and powerful religion.

This leads us rather close to Bataille without, nevertheless, coinciding with his interpretation. Some of his statements agree with this direction. For example, he writes that the ruthless business owner, making profits, devoting all his time to work, and perpetually extending his enterprises, was to the New World what the saint was to medieval Europe.[6] Bataille also states that the enterprise ignores humankind; its only god is growth.[7] Even if mere metaphor (but with such a comparison, how could it not be?), these formulations make of capitalism a religion in which god is growth for growth's sake, where devout and miserable penitents are the ordinary workers, and where the saints are the owner-capitalists who succeed in the expansion of their enterprises and the constant rise in their profits. They succeed at the price of a sacrifice, that of their lifespan, which is entirely devoted to work. But this sacrifice does not resemble, as Bataille insists, the glorious sacrifice of accumulated wealth. This wealth is an industrial and commercial benefit that is reinvested shortly to obtain more growth and profit. This is not an expense or a loss without economic return; it is an investment.

Finally, this is why Bataille does not see in "the reign of things" established by the industrial and capitalist world any experience of a return to intimacy and immanence and thus any religious truth.

III

Nevertheless, it seems that capitalist society is nourished by multiple tendencies, in part contradictory, and that we cannot, as do Weber and then Bataille, reduce the capitalist world to the successful secularization of

Christianity or even to the complete transposition of Christian belief to capitalist belief. Real capitalism is not the simple figure of an accomplished Calvinism. Capitalism is not homogeneous. Yet the contradictions of the Enlightenment era (the great Western democratic revolutions come from that era) have attracted the most attention. Some of these contradictions have been themselves inherited from this era. And we find them again in the spirit of capitalism, including today, under new and more developed forms.

In *The Philosophy of Enlightenment* (1932), Ernst Cassirer skillfully demonstrated the antagonism between Renaissance humanism and the Lutheran or Calvinist Reformation. Humanism and the Reformation agree on a common ground but, on a deeper level, are radically opposed. Renaissance and Reformation agree to confer a new value and a new religious primacy to terrestrial life. They also give a new value to spiritualization, that is, the internalization of faith. They replace the negation of the world with a transformation of the world. They promote action in worldly life and one's accomplishments by labor within one's profession. Nevertheless, despite this commonality between the humanist Renaissance and the Protestant Reformation, a deep abyss yawns between them. We return, with the origin of this opposition, to a religious dogma at the basis of Lutheranism and of Calvinism: original sin. Renaissance humanism, through its return to antiquity, to Plato, to the Stoics, favors the powers of mankind, the autarky of his will, against the yoke of the Augustinian tradition, which insists on the corruption of humankind and the role of grace. Humanists, even though they apparently remain in the Christian tradition, move closer to the old heresy of Pelagius, for whom humankind can free itself from sin by the sole strength of his free will.

This difference will have decisive repercussions during the Enlightenment, where original sin is the common target that unites the different tendencies of thought (whether Rousseau's or Voltaire's). The optimistic affirmation of the progressive evolution of human history (as in Turgot and Condorcet), the affirmation also of a hedonistic philosophy, the apologia of luxury and sensual pleasure (as in the young Voltaire), can only be based on the belief in the capacity of men to find happiness through their own strength. The Augustinian and Calvinist idea of a corrupted man, rotten, damaged, infected by Adam's sin, which prolongs in him as an incurable hereditary illness (in the harsh French language of Jean Calvin), cannot agree with this Enlightenment optimism that insists on the inner goodness of the human being.

There will be within the Protestant-dominated cultures that adhere to the "capitalist religion" a deep fracture, one not always visible at the beginning but more and more evident, between the spirit of Enlightenment, with its optimistic, rationalistic, utilitarian, hedonistic component, and another tendency, which is the consequence of the Calvinist heritage, for which ascetic discipline rather than the pursuit of happiness should guide human conduct.

This opposition was recently very well perceived and analyzed by Robert H. Nelson, who tries to interpret the various theories and positions of contemporary American economists as orientations conveying religious presuppositions. Thus, economics appears as a secularized form of theology, the gospel of our time, of which economists are the grand priests. "Economists played their most important role in American society in the twentieth century as theologians and preachers of a religion."[8] This religion is the one of the market and of profit.

In a general way, Nelson sees in American history two opposite conceptions, which more or less coincide with the opposition pointed out by Cassirer between humanism and the Reformation. This opposition continues today to have an effect on economic theories, even if the Calvinist tendency is not as well represented as the optimistic tendency of the Enlightenment. "In the broadest view, one might say that, intellectually and theologically speaking, much of American history has reflected a struggle between the pessimistic Puritan view of fallen, sinful humankind and the optimistic Enlightenment view of rational, utilitarian humankind."[9] According to Nelson, the great majority of American economists fall on the Enlightenment and progressive side of this divide, but others, such as Frank Knight, the most influential figure at the origin of the Chicago School, Milton Friedman's and George Stigler's professor—and one of the great mentors of George Gilder, the harbinger of the Reagan era—belong to this second current.

Gilder, an enemy of "secular culture," in his bestseller *Wealth and Poverty*, wanted to give a theology to capitalism. It is clear that his vision is radically individualistic and libertarian, where individual chance has a decisive place, one stamped by a kind of tragedy of destruction and of permanent reinvention that no organizational project of society could or should avoid. Without any doubt it should not be difficult to find a certain radical Calvinist inspiration, whatever may be this path of the influence. For Gilder, capitalism is essentially generous because the industrial and commercial supply may be compared to a gift without any assured return, comparable to the potlatch analyzed by Mauss. I have analyzed elsewhere this strange and unwilling encounter between Gilder and Bataille.[10] Nevertheless the poor (or, rather, the so-called poor, because according to Gilder there are no real poor in the United States) are simply bad Christians, and instead of receiving subsidies from the state, they should go to church to pray.

Friedman does not go as far as this, but he also conveys, via indirect influence (maybe partly independent of his own religious roots), an individualistic and libertarian tendency, one obvious in its conception of economic policy. He sees government as a major threat to freedom. The market should be the primary instrument for organizing economic activity in society. It would be desirable to deregulate the airlines, railroads, and the trucking and other transportation industries. The government should remove its support for various medical, legal, and other professional curbs on competition. In monetary policy, Friedman is a proponent of a floating exchange rate: the government should let the market determine the price of foreign currency.[11] In addition, one can find in Friedman a criticism of all that seems to resemble egalitarian policies that could weaken the responsibility of the individual for his own fate. It is significant that in *Free to Choose*, which begins by praising "the power of the market" and refusing "the tyranny of control," Friedman takes great pains to provide a detailed exegesis of the first words of the U.S. Declaration of Independence, to outline that in this inaugural document what is at stake, first and foremost, is to affirm "equality before God" (and only thereafter equality of opportunity) but not, in any case, to suggest, as some irresponsible intellectuals would like to pretend, that we could find support, on that basis, to critique the inequality of income.

Nelson again comes across the opposition between the optimistic Enlightenment and the pessimistic puritanical view in the antagonism between the MIT Economic School, dominated after the war by the figure of Samuelson (the author of the well-known introductory textbook *Economics*) and, on the other side, starting from the 1960s, the Chicago School (where following one another, though sometimes arguing among themselves, come Knight, Friedman, and Stigler).

In the first case, material advance was the route of a secular salvation on earth. God would not bring heaven to earth by means of some miraculous transformation of the world. Rather, God is economically oriented. The divine plan would operate through the economic forces of history, the productive resources of society, achieving a state of complete abundance that would bring new conditions in the relationships of human beings to one another.[12] In this optimistic scenario, the economist is an apostle and a preacher of scientific management and large government.

In the second case, the influence of a modern libertarian theory can be noted, one more puritanical and Calvinist in its origin, which explicitly rejects the orthodoxies of the progressive gospel and the prescription for the rational management of society. If this opposition corresponds to two historical and economical junctures of post–World War II America (the second corresponding to the Reagan era, with the ideas of Friedman or Gilder), it is also, according to Nelson, inherent to a permanent antagonism in American culture.

Such a view, soundly argued by Nelson, complicates the overly simple interpretation by Weber and by Bataille because it demonstrates a cultural contradiction within capitalism. There would be, fundamentally, two big tendencies that repeat, almost half a millennium later, the opposition between the Renaissance and the Reformation, or, two centuries later, between the Enlightenment's optimistic humanism and Protestant pessimism.

It is upon this previous contradiction that another contradiction in contemporary capitalism more recently grafts itself, one that Daniel Bell points out. He saw a conflict between a puritan ethic of hard work and soberness on one hand and a permanent appeal to consumer satisfaction on the other, satisfaction that makes possible, but also necessary, from a certain point, the capitalist production itself, as a requirement of its unlimited development. One could find here, under a contemporary and explosive form, the conflict between one of the tendencies of the Enlightenment (hedonism, utilitarianism, search for immediate terrestrial satisfactions, refusal of every sacrifice here below for the sake of a more dubious thereafter) and the Protestant Reformation, which maintains on the contrary a stern work ethic, an ascetic ethic of productive reinvestment.

Today, this contradiction within a consumerist society that stimulates the desire of the consumer by offering more and more seductions, by an *aestheticization* (and sometimes an *eroticization*) of the commodity, by a credit that no longer differs from the coveted purchase, has reached a critical point, introducing a new phase in capitalism, one that does not resemble the one analyzed by Weber or Bataille. In this postmodern capitalism, dominated by finance, by stock speculation, by the arbitrarily high salaries and bonuses (and, analogously, by the symptomatic arbitrariness of the prices of works of art)—in this capitalism dominated by the huge debt of private individuals or states, it seems that value has lost its ties with labor.[13] All payment or reimbursement is deferred toward the future, with exaggerated optimism. It is the intensity of the present desire (both subjective and manipulated) of the consumer that triggers a boom or a tumble of prices. The principle of the instantaneous auction, the mechanism of permanent stock exchange, dominates all domains. Fashion is everywhere. The fixed standards of value (ethic, aesthetic, and economic) have been smashed, as if capitalism had recaptured and integrated the utopias that had hoped to reverse capitalism's organizing principles. Now is the reign of the frivolity of values.[14]

It is significant that the economic theory of labor value, which was deeply rooted in a British Protestant tradition marked by Calvinism (Petty, Locke, Smith), yields the terrain, since the end of the nineteenth century, to marginalist theories of value satisfaction rooted in the Catholic terrain of Italy and France: Davanzati, Galiani, Turgot, Condillac.[15] These theories situate the source of commercial value in consumer pleasure and not productive labor. In this conception the difference between use value and exchange value is not radical because it is the use of the object (utility, anticipated satisfaction) that grants it its exchange value, a value that thus loses its "objective" basis in the labor time necessary for its production.

IV

This allusion to the Catholic source of the theories of value satisfaction gives me the opportunity for a remark. There is a great lacuna in the analysis made by Bataille of the religious phenomena imbricated in the origins of capitalism in Western society: Catholicism. Having postulated with Weber a concordance of principles between Protestant ethics and the spirit of capitalism, Bataille does not address the specific way a Catholic-dominant society enters capitalism. Catholicism, as a religion strongly attached to holy works and thus to unproductive expenses, is out of the analytic frame (of Hegelian inspiration) and definitively stays at the back of the movement that leads inexorably to a break between the order of things and a religious level of intimacy. Nevertheless there is much to say on the proper route of the secularization of Catholic societies. It is only possible here to indicate a few markers, sometimes in opposition to Bataille.

It is common knowledge that the most Catholic societies, when they secularize and modernize themselves, demonstrate Marxist tendencies (socialist or, often, communist) much stronger and longer lasting than in Protestant societies. Many interpretations of this fact are possible. We could outline the greater gap to make up for the spirit of economic realism, an adjustment that Marxism allows or promises. But, on the other hand, the tradition of a unified, all-powerful, centralized, and hierarchical church, the organizer of social and cultural life (education, places of worship, popular celebrations) and the source of care for the sick and the helpless (hospitals, poorhouses, and diverse charities), would continue under the guise of the socialist-type welfare state.

More deeply, the relations between Christianity (at its origin, a religion for the poor, the slaves, the oppressed, the sick, the humblest) and socialism (or communism) has been strongly underlined by Engels as well as by Nietzsche, who obviously draw from this comparison opposite philosophical consequences. Nevertheless, it seems that Protestantism, being in concordance with rising capitalism, placed Christianity on another path. It made of it a religion of bourgeois domination and therefore of commercial success. The affirmation of full individual responsibility for the acquisition of better social status by hard work, combined with the inscrutable decree of God concerning the salvation of the soul, seems to have diverted Christianity, via the Protestant bifurcation, from its egalitarian and Marxist inclinations. There are the reprobate, and there are the elect, and thus there is no equality of all before God.

Even if, in principle, this difference stays unknowable and even cannot be proven by works accomplished on earth, the faithful cannot prevent themselves from believing that there are some visible, terrestrial signs of election or damnation. With the development of capitalism they will easily find these signs in wealth or poverty, now considered as effects of individual morality. This dogma of predestination, coming from Augustine but accentuated and elaborated again by Calvinism in new circumstances, confers opposite and even concurrent destinies on individuals. This can explain the deep incompatibility between Protestantism and communism. On the contrary, Catholicism, which in its main tendency postulates that God gave humankind Jesus for the redemption of all and hardly insists on the difference between the two predestinations (in spite of long theological controversies, of which the *Ecrits sur la grâce* by Blaise Pascal gave us an interesting sample), will be more propitious to secularizations of a communist type.

Nevertheless, political and juridical equality have been earlier proclaimed by the Protestant spirit, the enemy of ecclesiastical hierarchy, of the theological authoritarianism of Rome, of the all-powerful mediation of the church in the relationship of the believer with God. This individual responsibility directs the Protestant spirit toward parliamentary government rather than conceptions that grant to the state and its administration all power of organization of public and private life. One knows very well how many Americans are defiant toward or skeptical of the state, the central power, "big government," Washington.

At the same time—and this is an important point—poverty received a very different signification in Catholic societies than in societies with a Protestant culture. In Catholicism, not only is poverty not perceived as a severe metaphysical defect; it can even be a way to reach a life nearer to sanctity, as shown by the vow of poverty of monks and the existence of mendicant orders.

If we take literally some sentences of the Gospel, the poor are closer to God and have a better chance of entering Paradise than the rich. In Protestantism, on the contrary, poverty is a sign of damnation; it is perceived as a vice—or a depravity, the result of a vice. The poor do not have the "marvelous dignity" that Bossuet, for example, acknowledges in them in his panegyric of Saint Francis of Assisi.[16] Moreover, Bossuet states, in this same panegyric, that, according to human law, the owner is fully proprietor of his wealth but that, according to the justice of God, it is necessary that these masters and owners be wary of believing that the poor have totally lost "this so natural right that they have to take in common bulk of goods all that is necessary for them."[17] Astonishing discourse coming from an honorable and celebrated bishop of King Louis XIV!

This communist proclivity of Catholicism that one cannot find in Protestantism contradicts, at least partially, some of Bataille's observations about "the similarities between Reformation and Marxism."[18] Bataille claims that Marx distinctly asserts what Calvin had only sketched because he entirely frees the world of *things* (the world of economy) of all elements that are exterior to the *things* (that is to say, to the economy). It is true, he adds, that Marxism notes at the same time that this liberation is also an enslavement and that thus it becomes a critique of capitalism. However, Bataille does not see that there is in Marx an optimistic and progressive dimension, the affirmation of a capacity of humankind to take in hand its historical destiny, which typically belongs to the spirit of the Enlightenment (Condorcet, for example) and that totally contradicts the dogma of double predestination, which introduces a difference in principle between individuals that is not compatible with the communists' postulates.

These brief considerations on the difference between Catholicism and Protestantism in the modern phase of secularization reveals a lacuna in Bataille's analysis, which is entirely focused, through a Hegelian and Weberian influence, on Protestantism. Nevertheless, this lacuna does not affect the general movement that Bataille draws toward a deepening secularization, which leads to a general acceptance of the industrial world and of its economic logic. But the domination of the so-called world of things leaves only to an "inner experience," very marginalized and individual, the relationship of intimacy and immanence, where he sees the essence of religion. This burning quest by Bataille, for a proper terrain of religion, outside the sphere of things, outside the productive economy, outside labor, bears witness that for him capitalism is not able to be a religion. There is a shortage. And one could point out that if in the line of Protestantism capitalism can be perceived or fully lived at the limit as a religion, it cannot be lived as such in the line of Catholicism (from which Bataille stems).

It is precisely this shortage, inassimilable to the Protestant logic of capitalism, which expresses itself in the work of the "Catholic" Georges Bataille. The erotic literature that he produces, his mystic experiences, his questioning of the utilitarian, his nostalgia for "glorious" and unproductive gestures (of which art and literature are a part), his fascination with sacrificial expenditures, are the many dimensions that the spirit of capitalism, in its Protestant hardening, excludes, eliminates, and ignores and that Bataille attempts to outlast on the level of art and thought under contemporary conditions. In doing that, he puts into question the limits of modernity, a claim that goes beyond his original anchoring in the terrain of Catholicism and that questions everyone who wonders about the effects of the extreme secularization of religion in contemporary societies.

Sacrifice as Ethics
The Strange Religiosity of Neoliberalism

SHANNON WINNUBST

> But it is no less striking that, in our day, with the custom of sacrifice in full decline, the meaning of the word . . . is still as closely linked as possible to the notion of a *spirit of sacrifice*, of which the automutilation of madmen is only the most absurd and terrible example.
>
> **—Georges Bataille, "Sacrificial Mutilation and the Severed Ear of Vincent Van Gogh"**

> Where we think we have caught hold of the Grail, we have only grasped a *thing*, and what is left in our hands is only a cooking pot . . .
>
> **—Georges Bataille, "The Bourgeois World,"** *The Accursed Share,* **vol. 1**

As we enter the second decade of the twenty-first century on the Western, Christian calendar, a new kind of rationality is fully taking root in U.S. culture. Despite ideological or political differences, we are all speaking the same language, drinking the same Kool-Aid, breathing the same air: we are all neoliberals, whether we even know what that might mean. Neoliberalism, which functions as a particular kind of rationality that is internalized by subjects and externalized by governmental practices, pervades our educational systems, saturates youth culture, dominates political discourse (despite one's party allegiances), and helps structure such intimate decisions as the choice of life partners, whether (and how) to rear children, where to live, how to work, and even how to have fun.[1] It seems to tell us who we are before we even know we are asking the question—indeed, it may even shape that exact question in the first place. It is everywhere and, just like Hegel's black cows, subsequently nowhere. Invisibly omnipresent, a phallic signifier par excellence: our new religion, if not our new god.

We are thus far from Nietzsche's dream of a godless world and its utopia beyond morality. But the form of our religiosity has fundamentally changed and no longer tracks along the arc of a slave morality. Indeed, we seem to be religious without a conscience, without a scale of good or evil. Turned inside out by this new social rationality of neoliberalism, as Foucault argues in his *Birth of Biopolitics*, into entrepreneurs and consumers, we no longer answer to guilt-inducing techniques: interiority is no longer a viable foothold for political manipulation, and transcendent law is no longer the proper or viable structure of ethical judgment.

Foucault insists that neoliberalism is not merely the latest ideological instantiation of capitalism. Situating it in a longer historical context than that of most contemporary scholarship,[2] ranging from eighteenth-century French and British economists[3] to German ordoliberals of the 1930s–1950s and the U.S. Chicago School of the 1960s and 1970s, Foucault argues that neoliberalism emerges out of an intensification of the fundamental fealty of liberalism: the separation of the economy and state. As such, he argues that it comes to function as a social rationality rather than as a more truncated, state-centric operation of abstract politics, economics, or ideology, and that it develops an astute genealogy of the transformations in economic practices and theories and their gradual rooting in our very concepts and practices of subjectivity. Just as his work in sexuality, criminality, and madness also traces, Foucault focuses on how this new social epistemology of enterprise comes to function as a social ontology with the causal power to produce new kinds of subjectivities. Namely, in the transformation from "the human" into "human capital," Foucault locates the emergence of a subjectivity that he hails as "one of the most important theoretical transformations in Western thought since the Middle Ages." He calls this a "subject of interests."[4] As neoliberalism takes root as a widespread cultural *episteme*, economic calculation—and all its attendant utilitarian epistemologies and individualist social ontologies—becomes the mode of rationality for self-reflection and the barometer for individual success.

When we read these lectures alongside Bataille, at least two related but absent domains of inquiry come to the fore: religiosity and ethics. As I will develop here, when read in light of Bataille's work on Protestantism in the first volume of *The Accursed Share*, we come to see that the neoliberal intensification of the separation of the economy and the state—which is arguably a more important decoupling than the more infamous church/state division celebrated in orthodox liberalism—sets loose a sense of "religiosity" in neoliberalism that does not at all resemble that of Protestantism and its insistent separation of the economy and the church. Thus, while Foucault does not attend explicitly to questions of religiosity, his analysis nonetheless exposes the strange religiosity of neoliberalism, wherein we bow down at one altar: the calculation of interests. But as Bataille's work on the ethical dimension of religious practices of sacrifice then exposes, this strange religiosity of neoliberalism also entails a strange transformation in ethics—so strange, in fact, that it more readily appears as an erasure of ethics altogether.

As this "religiously" endless calculation of interests becomes an obsessive social rationality, it absorbs all aspects of living into a flattened horizon of endless accumulation and endless enhancement of interests. It thereby comes to function as a circuit of interests that floats freely across the surface of relations without any social, historical, or ethical anchor. Whether our interests bolster a democratic or fascist state, whether they render us vulnerable or secure, and whether they sustain social relations or enhance an isolated egoism is all far beyond the purview of our pursuits. We are interest-seeking beings purely and solely. For example, as the work of Jodi Dean emphasizes, this externalized subject of neoliberalism is, despite vacuous claims to freedom, left utterly vulnerable to the whims of media, styles, fads, and trends: "*I must be fit; I must be stylish; I must realize my dreams. I must because I can—everyone wins. If I don't, not only am I a loser but I am not a person at all; I am not part of everyone.*"[5] As Dean writes, neoliberal identities are "incapable of establishing a firm place to stand."[6] Consequently, when violence becomes cool or disasters become fascinating, neoliberal subjects have no script with which to respond—they have no ethics, at least not any recognizable sort. By putting this constellation of dynamics into play with Bataille's work on the ethical dimension of sacrifice, I hope to suggest how neoliberalism might yet recuperate some possibility of ethical—and thus recognizably human—living.

The Calvinist Turn: The Separation of Church and Economy

When we think of religion, we do not readily think of political economy. But as Bataille's work shows over and over, the two are intimately connected: "religious activities," he writes, "absorb the excess energy of a society," which is how he describes the domain of political economy.[7] To analyze one is, for Bataille, always to analyze the other; not to do so is to miss the essence of each. When he charts the Protestant break from Catholicism in the first volume of *The Accursed Share*, therefore, Bataille places the true ontological break in the figure of Calvin, not Luther, precisely because it is Calvin who creates a theology for the political economy of nascent capitalism.[8]

While Luther infamously argued against the Catholic practices of usury and purchasing indulgences, the core of Luther's protest, for Bataille, was against the *use* of material wealth, not against the existence of luxury and wealth itself. The extravagant cathedrals and abbeys, the idle priests and monks were not abhorrent to Luther in and of themselves but as a perverse confusion of the economic and the religious domains. For Luther, the Catholic urge "to make the Church the earthly radiance of God" achieves precisely the opposite, reducing divinity to the base materialism of things: the church "had succeeded less in making earth heavenly than in making heaven banal."[9] Consequently, Luther insists on "a decisive separation between God and everything . . . that we can *do* and *really* carry into effect," resulting in a strictly negative system of theology and morality that sunders this material world from the transcendent realm that connotes true divinity.[10] This strictly negative system, however, does not fundamentally break from the view of the economy that runs through Catholicism. Just as the Catholic cosmology, whether through extravagant rituals, idle meditation, or squandering altruism, orients all productive resources toward the nonproductive glory of God, so too does Luther's protest against such "uses" of wealth still uphold the fundamental aversion to business and commerce that was inherent in the Catholic conception of the economy. For the more radical break that, albeit ironically, introduces a social ontology of commerce into the heart of Protestant theology, Bataille follows both Max Weber and R. H. Tawney and turns to Calvin.

Unlike Luther's "naïve, half-peasant revolt[,] Calvin expressed the aspirations of the middle class of the commercial cities."[11] Giving nascent forms of capitalism their theological scaffolding, Calvin "generally recognized the morality of commerce."[12] The difference from Luther turns on how to deal effectively with the production and accumulation of excessive, nonproductive wealth. Shorn from its Catholic meaning to glorify God, wealth becomes the hallmark, while never the cause, of God's grace for Calvin. He subsequently answers Luther's dilemma about how to reorient the meaning of luxury and wealth by taking, as Bataille puts it, "the overturning of values effected by Luther to its extreme consequence."[13] Recognizing the inherent production of excess as integral to the economic practices of capitalism, Calvin renders it theologically meaningful through, ironically, the praise of utility. His argument goes something like this: because we can only account for this plane of material existence, we must work diligently as God's creatures; if excessive wealth emerges from this useful labor, this is merely a sign of God's grace, not an achievement of our own work. The Protestant work ethic thus emerges in all its glory, so to speak, precisely as the negation of any such glory. As Bataille writes, "The true sanctity of Calvinist works resided in the abandonment of sanctity—in the renunciation of any life that might have in this world a halo of splendor. The sanctification of God was thus linked to the desacralization of human life."[14] Calvin completes Luther's corrective realignment of the religious and the economic domains—i.e., the separation of the church and the economy—precisely by setting the economic free from any transcendent religious meaning and, subsequently, as I will develop, also from any moral constraint. The gloryless activity of humankind becomes the only religious or moral mandate of Calvinist Protestantism: we are set loose to become all that we can be—namely, masters of commerce.

But in the present milieu of neoliberalism, this fundamental value of work and utility is fading from prominence. Although we may still pay allegiances to them, particularly as well-worn vehicles for xenophobic American nationalism, we reserve our true admiration for those who achieve economic success with the smallest effort or labor: the great entrepreneurial innovation is great precisely because it grants success with minimal effort. "Maximize interest, minimize labor": this becomes the mantra of these neoliberal times, severing grace from effort even more radically than the Calvinist sanctification of the Protestant work ethic. Despite ongoing lip service to those sacred cows of a work ethic and utility, we respond to their interpellation as a faint nostalgic call, heeding rather the kinetic circuit of interests, in whatever guise they may don: compulsive workouts at the gym; latest hip trends of diet or fashion; quick new fixes for enhanced mental stimulation, whether organic, synthetic, or virtual; and, of course, savvy market transactions, no matter the object or market of exchange. This is the "subject of interests" that Foucault describes as the fundamental change in subjectivity enacted in the ascendancy of neoliberalism in the early twentieth century. Foucault characterizes these "interests" as the bedrock for all decisions: "[the] principle of an irreducible, non-transferable, atomistic individual choice which is unconditionally referred to the subject himself."[15] Interests are those irrational and sometimes ineffable connections, whether positive or negative, we have to experiences; they are the reasons we care about things; they are what psychoanalysis calls cathexes. And in the milieu of neoliberalism, they are unhinged from any other register of evaluation, whether social, historical, or ethical. They become, in Lacanian terms, the pure circuit of the drive, deriving enjoyment not from the act of eating but from the repetitive stuffing of the mouth: compulsive repetition, indifferent to the object, supplants interior judgment as the motor of evaluation.[16] Neoliberalism carries the Calvinist break to its extreme, rendering commerce and the endless circuit of interests our god.

Sacrifice: An Ethics of General Economy

In its most general articulation, Bataille's cosmology suspends the human in a tripolar world: animality, sanctity, and thinghood. As a witness to the historical slide into pure thinghood that he diagnoses as the state of Western culture (politically, economically, ethically, and even religiously) in the twentieth century, Bataille valorizes the act of sacrifice as a reigniting of the lapsed poles of animality and sanctity. Sacrifice, especially as ritualized in the festival, offers a reprieve from this threatening reduction of humanity to thinghood. As Bataille writes in *Theory of Religion*, "The constant problem posed by the impossibility of being human without being a thing and of escaping the limits of things without returning to animal slumber receives the limited solution of the festival."[17] And the festival, in turn, "reaches the plenitude of an effusion only if the anguished concentration of sacrifice sets it loose."[18] Sacrifice thereby becomes the act that sets us free from thinghood precisely by reintroducing the radical discontinuity of the sacred into the limited economy of utility. Defined by destruction, we are horrified by sacrifice—and this is what signals our humanity. Unlike the "animal slumber" of an undifferentiated world, the profanity of the world of things is precisely its human character. When the sacrifice destroys this, even if only ritually, it simultaneously horrifies and allures us, just as we also find in practices of eroticism.[19] Sacrifice thus calls us out into the sacred that the profane world must hide, enacting a cosmological realignment that reinserts the world of allegedly pure thinghood into its tripolar relation with sanctity and animality.

In so doing, the act of sacrifice retrieves us from this slide into pure thinghood, returns us to our humanity, and thereby enacts the moment of ethics. Given our historical location, we are epistemologically and psychologically blocked from grasping this: we dismiss the possibility as an aestheticizing of violence. The violence endemic to sacrifice, however, is not only the immediate violence of killing or destruction, per se. The infamy attached to Bataille's biography and his alleged sacrificial experiments with the Acéphale in the 1930s, compounded by his early writings on sacrifice, have fueled a reading of Bataille as aestheticizing, if not fetishizing, sacrificial violence.[20] But especially as we see it taken up in later works, such as in the first two volumes of *The Accursed Share* (approximately 1947–1962) and *Theory of Religion* (1949),[21] where he explicitly argues that "death is not necessarily linked to it, and the most solemn sacrifice may not be bloody," the violence of sacrifice is not endemically connected to physical violence or biological death.[22] The fundamental violence of sacrifice is the tearing at the epistemological and psychological seams of the limited economy of thinghood and utility—the very seams that keep us from grasping sacrifice as the moment of ethics. Sacrifice entices our quiet suspicions that the world of things is not the totality of human experience. Intimately connected to practices of eroticism for Bataille, sacrifice engenders a reordering of the world so radical that we cannot think or know it. It intervenes violently in the order of thinghood, decapitating us and destroying the orders of temporality and epistemology that ground our subjecthood in such durable certitude. As Bataille realizes, "this is what gives the world of sacrifice an appearance of puerile gratuitousness."[23] But this is also what shapes it as the moment of ethics, transforming the act of sacrifice from a killing and destroying to a relinquishing and giving. The tearing from the limited economy of utility and thinghood is violent because mastery does not relinquish itself willingly. But the gift is to be "rescued from all utility."[24]

For Bataille, this comes as a relief: "Human life is exhausted from serving as the head of, or the reason for, the universe."[25] Writing out of the horrors of both world wars, he knows all too well the ethical monstrosities that come from the wholesale reduction of the world and experience to thinghood. Consequently, the gift of sacrifice is the reintroduction of the sacred into the Calvinist world of things. But this reintroduction does not come easily: it is experienced as violence in this post-Calvinist world. When Calvin completes Luther's "Copernican turn" of severing the human world from that of divinity, he also evacuates sacrifice of any eschatological meaning. We may use the language of sacrifice to describe some of our aspirations, such as "sacrificing" our time to work harder and harder or be a better and better parent or a more and more dedicated teacher, but this is only a truncated notion of sacrifice. Utility and diligence, the values at work in these examples, are already clearly demarcated and sedimented as humanity's highest values in the Calvinist world. Such a concept of sacrifice thereby operates within a preordained and secured teleology and merely offers a domesticated expression of sanctity. (Protestant churches, we should recall, are not filled with the bones of martyrs.)

The more radical meaning of sacrifice, lost to the Calvinist tradition and those it spawns, signals a vaulting over finitude. In the rituals of the Catholic mass and its iconography, for example, the figure of Christ embodies the ultimate sacrifice because it is the graphic sacrifice of finitude as flesh. As Catholics reenact this sacrifice weekly (and sometimes daily) in the core ritual of the mass, they enter into the fundamental risk that a sacrifice of finitude entails. To sacrifice finitude itself is to sacrifice all that we know. While Catholic theology assures the return on the gamble (namely, the entry into transcendent sanctity through such sacrifice) and thereby also inscribes sacrifice in a limited economy of prescripted meaning, the security does not emerge out of an epistemology of certitude. Modern instrumental rationality is not the vehicle for *sanctifying* martyrdom and mysticism as the most ethical ways of living human life.

We hear, of course, the Protestant protest loudly. From Luther and Calvin to the Hegel of the *Phenomenology of Spirit*'s preface to the Kierkegaard of *Philosophical Fragments*, the struggle to articulate an Absolute without the stain of finitude's demarcations echoes again and again. It is at the heart of the Protestant break from the natural law tradition of Catholic epistemology. When Luther and Calvin evacuate human life of any human trajectory toward divinity and thereby remove sacrifice from the horizon of social meaning, they do so through the valorization of an epistemology of instrumentalism and certitude. Planted firmly in this finite, material plane of existence, only one mode of consciousness matters: instrumental rationality. Sufficient and efficient to the domain of commerce, instrumental reason initiates and subsequently rules the limited economy that becomes the proper realm of human life. Living thus becomes a matter of calculation and rules, not of sacrifices or other nebulous expressions of unfettered eschatologies. Accordingly, as we see in widespread practices of various brands of Protestantism, religion splits into two domains to answer the quandaries of such calculations and rules: faith, which comes to function as a Kantian noumenal that demarcates the limits of reason, and morality, which becomes the domain of enforcing the rules granted by instrumental reason for a proper life. Quarantined to the domain of faith, the sacred is thus cordoned off from any contact with the secular world, preserving it precisely in and through its discontinuity from the overarching moralism, ruled by instrumental reason, that becomes the raison d'être of high religion.

When Bataille writes, over and over, of sacrifice as an inner experience, linking it to practices of intimacy and eroticism, he writes in a very different register. Even in the Catholic cosmology, sacrifice is a risk hemmed in and secured by a theology that preordains its meaning. But in religion as a human experience, not as a matter of theological epistemology and its security of transcendence, the risk is more radical—unsure, wide open, ateleological. This is its seductive existential force. Sacrifice is a kind of glue of religion for Bataille, but of religion writ large as a human experience. Granted, some forms of human religiosity still hold out the promise of a clear, if not theologically secured, *telos:* the religiosity of patriotism, nationalism, even racism, and also of particular forms of feminism, civil rights, and other so-called revolutionary social movements that call for sacrificial acts and unbounded conviction only on the basis of clear goals and aspirations. For Bataille, these are but domesticated human experiences of religion and sacrifice, with only a morality, not an ethics, attached to them. He is interested in more radical social movements, such as radical feminist or queer politics, that remain "utopian" at their core—literally having "no place" in current epistemologies and thus ateleological in their structure. In these "religious movements," sacrificial acts become crucial sites of social meaning making precisely through this unbounded, uncertain character. In Bataillean terms, they are moments of instantiating the general economy—not in the theologically assured modes of certified transcendence but in the modes of social sacrifice that are "ferociously religious."[26] As sites of social meaning making, sacrifices are crucial expressions of religiosity as the transcendence of current conditions into unfounded, pure hopes of better lives. A kind of motor of social movements, they express religiosity in an otherwise secular world.

Bataille's Sacrifice: Unknown and Undesirable

As modern subjects, we are multiply blocked from experiencing this kind of sacrifice. Epistemologically, we are trapped within the kind of knowledge that, as Bataille sees in Hegel, "is never given to us except by *unfolding in time*."[27] Bound to the limited economies of teleologies and utilities, modern epistemology is structured by and reduced to instrumental rationality, which subsequently locks us into the temporality of anticipation—the temporality that virtually all of Bataille's writings shun, ignore, and often undermine. When he writes of "unknowing" as "the miraculous moment when anticipation dissolves into NOTHING," we can hear the salient moment of all the many modes of human living to which Bataille is attuned.[28] His writing is absorbed by the effort to capture this moment in which we moderns come undone: eroticism, violence, "the grip of strong emotions . . . the deeply rhythmed movements of poetry, of music, of love, of dance,"[29] religious despair, mysticism, intimacy, competitive games, and—perhaps most of all—sacrifices.[30] These all share the decapitation of rationality that Bataille so craves and invites us to undergo.

But joining him is no mean feat: to aspire to do so is already to fail to do so. Intentions have no place in these moments that can never properly be achieved. They enact a different temporality, a different epistemology, and a different conception of desire and intentionality than those that dominate modern ontologies. We habitually understand the structure of desire as doubled: the child of both lack and excess, as Plato tells it so long ago, and driven by prohibition and transgression, as Freud codifies it. These two layers then double upon themselves to produce our normative concept of desire, wherein desire becomes the excessive, ongoing, even compulsive transgression against the lack that the law of prohibition (of God, of nature, of culture, of language) instills at its heart. The subject can thus only desire that which the law will always prohibit, thereby locking us into a sadistic law that produces a masochistic subject who cannot resist its attraction.

Caught up in a fundamentally epistemological disagreement, neither Catholic nor Protestant theology challenges this concept of desire or the subjectivity it spawns. For Catholic theology, this concept of desire explains the human condition as the endless struggle between prohibitions and transgressions. Sacrifices thereby attain their meaning and intensity as exalted transgressions of earthly and divine prohibitions. Martyrdom, the exemplar of Catholic sacrifices, enacts this convoluted logic incisively: it enshrines the transgression of the fundamental prohibition against taking one's own life as precisely the ultimate sign of a valuable human life. The Protestant turn away from sacrifice, however, does not break from this normative concept of desire as the vexed dance of prohibition and transgression. Rather, in keeping with the Lutheran and Calvinist cosmologies we have already encountered, the Protestant turn away from sacrifice is an epistemological disagreement: because we cannot know the law of God, we cannot find any meaning in acts that claim to transgress it. We can only grasp Abraham's plight as a limit to understanding—or, as Kierkegaard puts it, "the absurdity of faith." But desire remains structured as the play between transgressions and prohibitions, whether deemed transcendent because unknowable and hence "absurd" or reduced to the finite realm of the moral law.

Bataille's break from modern ontologies is more radical. When he writes of sacrifice as the moment of ethics, he breaks not only from modern rationalist epistemologies but also from this concept of desire as the vexed play of prohibition and transgression. As he portrays this kind of subjectivity in the aphoristic and delirious "Sacred Conspiracy" of 1936, "Man has escaped from his head just as the condemned man has escaped from his prison. He has found beyond himself not God, who is the prohibition against crime, but a being who is unaware of prohibition."[31] Simultaneously terrifying and alluring, this "monster" of André Masson's *Acéphale* enacts the horizon of meaning that is beyond prohibition and transgression—a horizon on which ethics is no longer determined by a transcendent Law. Despite the widely circulating image of Bataille as the thinker of transgression par excellence, I argue that this movement beyond prohibition and transgression enacts the ethics that Bataille finds in practices of sacrifice. To grasp them, we must suspend not only our modern epistemology of certitude and its attendant ontology of utility; we must also suspend our modern subjectivity of a desire that is cathected through the Law. Given that these are precisely the contours Foucault diagnoses of neoliberalism, Bataille's sacrificial ethics may offer a viable ethics for this contemporary milieu.

An Ethics of the Real

Bataille, of course, is no stranger to the powerful forces of prohibition and transgression. To the contrary, this is clearly at the heart of his reputation as the bad boy of French philosophy, the scandalous thinker of limits and transgressions. But I want to argue that Bataille's disposition toward the apparently totalizing grip of prohibition and transgression—or what Lacan might call the long reach of the Law—alters when we frame it in this larger break from both modernist, rationalist epistemologies and long-standing Western ontologies of subjectivity and desire.

In the second volume of *The Accursed Share*, Bataille develops an account of eroticism that emerges from the perspective of the general economy—that name he gives to his move beyond rationalist, teleological, instrumentalist epistemologies and their attendant ontologies of subjectivity and desire. In so doing, he recognizes and dwells on the necessity of these prohibitions to cathect and eroticize all kinds of subjects, objects, and activities. His exemplar, incest, is instructive for how he understands the historical yet necessary character of prohibitions. The incest prohibition against intergenerational sexual contact within biological families eroticizes the marital tie while ensuring the continued flow of erotic energy in this otherwise closed container. Functioning as a kind of generator of energy and force in an otherwise stagnant field, the prohibition sets centripetal and centrifugal forces into play by constructing a strict boundary at the heart of that field: it eroticizes the marital tie precisely as originating in exogamy. Prohibitions thereby function to eroticize particular realms of behavior and culture within human communities, but they do so in historically arbitrary, even if structurally necessary, ways. Moreover, they only function through the sporadic act of transgression, which, whether physical or psychological, becomes necessary to recathect those boundaries and the objects and subjects they constitute as valuable.[32]

As Bataille moves on to give a "general" account of eroticism, however, we begin to see how these various practices of prohibition and transgression are strictly the historical forms that particular limited economies assume in their respective expressions of eroticism. What incites erotic attraction varies across time and space, with a necessity that is only local to the closed economy in which it operates: religious taboos, economic codes, racialized barriers, educational systems, and, of course, norms of sexuality all eroticize various acts, objects, and thoughts differently at different times and places. The erotic world is, as Bataille puts it in terms now quite loaded with Kantian and Lacanian connotations for the question of ethics, "imaginary in its form."[33] But it is not thereby reducible to these historical forms. Eroticism, which absorbs so much of Bataille's thinking yet is so impossible to articulate discursively, exceeds such historical forms. Proclaimed as the exemplary field of sovereignty and "the accursed domain par excellence," eroticism exceeds the historical forms through which we experience it and, in that exceeding, resonates with the forms of religiosity and ethics that Bataille finds at the heart of practices of sacrifice.[34]

Lacanian terms may be unusually helpful here. In the Lacanian registers of the Symbolic, Imaginary, and Real, practices of prohibitions and transgression are necessary, but only at the level of the Symbolic. As the register through which language operates, the Symbolic calls us into subjectivity and thereby frames the horizon of our subjectivity as speaking, conscious selves. As Lacan describes in his early work, such as "The Mirror Stage as Formative of the *I* Function" (1949), "The Signification of the Phallus" (1958), and "The Subversion of the Subject and the Dialectic of Desire" (1960), the Law of the Symbolic locks us into the impossible pursuit of precisely that which we lose through the entrance into language (and signification, more broadly, as we find in the role of images in the mirror stage)—namely, an excessive, overwhelming sense of plenitude, which Lacan characterizes as the "jubilant activity" of a prelinguistic infant. As the phallic signifier that, in Lacan's transposition of Freudian schemas into the field of language, intercedes in the mother-child dyad to introduce the Law and thus complete the Oedipal triangle through granting entrance into language, the Symbolic frames the subject as a subject of desire that is grounded in the ontological break of the infant from the mother. Desire is thereby doomed to failure, haunted as it is by this ontological lack. Moreover, the law functions primarily through the rule of prohibitions, which locates subjectivity in a self-splitting double bind: its entrance into language severs it from the plenitude of prelingusitic/pre-Oedipal contiguity with the M/Other, yet the phallic law of language prohibits any return to this paradise lost. Subject to a sadistic law, the subject can only masochistically desire what the law will always prohibit.

On this (still fairly orthodox) reading of Lacan, the Symbolic thereby mediates our experiences of desire as historically and socially mediated structures of consciousness. But following an increasingly widespread reading of Lacan, especially his ethics, as rooted in the register that he calls the Real, rather than in the Law of the Symbolic, I suggest that this understanding of desire as the impossible yet endless pursuit of a paradise lost limits our grasp of what is happening in and through subjectivity: it truncates our field of vision to include only a concept of desire that is rooted in lack and cathected strictly through prohibitions.[35] It truncates our understanding of desire to the historical registers in which we live immediately, foreclosing access to past or even transhistorical forms of meaningful desire. It limits us to grasping subjectivity as only and always driven by this cruel, lacking desire (and all the normalizing effects thereof).[36]

Lacan's turn in his later work to the Real, especially as the site of ethics, shores up these limitations as the problem of what Bataille would call "a restricted economy"—that is, a limited perspective that insists on the universality of its claims without realizing its own finitude or the biases of its own partiality. By placing Lacan's turn to the Real alongside Bataille's turn toward general economies, I argue that the emphasis on the cathecting role of prohibitions and transgressions in both thinkers grants each of them a *limited* and *historical* diagnosis of subjectivity and desire. For both thinkers, this analysis captures a central, defining dynamic of the subjectivation of sociohistorical power. While never disavowing their respective analyses, however, each of them also explicitly recognizes the limited scope at work, albeit quite differently, in them. Alongside this historical analysis, then, each of them also aims to surpass it *through the creation of more expansive epistemologies and ontologies of the subject*—namely, the register of "general economy" in Bataille and "the Real" in Lacan. This aim to surpass the limited and historical diagnosis of subjectivity and desire is, so I want to suggest, driven by a fundamental question of ethics.

In *Sensible Ecstasy*, Amy Hollywood connects Bataille and Lacan in exactly these terms of their resistance to historical narratives, which both thinkers critique as endemically domesticating the violence, suffering, anguish, horror, and joy that defines human life. Locating the turn in each thinker as a turn toward ethics, she associates both Bataille's obsession with suffering and anguish (exemplified in his meditations on the Chinese torture victim in *Guilty* and *Inner Experience*) and the Lacanian Real (which she describes as emerging out of a rejection of the pursuit of phallic wholeness) "with that in history that is unassimilable to its meaning-giving and salvific narratives."[37] Hollywood thereby reads both thinkers as resisting the recuperative function of historical narratives as a primary obstacle to encountering the ethical. This focus on the limited and domesticating character of historical accounts, including their categories and discursive modes of communication, intensifies the connections I want to draw between Bataille and Lacan in two ways: first, it accentuates my argument that Bataille's insistence on the necessity of prohibition and transgression as the site of desire is merely a historical insistence—an analysis at the level of the Symbolic. Second, and more importantly, it reads Bataille and Lacan as locating ethics in the exceeding, however tortuously, of these historical parameters.

When Bataille fastens on practices of sacrifice as tearing at the seams of modern rationalist epistemologies, he sees in them this turn to the ethical. His various moves to think from a general economy then extend this impulse to articulate, in however oblique a manner, that which exceeds these limited epistemologies. That is, he exceeds the knowable/unknowable conundrum that divides Protestant and Catholic epistemologies, as I have portrayed them above. If we read this as (at least structurally) also surpassing the post-Kantian modern epistemology of the knowable/unknowable conundrum, we can once more draw connections to Lacan's Real—connections that begin to intensify the ethical dimension of such epistemological surpassing.

Explicating it in this Kantian dimension, Alenka Zupančič also locates the ethical dimension of the Lacanian Real in this exceeding of all knowability. Whereas Hollywood emphasizes the domesticating character of (especially modernist) epistemology itself, Zupančič returns us to the formative scene of Kantian ethics and the strange role of noumenal concepts within it, especially the desire itself for ethics.[38] For Kant, Zupančič reminds us, the unknowable characteristic of one's motivations to act ethically are precisely what protects the ethical from reduction to mere duty: the ethical act will always align with duty, and thus our originary motivation to act ethically will forever be obscured by the possibility that it is merely this insufficient motivation of fulfilling one's duty. The ethical motivation qua ethical can never be distinguished at the level of the act itself, since all ethical acts should also conform perfectly with duty (assuming the cultural law of the duty is itself ethical). Given this quandary, Zupančič uses the Kantian concept of "pure form" to describe this unknowable, indecipherable motivation as "a surplus which at the same time seems to be 'pure waste,' something that serves absolutely no purpose"—strikingly Bataillean language.[39]

For Bataille, this epistemic opacity indicates the excessive character of ethics in much the same way that Zupančič sees a Lacanian ethics of the Real. When Bataille sees in sacrificial acts a subjectivity that is not structured by desire, endemic lack, and transgression, he thus goes beyond a merely premodern critique of utility (as Žižek accuses)[40] toward an ethics that resonates, with all its emphasis on excess that surpasses containment, with Lacan's infamous description of the Real as "the lack of a lack."

If so, then ethics becomes that which is the effect of our actions but not the aim, *the jouissance that is always with us but never experienced*, an always lingering possibility but the rationally impossible,[41] and the limit to our aggression but not the quelling of such base impulses.[42] It is what Bataille sees as the necessary squandering of energy, through a radical surpassing of modernist epistemologies and ontologies of the subject, such that we not blow ourselves up.

And it appears, in ways I have merely suggested here, to be the only viable articulation of ethics in our contemporary milieu, saturated as it is with neoliberalism.

Bataille's Contestation of Interpretative Anthropology and of the Sociology of Religion

ALPHONSO LINGIS

Religions, rituals, and myths have been studied as social practices and institutions by the sociology of religion. The symbolic function and representational content of rituals and myths have been elaborated into theologies and studied by cultural and interpretative anthropology. And participation in rituals and the mental organization of individuals and groups by myths produce a distinctive experience.

It is this experience, "inner experience," that was the focus of Georges Bataille's writings. The phenomenological explication of this experience led him to contest the theological elaborations of rituals and myths in their dominant interpretations by cultural and interpretative anthropology and to contest the dominant conceptions of the sociology of religion.

Sacrifice and Mysticism

Bataille's conception of the sacred experience was guided by his reading of the Christian mystics: Angela de Foligno, John of the Cross, Teresa of Avila, Jakob Boehme, Catherine of Siena, Meister Eckhart, and others. These writings recounted the mystical experience and could be understood only by those who shared something of this experience. Bataille was attentive to moments in which such experience befell him. On the other hand, Bataille's reading in the anthropology of religion convinced him that sacrifice was the essential religious act. It was the experience of the participants in sacrifice that Bataille was concerned with. Bataille's conception of the sacred experience sees the experience of the participants in sacrifice as mystical and sees mystical experience as sacrificial.

A sanctuary, a sacred precinct, is a dark or radiant place marked out by prohibitions and taboos, separated from the profane sphere. To encounter there the sacred is to encounter the powers of what is separated from, what marks the limit of, the world of work and reason, of calculation and appropriation. These powers may later be represented in the guise of great beasts, demons, or deities, but Bataille affirms that first and fundamentally they are experienced as unapprehendable and impersonal powers.

Sacred precincts are places of sacrifice. Modern world religions, which have striven to rationalize themselves, regard sacrifice—of goods, other animals, of firstborn children—as traits of primitive and superseded religions. Yet, as Henri Hubert and Marcel Mauss argued, sacrifice is the most universal, perhaps the most fundamental, of religious acts.[1]

In a sacrifice something supremely precious—our finest harvest and livestock, our firstborn son—is set aside from all use, separated from the profane sphere. What is set apart from all profane use is separated absolutely, definitively, in being destroyed.

In sacrifice, the burning and killing reveals the separate, sacred power that limits the space of all work and reason. In a sacrifice of the food from the harvest, the violent, indomitable power of the flames blazes over human works. The knife that tears open the body of the sacrificial victim tears apart the protective hide or skin, exposing the writhing turmoil of spilled organs; it reveals the violence of a stag or boar taken from the wilderness— the inner violence of its life; it reveals anonymous untamed forces in the child. The knife of the shaman, the priest, or Abraham reveals the unintelligible core of life and the inner impersonal violence in the composition of living things.[2]

The sacrificial priest leaves the profane sphere to perform the sacrifice and acts in the name of the people. Bringing to him of their harvest and livestock, a beast of the wilderness, or their firstborn child, they participate in his deed. Those who perform sacrifice identify with the victim. The Aztec priests covered themselves with the blood of the sacrificial victims, excoriated them, and pulled the skin of the victims over their naked bodies. And we who consign to the sacred sphere our resources, the game from our hunt, our children, identify with them, identify with the victims. The stag or wild boar sacrificed would have sustained and nourished us. How could we not identify with our firstborn child, sacrificed to the mountain god Yahweh? At the moment of the blood sacrifice, the participants find their identity slashed with the knife. When the fire blazes upon the sacred victim, it blazes too on us.

Bataille focused on the experience of this identification. The participant in sacrifice exposes himself or herself to the unmanageable and incalculable powers that limit the sphere of work and reason and experiences extreme emotions of being lacerated. But this anguish is also exhilaration; ethnographers report that sacrifices are times of frenzied release of energies and elation. The communication continues in feasts where immense resources are consumed, and in saturnalia where participants abandon their sense of themselves and their controlling will, finding themselves possessed with the forces of pounding music and dance, with violent, erotic, excessive compulsions, and with the forces unleashed in the forests and rivers by night.

Bataille observes that ordinary emotions are addressed to objectives, accomplishments, obstacles, efforts, and frustrations in the sphere of work and reason. Extreme emotions are produced by breaking through barriers, transgressing prohibitions and taboos.

Bataille found that the mystical experience is unleashed by the apparition of an object that fascinates and absorbs the viewer. It could be anything—a cascade, trees seen in the fog from a car window, a flash of lightning. The ecstatic object has no necessary or meaningful connection with a complex of other objects or with one's own nature and goals. Ecstatic experience fixes on objects out of reach, things with which one can do nothing. An ecstatic object is also not some condensed image or symbol of perfection, peace, utopia, or the divine.

An ecstatic object captivates and focuses attention by its improbability, its impracticability, its multiple and conflicting facets. In classical metaphysics and in Husserl's phenomenology, each perceived object is doubled up with its idea or eidetic form; in an early essay Bataille sees objects doubled up with their shadows, reflections, and parodies.[3] Indeed, the idea of a thing is a parody of it. Lead is a parody of gold, air a parody of water, the brain a parody of the equator, coitus a parody of crime.[4] The vagina caricaturizes the mouth, the mouth caricaturizes the vagina, the buttocks caricaturize the breasts. The limp penis caricaturizes the tongue that extends to it, the extended middle finger caricaturizes the erect penis. The things also cast their shadows and their halos and their caricatures upon our body organs and parts. Our leoparded skin moves in the dappled light of the forest, the bonfire flames in our eyes. We snarl and hiss back at the mongrel dog, crouch as the wild dog sees the terrorized opossum before him. The august façade of the manor imposes its solemnity on the features of our face.

The ecstatic vision finds kinship with the ecstatic object. This object is like oneself in that it is disconnected from significance and function in the network of pragmatic or significant relationships. It exists in and for itself.

But it is undergoing a dramatic loss of its identity, multiplied in caricatures of itself, rent, in flames.[5] The ecstatic fixation on such an object conveys an overwhelming desire to join that object, merge with it, lose oneself in it, and senses too in anguish that the object is lethal. "I adhere to this point and a deep love of what is in this point burns me to the point that I refuse to be alive for anything other than what is there—for that point which, being together life and death of a loved being, has the flash of a cataract."[6] Bataille writes of seeing a tree struck by lightning and ecstatically joining it to such an extent that he felt himself within that tree, having become that tree. His arms were gradually lifted and their movement joined that of the limbs of the tree, which were now broken stumps along the height of the trunk.[7] The upper part of his body, above the solar plexus, had disappeared. Only his legs that were standing on the plank floor retained a bond with what he had been; the rest had become blazing fire. The flames were dancing and decomposing, retaining something of the character of an object situated outside of him.[8]

The ecstatic object is catastrophic.[9] Something immense, exorbitant, is liberated in it in all directions. It arises from an unreal, infinite void and sinks back into that void. Out of the fog trees emerge with an incalculable architecture and artistry of twigs and new-opening leaves, which mesmerize the eyes occupied with more than they could ever see, and then each tree sinks back forever into the night, never to be found again.

The ecstatic object opens onto a realm not tied together with instrumental interconnections or relations of intelligible interdependency. One finds oneself exposed to powers outside the realm of work and reason, uncontained by and destructive of work and uncomprehended by reason. The outer realm is encountered as the realm of the impracticable, the unutilizable, the unmanipulatable, a realm of darkness and emptiness. It is not the luminous heaven of celestial explanations but a realm of silence.

> Contemplating night, I see nothing, love nothing. I remain immobile, frozen, absorbed in IT. I can imagine a landscape of terror, sublime, the earth open as a volcano, the sky filled with fire, or any other vision capable of "putting the mind into ecstasy"; as beautiful and disturbing as it may be, night surpasses this limited "possible" and yet IT is nothing, there is nothing in IT which can be felt, not even finally darkness. In IT, everything fades away, but, exorbitant, I traverse an empty depth and the empty depth traverses me.[10]

Bataille's account of objects that open upon the outer zone yields a more concrete account of the beyond. The pine tree is also Bataille's body; the view into the stars is also a fall; the woman is an ethereal goddess and a hairy animal body. The outer zone is the place of these unstable reversals. Yet the substantiality of this zone buoys the experience and charges it with exhilaration.

In making contact with what is unappropriable in someone we make contact with him in his own being, and in making contact with what is unappropriable in things we make contact with them in their own being. "There is an element in it which one cannot reduce, which remains 'beyond expression,' but ecstasy, in this respect, does not differ from other forms: I can have, can communicate the precise knowledge of it as much as—or more than—that of laughter, of physical love—or *of things.*"[11] As things lose their apprehendable and graspable forms, they obtrude in all the alien force of their own being. The force of their being excites the energies of exhilaration. The dissolution of the subject of thought and action is the intimate experience of all beings in their alien existence.

In Bataille's account, the powers outside of the world of work and reason and the nothing—beneficent and malevolent—are conceived in a distinctive way. The outer zone is not the sacred or God unified as *mysterium tremendum et fascinans* but the indefinite multiplicity of reversals.

> What is sacred, not being based on a logical accord with itself, is not only contradictory with respect to things but, in an undefined way, is in contradiction with itself. . . . Inside the sacred domain there is, as in dreams, an endless contradiction that multiplies without destroying anything. What is not a thing . . . is real but at the same time is not real, is impossible and yet is there.[12]

The outer zone, depth of extinctions and reversals, is the domain of chance.

The experience of the outer zone involves a collapse of thought, of rational and reflective thought. Such an object can be given only in the imagination, Bataille affirms—but it can be given. "These great tides of miraculous possibility, where moreover the transparency, the richness and the soothing splendor of death and the universe are to be regained, presuppose the imagination joining together that which is never given except in parts."[13] The transition of the visual experience of an ecstatic object to the realm of indeterminacy and night is the very medium of the imagination. Dreams and nightmares represent this realm.

Thus Bataille finds the mystical experience to correspond to the experience of participants in sacrifice; there is intense absorption in the ecstatic object that opens upon the impersonal powers of what lies beyond the realm of work and reason, experienced in anguish and exhilaration, as the ecstatic object that held the viewer vanishes.

Communication . . . with our beyond (essentially in sacrifice)—not with nothingness, still less with a supernatural being, but with an indefinite reality (which I sometimes call *the impossible*, that is, what cannot be grasped (*begreift*) in any way, what we can't reach without dissolving ourselves. . . . It can remain in an undefined state (in ordinary laughter, infinite laughter, or ecstasy).[14]

In pragmatic action an object is envisioned in its capacity to move, displace, modify, or assemble other objects. As a tool, a means, an object is subjugated to the absent and future objective. The agent uses his body as a force to manipulate other objects, makes himself a tool in using tools, makes itself serve and servile. In discourse, the sense, force, and function of the opening word depend on the words to come. The present is subjugated to the absent, the future. In discourse the mind subjugates its present state to a future state, to the words that will determine the meaning and place of its present words. The mind makes itself serve and servile.

At the far end of the practice of understanding through discursive representation we discover a sacrificial ecstasy of the mind, austere and intoxicating. "In these incomprehensibly transparent states, the mind remains inert and intensely lucid, free. The universe easily passes through it. The object imposes itself on it in an 'intimate and ungraspable impression of déjà vu.' . . . Only this state takes comedy to an extreme limit; it is infinite volatilization, effortless freedom, reducing all things to the movement into which they fall."[15]

Bataille characterizes the experience of ecstatic objects as sovereign. In miraculous moments, a life is liberated from the servility in the world of work and reason, where the organism deals with implements in making itself an implement. This sovereignty is neither autonomy nor domination over others. Every healthy organism generates energies in excess of those it needs to maintain itself. Sovereignty is affirmed not in the use of these energies but in their superabundance and their intensity. In ecstatic moments they are discharged, imprudently, without calculation, without recompense. Ecstatic states, sovereignty, are transitory moments. "Autonomy . . . can't be a state but a *moment* (a moment of infinite laughter, or ecstasy)."[16] Sovereign moments are not achieved through work and reason; they occur by chance and are without expectation or hope. They are not states of fulfillment, totality, and serenity. "This sovereignty cannot even be defined as a good. I am attached to it, but would I be if I were not certain that I could just as well laugh at it?"[17]

Ritual and the Social Order; Myth and Existential Crises

Since the romantics, anthropologists have focused on the function of rituals and myths to consolidate and strengthen a community and its hierarchies. The sociology of religion, founded by Émile Durkheim, studies the progressive consolidation and differentiation of society and of religion. The anthropologist Roy Rappaport saw in ritual a society's means to limit the multiplication of meanings and deception that are intrinsic to language.

Anthropologists such as Claude Lévi-Strauss and Clifford Geertz focused on the intellectual function of religion. Sir James Frazer had seen in magic the conviction of universal causality and the uniformity of nature that will eventually give rise to the scientific method. Lévi-Strauss acknowledged that even small societies elaborate and transmit exacting observations and classifications of their environment and could have survived in often harsh environments only if they did so. They also elaborate myths to organize their observations and classifications with general symbols. But Lévi-Strauss affirmed there is nothing to be learned about the order of nature or the nature of reality from the study of myths.[18] He devoted himself to a formal structural analysis of the oppositions and combinations of terms in myths, persuaded that they instead reveal the fundamental structures of the human mind, structures equally operative in the rationality of the modern sciences.

For Clifford Geertz, the distinctive core of religion is belief in a sacred realm that is really real, real in some different sense and different way from the way the commonsense world is real. What makes people turn to this cosmic realm, Geertz says, are harrowing perplexities that confound common sense and understanding and threaten their ability to orient themselves and act effectively in the world.[19]

Geertz identifies three such crises. First, there is the inability to explain things such as the ravages of nature, volcanic eruptions, earthquakes, and plagues; the origin and place of humans in the world; and the portentous visions of dreams. The inability to understand or explain certain aspects of nature, self, and society with the explanations of common sense, science, or philosophical speculation makes people chronically uneasy. A quite trivial empirical event may bring us up against the limits of our ability to understand and raise the suspicion that we may be adrift in an absurd world. The religious perspective envisions a wider, cosmic order beyond the radius of the commonsense world, where explanations may lie.

A second existential crisis concerns suffering and erupts in illness and in mourning those we have lost in death. Geertz rejects the kind of positivist theory espoused by Bronislaw Malinowski, according to which religion is a collection of magical pseudoremedies and assurances that illness will be cured and the dead reborn. "Over its career religion has probably disturbed men as much as it has cheered them," Geertz points out, "forced them into a head-on, unblinking confrontation of the fact that they are born to trouble. . . . With the possible exception of Christian Science, there are few if any religious traditions . . . in which the proposition that life hurts is not strenuously affirmed."[20] The religious perspective envisions a wider, cosmic reality where physical pain, personal loss, worldly defeat, and the helpless contemplation of people's agony is explainable and thus becomes something that has to be and can be endured. It enables the sufferer to grasp the nature of his distress and relate it to the wider world. It gives resources for expressing our sentiments, passions, affections, and afflictions—the words but also the tone for lamentation, recollection, and compassion.

The third existential crisis that drives the religious perspective is the fact that we strive, that we have to strive, to work out some normative guides to govern our actions but see all too often that ethically correct behavior results in disaster while behavior that we can nowise approve of is rewarded. The religious perspective envisions a wider, cosmic history that accounts for the fallen or corrupt nature of our world that so often thwarts our efforts to live according to sound moral judgments.

Belief in the sacred realm is not adherence to statements but arises in experience—experiences of participants in ritual in which the powers of this realm are *presences*. Faithful to his conception of all experiences borne in perceptible symbols, Geertz sees these experiences mediated in tribal religions by the persuasive power of traditional imagery and in charismatic religions by the hypnotic attraction of an extraordinary personality. Geertz also recognizes supersensible experiences in mystical religions.

Bataille and Belief in the Sacred Realm

The Unknowable

Bataille recognizes the limits of common sense, science, or philosophical speculation to explain certain aspects of nature, self, and society. It is the experience of scientific theorists that their laws and theories do not close in upon themselves, comprehensively apprehending the universe as a totality, but open regularly upon the unknown and fragment into mutually nontranslatable disciplines. Language itself leads us to the frontiers and the depths where its words no longer take hold, where our mind finds itself empty, open upon nothing that words can grasp.

But whereas myths and theologies evoke a wider, cosmic order beyond the radius of the empirically comprehensible world where explanations may lie, Bataille finds that the sacred experience instead affirms the unknowable. In moments of austere lucidity thought discovers ignorance in itself. In fascination and anxiety thought plunges into the unknowable and has the sovereignty of a subject that exists in the zenith of intensity without objects. No longer subordinated to some anticipated result, its ecstasy is the ecstasy of a self-propelled and sovereign movement.

> I resolved long ago not to seek knowledge, as others do, but to seek its contrary, which is unknowing. I no longer anticipated the moment when I would be rewarded for my effort, *when I would know at last*, but rather the moment when *I would no longer know, when my initial anticipation would dissolve into* NOTHING. . . . [T]his way of going in the wrong direction on the paths of knowledge—to get off them, not to derive a result that others anticipate—leads to the principle of *sovereignty* of being and of thought, which from the standpoint where I am placed at the moment has this meaning: that thought, subordinated to some anticipated result, completely enslaved, ceases to be in being *sovereign*, that only unknowing is *sovereign*.[21]
>
> The thought that comes to a halt in the face of what is sovereign rightfully pursues its operation to the point where its object dissolves into NOTHING, because, ceasing to be useful, or subordinate, it becomes *sovereign* in ceasing to be.[22]

Bataille seeks these moments not only at the frontiers of theory but also in everyday life, when a train of thought stumbles, producing nonsense that breaks into laughter, and in the absurdity and speechlessness that breaks into sobs and tears. The objective of thought vanishes. Such moments are also the time of poetry, where common words designate in visible things the invisible and the uncanny. They also occur in eroticism, where the seriousness of action is parodied in teasing and seductive games and where speech disintegrates into nonsense, murmurs, moans, sighs, and laughter. The unknown is also the realm of chance, and it opens when we are struck with chance events.

Suffering and Ecstasy

Bataille does not seek to lay out the dimensions of a wider, cosmic reality to which physical pain, personal loss, and worldly defeat are related, are explainable, and thus become something that can be endured. Instead, he finds that the anxiety—the sense of inner disintegration and shattering, nothing supporting one, nothing to hold on to—is intrinsic to ecstasy. The ecstasy that finds itself sovereign in the void is not an experience of integration, wholeness, and serenity, of fulfillment of its desires, but instead an experience of shattering and anguish. Extreme emotions surge in transgression, in breaking through the boundaries and taboos of the social and natural world, and also in the shattering of inner boundaries between zones of the self. Instead of a crucifix, depicting the suffering of Christ that delivered humans from guilt and punishment, he kept on his desk a photograph of a young Chinese man condemned to the death of a hundred cuts, his body everywhere bleeding but on his face an expression of bliss.

The Moral Order in an Amoral Universe

Bataille does not seek in the sacred sphere the foundation of the moral order or the explanation for a fallen or corrupt nature of humans or of the world. He does not seek an explanation that could account for the discord between the moral order that humans have to strive to establish and the amoral universe.

The ethical separation of good from evil is not, as Friedrich Nietzsche affirmed, derived from the distinction between the socially useful and what is harmful to the herd, nor from the distinction between what is healthy and life affirming and what is degenerate and sick. Bataille sees it deriving from the separation of the sublime from the base. The human who stands upright rises from the earth where what dies and decays falls.

But Bataille finds continuity between the organism that expels its waste products and that expends its energies. Life in an organism is the movement to expel sweat, semen, urine, and excrement.[23] And it is the locus of production of excess energies, which have to be discharged. It discharges its energies in useless and unproductive movements and in play; it discharges its excess mental activities in idle fantasies, in outbursts of laughter before the unworkable and the absurd, in telling tales and writing books it does not read.

The "excremental constellation includes fire, thunder, the gods, ghosts, souls, lights and colors, money (value) and gold, jewels and diamonds, decomposing corpses, the sun."[24] The sacred, the separated, is also the expelled, which repels our approach. The sense of the wholly other, the heterogeneous, covers both what we expel and eject—fecal matter, spittle, urine, sperm, menstrual blood—and what repels or expels us—the sacred, the prohibited, the tabooed. "The identical nature, from the psychological point of view, of God and excrement should not shock the intellect of anyone familiar with the problems posed by the history of religions. The cadaver is not much more repugnant than shit, and the specter that projects its horror is *sacred* even in the eyes of modern theologians."[25]

A corpse sinks into decomposition, expelling blood, bile, bloated internal organs and glands, excrement, and stench. It is a locus of violence, where violence has struck, from without or from within, and where violence continues, bacteria, viruses, or tumors having assaulted the homeostasis of the body, releasing toxins that will break out of the organs and cells, contaminating the ground with infectious seepage and excrement, polluting the air with foul gases. It is seen to have strange powers alien to ordinary human life, it sickens those who are contaminated by it, it is haunted by a malignant spirit, it can bring curses and ill luck on those who violate it, who trample on its grave. It cannot be put to use but must be buried or burned, expelled from the surface of the inhabited world in clouds of smoke. Regarded with fear and awe, circumscribed with prohibitions, it requires respect and rituals. The desecration of a corpse is a sacrilegious act.

From earliest times religious cults surrounded death and corpses and sexual orgies. Sacred rites merge into scatological rites.[26] Hierogamy is recognized in the copulation of gods with the great or wily beasts and in the ritual copulation of priests and priestesses with deities and demons and with temple prostitutes. The sacrificial priests are covered in sweat and blood, their own and that of their victims. The Aztec priests excoriated their victims and pulled their skins over their own naked bodies. In casting spells, shamans and priests employ blood, menstrual blood, bones, fingernails, and hair of the supplicant or the victim, or blood, feathers, hair of scapegoat animals. How grubby are the idols covered with fermenting ghee and blood! Circumcision, circumincision, and clitoridectomy are performed on initiates. Devotees submit to painful and bloody scarifications, piercings, symbolic or real castration. Menstruation, childbearing, illness, and death have been covered with cardinal sacred rites. The release of sperm in sleep and in masturbation has been surrounded by taboos, as have vomit, urination, and excretion. Exalted places and personages are desecrated in carnival dissoluteness. In sacred times and places precious resources are erected, displayed, and left to decompose. People deliver vast quantities of food to be consumed in potlatch and in festive meals and drunkenness. They are times of orgy.

The sexual order of copulation and reproduction has been experienced as contact with powers outside of work and reason, powers that work by chance. Complex prohibitions and taboos have been elaborated around menstruation, copulation, and childbearing. Bataille, however, attends not to sexual acts but to eroticism—the elaboration of the eroticized apparition. Its purest and most extreme elaboration is in the sanctuary itself.

The temple maiden is taken from the profane world and clad in filmy garments and headdresses and jewels; she appears in processions and dances, moves in a twilight or moonlight with floating ethereal movements. Her filmy and impractical garb and ethereal movements both prohibit and incite violation. The priest or the outsider who violates the sanctuary, ravishes the sacred maiden, does not conquer or possess anything. He abandons his self-presence and separate identity, abandons himself to anonymous cravings and paroxysms that leave him depleted.

For morality, good is the preservation of humans in their nature, and violation of the space and integrity of others is evil. But for Bataille communication is the drive in an individual to break through the boundaries of his enclosed existence, and to make contact with another is to violate his space and his integrity, to break through his independence, autonomy, his nature—to intrude upon him, unsettle him, wound him. If the notion of good designates respect for the space and the integrity, the nature of others and the ensuring of enduring integrity through action, the sovereign moment is closer to evil than to good.

Ritual and the Social Order; Transgression

Society is conceived as an ordered totality in which each individual from his or her recognized place and with his or her energies and skills communicates with a common language and builds a common enterprise of habitats, prosperity, enduring institutions, and established knowledge. The sociology of religion shows how religion functions and serves the consolidation of this society. But the myths and rituals also engender heretics, break-off sects, eccentrics, scoffers, charlatans, and profiteers.

In and beneath this society Bataille sees the innumerable multiplicity of movements of what for him is communication: contact with other humans, other species, and things in what is unappropriable in them and by which they exist in themselves—movements that are a violation of others and violence within oneself.

Sociologists recognize that demographic changes, migrations, climatic and ecological changes, technological developments, and the consolidation of wealth and attendant inequalities that distort and hamper economic changes produce conflicts and political and economic reforms and revolutions. But, Bataille affirms,

Without a profound complicity with natural forces such as violent death, gushing blood, sudden catastrophes and the horrible cries of pain that accompany them, terrifying ruptures of what had seemed

to be immutable, the fall into stinking filth of what had been elevated—without a sadistic understanding of an incontestably thun-
dering and torrential nature, there could be no revolutionaries, there
could only be a revolting utopian sentimentality.[27]

Bataille separates revolution from utopian sentimentality and also from
mob frenzy; revolution has an aim that must be concrete and realizable,
although fraught with risk of failure and defeat. Is this to say that it must
serve a community united in a common enterprise, and regulated by morality, which posits the good as respect for being? Bataille rather requires a
community in the world of work and reason that is interrupted by miraculous moments of extreme experience. But there is no program for the institution of such a community: sovereign moments are not achieved through
work and reason; they are without expectation or hope. We can nowise
fabricate a sovereign moment from a servile state.[28]

To be sure, the satisfaction of needs and the consolidation of communities devoted to work and reason and the servitude they entail are inevitable. "Even if it is true that our lot is in part and fundamentally bound to
the faculty of subordinating the present to the future, it is bad to intoxicate
ourselves with tasks that we assume for that, bad to take pride in servitudes
that are simply inevitable."[29]

The Utility of Religion

Émile Durkheim saw religion as the fundamental social institution of humankind, one that gave rise to other social forms. The sociology of religion seeks to understand the function, the social utility, of religion. Bataille sees the utility of religion beginning in the association of sacrifice
with fertility. "The possibility of producing, of fecundating the fields and
the herds is given to rites whose least servile operative forms are aimed,
through a concession, at cutting the losses from the dreadful violence of
the divine world."[30] Sacrifice is taken to serve the sphere of work and reason. "The weakness of sacrifice was that it eventually lost its virtue and
finally established an order of sacred *things*, just as servile as that of real
objects."[31] The identification of the multitude in whose name the sacrifice
is performed with the victim, the experience of loss, wounding, laceration,
immolation, now recedes before the community as a common enterprise
collaborating in the sphere of work and reason. "Positively in fecundation,
negatively in propitiation, the community first appears in the festival as
a thing, a definite individualization and a shared project with a view to
duration."[32]

Sacrifice and orgy are viewed as expenditures useful for achieving victory in war. Those who exposed themselves to violence and death and survived acquired women, booty, and territory. Sacrifice, which involves sacrifice of oneself with the victim, will be interpreted as a means to achieve personal salvation in another life. Sacrificing oneself will also be seen as a means to achieve equality and justice for the community on earth. Throughout history, reasons were devised for an individual to make himself a sacrificial victim. These reasons indeed generated history, which is a history of the works and conflicts of communities.

Bataille sees society as an enterprise in the world of work and reason that gives rise to the religion that separates the outer zone into two separate realms. One part is depicted as beneficent to humans, holy, wholesome, and healing—a celestial realm. The beneficent celestial realm is conceptualized as integrity itself, a figure of totality. The celestial realm becomes a providential God who explains, consoles, and ensures ultimate justice.[33] All that provokes anxiety, fear, and horror is relegated to an inferior and demonic realm.

But, Bataille observes, the representation of gods and the central figure of God is a late development in religion. "The development of knowledge touching on the history of religions has shown that the essential religious activity was not directed toward a personal and transcendent being (or beings), but toward an impersonal reality."[34]

The religion that confirms and consecrates the consolidation of a community as an enterprise in the world of work and reason is also taken to serve the expansion of that community. Local religions confronted other local religions and later were confronted by secular, scientific culture, and as a result, as Max Weber noted, they have undertaken a work of rationalization.[35] Theologians sought to make the body of myths coherent and consistent and harmonize all the affirmations in their cosmic representations. Thought formulates the essence and inner nature of the divine in concepts of unity, simplicity, stability, and purity.

Today, deprived of faith in another life, stripped of hope even for an egalitarian and just community worth dying for, we have no motive for heading toward exalted and sacrificial states. We find ourselves in sovereign moments without reason and exult in them without pretexts. We live at the mercy of laughter that breaks forth from us and shatters us and of sexual excitements that fill us with anxiety. "Ecstatic raptures and the burns inflicted by Eros are so many questions—without answers—that we put to nature and to our nature."[36] Bataille's experience thus contests the contemporary psychology that seeks in religious experience a means for self-fulfillment.

Scientific anthropology seeks to determine essential traits that enable us to identify ritual, myth, and religion. Anthropologists study religions empirically as factors in the constitution of societies. The ritual representations and myths, also empirically observable, elaborated in religions are studied, disengaging their syntactical and semantic structure and determining their meanings. But the ritual and collective performances, and the language and representations and myths that a society elaborates, function in part to affirm the distinctiveness of that society. The ritual and myths, the religions of human societies, exhibit extraordinary diversity. Generalizations are to be viewed with suspicion.

Participation in ritual and the mental acceptance of certain mythical narratives also constitute a distinctive kind of experience. The study of this experience encounters problems about access to this experience and the limits of empirical observation. Georges Bataille long made this experience his central concern and his writings elucidate the religious experience from within. We can wonder whether "the religious experience" is not essentially diverse.

The Traumatic Secret
Bataille and the Comparative Erotics
of Mystical Literature

JEFFREY J. KRIPAL

> No creatures can reach God in their capacity of created things, and what is
> created must be broken for the good to come out. The shell must be broken
> for the kernel to come out.
>
> —**Meister Eckhart, Sermon 24**

> Had I not as a child been brutalized by whoever this was, I don't think that
> I ever would have been able to perceive the visitors.
>
> —**Whitley Strieber, *What Is to Come***

One of the most formative books of my intellectual training was Georges
Bataille's *Erotism: Death and Sensuality*, in the City Lights Books edition.
You know, the one with a photo of the face of Bernini's Saint Teresa on
the cover, moaning in divine ecstasy, as the Catholic mystical tradition has
it. Or in orgasm, as Jacques Lacan famously pointed out. Or both. I read
the book in 1987 at the strong recommendation of Bernard McGinn, who
told a group of us something to the effect that this book was probably the
most insightful philosophical treatment of erotic forms of mysticism ever
written.

That turned out to be an accurate assessment. But this was more, much
more, than a philosophical treatise. It was also a book implicitly suffused,
as Bataille himself insisted, with the author's own "inner experience." The
scientists, those arbiters of acceptable knowledge in this superficial day of
ours, can never truly grasp the significance of eroticism, for they can only
speak "from outside."[1] They can only objectify, and so they "know nothing

about these states on principle."[2] Bataille, on the other hand, seeks to speak from the inside, that is, from "the subjective experience of religion" and the general history of religions, without which, he claims, the true significance of eroticism can never be appreciated and understood.[3]

Being Bataille

I think it was this combination of the inner or experiential nature of the text in deep conversation with the comparative study of religion that I responded to most deeply. Whatever the draw, the book read like a blueprint of my own soul and its still immature, inarticulate intuitions and intentions. I was, after all, training to become a historian of religions who specialized in erotic mystical literature. I was training, in effect, to be Bataille.

I especially remember being struck—stunned, really—by the opening few lines of *Erotism*, which go like this:

> The human spirit is prey to the most astounding impulses. Man goes constantly in fear of himself. His erotic urges terrify him. The saint turns from the voluptuary in alarm; she does not know that his unacknowledgeable passions and her own are really one. The cohesion of the human spirit whose potentialities range from the ascetic to the voluptuous may nevertheless be sought. The point of view I adopt is one that reveals the coordination of these potentialities. I do not seek to identify them with each other but I endeavor to find the point where they may converge beyond their mutual exclusiveness.[4]

When I encounter these seven sentences today, almost a quarter of a century later, they read oddly like a back-cover synopsis that could have been used on almost any of my books. Apparently, I have not strayed too far from those original intuitions and intentions. I have gone nowhere.

The terror of the erotic and its subsequent concealment and censorship. The "cohesion of the human spirit" and its "potentialities." The deeper unity of the ascetic and the erotic. The refusal to collapse these spiritual and sexual potentialities into each other and a move beyond both into a deeper, more fundamental ground. The mirroring, coordinated structures of the sacred and sexual arousal around the social and psychological dynamics of taboo and transgression. These are the leitmotifs of both my work and I dare say my life experience, from the very first pages of *Kali's Child* (1995), a heavily censored, now tabooed book, to my most recent work on the paranormal in books like *Authors of the Impossible* (2010) and *Mutants and Mystics* (2011), where this both/and is reframed now via the bizarre mind-over-matter events of psychical and paranormal phenomena in both elite theory and popular culture. In effect, the "cohesion" and "coordination" of the mystical and the erotic have morphed into the "cohesion" and "coordination" of the mental and the material.

The Traumatic Secret

But this deeper unity of the real beyond the dualisms of our cognitive hardware and cultural software is not the whole story here. There is also the question of just *how* an individual experiences what Bataille confessed as "the continuity of being." There are, of course, no hard and fast rules here. There are countless catalysts and correlates (I would not say "causes"), from the charismatic presence of a teacher or saint, through a profound engagement with a sacred text or ritual tradition, to a car wreck or sunset. Nevertheless, there are some definite patterns in comparative mystical literature, including what I have called a "comparative erotics." Much of my work has orbited around the erotic patterns generated by male sexual orientation and religious desire, the privileging of homoerotic structures within orthodox male mystical literature, and the exiling of male heterosexuality as heretical or at least heterodox within the same. Another pattern, which is the focus of the present essay, I have never quite named, but I would like to do so now. I want to call this pattern within my comparative erotics the *traumatic secret.*

By the traumatic secret I mean to signal the observation that in many cases the mystical event or altered state of consciousness appears to have been "let in" through the temporary suppression or dissolution of the socialized ego, which was opened up or fractured (either at the moment of the mystical event or earlier in the lifecycle) through extreme physical, emotional, and/or sexual suffering, that is, through what we would today call in our new psychological code "trauma." Such a model, at least as I am employing it here, does not reduce the mystical event to the traumatic fracture but rather understands the trauma as a psychological correlate or catalyst of the mystical state of consciousness. Put a bit differently, the traumatic fracture does not "produce" the mystical state; it "allows" the state to appear through the otherwise stable and solid defense structures of the ego. Which is not to deny that the state of consciousness "let in" is also laced with all sorts of cultural, linguistic, historical, and psychological details. It almost always is. These, after all, are precisely the features of the biological and cultured medium through which the state of consciousness manifests itself: the human being.

There are at least three reasons that such a traumatic secret has generally remained secret: a neurontological reason, a psychological reason, and a moral reason.

The first and most basic neurontological reason is that these mystical states appear to be accessing (or letting in) states of consciousness that have nothing to do with the linguistic processing, cultured ego, or cognitive processes located primarily, but by no means exclusively, in the left brain: they are literally "beyond language" and "beyond culture" and so "unspeakable" or "secret." I must add here that they have become even more secret, even more damnable, in our present intellectual climate, whose absolute commitments to materialism, mechanism, causal explanation, constructivism, and contextualism (all left-brain cognitive styles, again) result in a refusal to acknowledge, even entertain, the existence of any dimension of human experience outside the reach of culture, cognition, and language. Such states are not only secret now. They are also impossible.

The second, psychological reason is more simple, as it involves the likelihood that the individual is only vaguely aware of the connection between the earlier trauma and the later mystical event. The connection or coordination, in other words, remains largely unconscious, to employ a Freudian framework.

Third, and finally, such a dynamic remains secret because it suggests a counterintuitive and morally difficult idea, namely, that profoundly positive religious experiences can possess psychological catalysts and correlates that are morally reprehensible or physically horrific. To put it most starkly, it very much looks like a history of sexual trauma can and sometimes does help create the psychosexual foundations of a great mystic.

Again, I must repeat, it does not follow that the mystical life so catalyzed is "nothing but" a symptom of the earlier sexual trauma any more than a life transformed by a near-death experience of transcendence and light is "nothing but" an expression of the car accident or open-heart surgery. The terror and trauma of the car wrapped around the tree or the chest cavity split open like a grapefruit does not "cause" the mystical experience, but it is doubtful indeed if the experience would have happened without the earlier physical traumas. Transcendence and trauma, it turns out, are very much coordinated, just as Bataille argued.

One can, of course, experience the one without the other. I am perfectly aware that most forms of trauma are simply destructive and result in no experience of transcendence whatsoever. I am not here to romanticize trauma of any kind. Not at all. I am also perfectly aware that some experiences of transcendence display no traumatic features. I am not here to issue inappropriate generalizations. I am simply observing that sometimes, and remarkably often in the mystical literature, these two modes of human experience appear to occur *together.*

This traumatic secret was only whispered to me in my early graduate years, and then only in fairly abstract theological terms, like in all those places in Bataille's texts in which he points out that the central icon of Catholicism, particularly in its medieval devotions, is a gruesomely suffering man on a Roman instrument of torture on his way to resurrection. In short, the central mystery of Christianity involves a traumatic fracture of the most extreme kind opening up to a salvific and fantastically positive form of transcendence. Since I grew up in a small Midwestern town and church with just such an image at its liturgical and iconic center, that was a very convincing, if not entirely surprising, point.

What surprised me is how often the same insight returned with other religious materials. Indeed, over the last three decades, I have encountered the traumatic secret over and over again in virtually every single corpus or community that I have engaged in my scholarship (which probably tells us as much about me as these communities). It has also—and this is very important—played an especially central role in my private correspondence with readers of my work who have written, out of the blue, long intimate letters about the intertwining complexities of their sexual and spiritual lives and how they came to some new understanding, some new healing, after encountering my analyses of mystical experience and its correlation with sexual trauma. These private letters constitute what a professional journalist would call the "deep background" of the present essay—*deep* as in unspoken but incredibly informative, deliberately concealed but also very much a part of the revealing. These invisible women and men, their sufferings, and their inner experiences have been some of my most effective teachers. They are the silent coauthors, the haunting ghostwriters, of my published writings on the comparative erotics of mystical literature, and I seek to honor them here with what I hope is an act of simple clarity and frankness.

Reading Bataille

There are many things that can be said about Bataille's *Erotism.* One of them is how profoundly out of step the text is with the discipline's present commitment to historical and cultural specialization and its common allergic reactions to robust comparativism and radical (read: universal) theorizing. Bataille would have none of this. "The specialist can never tackle eroticism," he observed.[5]

And the scandal continues. "Nothing binds me to a particular religion," he wrote.[6] "I have to pick my way along a lonely path, no tradition, no ritual to guide me, and nothing to hinder me, either. In this book of mine I am describing an experience without reference to any special body of belief, being concerned essentially to communicate an inner experience— religious experience, as I see it—outside the pale of specific religions."[7] His was a religion of no religion. Accordingly, the philosopher looked forward to a time, just beyond his own historical horizon, in which he imagined that serious religious people would no longer rely exclusively on this or that religion, but draw on the total resources of the history of religions to shape their own personal mysticisms. "The time is coming, uncertainly enough perhaps, when with any luck we shall no longer need to wait for the decision of other people (in the guise of dogma) before attaining the experience we seek." That time had not yet come, of course, but it was close. For now, it was enough that people like Bataille could "freely communicate the results of this experience."[8] Hence *Erotism*.

The philosopher considered such inner experiences central to the writing of any adequate history of religions, for "without private experience we could discuss neither eroticism nor religion."[9] More radically still, without "the advantages of deep experience," the historian is condemned to produce a body of work that can only "lead to a lifeless accumulation of inert facts churned out in no sort of intelligible order."[10] It did not, however, follow for Bataille that the historian should freely confess and describe his or her own inner experiences in the scholarly text. These should be drawn on boldly, for they are the true sources of the historian's insights and organizing ideas, but they should seldom be explicitly invoked as such.[11] Another kind of "deep background."

Then comes the central argument, namely, that eroticism is intimately linked to death in that both processes lead to the dissolution of the person—temporarily or permanently—in an all-encompassing unity or ground, what Bataille calls the "continuity of being." In short, both eroticism and death are intimately linked to mysticism, mysticism here understood in the sense in which negative, apophatic, or mystical theology performs it: as a negation of name and form toward a unity or fusion with some absolute beyond language and logic.[12] Because "the divine is the essence of continuity," mysticism becomes the privileged form of religious experience for Bataille.[13] He thus variously describes mystical experience as "man's only pure experience," as "that ultimate in human potentialities," and as "the furthest frontier of human experience."[14]

Bataille's mysticism can best be understood by placing it in the context of his larger philosophical system, which revolves around a set of binaries that might be mapped like this:

profane order	sacred order
discontinuity of being	continuity of being
life	death
individuality	mystical union or absorption
law and taboo	transgression and sin
work day	holy day
rational thought	mythical thought
rationalism	mysticism

Bataille is especially sophisticated here, for he does not imagine one set of poles without the other. In a word, his thought is rigorously dialectical. He invokes Hegel to acknowledge this, and it is clear that, as William James had earlier intuited of Hegel (in a state induced by nitrous oxide), Bataille sees the Hegelian dialectic as essentially mystical in structure and intent.[15] And why not? According to Bataille, Hegel drew his knowledge of the dialectic from figures like Meister Eckhart and Jacob Boehme.[16] Hence lines like this one: "We are faced with the paradox of an object which implies the abolition of the limits of all objects, of an erotic object."[17]

In this same dialectical spirit, Bataille observes that transgression derives its power from the taboo; that the transgression does not remove the taboo but suspends, completes, and transcends it; and that taboos were put in place very early in the development of human society in order to enable work and the construction of a social order.[18] Humanity, in fact, begins for Bataille in the act of saying "No" to the superabundance, violence, and nonrational, nonpragmatic nature of the real.[19] Similarly, sexual taboos must not be misunderstood as simple superstitions. We cannot get rid of them, as our humanity depends on them.[20] In a similar spirit again, he is also constantly reminding his readers that the dynamics of sexual arousal and desire depend on the taboo, on the forbidden and the hidden.

Once these dialectical binaries are set up, the question immediately arises how an individual or community might attempt to pass from the list on the left to the list on the right. We can isolate at least four basic answers to this question: one metaphysical, one sexual, one spiritual, and one ritual—that is, death, eroticism, mysticism, and sacrifice.

Death. For Bataille, death is quite simply the return of a discontinuous being back into the continuity of being, which remains completely unaffected by the death of individuals.[21] We come and go. Reality remains what it is, always and everywhere.

Eroticism. Sexuality mirrors or replicates this death-as-continuity both biologically and psychologically. Biologically speaking, sexuality is clearly aimed at reproduction, and reproduction is the flipside of death (since without death there would be no need to reproduce). So sexuality brings more discontinuous beings into existence even as it arises from the fact that all of these beings will be absorbed back into continuity (the dialectic again). Psychologically speaking, sexuality is not eroticism. Eroticism is a much more complex and fundamentally human phenomenon for Bataille to the extent that it secretly seeks a temporary dissolution of those human constructions we call selfhood and society. This desire for continuity is signaled in the "decisive act" of stripping naked and the "obscene" intuition of "a sense of a state of continuity beyond individuality," but it finds its fullest expression in the sexual ecstasy of orgasm—that "little death" of which the French so accurately speak.[22] (English speakers, we might answer back with a grin, possess their own linguistic intuitions, with a more theological ejaculation: "Oh God, oh God, oh God!")

Mysticism. Most fundamentally, eroticism is an expression of "our obsession with a primal continuity linking us with everything that is."[23] This is most easily seen in religious forms of eroticism, that is, in mysticism, where we find "the fusion of beings with a world beyond everyday reality."[24] Bataille is refreshingly sophisticated, which is to say refreshingly dialectical, here. He does not reduce mystical experience to simple sexuality, as he finds in authors like James Leuba, but neither will he leave unchallenged all those pious attempts to read erotic mystical language as simple metaphor, as if such texts possessed only "transcendental significance."[25] Here he quotes a most remarkable line (which I employed in my *Roads of Excess* and have never forgotten, even twenty-five years later) of St. Bonaventure, which reads *in spiritualibus affectionibus carnals fluxus liquore maculantur,*[26] which Bataille will later partially translate a few pages down as "sullied with the liquid of the carnal flux"[27]—in short, a kind of wet dream sometimes occurs "amidst the spiritual affections." The mystic comes—sexual fluids flow. "I do not imagine that they are mistaken," Bataille reflects: "these accidents show nevertheless that basically sensuality and mysticism are akin."[28] Which, again, is not to say that they are the same. It is more that one system can easily set off the other, as we will see below.

Sacrifice. Bataille observes that human beings generally hedge their bets when it comes to their desire for the continuity of being: they certainly desire some contact with the sacred order of continuity, ecstasy, and mystical experience, but they also want to survive and exist as discontinuous beings outside that order. Basically, they want it both ways, and ritual violence allows them to do this. Sacrifice, for Bataille, represents this compromise between the sacred and profane orders. It allows a kind of transition from the latter to the former, but from a safe distance, as "a solemn rite."[29] Bataille intuits a deep linkage or coordination between sacrifice and mystical experience, as both attempt to reveal the sacred realm of the continuity of being: "Although clearly distinct from it, mystical experience seems to me to stem from the universal experience of religious sacrifice."[30]

It should be further observed that, in this model, "divine continuity is linked with the transgression of the law on which the order of discontinuous beings is built," hence the sacred is accessed ritually and mystically primarily through the violation of taboo, otherwise known as "sin" in Christian theology.[31] Little wonder, then, that in Christianity the sacred is so "readily associated with Evil."[32] Here Bataille's thought echoes Rudolf Otto's model of the sacred as a numinous presence at once alluring and terrifying, at once positive and negative.

Reading with Bataille

After I read and assimilated Bataille's *Erotism* in the late 1980s while studying the history and theology of Christian mysticism with Bernard McGinn, I never again returned, at least in any full fashion, to that book or Bataille's work in my writing. Which is not to say, at all, that all of this did not continue to influence and shape what I chose to write about. Looking back now, I realize that in actual fact Bataille was a constant companion of mine, alongside many other conversation partners, from William Blake and Sigmund Freud to Mircea Eliade, Wendy Doniger, Ioan Couliano, Gananath Obeyesekere, and Sudhir Kakar.

I could list dozens of these Bataillean moments in my work, but four stand out as particularly obvious.

1. *The House and the Latrine.* My first book, *Kali's Child*, was my dissertation, a close textual study of the nineteenth-century Hindu saint Ramakrishna in the original Bengali sources. The book was structured around the iconographic features of Kali, a goddess Bataille knew well and who could easily be described as the Hindu deity of "Death and Sensuality." Indeed, for Bataille, the Hindu Tantra (what he called "tantrism") was one of the closest and most precise religious descriptions of his philosophy of eroticism and mysticism, especially as it involved his speculations about how the sexual and spiritual systems can activate the other:

> If my reasoning has been followed it will be apparent that with intentions and key images analogous in both spheres, a mystical impulse of thought may always set off involuntarily the same reflex that an erotic image would. If this is so the converse must also be true. Indeed Hindus do base their exercises in tantrism on the possibility of

inducing a mystical crisis with the help of sexual excitement. . . . they pass from the carnal embrace to spiritual ecstasy.[33]

I will not rehearse here all the aspects of my own initial book on a very similar theme with the Bengali materials. Here it is enough simply to observe that one aspect of my argument involved positing a series of links—Bataille would say coordinations—between childhood and early adult trauma, mostly of a sexual nature, and the saint's later and most remarkable ability to dissociate in almost any context in order to enter various extremely positive ecstatic modes of consciousness and altered states of energy.

In the last chapter, dedicated to Kali's shameless extended tongue, I explored how some of these ecstatic states were explicitly connected to what the saint himself described as a kind of haunting of his bowel movements and the related fashion in which he described the path of Tantra as the "dirty path," the path of the latrine. One can enter the house of mystical experience, the saint pointed out, through many means. The front door works, but so does the back latrine. Taking up Ramakrishna's own imagery, I reflected on what I saw, and still see, as the coordination of sexual trauma and mystical states in the life of the saint:

> Ramakrishna's life, then, *was* tragic, but it was also ecstatic. The abuse he seems to have received as a child and young adult *was* reprehensible, both to him and to us, but it was also connected, in ways we do not yet understand, to his later mystical realizations. Once again, it is absolutely crucial to recall Ramakrishna's dogged insistence that the House of Mystical Experience can be entered through something as horrible as a Latrine. The House *can* be entered through the Latrine, but this does *not* mean that the House, once entered, is nothing but a Latrine. Whatever we think of such an entrance, the possibility remains that, under the proper conditions, even the Latrine might very well open up into a very large and very wonderful House. The ethical and religious implications of such entrances, both for the researcher who digs them up and for the culture that symbolically supports and yet publically denies them, remain to be addressed. I would hope in the meantime that researchers could be sophisticated enough to keep the admittedly troubling conditions of entrance and that which is entered distinct in their discussions. Only then will we be able to share both Ramakrishna's deep disgust with certain aspects of his own latrine-like entrance and his obvious joy at truly being in the House.[34]

Although the book has been endlessly reviewed, celebrated, and excoriated, no scholar, to my knowledge, has really addressed the book's Bataillean patterns. The traumatic secret remains just that: a traumatic secret.

2. *Two Suicide Conversions.* I pursued these same truths again in the lives of scholars of mysticism in *Roads of Excess, Palaces of Wisdom* (2002) and again in the dissociative states, divinizing experiences, and healing ministry of the Jesus of the gospels in *The Serpent's Gift* (2007). For example, in the former book, I showed how the French scholar of Islamic mysticism Louis Massignon was converted to the study of the tenth-century heretical Sufi al-Hallaj as he tried to kill himself, probably because of his repressed and morally tortured homosexuality. Al-Hallaj, Massignon firmly believed, actually intervened on his behalf over the centuries, that is, parapsychologically outside of time, in the midst of his suicide attempt. Ramakrishna, by the way, was similarly mystically transformed, in an ocean of light, amid a suicide attempt, probably for very similar psychosexual reasons. Both men used a knife.

3. *The Human Potential of Mind at Large.* The traumatic secret appeared again, if in a different form, in my next book on the human potential movement, *Esalen: America and the Religion of No Religion* (2007). Particularly influential here was the British American novelist Aldous Huxley. Huxley probably had more influence on the human potential movement as a whole than any other single person. It was he, for example, who coined the expression "human potentialities" (although Bataille had already used it in his description of mystical experience as "that ultimate in human potentialities," as we saw above) after which the movement was eventually named. Part of this influence stemmed from Huxley's early appreciation of Hindu and Buddhist thought. Part of it, maybe most of it, also stemmed from the fact that he was instrumental in bringing a new word into the English language (*psychedelic* or "mind manifesting") and helped catalyze a wide-ranging, decades-long discussion of the mystical potentials of sacred plants and manmade chemicals through his little Blakean tract *The Doors of Perception* (1954).

It was in this same book that the famous writer picked up a notion developed in the British and American psychical research traditions, particularly by Frederic Myers and William James, and applied it to the psychedelic situation. Enter the filter or transmission thesis. Put simply, much too simply, the filter or transmission thesis suggests that consciousness is filtered, translated, reduced, or transmitted through the brain and not produced by it. Mind is not the brain, but Mind is indeed filtered or individuated through the brain with all its mind-boggling evolutionary, neurological, psychological, cultural, linguistic, emotional, political, and historical complexities. We are local context and construction, *and* we share a kind of human consciousness that is universal and irreducible to any local context or construction.

It is important to realize that the early psychical researchers were forced into the filter thesis by their extensive ethnographic data on psychical phenomena, which in turn revolved around a single theme: death, that ultimate trauma, that final dissociation. Telepathy, for example, was coined in 1882 by a Cambridge classicist who intended to express through the neologism the fact that most dramatic telepathic communications occur between loved ones within extreme emotional states: hence the neologism, *tele-pathos*—"pathos at a distance." This was no matter of something as stupid as card guessing in a laboratory or as colorless as playing the stock market for material gain. These events rather were symbolic communications, often through dream or waking vision, between family members at that most poignant and most terrible of all human moments. This, in short, was another expression of the traumatic secret.

The early Cambridge researchers employed thousands of death narratives to explore such an idea, but for the sake of illustration, consider one that I recently included in a textbook on how to compare religions, from the forensic pathologist Janis Amatuzio.[35] In her *Beyond Knowing*, a book on the survival of bodily death, Amatuzio explains how she encountered a very troubled hospital chaplain in the course of her work one evening. He asked to go back to her office, where he then asked the doctor if she knew how they found the body of a young man recently killed in a car accident. She replied that her records showed that the Coon Rapids Police Department had recovered the body in a frozen creek bed at 4:45 AM. "No," he replied. "Do you know how they *really* found him?" The chaplain then explained how he had spoken to the man's wife, who related how she had had a vivid dream that night of her husband standing next to her bed, apologizing and explaining that he had been in a car accident, and that his car was in a ditch where it could not be seen from the road. She awoke immediately, at 4:20 in the morning, and called the police to tell them, with absolute certainty, that her husband had been in a car accident not far from their home and that his car was in a ravine that could not be seen from the road. They recovered the body twenty minutes later. Significantly, the wife insisted that this was no ordinary dream and that her husband was really standing there. In short, it was a physical or quasi-physical experience; it was a kind of resurrection apparition.[36]

This is a modern story of trauma to transcendence, but it is not an unusual one, and it is precisely narratives like this that produced the term telepathy (with dreams a particularly common medium of the telepathic communication), the filter thesis, and, eventually, the human potential idea of Mind at Large. Huxley, for example, knew this earlier psychical research literature well and borrowed the filter thesis from it to do some different work. Basically, he used it to explain how a chemical substance like, say, mescaline could result in mystical experiences yet not be the chemical cause of those states. He pointed out that one of the brain's main functions is not to take in all available sensory data, but to keep most of it at bay, and then to heavily process the data allowed in so that the human being can function in the world. There is way more "out there" than we can possibly process, including, he speculated, entirely different states of consciousness and being. James, of course, had said more or less the same thing in *The Varieties of Religious Experience* (again, because he had known such states while on nitrous oxide). What mescaline did, Huxley suggested, was temporarily shut down the brain's filtering and normal cognitive functions. Once the filter is suppressed, of course, all that other stuff can come rushing in, including something Huxley knew and called Mind at Large.

Mind at Large was the ultimate human potential for Huxley. It is what we *are* beyond our little individuated egos and all their linguistic, cultural, religious, and ethnic conditionings. It is how a dead husband can telepathically communicate with a sleeping, dreaming wife. It is what sometimes manifests when the brain and its ego are sufficiently traumatized. It is the true Subject of mystical experience.

This, by the way, was not the first time that he had suggested such a thing. Already back in *The Perennial Philosophy* (1945) he had employed a telling chemical metaphor that we might now recognize as an early traumatic model for the mystical:

> Nothing in our everyday experience gives us any reason for supposing that water is made up of hydrogen and oxygen; and yet when we subject water to certain rather drastic treatments, the nature of its constituent elements becomes manifest. Similarly, nothing in our everyday experience gives us much reason for supposing that the mind of the average sensual man has, as one of its constituents, something resembling, or identical with, the Reality substantial to the manifold world; and yet, when that mind is subjected to drastic treatments, the divine element, of which it is in part at least composed, becomes manifest.[37]

Huxley's boiling or "drastic treatment" is my "traumatic secret."

4. *Cracking Open the Cosmic Egg.* Most recently, the traumatic secret returned again in my work on the paranormal and popular culture, particu-

larly in *Mutants and Mystics* (2011) and my final chapter study on the horror writer–turned-visionary and mystic Whitley Strieber. Strieber is easily one of the most psychologically astute mystical writers I have encountered. He is as blunt and frank about the sexual and even rape dimensions of his abduction experiences as he is about how his later adult encounters with subtle beings, whom he calls simply "the visitors," were somehow related to a horrendous physical trauma that he believes he suffered on a military base as a young child (as a subject in an experiment). Indeed, he has shared with me that he is now convinced that, had he not been brutalized as a child, he would have never been able to perceive and experience the visitors. Exactly as I argued with respect to Ramakrishna, however, he does not reduce his later physical and mystical encounters with the visitors to his childhood trauma. Rather, he suggests that such overwhelming trauma can "crack open the cosmic egg" and so reveal a "hidden reality" of unimaginable scope. In short, he offers us another version of the traumatic secret.

Strieber, it should be pointed out, is also not alone in his brave linking of childhood trauma and the adult experience of alien abduction. The psychologist Kenneth Ring has similarly written about the links between early childhood trauma and a later psychic sensitivity to alternate realities, as displayed in individuals who have experienced either a UFO encounter or a near-death experience, the phenomenology of which, he demonstrates, are eerily similar.

There are very few things that can be said about the psychological makeup of individuals who have experienced what they understand to be alien abductions. Contrary to the debunking propaganda, these experiences occur across the demographic and educational spectrum, from farmers and construction workers to writers and intellectuals and at least one Nobel Prize–winning biologist.[38] According to Ring, however, there is one fairly clear psychological pattern in the abduction literature: a positive correlation between childhood sexual trauma and later adult abduction experiences. Ring's nonreductive argument is essentially identical to the one I advanced in *Kali's Child* with respect to Ramakrishna or that Strieber advanced with respect to himself. Listen:

> My argument begins with the proposition that a history of child abuse and trauma plays a central etiological role in promoting sensitivity to UFOs and NDEs. My second assumption . . . is that growing up under such conditions tends to stimulate the development of a dissociative response style as a means of psychological defense. . . .

By doing so [that is, by "tuning out"]—and this is my third assumption—he is more likely to "tune into" other realities where by virtue of his dissociated state, he can temporarily feel safe regardless of what is happening to his body. In this way . . . dissociation would directly foster relatively easy access to alternate, non-ordinary realities.[39]

Ring is careful to suggest that "this kind of attunement" is "not a gift of dissociation itself, which only makes it possible, but of a correlated capacity, that for what is called psychological absorption." Hence "it is the ability to dissociate that governs access to alternate realities," but these alternate realities cannot be explained by the psychological mechanism of dissociation.[40] We are back to the filter thesis and the traumatic secret.

Simple Impossible Thoughts

So what do the sexual traumas and ecstatic states of an avatar of God, the parapsychological conversion of a French Islamicist amid a guilt-ridden suicide attempt, a mescaline-induced altered state turned countercultural classic, and a famous twentieth-century abduction experience all have in common? Simple. They represent different ways that the brain as filter or transmitter is temporarily taken offline or suppressed. They represent common life traumas that can suppress (or temporarily destroy) the stable sense of self and thus act as "triggers" for mystical states. To invoke Bataille, they represent ways that the discontinuous being can be "sacrificed" and temporarily enter the continuity of being.

The same traumatic secret also explains why something like a car wreck, a psychopathological condition, or a stroke can all also produce a mystical state *and* why that state cannot be reduced or fully explained by the Toyota Camry wrapped around the tree, the schizophrenic condition, or the damaged brain. It also explains, as Bataille knew and said so well, why the scientific method is impotent before such states and can only, falsely, claim that they do not exist, that they do not happen. Truly to understand such states, after all, one must know them within one's own inner experience. As soon as they become "objects," they disappear; they become artifacts, contexts, discourses, functions, and so on (which, of course, they also are).

There is a very obvious problem here. The truth is that we have no reliable and replicable access to what Aldous Huxley called Mind at Large. We have no safe way to shut down the filter or transmitter of Mind. Because of this, the conflation of consciousness and brain states or cultural conditions is more or less perfect, complete, and unassailable. Hence the assumption that consciousness and culture or cognition can be reduced to or identified with one another in our scholarly methods and assumptions. Such a conflation is certainly understandable enough. We study what we as social egos have easy and reliable access to, not what we do not have access to and can only know once or twice in a lifetime, if at all.

Hence the traumatic secret.

Foucault's Sacred Sociology

MARK D. JORDAN

In Foucault's own genealogy, no bloodline is more difficult to draw than the one running to Bataille—unless it is their joint descent from Nietzsche. Facts about their shared circumstances are not hard to come by, nor is literary evidence of Foucault's readerly admiration (though it did not lead him to seek out the living author). The note presenting the edition of Bataille's complete works is signed by Foucault, who calls him "one of the most important writers of his century."[1] Still, the obviousness of biographical proximity and the banality of editorial praise conceal the difficulty of describing generational exchanges among such ironic readers of Nietzsche.[2] Foucault suggests more when he writes, "We owe to Bataille a great part of the moment where we are." The "we" in academic French often means "I": the moment where *I* am. "But what remains to do, to think and to write, that without doubt also owes much to him, and will for a long time. His work will grow." Certainly it grew in Foucault—and long after his so-called literary period.

A few years earlier, Foucault had written an essay in the double issue of *Critique* devoted to the memory of Bataille.[3] That essay, "Preface to Transgression," appears alongside pieces by Bataille's collaborators: Blanchot, Klossowski, Leiris. It is an obvious place to begin any description of Foucault's descent from Bataille, especially on questions about religion.[4] But the essay is no more than a beginning, because it makes clear that Bataille's legacy persists not only in the texts he wrote but in the religious projects he imagined. "His work will grow": by commenting on text and by enacting religion.[5]

"Preface to Transgression"

Foucault's memorial is a palimpsest of Bataille's languages—of lexicons, genres, structures, and erotic plots. Foucault often writes by a kind of mimesis. He would open his inaugural lecture at the Collège de France by wishing that his voice could blend in "surreptitiously" with a preceding voice, which he concludes by identifying as Hyppolite's.[6] With more intimacy, Foucault here rehearses Bataille's technical terms as if they were his own. Sometimes he italicizes them: *interior, sovereign, inner experience, extreme of the possible, comic operation,* even *meditation.* At other times he arranges the terms in heuristic patterns: sacrifice, ecstasy, communication appear as modes of a single cultural operation. But Foucault also pretends that Bataille's words are so familiar that they can be quoted without citation—as if from memory. (The essay's original version contains no footnotes.) From beginning to end, the essay speaks about experience without quotation marks and in a variety of contexts: the experience of sexuality, of transgression, of contestation; sovereign experiences, experiences essential to a culture, experience that has lost language. These phrases are not quotations: they are reenactments or, better, persuasive variations.[7]

Foucault also vivifies Bataille's images and symbols. He quotes passages that speak of the immense and silent sky; of crushing, endless night, pierced sometimes by a cry or a laugh, by stellar apparitions and strange lights, or by nothing. We overhear Bataille narrate stupor and drunkenness, copulating bodies that become earth, the desperate heart and the monstrous eye.[8] Foucault fuses these images with his own imagination of power. From *History of Madness* on, Foucault favors spatial metaphors when describing power. He contrasts techniques of exclusion and confinement or grid making (*quadrillage*). He claims that new forms of power arise between existing structures, in the meshing of their gears. He coins "heterotopia" to name a quasi-outside that is set apart within a system of power. Even Foucault's favorite technical term for power structures or mechanisms, *dispositif,* can refer to battlefield positions or military arrays. So too, in this memorial preface, Foucault represents Bataille chiefly in terms of space: the empty space of thin limits; the cultural space in which we act and speak; the space in which the sacred plays, appears, vanishes. In all these locutions, we hear at once a representation of Bataille and a reiteration of the guiding image from Foucault's *History of Madness,* published only two years earlier. There Foucault proposes to write a history of the "*limits*" by which a culture defines itself in rejecting something as its "Exterior": "this hollowed-out void (*vide creusé*), this white space by means of which it isolates itself designates it as much as its values." Again, "the plenitude of history is only possible in the space, both empty and peopled at the same time, of all the words without language."[9] The verbal echoes between the preface to transgression and the original preface to *History of Madness* are so strong as to make it seem that Foucault is ingesting Bataille into his book—if he is not inscribing his book within the corpus (the written body) of Bataille.

Foucault's appropriative mimesis of Bataille moves up from terms and images to other textual elements. The essay's genre is indebted to Bataille's habit of composing prefaces to his own works. For *Madame Edwarda*, Bataille drafted multiple prefaces, finally settling on one that distinguished him from "Pierre Angélique," the novel's pseudonymous author and protagonist.[10] For *L'Abbé C*, Bataille supplied an unsigned narrative preface that explains (that is, concocts) the finding of the manuscript for the rest of the book.[11] And so on. Foucault locates these prefatory devices among the strategies that Bataille uses to "fracture" his authorial subject. They go along with other techniques for creating distance between thinking and writing—techniques like the alternation of fiction and reflection, the twisting of compositional time, and deliberate oppositions between speech and speaker. So too Foucault's "Preface" means not so much to provide easy access as to prepare for an effect to be achieved through Bataille's writing. Foucault is not writing a preface to *texts* but to their evocation and performance of an experience. It is titled, after all, a "Preface to Transgression." For us—for Bataille, Foucault, their readers—transgression "prescribes not only the sole manner of finding the sacred (*le sacré*) in its immediate content, but of recomposing it in its empty form, in its absence thus rendered brilliant."[12] This is a preface on the way to recomposing the sacred through its absence.

The structure of Foucault's essay resembles Bataille's fragmentary discursiveness in *Érotisme* and *Les larmes d'Éros* more than his own taxonomic schemas. If Foucault often composes in dense outlines, this essay retraces the "detours and returns" that it discovers in Bataille's corpus, walks the "labyrinth" that it finds there. Indeed, the essay has a deliberately circular structure, both topically and narratively. It is divided topically into five sections, each of which views Bataille's transgression from a different angle, as if moving around a tableau. Each section ends by pointing to what follows it, so that the reader is directed to gaze both at the tableau and at the labyrinthine circuit around—the circuit that limits it.

The first section links "our" contemporary discourse about sexuality to the proclamation of the death of God. That absence opens an empty space in which sexuality becomes the thin form of limit: the limit for conscience or consciousness (since sexuality is the meaning of the unconscious), for law (since incest is the only universal prohibition), for language (since desire and its consummation fall into silence). Bataille's accounts of transgression reveal not only the intrinsic connection between our speech about sexuality and our proclamation of the death of God but the very meaning of our having killed God. Indeed, Bataille means by erotism "an experience of sexuality that in itself links the surpassing of the limit to the death of God."[13] Beneath both the new language of sexuality and the old Western languages of God there stands the "singular experience": transgression. But we do not yet have the language for it. We need a language beyond dialectic. In Bataille's writing, Foucault adds in a final couplet, we have only "the charred stump, the promising cinder."

The second section traces the mutual implication of limit and transgression, their necessary union in the violent instant of the crossing. It draws an analogy from the nonpositive affirmation of transgression to a distinction in Kant's *Critique of Pure Reason*.[14] But Foucault does so to situate Bataille's thought of transgression after Western philosophy's long preoccupation with contradiction and outside its recognized borders. Foucault connects transgression with Blanchot's notion of contestation: both gesture toward an experience that puts everything in question but not by mere denial. Transgression is "the solar reverse of satanic negation; it has a part linked to the divine (*le divin*), or rather it opens, from the limit that indicates the sacred (*le sacré*), the space where the divine can happen."[15] Western philosophy has led to this point and turned away from it—until Nietzsche, whose narratives gesture toward this language-after-contradiction, beyond dialectic. Philosophy's return to discursive language after Nietzsche is a reversion. Only the writers of extreme language—Bataille, Blanchot, Klossowski—can show transgression, mostly through what we call the "erotic."[16] Erotic philosophy takes different forms: against Sade's loquacious alternation of philosophic discourse and erotic tableau, Bataille displays rather the subject's failure to speak—shows the subject "stretched out on the sand of what it cannot any more say."[17] This speechlessness is condensed in Bataille's famous image of the reversed eye, the eye turned upward or inward by orgasmic ecstasy and by death.

The third section of Foucault's essay places the failure of language once again into a history of Western philosophy. The transit beyond dialectical language is the moment at the end of an epoch—or before it, at the dawn of Greek thinking. Or it is the (repeated?) moment of Zarathustra's arrival? Bataille writes into the void left by the murder of God, onto the growing desert of nihilism, but also into the Nietzschean geography peopled by Zarathustra, his shadow, his monkey, a braying donkey, the overman, Dionysus, Christ. After Nietzsche's collapse on the streets of Turin, this geography can seem a theater of madness. The void opened by God's absence, enacted by the ritual of empty transgression, is the disruptive possibility of the mad philosopher. (Do any of Bataille's protagonists not flirt with madness—or copulate with it?) More: it is the sacrifice of the philosophic speaker. Bataille's writing performs the philosopher's spectacular execution, his *supplice*. His very writing of his experience is inevitably a *supplice*. (What is often decried as the density of Foucault's writing in this essay might be better conceived as contortions or convulsions of discursive language.)

The essay's fourth section begins by describing Bataille's language as one of boulders, of sheer cliff faces, but also as a circle that points back to itself and folds over itself. Bataille's language is an eye: a globe of night circling a void in which there is both light and emptiness. For Bataille, the eye acts in the transgressive instant. It can be plucked out or turned inside, where it finds not superior inwardness, not a deeper night, but its prior engagement with death. Foucault quotes the scene in *Bleu du ciel:* as the narrator and Dorothée copulate among tombstones on All Souls, funerary candles become stars, earth becomes heaven. The plucked or reversed eye is language at the moment when it erupts beyond its confines: "laughter, tears, eyes turned up in ecstasy, the mute and bulging horror of sacrifice."[18] (The revolving eye is the condition of Bataille's writing—and the shape of Foucault's essay.)

The final section begins by announcing our century's discovery of gestures that consummate and consume: expense, excess, limit, transgression. The "sky of unreality" under which Sade placed sexuality, its doubled relations to transgression, indicates the impossibility of describing it in dialectical terms. Indeed, its arrival announces the need for a language beyond contradiction. Erotic writing shows the violent circle of this new language that puts language into question. "Sexuality is not decisive for our culture except as spoken and in the measure that it is spoken. It is not our language that has been, for at least two centuries, eroticized; it is our sexuality that since Sade and the death of God has been absorbed into the universe of language, denatured by it, placed by it in that emptiness where it establishes its sovereignty and where it ceaselessly poses, as Law, limits that it transgress."[19] In the linguistic consequences of that absorption, we encounter both the absence of God and our death. Foucault calls on a passage from Leiris to liken the space of this encounter, which is the space of Bataille's writing, to "the white beach" of a bullring. He ends with the famous scene at Seville's bullring from *L'histoire de l'oeil.*

The memorial essay's structure is thematically and metaphorically circular. It begins and ends with the emptied space in which sex is denaturalized and absorbed into (circling, failing) language. A circular structure and circular metaphors or images are entirely appropriate for a work that praises and repeats Bataille's interest in Nietzsche's Zarathustra, the prophet of both the death of God and eternal return. But the structure is also narratively circular so far as it stages a single episode of erotic transgression. Its first and last quotations from Bataille are bookends of erotic suspension and consummation. The first quotation is from an episode in *L'Abbé C* where the priest, Robert, kneels down before Éponine to recite a penitential psalm. When she wakes from her reverie to notice him, she is almost bowled over by laughter, turning to fall against a balustrade. The wind lifts her coat to expose her bare ass—the first thing the priest sees as he raises his eyes heavenward. A transgressive gaze but also a suspension of erotic action: in this excerpt, he only gazes. Foucault's essay ends by quoting the scene in which the matador's eye, gored out, becomes by analogy the bull's testicle that Simone inserts underneath her dress. The sky overhead liquefies—as urine, as if urine. The "unseizable moment" brings back a memory of their earlier partner (and victim), but it also completes a touch: "*Il me sembla, dans cet insaississable instant, la toucher,*"[20] where the *il* is at least the matador's eye, the matador himself, the bull's horn and perhaps the narrator.[21] There are many allusions here—not least to Nietzsche's *Zarathustra.* That rewriting of the Gospels ends with a scene in which Zarathustra, blinded by a sky turned to doves, reaches out to touch his companion-lion's fur—before he descends the mountain (again) as the Sun. But Foucault's last quotation from Bataille, which replaces his voice in the conclusion, also consummates the erotic action suspended in the first quotation. The line of the erotic limit is crossed so that it can be crossed again.

Certainly Foucault's essay carries forward the work of Bataille. It also predicts the later work of Foucault. It is tempting to read forward from its description of sexuality to volume 1 of Foucault's *History of Sexuality,* with its mockery of easy liberation, its preoccupation with speaking sex, and its final gesture toward another regime of bodies and pleasures that cannot yet be spoken—certainly not in the throbbing prose of D. H. Lawrence. But Foucault's memorial essay signals another direction—backward to the project in which the names of Bataille, Klossowski, and Leiris were originally linked. In that project, a preoccupation with religion was explicit. It was also sometimes enacted around a "blasted stump."

A College of Sacred Sociology

In July 1937, the third issue of *Acéphale* published a short declaration about "sacred sociology." The list of signatories for the declaration differed from the editors and contributors to the magazine, but there was also an important continuity—as there was from that magazine (or perhaps 'zine) to Bataille's earlier editorial work on *Documents*. Among *Acéphale*'s editors and contributors were Bataille, Roger Caillois, and Klossowski. If their contributions to it were diverse, they shared a commitment to the study and practice of religion as antifascist politics.

Religion is central to *Acéphale*, which carries the subtitle "Religion, Sociology, Philosophy." Its emblem, drawn repeatedly by André Masson, is a naked, headless man whose entrails are exposed, whose genitals are covered by a skull, and who holds in one hand a "sacred heart," in the other a sacrificial knife.[22] The headless man is at least both victim and priest—a priest who has made himself victim and victor by cutting off the heady God of prohibitions, of hierarchical authority. The work of this little magazine is then a religious rite. So it declares, inside its front cover, using boldface, capital letters: "We are fiercely religious." This means: we repudiate the God who has been used to swallow up life by tyrannical management in order to recover the God of erotic-religious ecstasy, the God who stands beyond both secular productivity and prohibition.

These dramatic declarations and illustrations are gestures against fascist political movements, which the editors see as falsely religious. Above the declaration "we are fiercely religious," there is an aphorism from Kierkegaard: "What has the face of politics and imagines itself to be politics will be unmasked one day as a religious movement."[23] This might express the prophetic hope of the group gathered around the magazine, but it is also unmasks the mechanisms of fascism. Fascism is the extreme of monocephalic society, in which the single head is a pinnacle of absolute authority represented as divine.[24] Fascism attempts to contain God within the military camp of a single nation.[25] Fascism scavenges older religious traditions, Christian and pagan, to make a church of its nationalized racism.[26]

How to fight the concealed religious energy of fascism? By taking back its supposed sources, such as Nietzsche. By unmasking its true character as decayed monotheism. But most of all by setting up a countercommunity in which the religious energies can be deployed against it—not in service of the more complete imprisonment but of a transformation of human selves and communities into something new. The magazine was in fact related to, though hardly identical with, a secret ritual community that sometimes met by a lightning-blasted oak tree in the forest of Marly—one reference of Foucault's "blasted stump."[27]

All of this frames that announcement of a public community in the issue of July 1937: "Note about the Founding of a College of Sociology."[28] The announcement begins by regretting how little agreed progress has been made in the study of "social structures." Its students haven't sufficiently modified their presuppositions and methods in view of their own discoveries. In particular, they have failed to reflect on the resistance that disclosures of social functioning must encounter. The representations that animate society are necessarily "contagious and active." Exposing them elicits resistance. In order for the study of social structures to proceed more seriously, it will be necessary to develop "a moral community" stronger than ordinary scholarly networks, more adept at handling the "virulent character" of social representations. This moral community doesn't demand unanimity of motive or purpose from those who want to join it. Its sufficient basis is a "preoccupation" with the "more precise knowledge of the essential aspects of social existence." The name for this knowledge is "sacred sociology, so far as it implies the study of social existence in all those manifestations where there comes to light the active presence of the sacred."

Some glosses may be helpful. The public group's founders, who possessed considerable classical learning, called it a "college" not to copy academic institutions but to recall ancient religious ones.[29] A *collegium* was in ancient Rome first of all a body of priests with civic functions. Some founders of the "College of Sociology" later likened it to a "religious order."[30] That translation may help our modern ears, but it misses the Roman sense of priestly college—in which there is no separation between priestly sacrifice and civic order, in which priestly functions make the civic possible.

What about "sociology"? The quickest answer is that the founders shared enthusiasm for the work of Durkheim and Mauss—for a certain understanding of the opposition of sacred to secular but also for an analysis of the elements of religious life, of myth, ritual, sacrifice, gift.[31] The group proposed a college of *sociology* because they saw in ethnographic studies of archaic religious practice a site at which they could gather insights from psychoanalysis or inspirations of experimental art for political action against the empty efficiency of modern life that breeds fascism. That is why "sociology" had already appeared as the second term of *Acéphale*'s subtitle, right next to religion.

This appropriation of sociology was controversial among the members of the new college. When they broke with one another two years later, thus dissolving it, a stated reason was disagreement over fidelity to the sociological method of Durkheim and Mauss. Leiris wrote to Bataille to complain that the work actually being presented at the college's public lectures repeatedly committed "very serious infractions of the rules of methodology established by Durkheim."[32] Certainly the expectation that Bataille held for a convincing sociology—for an effective understanding of the bases of the social—diverged increasingly from any common understanding. But it is important to see this as a disagreement about sociology rather than as its repudiation—as a disagreement over how to reply to the "sociological sphinx," as Bataille says at the last of the public lectures, when he was left to assert his understanding alone.[33] The splits within the group show that such knowledge will increasingly not resemble what universities accredit as sociological knowledge. It will increasingly both engage and enact the socially forbidden topics of sexuality and death. So far as it registers sacral processes, its own representations become sacral—indeed, become as macabre and pornographic as Masson's headless man.[34]

The short-lived experiment in sacred sociology may have failed of its stated purposes, but I underscore them not least to read them forward into their reception. If the group had continued, what would have become of the project of sacred sociology? One answer is obviously to be found in the later writing of its participants. Bataille, Caillois, and Klossowski went on to write major works about religion, in genres ranging from academic analysis to the mythological novel. But another answer would be to look for the persistence of the project in writers of the next generation, especially Foucault. To think about Bataille, Foucault, and religion, it is important to read the older project forward into Foucault's books of the 1970s—to volume 1 of his *History of Sexuality*, of course, but, more immediately, more strikingly, to *Surveiller et punir*, which we know in English as *Discipline and Punish*.

Foucault's Sacred Sociology

Discipline and Punish opens with a grisly tableau, the prolonged public torture of Damiens, condemned in 1757 for attempting to assassinate Louis XV. The first twelve paragraphs of the book are extended quotations from archival descriptions of the public torture—the published trial proceedings, a newspaper account, firsthand testimony by a police official. Their combined effect is to affix this gruesome image to the front of the book—just where *Acéphale* liked to put its image of the disemboweled priest-victim. Or to remind us of Bataille's fascination with the photograph of the Chinese execution by "a hundred cuts."[35] But in *Discipline and Punish*, the figure of the tortured body is only the first panel of a diptych, the first of two icons. The second image is a set of rules for a house of young prisoners, published in 1838. The rules determine every period of the day—not for punishment, of course, but for rehabilitation.

One of Foucault's purposes in juxtaposing the two images is to ask how we understand the change from gruesome public executions to lifelong rehabilitation—and whether we must understand it entirely as progress. Another purpose is to display two kinds of religion, just as was done in *Acéphale*, though the contrast is different. On one side, for Foucault, the liturgical Christianity that attends and justifies the public torture of Damiens. On the other, the legal-clinical religion that manages young inmates within the model modern reformatory. Christianity does of course appear in the reformatory. The rules require "moral or religious reading," then the public recitation of a passage from "some instructive or uplifting work," followed by "evening prayer."[36] But these Christian elements are only instruments in the service of another sort of theology—what Foucault here calls the theory of modern penality and which he will soon associate with the new religion of psychiatric power.[37]

The torture inflicted on Damiens is called in French *supplice*, the French descendant of the Latin *supplicium:* an offering or sacrifice, both the action of sacrificing and the thing sacrificed. Foucault shares the word and the sense of its etymology with Bataille, who uses it as an analogy and a religious allegory to frame his decisive discovery of what he calls "inner experience."[38] For Foucault, *supplice* as practiced under the French monarchy is a bodily spectacle in which Christianity has its required functions. Christian figures are indispensable performers in the event—not least the confessor who accompanies the condemned. The judicial torture is performed at Christian sites—often in front of a major church or shrine. It is punctuated by Christian speeches—by admonitions, confessions, cries for divine mercy. Indeed, Foucault says, this judicial torture is meant to assert the interconnection of divine and human judgment: it is an earthly anticipation of eternal punishment—a theater of hell. So Foucault frequently describes the *supplice* in religious terms, as a "ritual" or "liturgy."[39] At some public executions, the accused becomes not only a popular hero but a popular saint.[40] The gallows is both a scene of contrition and a coercive summons to sanctity.

To talk about the suffering body of a condemned criminal as the protagonist in a theater of hell that teaches divine truth is to summon the memory of a very particular execution—as Foucault and Bataille both know. On certain theologies they would have heard growing up Catholic, the *supplice* of Jesus' crucifixion is cited on every Catholic altar. The sacrifice of any Mass is the reperformance of a *supplice*. Bataille recalls such theology in many places but perhaps most extensively in that section of *L'expérience intérieure* entitled "Le supplice." The section extends *supplice* by punning on its relation to "supplication" and "sacrifice" but also by gesturing repeatedly, for contrast, toward Christ's suffering and its Christian repetition as ritual and as willed imitation. In *Discipline and Punish*, Foucault's section "Le supplice" is not so explicitly theological, but it does evoke the Crucified One stretched out behind Damiens—not least by emphasizing the Bataillean word as a section heading and central topic.

Compare this latter-day crucifixion with the second panel of Foucault's diptych, with the rules for the model penitentiary, which were published only seventy years after the public torture of Damiens. Foucault notes a few references to Christianity in those rules, but he means mostly to suggest that the embodied spectacle of redemptive punishment has been replaced by rational calculation of endless rehabilitation—in which an early diagnosis of criminal tendencies can lead to one's being confined under expert supervision for as long as it takes to treat them. In the name of rational reform, for the sake of overcoming the barbaric excess of the old monarchy and its unreformed religion, the modern state creates a vast system for controlling criminal tendencies.

In Foucault, many paths of thinking lead off from this contrast between the religion of the two panels—between the embodied spectacle of punishment and the rational regime of rehabilitation. We might think with him that the disappearance of the body—especially the disappearance of spectacles of the suffering body—leads to the rationalization or restriction of the very idea of religion. Or we could think with Foucault about the transfer of religious powers from the church to the state. The modern state apparatus has become more ecclesial, more churchly, has taken over the functions of Christian worship more directly—yet not in the manner of the ancient Roman priestly colleges.

However we pursue these thoughts, we must notice that the new religious system, what Foucault calls the "disciplinary" society, does not abandon ritual. It gives up certain spectacles like public torture—at least it professes to do so. But it does so only for the sake of extending ritual to every part of life. This is the point of the second image: the regime of the model reformatory ritualizes every moment of the day. It writes rubrics to control, so far as possible, every action of its inmates. Modern discipline does not abandon ritual. It extends ritual—in correctional facilities, on factory floors, in schools, even in churches. Disciplinarity as Foucault describes it totalizes ritual—by borrowing lessons learned in the confined space of the monastery. So Foucault will say in *Discipline and Punish* that modern society generalizes the techniques of the monastery, that a modern school is another monastery, that the modern timetable is the monastic *horarium* or schedule—in short, that vowed asceticism has become universal exercise.[41] Once established, the modern penal system even makes its own calendar of saints. Foucault singles out the death of a child inmate at the penal colony of Mettray. The boy's last words, reported by the colony's chroniclers, are: "What a pity to have to leave the colony so soon!"[42] Foucault calls this child the "first penitentiary saint." A saint who regrets having to leave the penal system because it offers such blessedness. If only one could be a prisoner within it forever! Foucault is ironic here, but he also means to indicate how far systems of state discipline supplant churches.

We can hear in Foucault's story about the new religion of discipline a more discursive version of the critique of fascism in *Acéphale* and the Collège of Sociology. But notice what seems an obvious difference between Foucault and Bataille at the time of the Collège: Foucault proposes no community, not even the floating editorial board of an ephemeral magazine, through which to resist the new disciplines of the state, the tyrannies of Enlightened religion. Some readers conclude that Foucault leaves no room for resistance and fault him for pessimism. Foucault instead acknowledges the difficulty of speaking resistance, of depicting alternatives, when all language and every image, including the religious, have been colonized by disciplinary power. For Foucault, as for Bataille, the representation of resistance, the articulation of resistance, may require that language and iconography be broken apart—be pushed to some extreme. For Foucault, perhaps as against Bataille, the extremity of language is no longer the macabre and pornographic. Those territories too have now been colonized by disciplinary power. Whatever possibility may remain for representing human life otherwise may lie in irony or in the avowed folly of reverie, in fantastical stories of a utopia that might instruct a heterotopia, in the prospectus for a *collegium* that could never be founded but must still be memorialized.

In the last pages of *Discipline and Punish*, at the opposite end from the diptych that begins with the torture of Damiens, there may be ghostly tracings of another picture of human life. It comes from the Fourierists, these extravagant social critics whom Foucault keeps quoting. Indeed, he twice notes that he is copying from the Fourierist newspaper *La Phalange*.[43] The second instance is the last text quoted by Foucault in this book—and so the exact structural complement to the archival accounts of the public execution of Damiens. *Phalange*: it derives from an ancient Greek military word, *phalanx*, and it was later picked up by various fascist groups in the twentieth century. But in the 1840s, the enthusiastic utopians took their title from Fourier's name for the ideal community, constructed by the exact calculation of human differences and by their balancing in economic, sexual, and ritual harmonies. (This can also be understood as the parodic ultimate of discipline so far as it is its reversal, its excess.) Fourier's vision is religious not only in its projection of a complex ritual system, with its own mythology, but in its eschatological predictions. To bring forward Fourier at the end of *Discipline and Punish* is an ironic gesture toward a speech, an imagination in which it might yet be possible to represent a communal alternative to present power. Does the allusion to Fourier then become a tacit gesture toward something like that other "Acéphale," which practiced rites before a "blasted stump"? Or is it, in its irony and utopian excess, an affirmation of the impossibility of that group's ever being able to be—or to say—what Bataille imagined, even at the limit of the possible?

In Foucault, Bataille's work grows by saying less—especially about community or communication in the emptiness before the sacred.

Bataille and Kristeva on Religion

ZEYNEP DIREK

> It is indeed true that this Death, and this Desire, and this Law can never meet within the knowledge that traverses in its positivity the empirical domain of man; but the reason for this is that they designate the conditions of possibility of all knowledge about man.
>
> —Michel Foucault, *The Order of Things*

Introduction

This essay concentrates on Bataille's and Kristeva's readings of religion in order to discuss what religion signifies for them. Both Bataille and Kristeva interpret religious signification in terms of desire, law, and death. They understand these forms of human finitude as heterogeneous experiences of life. The role that abjection plays in their conception of religion will be my focus, and I will point to the respects in which their reflections on abjection differ. While Bataille sees, in religious expression, the ambiguity of the erotic object that is desired in its very horror, Kristeva interprets the same ambiguity in terms of the abjection of the mother, in terms of which she offers a critique of the Freudian and Lacanian accounts of the psychoanalytic development of subjectivity.

The first section considers the significance of Bataille's thought in Kristeva's early career. The second section explains how Bataille's conception of religion in *The Accursed Share* and *Erotism* differs from his early reading of religion in *Theory of Religion*. The third section concentrates on the essence of religious experience for Kristeva and attempts to show how her reflection on abjection relates to, and differs from, Bataille's. While they have intersecting accounts of religion with common elements, Kristeva strives to distance herself from Bataille in *Powers of Horror.*[1] In "Bataille and the Sun, or the Guilty Text" (in *Tales of Love*), we see why Bataille can no longer be a major source of inspiration for Kristeva. Bataille affirms the sexual excesses of the maternal desire and names his mother "closer to God" than anything he had seen "through the window of the church."[2] The fourth section makes a general assessment of the extent to which Bataille's thought is relevant for Kristeva after the 1990s. Kristeva reads Bataille, first, as offering the possibility for a revolution in poetic language, then, as a thinker of revolt, but finally, in her later works, as a thinker of transgression, which leads her to distance herself from him. The conspicuous impoverishment in Kristeva's intellectual relation to Bataille deserves attention and needs explanation. As Sara Beardsworth points out, Kristeva's reflections are marked by her worry about the modern values of her own society, and, after the 1990s, these worries seem to increase even more and lead her to concentrate on ways of diminishing psychical suffering.[3] This is when Kristeva returns to the religious and finds in it the possibility of reconciling oneself with the law of the father. The Christian religion becomes the fulfillment of this reconciliation par excellence because it represents God as a good, loving, and forgiving father. Her late reflections on religion make one think Kristeva has moved a great intellectual distance from Bataille: she now sees him as a transgressor, a psychotic, a victim of an excessive mother, and a soul who suffers from the weakness (or absence) of the paternal function. In the final analysis, Bataille's atheological reflections on religion cannot redeem us through reconciliation with a symbolic father. For Bataille, Madame Edwarda, an old and mad prostitute, is God. In contrast, Kristeva turns to a classical and conservative account of religious experience: religion as a relation with the father, who helps reinstitute stability in the subject's personal and social life.

The Significance of Bataille for Kristeva in the 1970s

Bataille, as an intriguing figure of poetic language, pervades two of Kristeva's early works, namely, *Revolution in Poetic Language* and *Polylogue*. As is well known, he was a source of inspiration for members of the *Tel Quel* group (to which Kristeva belonged), in their projects to rethink subjectivity as excess and to explore the political implications of this new notion of subjectivity. In her 1973 essay "Bataille, Experience, and Practice," Kristeva relates the main preoccupation of Bataille's thought to Hegel's *Phenomenology of Spirit*. She argues that Bataille challenges the notion of the subject in Hegel's idealism with a different experience of negativity. In part A of *Phenomenology of Spirit*, "Consciousness," Hegel presents three different shapes of consciousness, each relating to their own correlative objects, which are presumed to exist separately from consciousness. The intentional relation between these shapes of subjectivities and objectivities are mediated by spiritual essences that deploy themselves in a negative movement. In this movement, Hegel's task is to show that the individual subject's particularity is overcome and that subjectivity reveals itself to be the very movement in which the spirit, the universal subject, knows itself. In Kristeva's reading of Bataille, he interrogates what Hegel fails to think in a radical way, that is, the individual subject's relation to negativity. Hegel thought through subjectivity as knowing, but he failed to account for the relation to negativity of the subject as "not knowing" (*non-savoir*). In "Bataille, Experience, and Practice," Kristeva claims that Bataille's new relation to negativity—understood as an experience and a practice—can, at once, escape the nihilism of modernist literature and sketch a new Marxist and dialectical attitude toward subjectivity. Her first interest in Bataille is determined by the fundamental question of structuralist linguistics: How is signification possible? She rethinks the play of signifiers—their dynamic movement in which infinite substitution is possible, their *ration supplémentaire* for the absent center (the absence of a transcendental signified)— as negativity. This negativity would not lend itself to a conceptual determination in terms of an *arche* (origin) or a *telos* (end). For Kristeva, meaning is produced and destroyed by a negativity underlying the signifying of a speaking subject. As Lacan says, "it speaks" (*ça parle*) through the speaking subject. According to Kristeva, "it" not only refers to a movement of the play of signifiers, to their substitution and combination, but the negativity of the movement of signification must also be conceived as a fundamental opening to the nondiscursive real, an economy of life as a heterogeneous movement. This is to say, the early Kristeva turns to Bataille for her attempt to rethink Lacan's structuralist interpretation of the unconscious. Structuralism deprives itself of access to the nondiscursive real; Bataille's rereading of Hegel can provide us with the needed opening. Thus, from Kristeva's point of view, Bataille is the first thinker of this very negativity in which the semiotic elements of meaning make their appearance at the symbolic level. Clearly, Kristeva reads Bataille for her own philosophical project. She believes he is an intellectual resource to whom she can appeal to reinterpret the negativity of the movement of signification while avoiding idealism and teleology. Bataille helps Kristeva move beyond both structuralist and phenomenological accounts of meaning.

It is necessary to start with this background on the intellectual relationship between Bataille and Kristeva because it shows his initial importance to Kristeva. Nevertheless, my focus here is not the question of the speaking subject in relation to the negative movement of signification: instead, I take up the question of how their reflections on religion relate to, and differ from, one another. I do not claim to exhaust all the interesting aspects of their intellectual relationship. Nonetheless, it is to be kept in mind that Kristeva's relation to Bataille has a history and that this history has its own extraordinary moments. In the first phase of Kristeva's relation to Bataille's works, he appears to her as belonging to the group of writers, including Artaud and Mallarmé, who were thinkers of "limit experiences" for her. In such experiences, madness could say itself at the level of consciousness and, in so doing, put the values of modern society into question. Kristeva does not want to celebrate psychosis—as, for example, Deleuze and Guattari did in *Capitalism and Schizophrenia*—because psychosis implies suffering and death by suicide.[4] Her attraction to discourses like Bataille's lies in the way a force or desire pushes language, which is dominated by logic and grammar, to its own critique. This critique amounts to questioning the prevalence of subjectivity as the solid ground of all significations. And, in this period, Kristeva is concerned with describing subjectivity as something that comes into being, and dissolves, in the movement of negativity.

Bataille on Religion

For Bataille, religion has a history and is part of the secret of human existence. In monotheisms—in which God becomes unique, exclusively good, and transcendent—and in onto-theologies that follow from them, this secret increasingly fades into oblivion. I begin by giving Bataille's overall argument in *Theory of Religion* before discussing how religion comes to the foreground as a phenomenon of economy and abjection in *The Accursed Share*. I take *Erotism* to be further developing this idea of the sacred as taboo or abject, by describing the relation between the erotic and the religious in terms of transgression and inner experience. In other words, *Erotism* explores a perspective already opened up in *The Accursed Share*.

Theory of Religion lays out the genesis and development of religion by asking anthropology's fundamental question, which concerns the transition from nature to culture. The humanity of the human originates in this transition, which Bataille locates in the opposition between immanence and transcendence. The world of things, individuals, work, utility, and action transcends the "life of immanence."[5] Originally, humans were animals—living as immanent to nature, still lacking the dimension of transcendence. They became properly human, as distinct from the rest of animal life, by transcending that immanence, thereby constituting the human world. The term "human world," as I use it, not only encompasses the profane world of work and utility but also the sacred world. In *Theory of Religion*, the sacred and the profane realms come into being at once and participate in one and the same dialectical process. Bataille seems to give different accounts of what constitutes transcendence at different moments of his itinerary. I contend that the account in *The Accursed Share* and *Erotism* goes beyond the account in *Theory of Religion*.

Theory of Religion carries out a reflection on transcendence in terms of the use of instruments and work. Work and the consciousness of death are considered as equiprimordial elements that open up a realm of transcendence. In *Theory of Religion*, the secret of religions is the unconscious nostalgia we feel for immanence, our lost intimacy with nature.[6] Immanence is immediacy, sensibility, corporeal communication, and the absence of individuality, whereas transcendence is distinction, separation, individuation, objectivity, subjectivity, and intelligibility. Bataille makes use of these oppositions in order to erase them: his discourse feeds on the awareness that humans, in their very transcendence, are outside as well as inside animality. Therefore, there is no nostalgia for what we have lost; there is instead an unconscious desire for communication with the rest of life. Religion is a symbolic transposition of a sentiment about the internal relations of all living beings. Thus, it gives, at the symbolic level, what we have broken with in the profane world. The sacred world both negates and counterbalances the profane world in which life suffocates from subordination to utility. Broadly speaking, the sacred world has a double function in relation to the profane: it secures the boundaries of the profane world, and it does so precisely by overcoming the profane economy through sovereign mystical experiences. Religion sublates immanent communication to a transcendent symbolic level, functioning to interrupt the world of utility and work and culminating in the dissolution of individuality. Thus, it overcomes the separation of beings from one another. Religion is a mediated experience of primary intimacy with animality, which is the greatest value that man lost in subordinating his life to work and utility. This value is about sovereignty, which gives the possibility of a relation beyond utility—with oneself and with others—that Bataille names "communication."

The second important moment in Bataille's reflection on religion appears in the second volume of *The Accursed Share*. This text can be read as a new attempt to answer the fundamental question asked in *Theory of Religion*. *Theory of Religion* conceived religion as an institution with a temporal origin that is undergoing a development whose different forms can be seen as more or less continuous. In this work, Bataille accepts the equiprimordial consciousness of death and of work as the double source of the sacred and the profane worlds. The novelty of *The Accursed Share* lies in the influence Claude Lévi-Strauss's anthropology has on Bataille's reflection on religion. This perspective is fully developed in *Erotism*. Through Lévi-

Strauss, Bataille realizes that eroticism is the third most important factor, which must be included in his account of human transcendence.[7]

In *The Accursed Share*, Bataille takes history to be the history of man's alienation from his own being. Although he borrows terms from the Marxist tradition, such as "alienation" and "reification," he reinterprets them as "abjection," "abhorrence," "disgust," and so forth. According to this view, alienation starts with abjection and culminates in man's enslavement to the capitalist system—his subordination to work and utility and the enclosing of life within the sterile limits of bourgeois housekeeping. Life's abjection manifests itself in the stringent requirement of sterility, excluding abject things, predominantly human bodies. From a Bataillean perspective, abjection plays a constitutive role in the disciplining of bodies, the rigidifying of their borders, their gendering and racialization, and the exclusions that follow therefrom. Abjection serves to reify bodies in order to subordinate them to productive work. Disgust from the heterogeneity of life itself precedes the abjection of bodies that do not conform to the world of work and utility, and this also accords with the Foucauldian idea that capitalism and the modern power feed on the life energy of the living body. Abjection contributes to securing the limits of a world of work, which is also a world of class difference and oppression; however, this is not the only level on which it functions. As the profane and the sacred worlds are co-original and belong together, abjection must also play a constitutive role on the level which the sacred is constituted.

Bataille analyzes history in economic terms, focusing on the necessary consumption of "the accursed share" in diverse historical worlds. Marx was right to claim that economic laws govern history; however, he did not have the insight that sovereign consumption, not production, is the value of all values. As is well known, Bataille inverts Marx, turning to a study of the means and relations of consumption rather than those of production. His political economy presents history as a domain in which the boundaries of immanence and transcendence change unceasingly and are constantly redrawn. In this very shifting of boundaries, the history of the profane world intersects with the history of the sacred and cannot be separated from it. Bataille's anthropology pays special attention to the intervals in which consumption takes an excessive form of destruction and wasting away, thus suspending the orderliness of the profane world of work. Although influenced by Marcel Mauss's reflections on potlatch, his task is not limited to reflecting on the structures or relations of exchange that underlie society. In his attempt to rethink the economy of consumption as an economy of life, he goes beyond the limits of anthropology toward an ontological analysis.

In *The Accursed Share*, Bataille understands "general economy" as an economy of energy based on the exuberance of living matter as a whole. The fundamental problem of general economy, namely, excess resources, shows itself from the point of view of general existence.[8] The general existential problem is posed by the essence of the biomass, which must "constantly destroy (consume) a surplus of energy."[9] "The accursed share" is an economic term with the utmost ontological significance: it refers to the excess energy invested in the growth of an organism, but—when growth has reached its limit—it must, willingly or unwillingly, be spent without profit, gloriously or catastrophically. Clearly, the basic axiom of Bataille's political economy concerns the living organism, the body, which is both grounded in and receives its excess from the play of energy on the globe. The body's belonging to the play of energy on the earth underlies human reality. Bataille argues that life, as the source of the bodily forces that sustain the worldliness of the world, cannot fit within the boundaries these structures draw for it. The inscription of the body within the play of energy in earth and world, domains of excess it cannot always cope with, is the ontological starting point for an understanding of Bataille's distinction between "general economy" and "restricted economy."

In the first volume of *The Accursed Share*, religions, too, are reflected upon in terms of this general economy. Bataille conceives religious experience, within this economic and ontological framework, as an experience of sovereignty. The question of sovereignty concerns the humanity of the human being. The human being's essence cannot be found in its striving to remain in being, to consume merely to satisfy needs. A being limited by its most stringent needs is not only less than a human being but is, by definition, an impossible living being, a paradox. Consumption in the general sense is crucial for an understanding of man's essence. Man's most important issue is not to persevere in being, having a guaranteed future for its needs, but "sovereignty." Sovereignty is not about being self-sufficient: mastery over the economic conditions of life could still be slavery, if it sacrifices all life to work. Sovereignty is a consciousness of self that is made possible by the expenditure of energy, consumption beyond the care and worry for survival. In that sense, limit experiences—such as erotic experience, sacrifice, laughter, and death—are consumptions. These experiences are "sovereign experiences" not by their explosive nature as expenditures of energy without return but by their function to make possible a new relationship with life, which the profane world schematizes. Sovereign experiences transgress the boundaries of the profane world; as interruptions, they are the moments that make the world of utility dissolve: they are ways of exiting the world even while still belonging there. Thus, sovereignty is a belonging without belonging to the human world of work—transgression. For example, the phenomenon of festival is the negation of attachment to the profane world, a temporary suspension of the validity of the laws of restricted economy, which thereby liberates the sacred from calculation. Insofar as the sacred is the refusal of subordination, entrance to it will be by insurrection or revolt rather than submission. One cannot belong to the sacred by surrendering to the ways of the world, which compel the majority to give themselves to servitude. The relation to the sacred has a dimension of revolt, which is why the sacred is the negation of negation. While this double negation does not return us to the originary realm of immanence, it does reinforce our connection with life as the ground of existence.

Given that the second volume of *The Accursed Share* is obsessed with figures of abjection, the question of abjection's role in Bataille's account of religion must be addressed. Even though various figures of abjection dominate this volume, the relation of the religious to the abject is only generally framed, and Bataille focuses more on the relevance of abjection to the constitution of the profane world. In modernity, man experiences himself as a subject who knows a world of objects. The predominance of the theoretical relation to objects makes the subject overlook his own corporeal being. Enclosing the body's natural functions inside walls indicates our shame in the face of fluidity.[10] The body is shameful; we pretend nothing flows from it. Characterizing as abject all that exits the body is a necessary condition for the body's objectification; this objectification conditions the invention of the subject as a separate, rational being capable of disembodied vision. The abjection of the living body as such—and, arguably, the female body, bodies that would be unintelligible according to heteronormativity, and the mother's body to which the event of birth refers—is inscribed in the very structure of subjectivity, as modernity conceives it. Bataille thinks subjectivity, as constituted by abjection, is tied to the loss of sovereignty and to humanity's surrendering of the naked surplus of existence to restricted economy.

In *The Accursed Share*, abjection lies at the foundation of restricted economy. It is accounted for with reference to two limit experiences. We feel disgust for what remains of consumption, its corrupting residues, the excremental, the putrefying garbage, the corpses of animals and humans, which are abandoned to nature without sacralization; the biological material, which the natural processes decompose before its absorption in the global play of energy. In that sense the abject is the organic matter as presently inhabited by death and productive of other forms of natural life. In the decaying abject, life is on the threshold of reawakening: one form of life transforms itself into others through death. This is the movement of the organic life in its general economy. Second, not only death but also birth is abject because the event of birth involves another transition from one form of individual life into another. Bataille says: "It is clear that we are sorry we came from life, from meat, from a whole bloody mess. We might think, if need be, that living matter on the very level at which we separate ourselves from it is the privileged object of our disgust."[11] Birth and death are similar movements; the only radical difference between them lies in the fact that the being that gives life to another being may endure the genesis of another living organism. However, the death of the parent organism is implicated in the birth of the offspring. Both corpse and its sexual organs are abject, and Bataille thinks they are not without relation:

> In theory, the sexual organs have nothing to do with the disintegration of the flesh: indeed their function places them at the opposite pole. Yet, the look of the exposed inner mucosa makes one think of wounds about to suppurate, which manifest the connection between the life of the body and the decomposition of the corpse.[12]

The abject is horrifying, yet it is the other side of desire, as "horror conceals always a possibility of desire."[13]

There is an anxiety to abjection, an anxiety caused by the failure to separate neatly life and death into discrete events. Abjection is the limit experience in which life presents a challenge to the human world. The restricted economy of the human world is governed by the principle of the radical separation of life from death. On the other hand, the general economy of life shows the illusory pretence of that separation. Abjection is a reactive feeling we have when faced with the interlacing of life and death. We cannot reckon with the fact that life comes from death. "One day this living world will pullulate in my dead mouth,"[14] writes Bataille, thus denouncing the state of mind that is anxious to protect the limits of the profane world; our effort to keep sterile life separate from filth is not only a separation of life from death but also a refusal to attest to, and affirm, their intimate relation. The abject is a domain of not knowing, a domain in which immanence returns via the remains of the human world.

Although Bataille's description of abjection in *The Accursed Share* aims to establish that it is part of transcending the profane world, that the religious realm is opened by the very ambiguity of the desired and horrifying abject belongs within the general framework. *Erotism* supplements *The Accursed Share*, putting an account of religion in the foreground. Its fundamental thesis is: "Whatever is the subject of prohibition is basically sacred."[15] The relation to an abject thing seems different from the relation to a sacred thing, for the latter is an object of respect whereas the former is not. Both experiences are horror in the face of a forbidden object.[16] Bataille clarifies that religion, more than being about rules, is about transgressing rules. Terror and nausea are affects that accompany transgression. "Sin is transgression condemned."[17] Furthermore, Bataille shows how mystic experience (divine love) intersects with erotic experience (sensual love). Erotic experience has the irreducible ambiguity of accommodating both horror and desire, which are also present in the spirit's mystical experience. There is no eroticism without prohibitions and their transgression. Likewise, we become aware of our unity with the sacred world by way of violent agitation, prohibition, and transgression. Hence, eroticism and religion are understood in terms of "contradictory experiences of taboos and transgressions," which *Erotism* refers to as "inner experience" and which is not "an experience of clear consciousness."[18] Nevertheless, the way the abject relates to religion is radically different from the way it relates to the human world of work. Abjection helps rigidify the borders of the profane world by separating life from death, but the sacred realm is par excellence a fluidity of life and death, of transformation of life into death and death into life. In the religious sphere, we are fascinated with those transformations that horrify us in the world of human affairs. Indeed, for Bataille, religion is not the revelation of a divine being who is creator of all things, nor is it something to believe in; rather, it signifies the general movement of life, in which life and death pass into each other.

Kristeva on Religion

In the 1980s, Kristeva publishes a trilogy—*Powers of Horror* (1980), *Tales of Love* (1983), and *Black Sun* (1984)—in which narcissism is her main focus. It is in this framework that she starts to reflect on what religions may signify when interpreted from a psychoanalytic perspective. In *In the Beginning Was Love: Psychoanalysis and Faith*, an essay from 1984, Kristeva makes clear that she is interested in religion as an analyst. She reads the Credo (Symbol of Apostles) not as a representation of Christian dogma but as signifying phantasms that reveal desires or essential traumatisms.[19] In doing so, she follows Freud, who, in *Totem and Taboo*, translates religious expressions into symbolic expressions of the desires and frustrations of the human psyche. Kristeva contributes to this strategy by distinguishing between the semiotic and the symbolic. Religious significations are the semiotic manifestations of impulses at the level of symbolic forms. In other words, processes of signification that precede and escape the subject (in the classical sense, as a conscious subject of intentional acts) are at work in religious significations.

These are unconscious processes that signify desire, in its intimate connection with the horror of death and against the law that prohibits its satisfaction. Religious ecstasy upsurges from the negative movement of desire, which creates and dissolves a transient subjectivity. It is noteworthy that, in contrast to Freud (who accounted for the prohibition of incest in terms of patricide), Kristeva argues that the sacred has its source in abjection, which calls for the primacy of symbolic matricide.

How is Kristeva's predominantly psychoanalytic approach related to Bataille's philosophical anthropology? As I have noted, her take on religion is influenced by Freud's interpretation of it in *Totem and Taboo*, which is a fascinating reflection that makes ethnology and psychoanalysis illuminate each other. As Foucault notes in *The Order of Things*, these two disciplines are countersciences, which he contrasts with human sciences that concern themselves with the ways men *represent* their relation to life, labor, and language to themselves. Psychoanalysis and ethnology differ from such human sciences as economy, sociology, and philology by making contact with forms of human finitude (specifically, law, desire, and death), that is, with the unrepresentable limits of the human experience of existence.[20] Even though Bataille's reflection draws more heavily from anthropology and Kristeva's from psychoanalysis, the difference between them is not sharp. Kristeva sees the psyche as an interface between the individual and the social world. Psychoanalysis and anthropology are intersecting discourses. Religion is a realm of macrophantasms; psychoanalysis investigates how such macrophantasms reflect microphantasms. For example, Kristeva sees a sexual desire that denounces itself by deforming its object in prayer.[21] Broadly speaking, Bataille's and Kristeva's reflections on religion, with their focus on the abject as the source of the sacred, are akin because they both make contact with the above-mentioned forms of human finitude. Moreover, this contact appears in religious signification: religion is not a realm of representations but of significations.

Nevertheless, the role Kristeva assigns to Bataille in *Powers of Horror*, his strictly restricted place in her text, is puzzling. She ignores Bataille's obsession in *The Accursed Share* with terms such as "disgust," "abhorrence," "repulsion," "repugnance," and "abomination" and relegates his reflections on the co-origination of the profane and the sacred in abjection to "anthropologists' findings." Problematically, Kristeva chooses to ignore the philosophy of life, the heterology orienting Bataille's relation to those findings. She evokes his name three times, but she only makes one serious reference to his work. Her third chapter, entitled "From Filth to Defilement," begins with an epigraph taken from his essay "Abjection et les formes misérables."[22] Written in 1933, this essay does not directly concern the relation of abjection to religion but aims at a political analysis of abjection. I shall briefly discuss it here, in order to raise the question whether Kristeva gives a reductive, if not distorted, treatment of Bataille's notion of abjection.[23] Indeed, in *Powers of Horror*, Bataille's name marks a crucial moment that enables us to distinguish between Bataille's and Kristeva's treatments of abjection. Kristeva herself comes to a limit: a limit forming part of her description of abjection, in which it is difficult to recognize the border between self and the other and, in this case, that marks the border between Kristeva and Bataille. She refers to this essay in order to demarcate her account of abjection from Bataille's. There, Bataille reads the forces of fascism as forces of abjection and, thereby, responds to a historical context marked by the rise of fascism. He provides an analysis of oppression through abjection, noting that oppression cannot be explained by immediate coercion. The oppressed classes are first constituted as wretched, miserable, and abject by the prohibition of contact. He then asks how these classes can subvert fascism and protect themselves from it. It is remarkable that Kristeva abstracts from this context when quoting Bataille: "Abjection . . . is merely the inability to assume with sufficient strength the imperative act of excluding the abject things (and that act establishes the foundation of social existence)."[24]

Here, Kristeva focuses on "the inability to assume with sufficient strength the act of excluding the abject things." She makes this incapacity a structural part of the logic of prohibition founding the abject and draws support from Bataille for this point. She writes:

> The logic of prohibition, which founds the abject, has been outlined and made explicit by a number of anthropologists concerned with the defilement and its sacred function in so-called primitive societies. And yet Georges Bataille remains the only one, to my knowledge, who has linked the production of the abject to the weakness of that prohibition, which, in other respects, necessarily constitutes each social order.[25]

Kristeva attributes weakness to the prohibition, but Bataille understands that the failure to assume the imperative to exclude abject things is a result of the social and material conditions of the poor (if not a consequence of physical and mental incapacities). The miserable do not have the material and social conditions necessary to obey the prohibition. They are dirty because they have no means to be clean. For support, Bataille refers to a child who cannot be blamed for appearing ignoble. One must attend to the rest of Kristeva's reference to Bataille to learn why and how she demarcates herself from him: "The act of exclusion has the same meaning as social or divine sovereignty, but it is not located on the same level; it is precisely located in the domain of things and not, like sovereignty, in the domain of persons. It differs from the latter in the same way that anal eroticism differs from sadism."[26] Kristeva interprets these sentences to mean that, for Bataille, abjection concerns the subject/object relationship and not the subject/other (subject) relationship. However, Bataille does not say that abjection does not play out in relations between people. His overall argument is that the abjection of things underlies and makes possible the abjection of persons. Abjection establishes both the individual sovereignty of the oppressor on the social level and divine sovereignty. The distinction between "anal eroticism" and "sadism" is central to accounting for the difference between the levels on which abjection of people may occur. Anal eroticism refers to the oppressor's exclusion of the miserable (or wretched) classes to the level of abject things. These things have no worth and therefore can simply be cleared away. In sadism, on the other hand, the oppressed other is also desired in person, which is why sadism is divine sovereignty—beyond the sovereignty of social oppression. Although abjection of things founds both the profane and the sacred (divine) worlds, divine sovereignty cannot be reduced to the abjection of things because in sadism the other is not reduced to a thing: hence, the religious realm must also be understood in terms of a specific type of abjection that operates between people. This explains why, in *Erotism*, erotic experience plays an exemplary role in shedding light on the religious.

Kristeva closes the political and religious horizons of Bataille's essay in order to argue for her specific thesis about abjection, which enables her to distinguish her position from his. Kristeva's discussion of abjection emphasizes that in abjection the "I" comes to a limit at which it gives birth to itself through "the violence of sobs, of vomit."[27] I extricate myself from the abject at the limits of my condition as living being. Hence, abjection is both about a loss of identity, system, and order and about identifying oneself through separation. Ultimately, primal repression "appears through the gaps of secondary repression."[28]

The contrast between this structural analysis of the human psyche and Bataille's historicopolitical analysis of fascism is sharp. In *Powers of Horror*, Céline—whose compromise with fascism is a historically known fact—is the main literary figure, and abjection supplies Kristeva with the theoretical framework for interpreting Bataille's work. It is quite puzzling that, in developing a theoretical framework for Céline, she marginalizes Bataille both as a thinker of abjection and as a thinker of fascism. For example, she does not even mention his 1933 text "La structure psychologique du fascism." One may think Kristeva distances herself from Bataille because she understands herself as thinking through abjection in the subject's relation to the other and, more specifically, the *mother*.[29] At the level of personal archeology, the original event of abjection occurs in the mother-child dyad: "With our earliest attempts to release the hold of *maternal* entity even before ex-isting outside of her, thanks to the autonomy of language. It is a violent, clumsy breaking away, with the constant risk of falling back under the sway of a power as securing as it is stifling."[30] In *Powers of Horror*, abjection is the very experience that precedes the subject-object divide and conditions the coming into being of both subjectivity and objectivity. The child must abject the mother and separate himself from her. The constitution of the child's corporeal subjectivity and the objectivation of the objects, self-relation, and object relation follow from that separation. Now, these remarks could imply that, at the foundation of the fascistic identificatory exclusion of other human beings, one finds the abjection of the mother, but I am not sure Kristeva really makes this claim. And, if she does, then she takes a political risk: if abjection is structural to the human psyche, then fascism, racism, sexism, religious discrimination, and such would be necessary to social identification.

Let me return to Kristeva's reading of religion. For her, religion confronts us with the unrepresentable limits of the psychic experience. In "Reading the Bible" in *New Maladies of the Soul* (1993), she argues that structuralist readings of the Bible are silent about the dimensions in which religion gives expression to the limit experiences of suffering and desire.[31] These various experiences refer, in the last analysis, to desire for the mother, which must be renounced because of the prohibition of incest. She attends to other forms of prohibitions, such as those concerning nutrition in Judaism, and connects this anxiety for purity with the primordial preoedipal horror during the child's separation from the mother. The religious limit experience sublates the moment of the abjection of the mother, which is the original experience of ambiguity when desire and horror (disgust) are present at the same time. Abjection gives birth to the mother as a being that is both debased and exalted. Kristeva notes that anthropologists, including Bataille, are aware of this ambiguity as a characteristic of taboo, but—avoiding him in delicate ways—she relies instead on Mary Douglas. Douglas focuses on the purification rituals that see menstrual blood and excrement as pollutants. On the basis of Douglas's findings, Kristeva explores the role of the maternal in the genesis of the sacred. Indeed, Freud had already suggested that excrement, as that which separates from the body, could signify birth, the original event of separation from the mother.

Like excrement, the mother poses a threat to the identity of the body, to its autonomous corporeal limits. Failure to separate oneself from one's mother implies death and destruction, and—in a society where the paternal function is no longer strong—the whole society feels threatened by the abject. As Sara Beardsworth argues, "The presence of purification rituals in a society . . . points to the weakness or demise of the symbolic function, paternal function."[32]

Kristeva's reading of religion irreducibly features an emphasis on the essential possibility religion offers us. Religion, as a symbolic system, is fundamentally about the law of the father, which is why it offers us the possibility of reconciling with that law. For Freud, our civilization is neurotic, and Lacan explains that we must enter the symbolic system as castrated subjects because the privileged signifier of the phallus organizes desire. Kristeva shows that the abjection of the mother precedes the dialectic of need, demand, and desire—that is, her constitution as an object of desire. We suffer not only because we become aware of our own limits in the castrating discovery that our desires go further than our powers but also because our very identity is constituted by a threat. The mother gives life, but death also comes from her as she threatens the child with psychological and emotional absorption. Kristeva argues that a relation to a loving and forgiving father may contribute to our struggle with narcissistic sufferings: although she questions the role of the feminine in religion and understands the sacred in terms of abjection, at root, religion offers the possibility of psychically reworking the relation with the father. She is convinced the subject suffers much more without the means for a loving relation with the father. Religion offers such means at the symbolic level. In *In the Beginning Was Love: Psychoanalysis and Faith*, she writes:

> More than any other religion, Christianity has unraveled the symbolic *and* physical importance of the paternal function in human life. Identification with this third party separates the child from its jubilant but destructive physical relationship with its mother and subjects it to another dimension, that of symbolization, where frustration and absence, language unfolds.[33]

Kristeva's priority is to find the cultural resources that may help the subject achieve psychic well-being by offering the possibility of becoming a speaking subject. Religion can be such a resource because it makes it possible to affirm the relation with the father, with his law. Inasmuch as Kristeva's interpretation of religion culminates in a well-known psychological affirmation of religion (religion offers comfort through a relation with an almighty father), she feels the need to distance her own interpretation of religion from Bataille's. This need is apparent in *Tales of Love*, which includes a short piece on Bataille's *My Mother*. At stake in this short essay, entitled "Bataille and the Sun, or the Guilty Text," is precisely Bataille's affirmation of his relation with his mother—more sharply, his deification of her. Bataille writes:

> Most often it seems to me that I adore my mother. Could I have ceased to adore her? Yes: God is what I adore. And yet I do not believe in God. Am I then crazy? What I only know: If I laughed in the midst of tortures, fallacious as this might be, I would answer the question I asked while looking at my mother, the one my mother asked while looking at me. What is there to laugh about, in this world, outside of God?[34]

Bataille's identification of his mother with a God in whom he does not believe but sovereignly affirms in laughter is even clearer here: "Death, in my eyes, was no less divine than the sun, and my mother, through her crimes, was closer to God than anything I had seen through the window of the church."[35] In this brief text on Bataille, Kristeva takes him to be a psychotic going through the turmoil of a passion at the sight of "the naked, sublime, or disgusting body of the loved one."[36] Bataille's meditation on the sublime is a "paradoxical meditation": God is revealed through obscenity or destruction, a "deadly, or simply painful and abject medium." For Kristeva, Bataille's God is the almighty feminine libido who knows no limits. Affirming such a feminine libido generates disgust with the self, guilt, solitude, and suicide. Kristeva categorically refuses to give any value to Bataille's interpretation of this libido as God. For Bataille, the self attains sovereign joyful ecstasy in adoring such a God, and, in that adoration, the general economy of life that sustains all beings is affirmed. Although she never confesses it, Kristeva's problem is that religion appears through the transgression of the father's law in Bataille. The name of the father is entirely absent from Kristeva's discussion of Bataille's understanding of religion in *My Mother*. She does not comment on the father's insignificance to the adoration of God for this text. She repudiates Bataille's text without saying a word about the absence of the father. One might say that what irritates her in Bataille is not only the father's absence but also the denial of religion as *re-ligare* to the father. Her silence about the father's absence affirms her faith in the father's protective power against the mother's potential dangers. "Bataille and the Sun, or the Guilty Text" marks Kristeva's break from Bataille's thought and explains why she refers to Bataille less in her later works.

Transgression, Revolution, and Revolt

What are the political implications of Bataille's thought for Kristeva? Her reading of Bataille shifts from a politics of revolution (which is now impossible) into a politics of revolt (which is becoming meaningless) and leaves behind just a politics of transgression (which is already obsolete).[37]

For Bataille, the transgression, as erotic experience of the law of restricted economy, reveals the truth of existence as communication. In *Inner Experience*, the negativity of communication leads me to renounce my *ipse* and to reject to submit to knowledge an erotic encounter with a fellow being (*semblable*).[38] Erotic communication articulates itself in language as poetry, generosity of silence, or a sacrifice of words rather than as logical discourse.[39] Bataille thinks of "inner experience" as a relation with the heterogeneous in terms of both "revolt" and "revolution." He insists that revolution can be otherwise than a restitution of homogeneity through abjection, and Kristeva shares his thinking of revolution formulated in terms of the heterogeneous. In the 1970s Kristeva is a Maoist for whom the renewal of social and communal existence means "revolution." In 1973, she already outlines her major interest in the relations of sexuality-language-thought as an interest in the possibility of social communication. In contrast to depictions of Bataille as an extravagant thinker of human sexuality who has an unconvincing, even absurd view of politics, in the 1970s Kristeva sees Bataille as a political thinker. Note, however, that the term "revolt," which pervades Kristeva's writings in the 1990s, occurs only once in "Bataille, Experience, and Practice," and it is not used in the same sense. Kristeva often questions the revolutionary potential of her account of signification.

In the 1980s, she gives up her aspirations for revolution and—with the trilogy *Powers of Horror, Black Sun*, and *Tales of Love*—turns to an analysis of narcissism. Bataille remains a source of inspiration for Kristeva's theorization of the sacred, religion, erotic, abjection, language, revolt, and such, but now she disavows his legacy and seeks to distance herself from his thought. As we have shown, both Bataille and Kristeva take the idea that the sacred is originally that which is dirty, the taboo, seriously. They share an interest in "abjection": for Kristeva abjection primarily refers to the event of the separation and identification of the corporeal subject; for Bataille, abjection is part of the movement of transcendence through which the profane and the sacred worlds come into being. From Bataille's point of view, Kristeva's drives and their semiotic fluidity flow with the erotic energy that pervades the general economy of life. His task is to show, against Hegel, that religion cannot be submitted to the philosophy of the concept, absolute knowing, but it helps us rethink the subjectivity of the subject.

Likewise, in *Sense and Non-Sense of Revolt*, Kristeva challenges Lacan by saying that, even though psychic life may have been organized by language, we cannot reduce its dynamism to its symbolism.[40]

Their continuity of thought is probably best assessed by tracking the term "heterogeneous" in Kristeva's text. Doubting whether the relation to the heterogeneous can produce a revolution, Kristeva thematizes the difference between "revolt" and "revolution" in *Sense and Non-Sense of Revolt*. Having already given up a reflection on revolution in the 1980s, Kristeva makes another distinction between "religious revolt" and "aesthetic revolt" in the 1990s and claims that "religious revolt" is no longer viable.

The question arises whether Bataille becomes a thinker of revolt for Kristeva in the 1990s. In *Sense and Non-Sense of Revolt*, she says that the twentieth century is pervaded by the figure of the intrinsically contesting intellectual and that erotic literature is a subversion of that contestation. She makes Bataille's *The Blue of Noon* a significant example of that literature.[41] While she finds this "transgression" fascinating, Kristeva questions whether it still makes sense at the end of the century. Why is Bataillean transgression no longer viable? "The dialectic of law-transgression" or "the logic of interdiction-transgression" depends upon a space of pure and stable values; indeed, this logic or dialectic organizes the religious space and arts that stem from it.[42] We no longer have such a pure space of values: "transgression" is appropriated by the capitalist market economy in order to transform us into better consumers, and the paternal function is in peril. According to Kristeva, religion provides smooth, nonviolent phantasms, charged with a certain dose of aggression, and flattens the obscure desire to enjoy revolt. In a sense, priests and "horse-boys" are complementary figures that dialectically presuppose each other. In religion, one can satisfy one's side of "horse-boy,"[43] but "religious revolt" has now become impossible because the paternal function is rapidly weakening.[44]

It is remarkable that Kristeva ties her concept of revolt to Freud's genealogical account of the symbolic system. Revolt occurs in a symbolic system that implies patricide, the abjection of the mother or the evacuation of the feminine, the fundamental social contract between brothers, and the experience of the sacred. It signifies because of this prehistory, which Freud conjectures in *Totem and Taboo*. At times, Kristeva speaks as if "revolt" appeases the excluded brothers, who do not feel they have sufficiently benefitted from the social contract, and, if the revolt is successful, may result in their inclusion in the system. In sum, "religious revolt" gives the possibility of reworking and repeating the relation with paternal authority. At stake in "revolt" is a radical experience, a reorganization of our psychic life. Revolt is not a return to the past but a displacement, a modification, of the past.

Its temporality is that of the future anterior, for it is a "reformulation of our psychic life."[45] Revolt is defined as a process of signifying (*un procès de significance*) of the speaking being, opening such a being to its own being by a reformulation of its psychic life. Kristeva connects what we can call a struggle for recognition between brothers with a general semiology (her account of the semiotic break and fluidity within the symbolic). The point is that revolt thus organizes psychic life and helps renew political and social institutions, making them more inclusive.

In *Sense and Non-Sense of Revolt*, Kristeva concerns herself with the possibility-impossibility of a revolt beyond the dialectic in which transgression presupposes the purity of law. Her objection to the grid "law-transgression" explains why Bataille is not a central figure here and why Kristeva prefers to ask the question of revolt of other literary figures or thinkers, such as Aragon, Sartre, and Barthes. Could not Bataille be taken as a thinker of "aesthetic revolt?" Unlike the early Kristeva, the later Kristeva seems reluctant to see Bataille's practice of signification as providing the resources for renewing the symbolic system. While his influence on her was substantial in the past, in the 1990s she seems to situate him as a thinker of transgression and not of "aesthetic revolt." As her worry about nihilism grows, she comes to suspect the very possibility of any revolt. Modern nihilism has transformed our relation to law and made us indifferent to our own psychic life; new patients appear with new sicknesses of the soul. Thus, in the twenty-first century, Kristeva sees Bataille as a historical, even nostalgic, figure of transgression from the mid-twentieth century.

Let me remark that this supports a poor reading of Bataille. Bataille continues to inspire contemporary critical theory but is often oversimplified as a thinker of "transgression" who acknowledges the necessity for the existence of prohibitions and sexual taboos and claims that their transgression helps the realization of human potential.[46] He is also presented as pursuing an erotic experience, understood in purely heterosexual terms, that makes possible an experience of the totality of being.[47] Such characterizations of his thought enclose Bataille within the simple grid of "law-transgression" and set his complicated philosophical relation to Hegel's idealism aside, entirely neglecting the question of signification and language in its relation to negativity, which is central to Bataille's literary efforts. Such oversimplifications have no understanding or account of what is so challenging in Bataille, namely, his writing. In contrast to the trend of underrepresenting Bataille's thought in order to dismiss it as extravagant and politically useless, Kristeva's early reading of Bataille is still important for a more philosophically interesting view of his thought. She concentrates on the "immediate experience" in Bataille and understands it as the nondiscursive, immediate experience of life that already exceeds the unified subject. She is interested in whether this nonknowledge can be an affirmative moment in the process of signification and serve to question the power relations of social structures. She holds that the semiotic fluidity of the forces within the corporeal being that lives within a social and familial world can enable, or motivate, a discursive expression in the symbolic. For her, Bataille's writings are valuable because he both acknowledges the thetic break and offers an outlet from the level preceding it. Thus, his writings provide resources for the renewal of social and communal existence. This reading is attractive because she focuses on the question of meaning/signification, taking his contestation of Hegel's idealism (by reopening the problem of the relation of lived experience to language) into account, and then addresses the problem of a social and political transformation of human existence in the world. She reflects on Bataille's inner experience insofar as it involves an intersecting of sexuality and thought. In *Revolt She Said*, she remarks that French thought is, in general, characterized by corporality and sexuality. Bataille is one of these French thinkers who take sexual experience in its copresence with thought into account. Kristeva's characterization of French thought in general applies a fortiori to Bataille: "a strange valorization of a very particular psychic life, inasmuch as it is sustained by sexual desire and rooted in bodily needs."[48] The task of such a valorization is not to deny transcendence, which it exhausts, but to make it incarnate and bring "such incarnate transcendence back into meaning."[49] As Kristeva says in 2002, Bataille interpreted erotic experience in terms of a nonreligious sacred, but this elaboration of sexuality was a way of liberating speech in order to join private enjoyment (*jouissance*) to public happiness.[50] Nonetheless, some of her later remarks on Bataille may also reinforce simply dismissing Bataille's thought. It seems to me that she now seeks redemption in art and psychoanalysis, and what she describes as "aesthetic revolt" sounds like a return to romanticism.

Bataille, Teilhard de Chardin, and the Death of God

ALLAN STOEKL

It is well known that Georges Bataille, already by the 1930s, was a major proponent in France of the notion of the "death of God." And since he also was a strong proponent of the rereading of Nietzsche—at a time when many French readers assumed that Nietzsche was simply a "fascist" philosopher—one can assume that Bataille's mortal God was largely derived from Nietzsche. But what does Bataille mean, aside from a quick and too easy reference to Nietzsche, when he writes of divine mortality? What are the larger political, ethical, and philosophical stakes of his position? Most important, what might the interest of Bataille's death of God be in an age of poststructuralist and postmodern concerns with the *virtual*? I would like first to consider some of the larger implications of Bataille's divine mortality, especially in the context of modern Protestant theology, and then turn to a surprising connection with a Catholic theologian who was Bataille's contemporary—Pierre Teilhard de Chardin—to consider the ways in which the Bataille-Teilhard connection allows us to think of atheology in the era of the virtual.

Mark C. Taylor, in his compelling recent book *After God*, notes the strong public fascination in the English-speaking world, in the 1960s, with a "death of God" theology.[1] Taylor notes that an issue of *Time* was devoted to this topic in 1966, and, no doubt, the *frisson* offered by the awareness of a divine mortality harmonized nicely with the contemporaneous challenges posed to political and social orthodoxies by writers, film makers, rock musicians, and so on. The so-called fundamentalist view of God so typical of American religiosity, it was assumed by the editors of *Time*, was being severely challenged by a rather exotic and paradoxical theology that announced not God's centrality—after all, his very trustworthiness is proclaimed on American coins and banknotes ("In God We Trust")—but his mortality. To challenge God, then, was of clear social and political import. Taylor notes that much of this concern was fueled by several eloquent books written by the Protestant theologian Thomas J. J. Altizer. Altizer wrote, in his 1966 book *The Gospel of Christian Atheism*:

> Refusing either to deny the Word or to affirm it in its traditional form, a modern and radical Christian is seeking a totally incarnate Word. When the Christian Word appears in this, its most radical form, then not only is it truly and actually present in the world but it is present in such a way as to be real and active nowhere else. No longer can faith and the world exist in mutual isolation: neither can now be conceived as existing independently of the other.[2]

We realize that in fact the death of God in Altizer is no such thing: it is merely, as Taylor would call it, the Hegelian option, in which "the Infinite is immanent in the finite and religion is a feeling of primal unity, which closely approximates the enjoyment of art. . . . The end of history is an organic whole in which every person becomes a member of an ethical community."[3] Against this is the tradition of Kierkegaard, where God is "infinitely and qualitatively different."[4]

God is only relatively dead, then, in "death of God" theology. He is nevertheless quite present, immanent, if we see him in every one of our daily practices and judgments. In this sense the immanent, "dead" God will also be a political God, one not far removed from the divine motor of liberation theology and the Catholic Worker movement.

This Protestant Hegelian tradition certainly influenced Bataille—as we'll see, there is a major rewriting of Hegel in Bataille—but the French tradition of the death of God, long preceding Zarathustra's proclamations, is also very important. This tradition sets us on another track, one taking us away from the immanent/transcendent opposition and leading us toward what I will call, by the end of this essay, the "virtual" death of God. This French tradition argues for the radical absence of God, his *fictionality.* God doesn't exist as immanent presence in our lives, and he simply doesn't "exist."

He is, instead, a fiction, a con job, a lie. This argument was very strong during the French Revolution; it followed from Enlightenment authors such as d'Holbach and La Mettrie, radical materialists who were content to argue that fully explicable means alone caused the rise of physical beings and conscious minds. A number of revolutionaries actually sought to disband the Church and establish "Temples of Reason" that celebrated the absence of God and the overwhelming importance of that which is, apparently, least divine: human reason. The Marquis de Sade pushed this tendency furthest, arguing that the only true pleasure in life is physical (in this he followed d'Holbach) and that physicality arose from following the dictates of Nature, which commanded violent pleasure, such as murder (in order to repopulate continuously the earth—not necessarily with humans). And not only murder, but the ever-repeated murder of a fictitious God in and through blasphemous orgasm.

Bataille, like most avant-garde authors of the 1920s and 1930s, was enormously influenced by Sade, and his atheism owed much to the "divine Marquis." Sade's atheism turned on a major feature of Enlightenment reason: its rigorous logic could be construed as a mechanical and efficient thing that functioned, like clockwork, irrespective of human needs and pleasures. Law was for Sade the extreme example of this: law turning in a void, as a program that ignored the needs and desires of citizens, could be seen finding its greatest accomplishment in the Terror of Robespierre. Himself almost becoming a headless victim of the "Incorruptible," Sade on the contrary held that Law, if it were to exist at all, should reflect *only* particular human desires and passions: for this reason laws should be "mild," and murder should be tolerated and even encouraged. For Sade the ultimate physical pleasure was to be found in orgasmic cursing of the nonexistent God—the divine embodiment of Robespierre's harsh laws.[5] Thus there was a conflation early on between Law and (Robespierre's) God; the official God was, for Sade, a cruel, distant figure, torturing and killing humans thanks to an implacable Law. Ironically enough, the Catholic God was linked in Sade's conception to the God of Reason, who was also, then, the God of the Terror; to lose God, who was in the end as fictional as all those purely programmatic laws, one must listen to Nature and do her violent and intensely pleasurable bidding. This alone—the endless death and rebirth cycles of "Nature," aided and abetted by the Sadean villain—would allow the constant regeneration of the earth, and this alone would be to follow the dictates of reason—but this time a passionate reason, not the cold and bloodless reason of the Terror.

Bataille's death of God, then, following Sade, involves an eroticism that touches on, that is even indistinguishable from, death. But he tweaks Sade in that, while affirming the jouissance/death linkage, he ties it to the death of God not as simple absence of God, or as the derision of a God who is a perfect victim only in his fictionality, but as the point at which God is *present* as his *absence* in this eroticized death. In other words, God is the fiction proclaimed by Sade, but, while for Sade he was *only* a fiction, an erotic phantasm, no more real than an inflatable doll, for Bataille he is the space, the eroticized hole, where God is missing but around which everything continues to turn and lose itself. God is not just absent or dead in general, not just a convenient, delectable, and hated fiction; he is the void of his place around which creation is still structured. But precisely because there is no God, any full knowledge or experience of God will be inseparable from an impossible "experience" of eroticism or death—that is, God's radical absence, of the negativity of death-bound and useless pleasure He can no longer serve to limit. It will also be an "experience" of an eroticized philosophy of the death of God *as* fiction (here we are still in Sade territory) but also of the "experience" as a kind of mystical event, since God's absence is not abstract (He is not a mere formal principle of Law, much less a parodic character in a pornographic skit) but is violent and "lived" (to the point of death). This might make Bataille a kind of existentialist, if one could contain this experiential aspect within a constructive model of life, but as Bataille himself points out, his inner experience is neither inner (within a single "person" or "self"), nor is it an experience (a lived event on the part of a limited consciousness or will somehow tied to a finite body).

So for Bataille the death of God is inseparable from the perspective of both a philosophical-structural analysis *and* an erotic fiction. This implies two different genres of text often conflated in Bataille, explicitly or implicitly. One is a rewriting of a philosophical work; the other is a refashioning of an erotic one. And the two categories intermix, leading to a kind of hybrid eroticized philosophy, or to a philosophically tainted eroticism. Here, too, as with the rewriting of Sade, Bataille is working in an eighteenth-century mode, an era in which many works of fiction blended eroticism and philosophy—not just in Sade, in works like his *Philosophy in the Bedroom*, but also in huge bestsellers of the time such as *Theresa the Philosopher* (possibly by the Marquis d'Argens).

For the first type of writing—philosophy that moves into the domain of eroticism—I would cite the "Hegel" section of Bataille's *Inner Experience*.[6] Here I would note the connection Bataille makes between the circularity of Hegelian knowledge, the role in it of vision and the blind spot, and, finally, ecstasy as precisely the point, the blind spot, at which knowledge is lost in nonknowledge.

Bataille first poses the Hegelian endpoint, where the perfect Hegelian reader, reading and "miming" absolute knowledge, becomes God. This ultimate immanence, the point at which one completes the double "circle" of becoming conscious of self (human knowledge) and of becoming everything, results for Bataille not in immense freedom, or deliverance, or blessedness (in the everyday)—as Altizer might argue—but rather in a state of imprisonment. One realizes with anguish that "I know that I would know nothing more than I know now."[7]

The problem is that to become God one must know everything, including that one's knowledge is complete. That's fine, but completeness implies, for Bataille at least, the presence-in-absence of an element that remains outside; if nothing were outside, after all, one could not speak of the complete (hence the finite, the closed circle of knowledge). Bataille draws finitude out of absolute knowledge; in so doing he posits a more radical negativity than that recuperated in the Hegelian system (all the evil, violence, and death necessary for the completion of the circle).[8] Hence circular knowledge depends on definitively exterior negativity that can only be "known" *as* exterior; to complete absolute knowledge one must incorporate a negativity so radical it subverts the possibility of that completion. This protodeconstructive negativity therefore serves as the completion point of the circular dialectic at the very point at which it ruptures it: "absolute knowledge is definitive non-knowledge," Bataille states.[9]

Bataille then shifts metaphors, moving from the circular knowledge that perhaps conjures up images of a completely explored globe to that of an eye. The eye is also, of course, circular, spherical, with an opening in front (the pupil) that lets in light and a point at the back at which that light is focused (the retina). Now we know that for Bataille the novelist the eye is the eroticized body part par excellence; in *Story of the Eye*, Bataille's heroine, Simone, places the enucleated eye of the murdered priest in her private parts, where it continues to stare in a rather uncanny manner. In "Hegel," the eye is perhaps more philosophical than erotic, but we could also say theological, because the completion of its circularity is the very point at which God as totality dies. Bataille writes:

> There is in understanding a blind spot: which is reminiscent of the structure of the eye. In understanding, as in the eye, one can only reveal it with difficulty. But whereas the blind spot of the eye is inconsequential, the nature of understanding demands that the blind spot within it be more meaningful than understanding itself. . . . To the extent that one views in understanding man himself, by that I mean an exploration of what is possible in being, the spot absorbs one's attention: it is no longer the spot which loses itself in knowledge, but knowledge which loses itself in it. In this way existence closes the circle, but it couldn't do this without including the night from which it proceeds only in order to enter it again.[10]

This is the movement that Bataille calls "circular agitation": the completion of the circle, the arrival at knowledge, which by implication is the point of maximum vision, the retina as what it sees, is incessantly reversed in nonknowledge, the impossible perception of what cannot be perceived, known; this is the blind spot of the retina, a blind spot that gets monstrously large and "swallows" the knower, God, in a recalcitrant "night." The completion of the globe of God, man, and knowledge is necessary but also impossible in the sense that this completion is reversed into the blind spot of all the moments of existence that are resistant to knowledge: "poetry, laughter, ecstasy," and presumably eroticism as well, since Bataille compares leaving this "night" to "leav[ing] a girl after love."[11] This process is repeated indefinitely because not only is knowledge reversed (or, using a more Marxian metaphor, inverted) into nonknowledge; by knowing, by writing this process, nonknowledge is itself reversed into knowledge, which is in turn reversed—and so on, to infinity.

One has the sense that Bataille is playing with us: not only is he "miming" Hegel; the "eye" of understanding is his plaything, just as much as the priest's eye is the toy of Simone. He is rolling this eye around, eyeballing it, sticking it in his eye socket and seeing with it, then pulling it out and thoroughly enjoying its blindness, *seeing* its blindness, seeing *only* its blindness from the inside out. And then back in and on again. All that is terribly sexy, especially since, almost like a teenager playing self-suffocation games, he mimes, relives, the greatest consciousness, Hegelian (post-)divine knowledge, and then always again morphs it into a kind of passing-out of God-sanctioned truth, understanding's blackout in ecstasy, orgasm, or whatever. And the risk, the imperative, of death runs through the circle, through the knowledge of the eye as toy, just as it thrills the kid playing with that rope.

So we have these two points, of vision and blindness, which complete the circle while opening it out. One thinks of the oculus of the Pantheon in Rome, now admitting light and illuminating the interior of the temple, now a source only of a darkness that fills and renders unknowable the abode of the gods.

Bataille's erotic text takes a very different direction from Sade's. Rather than invoking a fictional God exclusively *as* fiction, cursing him, and then finding in that the ultimate pleasure, Bataille creates a number of scenarios in which God is invoked, defined, made "present" in the text through the word, incarnated as a character, and *then* is defiled in his nullity. Once again, central to this operation is the principle of the focal point, the node that centralizes divinity only in order to reveal its radical absence. God is not just the central character, the ultimate victim (as he is in Sade) in an erotic fiction; he is and remains the organizing principle, the origin and end of creation, its ultimate knowledge, but all the while absent from that immanent position, dead in the largest sense. He has been sacrificed but his sacrifice always goes on; in the closing movement of the circle, he is over and over sacrificed, put to death in the revelation of his nullity at the very moment the circle always again snaps shut; erotic delirium is limited (put to good use); and knowledge becomes absolute.

Bataille's technique, noted a long time ago by Barthes in his reading of *Story of the Eye*, involves metonymy, the trope by which parts stand in for wholes, always suggesting another whole that in turn is part of another. The story, then, if we can call it that, of the death of God in Bataille is this story of transpositions, of textual drift, of the movement of words beyond their limits.

Bataille's *récit Madame Edwarda* is, along with *Story of the Eye*, perhaps the best-known instance in which the author puts into play eroticism and what we could call the death of God. Early on, in his preface, he sets the terms in relation to each other:

> This story sets in motion, in the plenitude of his attributes, God himself; and this God, nevertheless, is a hooker [*une fille publique*], in every way the same as the others. But what mysticism could not say (at the moment it said it, it failed [*défaillait*]), eroticism says: God is nothing if he is not the going-beyond of God in all senses; in the sense of vulgar being, in that of horror and impurity; finally in the sense of nothingness. . . . We cannot add to language, with impunity, the word that goes beyond words, the word God; at the moment we do it this word, going beyond itself, destroys its limits vertiginously. While it retreats before nothing, it is everywhere where it is impossible to reach it, it itself is an *enormity*.[12]

We might ask at this point what the *fille publique* has to do with a word whose meaning is the destruction of the limits of the word, and of all words. I don't think Bataille is getting at the idea that God is immanent in the prostitute, as He would be in any other living being (in Protestant "death of God" theology). Rather, the link could be the word "enormity," which in French—*énormité*—has the sense of monstrousness. The word God is monstrous not because it indicates a thing, a divinity, that is huge, beyond measure—something we could relate to an esthetics of the sublime—but rather because as a word it destroys the limit of finite, bounded, comprehensible, and useful terms. And the prostitute is God because she, too, violates the limits of socially sanctioned and useful sexuality (the family, sexual and social reproduction, etc.). Madame Edwarda is the incarnation, so to speak, the immanence, of the violation of those limits, even of their overthrow. In this sense, Bataille ties divine prostitution to a kind of "base sacred" that requires the expenditure not of mere money but of the boundaries of stable social order (rather than reaffirming them, as a more conventional sacred would do). Madame Edwarda is God in her death-bound limitlessness.

We face a rather strange situation, then, in that we have a character—the prostitute, Madame Edwarda—who is the incarnation not of God but of the death of God, which is the death of language, of the word. Madame Edwarda is the nodal point in which the limits of language, the limits of the world, the coherent, cold, legal world, are broken, in which the word and the world are revealed as limitless. And once again this is done through the sight of a blind spot, a vision of that which makes all else possible but at the same time stares back as the void in which all is lost.

The narrator, Pierre Angélique, meets Madame Edwarda at a bordello near the rue St. Denis. In front of a crowd of patrons, she immediately singles him out:

> You want to see my "rags" [mes guenilles]?
>
> My hands gripping the table, I turned toward her. Sitting, she held high one splayed-out leg: to better open the slit [la fente], she pulled the skin back with both hands. So the "rags" of Mme Edwarda were looking at me, hairy and pink, full of life like a repugnant octopus. I mumbled softly:
> —Why are you doing that?
> —You can see, she said, I am GOD . . .
> —I'm crazy . . .
> —No, you have to look: look![13]

Later, when she commands him ("in front of the others") to kiss her "living wound" (plaie vive), her nude thigh caresses his ear, and he seems to hear "the sound of the sea, you hear the same sound putting your ear next to large shells."[14]

The narrator, then, is caught, before Madame Edwarda, in a situation in which he confronts God not as a mere divine being but as an incarnation of the violation of limits: in language, in the sight of the "slit" that stares blindly back, and in the experience of an auditory void, the resonance of the sound of nothing. Rather than a linear metonymic series, as Barthes would have it, I think we could argue that this is instead a circular or even spherical movement, in which each term is substitutable for another but also in which each points back to, and returns us to, the preceding: the word God, Madame Edwarda as God, the "slit," the regarding eye that looks at and is stared back at, her thigh, the empty shell, the sound of the sea. And back to the word God, infinitely. Word, eye, gaze, and *fente* are identified; each breaks the limits of itself, of others ("You see, I am God"). Following Bataille's introduction, we can say that "in the beginning was the word," but the word is not transcendent: it is the violation, the transgression, of language and its limits, and that transgression can only be a series—infinite but circular, but open-ended (the oculus)—of figures, of terms, whose integrity is itself incessantly violated. It is circular, spherical, but we should add torn open by a slit, the point of nonknowledge, and thus leaking or shedding meaning, or seeing it evaporate: the word as the voiding of the limits of the word.[15]

This death of God is particularly virulent because, rather than esthetic (as Altizer ultimately would maintain), it is the dissolution of the limits that make language possible. It depends on those limits—it is after all a word—but it breaks them and spins out an indefinite series of terms that function together—an old-fashioned critic might call it "Bataille's universe"—but that can never be totalized in a coherent (transcendent?) whole. We might think of it as a network—an obscene, defiant network, one that poses a parodic (because doubled, repetitious) knowledge—and a grouping, without ever being finalized or finalizable.

Mark C. Taylor has termed this kind of grouping "virtual," and he proposes it as an alternative to the simple transcendent/immanent model that has conditioned Christian theology for many centuries. In *After God* he writes:

> What poststructuralists cannot imagine is a nontotalizing structure that nonetheless acts as a whole. But this is precisely what complex adaptive networks do. . . . Decentralized, distributed and deregulated networks have an identifiable structure that is isomorphic across media and have a discernable operational logic, which, though different from binary and dialectical systems, can nevertheless be clearly conceived and precisely articulated.[16]

Here, miming Bataille, we might ask: how are they to be so precisely articulated? This is the question Bataille poses to a deconstructive theology of the sort that Taylor proposes. Bataille's God does not guarantee clear conception and precise articulation; on the contrary, he is precisely the violation of those limits. Yet this notion of vast networks recalls the constellations of terms that Bataille charts around and out of God, but they are indeed structured in such a way that they pose a kind of movement—a rhizome, to borrow a term from Deleuze and Guattari—that both finds

God—the nodal point of the eye—and always again loses Her, in Her constitutive blindness, Her slit, Her death (Bataille explicitly links God's [non]immanence to Her "rags," not to any phallic principle of closure or completion). God, as the word that undoes all language, both has a crucial position in any written work that attempts to write Her—but at the same time She is only one term among many, lost in a spherical labyrinth of metonymic positions and conjunctions.

Taylor goes on to associate these networks with the virtual and, by implication, with the vast system of the cyber and Internet reality:

> Never present as such, the gift of the present is present by that which arrives by not arriving. [Its] proximity renders all reality virtual. The virtual is not simply the possible but is the fluid matrix in which all possibility and actuality arise and pass away. Always betwixt and between, virtual reality is neither here and now nor elsewhere and beyond, neither immanent nor transcendent. To the contrary, the virtual is something like an immanent transcendence, which is inside as an outside that can never be incorporated.[17]

With this, we are back at the "nonknowledge" of *Inner Experience*, the blind spot definitively resistant to all incorporation, indeed the impossible point that shatters all constructive limits, which is nevertheless integral, as "absolute knowledge," to the coherence of the entire circular edifice (or to the spherical eye). Hence, perhaps, the "fluid matrix," but, pace Taylor, "matrix" implies (maternal) generation, whereas Bataille's "system" of non-knowledge can only parodically pose a mortal and moist orb.

At this point I would like to consider a bit more fully this idea of the virtual as a mode of Bataillean nonknowledge. I think one way we could frame Bataille's project as "virtual" is to see it in the context of Teilhard de Chardin's model of evolution and the noosphere. Now I realize that at first glance it might seem paradoxical to link Bataille's atheology to a Christian model in which a higher (cosmic) consciousness is derived from the complexity of the spherical "thinking skin" of the earth. But if we consider both projects together, some interesting connections will appear.

Teilhard was a paleontologist, and his theory explicitly attempted to link the evolution of species to a kind of second coming of a larger, divine consciousness. His basic thesis was that all the way from simple atoms to more complex organisms, the evolution of creation tended toward complexity, and that out of complexity consciousness arose. Thus simple flat organic structures, like leaves, gave way to the inward turning or circular-spherical structures of animal's brains. Human evolution in turn showed clearly that each new version of the hominid line not only had a larger brain but a brain that curved in upon itself more thoroughly; the folds of the *Homo sapiens* brain allowed it to become exponentially more complex, as its inner surfaces were extended. More and more folds meant more complexity and the possibility of more connections. At a certain tipping point, which Teilhard associated with the number ten billion, a quantitatively new state arose: consciousness.

Teilhard was not willing to stop at the development of consciousness; he posited beyond individual human awareness a much larger consciousness that would arise when all of humanity turned in on itself, so to speak, when the surface of the earth became a giant thinking organ, thanks to the enhanced communication capabilities brought about by modern technologies. In essence each person would become like a brain cell, and a higher-level planetary consciousness would arise as all these brains thought together in spherical completion. He characterized this consciousness, the point of convergence of all the consciousnesses of the world, as the Omega Point. This point is both the endpoint of all evolution, and at the same time it is irreducible to the individual consciousnesses that precede it. Teilhard writes:

> We are now inclined to admit that at each further degree of combination *something* which is irreducible to isolated elements *emerges* in a new order. . . . While being the last term of its series, it is also *outside of all series*. Otherwise the sum would fall short of itself, in organic contradiction with its whole operation. When, going beyond the elements, we come to speak of the conscious Pole of the world, it is not enough to say that it *emerges* from the rise of consciousness: we must add that from this genesis it has already *emerged;* without which it could neither subjugate into love nor fix in incorruptibility. . . . Autonomy, actuality, irreversibility, and thus finally transcendence are the four attributes of Omega.[18]

Teilhard the theologian is careful to maintain that the Omega Point— God, in short—as higher consciousness is not merely the product of the complexification of the globe; one has the sense that there is an "always already" at work here. In other words, for the Omega Point to be eternal, immortal, timeless, the creator—all the attributes of the Christian God—it must have "always already" emerged from time and space. After all, in Christian theology it was God who created the world.

This is hardly orthodox Catholicism, of course, but Teilhard is attempting to return the Omega to a divine transcendence. We might recall here Bataille's notion of the "right-hand" sacred, the sacred that is heterogeneous to the closed economies of the world but that, at the same time, through its very exteriority, guarantees their workings, gives them an origin point of being and an endpoint of meaning. Indeed Teilhard says that as the "last term" of the series, the Omega is "outside all series." It has to be. If it were merely *one more* term, the series would only be relative, contingent; it could not be totalized in and through a divinity.

But I want to note one more thing that characterizes this Omega Point. It is the breaking down of limits. For the higher consciousness to emerge, the limits of individuals must be abolished. Teilhard makes the obvious analogy with love: if the Omega Point is the highest point of love, then we first know its truth, its power, through the personal, physical experience of earthly love. Teilhard writes: "At what moment do lovers come into the most complete possession of themselves if not when they say they are lost in each other?" And "if ['personalizing by totalizing' can be repeated] daily on a small scale, why should it not repeat this one day on world-wide dimensions?"[19]

Teilhard links the earliest development of organic molecules with the later emergence of the noosphere: he writes of the "*double related involution*, the coiling up of the molecule upon itself and the coiling up of the planet upon itself."[20] Now one could make the obvious connection between the noosphere and the Internet; in the Internet, just as in the noosphere, one can imagine the emergence of a higher complexity as vast numbers of isolated cells—people—are brought together, processing and becoming aware of seemingly infinite amounts of information, all in "real time." Thus many see the noosphere as a precursor of cyberspace, a unified and conscious space that is nevertheless "virtual," not so much materially present as existing on a higher level, more real than real, that of the space of information and awareness that floats over the earth and into which enter millions of consciousnesses, heretofore independent and now fused.

But if one could argue that Teilhard anticipates the Internet, one could also say that he misses its point entirely. Teilhard is still a man of the 1920s and 1930s, and at times his unification of souls in a vast and unitary consciousness seems to resonate more with the emerging ideals of fascism (every identity lost in a higher unity) than with a virtual reality that is both a "thinking sphere" and in which freedom and independence reign. I would argue that if, as Taylor states, there is a kind of virtual divinity emerging, it is that of a noosphere-Internet that owes more to Bataille than to Teilhard.

By this I mean that, though Teilhard proposes the noosphere, Bataille is much closer to a "virtual" reality emerging out of cyberspace. One can establish numerous connections between Bataille and Teilhard. Bataille too has his "thinking spheres," but as I've argued, they are ruptured rather than totalized at their Omega Points—which Bataille calls their blind spots, their points of "nonknowledge." Bataille's noosphere is one of heterogeneous objects, bodies with orifices, "God" and "Hegel," words that destroy the limits of words. Where Teilhard sees love leading to the loss of individuals in one another, Bataille proposes an eroticism, a "communication," that results not in a higher union but in an open-ended, proliferating series of openings, of (w)holes, of transgressions. The virtual in Bataille, then, his Internet, resembles more closely what has emerged, than does Teilhard's, yet it derives from it, it reverses it in a "black night." Yes, there is a knowledge of the Internet, we might even say an "absolute knowledge" of immediacy and certainty in which the known turns in on itself, completes itself. But the completion point, the Omega, is not an easy totalization, a sacred point both capping and escaping the sum total of consciousnesses. Bataille's completion point is an open wound, the point of decapitation;[21] his Omega the abyss into which totalization fails and falls; it is the virtual as Taylor describes it, "betwixt and between, neither here and now nor elsewhere and beyond," but aroused and unlimitable. It is the rupture of the limits of any coherent terms, such as elsewhere and beyond, but also total, superior, irreversible, actual, under the aegis of the word God. "Circular absolute knowledge is definitive non-knowledge." The thinking sphere of the earth is a sphere of loss, of blindness; it "communicates ecstasy," as Bataille puts it in *Inner Experience*, with the emphasis either on ecstasy—the violation of the limits of self-satisfied knowledge—or on communication, the violation of the limits of beings, in eroticism or death.[22]

One commentator has affirmed the connection between the noosphere and the Internet—it probably occurs to everyone who reads Teilhard—but she objects because the pristine, new world of the Internet has been sullied by the "old" world of commerce, corruption, and pornography. "Pornography is also rampant. The virtual world has turned out to include all of the unsavory elements of the physical world."[23]

I have no interest in defending porn as it is produced and sold through the Internet. But the question of cybereroticism does allow us to think the virtual in a different way. If the Internet is divine—if it is the noosphere of the death of God (in Bataille's sense)—then what of the eroticism of the noosphere? Teilhard would have "love"—which might include the erotic—subsumed by the divine, subsumed in the Omega Point. Bataille, on the other hand, would argue that it is the immortality of the divinity that is lost, that incessantly "dies" in the orgasmic "rags" of that which stares back, blindly.

In this context we might consider a question concerning the Internet: is cybersex sex? With this question as a title Louise Collins has written a brilliant article discussing the conundrums of many of the varieties of cybersex. I will cite one type here, which is relevant, I think, to our concerns with the eroticized noosphere. It is the MUD, the "Multiple User Domain/Dimension/Dungeon." In it one

> assumes a named, fictional persona ("Pooh") by posting a self-description that need not match one's actual appearance, character or species ("a stout and reliable bear"). I type speech, actions and reactions that are meant to be attributed to my persona, "Pooh," not to me, "the author of the Pooh character." For the sake of erotic arousal, I may initiate an encounter in the MUD between "Pooh" and another person, "Piglet," scripted by another pseudonymous author. As Elizabeth Reid comments, "Who it is that is communicating becomes unclear, and whether passion is being simulated or transmitted through the MUD becomes truly problematic."[24]

One can certainly argue that this uncertainty, this textualization of sex, is "postmodern," what with eroticized selves communicated as fragmentary functions of narration and simulation. But what strikes me is that this is just a version, on a planetary scale, the scale of the noosphere, of the eroticized writing that Bataille engaged in works like *Story of the Eye* and *Madame Edwarda*. Remember that those works were "erotic" but that they also owed a lot to the philosophical pornography of Sade. It seems hard to imagine reading *Madame Edwarda* as a "one-handed text," but until not very long ago works such as this, by Bataille, were in fact sold "under the counter" in France in clandestine printings with a pseudonymous author ("Pierre Angélique" is also the "narrator" of the story). Who are we to second-guess the French authorities? In any case, in Bataille's fiction we have the same questions as arise in the MUD: there too the author is the narrator, under a pseudonym. And in Bataille the story is largely the recounting of events in which people take on fictional personae: Madame Edwarda is God, Pierre Angélique is Hegel (via the introduction, written by "Bataille"). The reader gets into the game, miming Bataille miming Hegel (one attains nonknowledge through Bataille the same way that one attains absolute knowledge through reading Hegel: by miming it). Or miming Bataille miming Madame Edwarda miming God. And in all this miming, somewhere, there is eroticism, maybe even some kind of weird stimulation, physical, textual, divine. One communicates, in other words, in and through the fictional, eroticized text, taking on and reshuffling personae. One "plays" with oneself with—in and out of—the text. In fact if we go back to Sade that's where a lot of the "obscenity" comes from—from the imaginary identification on the part of the reader with the fictional "monsters" depicted (and not least with the absent, phony God, the ultimate villain and victim). In the same way, we identify with *all* the fictions, *all* the monsters, philosophical and otherwise, in Bataille.

Perhaps the MUD is nothing more than this, although elaborated on a planetary scale, the scale of the noosphere. The limits of the word have been broken; it resonates across the surface of the planet through risible erotic and deified personifications. (Who could be more divine than Piglet? After all, in a footnote to his introduction to *Madame Edwarda*, Bataille writes: "God, if he knew, would be a pig.") Today the Omega Point may be precisely the point of eroticism where the identity of the fictional "author" of the erotic/philosophical/sacred scenario is the least knowable (in any sense of the term). In cybersex, Bataille's "virtual" death of God has become planetary.

Does the Acéphale Dream of Headless Sheep?

JEREMY BILES

> *Dreams*—Either we have no dreams or our dreams are interesting. We should learn to arrange our waking life the same way: nothing or interesting.
> —**Friedrich Nietzsche,** *The Gay Science*

The Dreaming Dionysus

Writing in a 1937 issue of the short-lived journal *Acéphale*, under the double heading "Nietzsche Dionysus," Georges Bataille proclaims, "The very first sentences of Nietzsche's message come from 'realms of *dream* and *intoxication.*' The entire message is expressed by one name: DIONYSUS.'"[1] In placing Nietzsche's "entire message" under the sign of Dionysus, Bataille would seem to be eliding from Nietzsche's account the god Apollo, with whom the German philosopher had associated dream. More precisely, however, Bataille is here enacting a Nietzschean transvaluation of *The Birth of Tragedy*, affiliating dream not with the god of light and placid forms but with the god of intoxication, excess, and death. The eponymous "monster" that emblazoned the cover of *Acéphale*—the monster "reunit[ing] in the same eruption Birth and Death"—is likewise a transvaluation of Dionysus, in whom dream and intoxication now converge in a "rapturous escape from the self."[2] Heralding the advent of this headless monster and the "ferociously religious" sensibility it bodies forth, Bataille writes: "I was no longer able to doubt that the lot and the infinite tumult of human life were open to those who could no longer exist as empty eye sockets, but as seers swept away by an overwhelming dream they could not own."[3] The sacred monster not only solicits intoxicated dispossession; it also affirms "the absolute power of dream."[4] *The Acéphale is Dionysus as the god of dreams—the dreaming Dionysus.*

André Masson, *Acéphale*. © 2014 Artists Rights Society (ARS), New York / ADAGP, Paris

To recognize the Acéphale as the dreaming Dionysus opens two intertwining paths I wish to follow in these pages. First, revealing the important
but often eschewed place of dreams within Bataille's writings will provide
a corrective to the prevailing interpretation of Bataille as betraying a dis-
dain for dream and the powers of the unconscious. This erroneous reading

emerges from an oversimplifying account of Bataille's fraught relationship with surrealism, a movement that, as conceived by André Breton, sought to synthesize dream and waking reality. Redressing this misperception of Bataille by discerning his Nietzschean transvaluation of the dream, with its courting of contradiction, opens the second path: an investigation into the resources in Bataille for engaging dream. In adumbrating a heterological approach to the dream, I want to reveal how Bataille's writings draw upon but also exceed the Freudian analytical approach in their provocations to sacrificial ecstasy. In doing so, I hope to demonstrate that dream and the sacred are not merely analogous but in fact coincide in Bataille's thought. To dream with Bataille is to relinquish oneself to the sovereign and sacrificial power of the dream, the power that animates what Bataille calls the "religious sensibility."

Sacrifice and the Ambivalence of the Sacred

Though it has gone largely unrecognized in the critical literature on Bataille, dream and the unconscious are intimately related to the sacred in Bataille's thought. Understanding this connection requires an account of Bataille's conception of the sacred as an ambivalent force that, when accessed through sacrificial acts, engenders an ecstatic loss of self. This loss of self corresponds with Bataille's idiosyncratic notion of sovereignty, which is related to an escape from the "servile" world of instrumental reason—the sphere of the profane.

In conceiving of the crucial category of the sacred, Bataille follows Émile Durkheim, who posits a rigorous distinction between the sacred and the profane in his landmark study *The Elementary Forms of the Religious Life.* There Durkheim writes that "all known religious beliefs . . . present one common characteristic: they presuppose a classification of all the things, real and ideal, of which men think, into two classes or opposed groups . . . profane and sacred."[5] This classification amounts to an "essential duality," a radical heterogeneity of the sacred with respect to the profane.

Durkheim's dualistic sacred is the very "matrix of [Bataille's] thought."[6] Bataille, however, extends and modifies Durkheim's account, arguing that this dichotomy arises in conjunction with the advent of labor. He relates labor to the emergence of the subject/object dichotomy in human consciousness, suggesting that "the positing of the object" as a separate *thing* occurs "in the human use of tools."[7] Subordinated to the one who uses it, a tool is assigned a utility, a *telos* beyond its immediate existence, and thus it takes its place within a newly emergent sphere of discontinuous objects that now includes oneself.

With the rise of self-consciousness, of oneself as a distinct, "discontinuous" individual, also comes the fear of death and the corresponding desire for durable existence—an existence that the subject vouchsafes to instrumental reason. Bataille identifies the realm of instrumental reason and its dedication to work—work intended to guarantee the preservation of the individual self—with the sphere of the profane; it is the realm of discontinuity. In the profane sphere, humans are subject to the laws of work and rational utility, which see objects in terms of use and their fitness for ensuring the durability of the individual self. In this sense, work *subjugates* one to some future aim or goal that defers experience of the present moment.

The sacred, on the other hand, is characterized by a sense of sovereignty not subordinated to future ends or goals. It is the sphere of transpersonal continuity, which objects, in their distinct forms, transcend. Accessing the sacred demands the transgression of prohibitions that maintain the utilitarian order of the "real world" of objects and discrete individuals. Sovereignty is thus linked with transgressions through which sacred excesses—ecstasy, tears, laughter, erotic effusions—erupt. Far from a quest for masterful control, sovereignty entails ecstatic abandon—the rupture of the closed, individual self as formed through social prohibitions and work.

Sovereignty is thus expressed in fleeting experiences of explosive affectivity. Erotic experience exemplifies Bataille's conception of sovereignty, for it "always entails a breaking down of established patterns . . . of the regulated social order basic to our discontinuous mode of existence as defined and separate individuals."[8] The risk upon which eroticism is predicated is a "conscious refusal to limit ourselves within our individual [or discontinuous] personalities."[9] By upsetting "the physical state associated with self-possession, with the possession of a recognized and stable individuality," the erotic experience brings the subject violently outside of itself, into an experience of continuity with the other.[10]

Bataille attributes to such sovereign moments of energetic, affective expenditure a sacrificial character. "The principle of sacrifice is destruction," he writes, "but though it sometimes goes so far as to destroy completely . . . the destruction that sacrifice is intended to bring about is not annihilation. The thing—only the thing—is what sacrifice means to destroy in the victim. Sacrifice destroys an object's . . . ties of subordination; it draws the victim out of the world of utility" and into the sphere of the sacred.[11]

Born of the anguish attendant upon loss of self yet opening onto ecstasy, the sacred is deeply ambivalent. Again following Durkheim, Bataille conceives of the sacred as not only in opposition to the profane but internally divided between what are often termed the "right" (or right-handed) and "left" (or left-handed) aspects of the sacred—the beneficent, purifying, vital sacred and the dangerous, decaying, morbid sacred, respectively.

Bataille advances this "duality of the sacred," extending and radicalizing the features of the "two opposing classes" observed by Durkheim: *pure and impure*," vivifying and decaying.[12] According to Bataille's account, the right sacred amounts to a transcendent projection of the profane world; it is rational utility elevated to the level of God or some other exalted figure. Such figures of individualized power are "higher forms" attesting to a will to *individualization:* the durability, stability, and extension of the self into a future in which death is indefinitely deferred. In this way, the right sacred is akin to the Apollonian aesthetic sphere exposited in Nietzsche's *Birth of Tragedy*—a realm in which stable forms (enduring, plastic structures) are divinized.

The left sacred, by contrast, is the Dionysian dimension of the sacred; it is not accessed in transcendence but activated through the transgression of prohibitions that keep the profane world intact. Whereas the elevated, Apollonian consciousness seeks stable and enduring forms, the disciple of the monstrous, left sacred revels in "ruptur[ing] the highest elevation, and . . . has a share in the elaboration or decomposition of forms" attendant upon intoxication, madness, and artistic profusion.[13] Excessive and transgressive, the left sacred is that which escapes assimilation or systematization. In this way, like the chthonic god with which it is affiliated in Bataille's thought, the left sacred is a "low value" that disrupts both the rational order of utility—the "real world," conditioned by telic thought and dedicated to useful projects—as well as its divinized counterpart, the right sacred. It is at once activated by, and provokes the death of, the closed, individual self—the death that grants the experience of continuity.

For Bataille, the sacred is thus a realm of "perpetual strife" recalling Nietzsche's dialectic in *The Birth of Tragedy*. But Bataille's conception of the sacred places an accent on the Dionysian, or left, aspect of the sacred as the very principle of contradiction. The sacred is "not only contradictory with respect to things but . . . is in contradiction with itself."[14] Bataille sees in the right sacred dangers to which the forces of the left sacred must respond. In combating the individualizing and eternalizing inclinations of the right sacred, Bataille wants to disclose and activate the corruptive, subversive, and death-dealing forces of the left. To be sure, it is the left sacred that inspires Bataille in describing the religious sensibility he theorizes and attempts to provoke in his readers. Like the Acéphale, itself a monstrous embodiment of contradiction (man and god, birth and death "united in the same eruption"), the religious sensibility Bataille seeks is contradictory, issuing in ambivalent affective effusions that lacerate the closed individual: anguish and joy, horror and bliss.

In this way, Bataille's analysis of the sacred recalls Freud's account of the unconscious, with its ability to sustain contradiction, and it is on this point that Bataille's critical difference from Breton becomes apparent.[15] According to Bataille's Nietzschean reading of Freud, the unconscious revels in contradiction, "not only court[ing] the transformation of everything into its opposite but hold[ing] both of these things together, at once."[16] Bataille believes that "contradiction is not negative: inside the sacred domain there is, as in dreams, an endless contradiction that multiplies" prolifically.[17] In fact, Bataille's theory of the sacred, with its embrace of contradiction, significantly coincides with (and is undoubtedly inflected by) Freud's formulation of the unconscious.[18]

Marshaling a Nietzschean embrace of strife and contradiction, Bataille regards the unconscious as the site of "heterological" forces expressed in contradictory emotional discharges; it also generates ambivalent images and moods that, if affirmed and not suppressed, may interrupt the world of rational utility. André Breton, by contrast, exhibits a Hegelian sensibility and therefore finds in Freud's theory grounds for interpreting the unconscious as a space of psychic resolution of opposites. These opposed readings and valuations of the Freudian unconscious will animate Breton's and Bataille's respective treatments of the dream. Whereas Breton's will to synthesis poses the dream as an expression of satisfied desire—what Freud famously referred to as "wish fulfillment"—Bataille will wend a left-handed, Nietzschean path through Freud, seeking to activate and embrace the monstrous and contradictory aspects of the dream, beholding and deploying dreams as provocations to an experience of desirous self-laceration on the level of the sacred.

Domesticating the Dream: Bretonian Surrealism

The passing attention that has been paid to the place of dream in the thought of Bataille has come largely in the context of Bataille's polemical relations with Breton and Bataille's wider critiques of surrealism. The reticence on this subject in the literature on Bataille has to do at least partly with the fact that Bataille himself did not write on the dream in a sustained manner; unlike Breton, whose *Communicating Vessels* was to become among the most important modern texts on the dream after Freud's *Interpretation of Dreams*, Bataille's evocations of dream are fleeting and far-flung.[19]

Yet I want to suggest that the role of the dream in Bataille's thought is at once more crucial and more pervasive than has previously been recognized. I see the dream as a hidden, almost occulted, element in Bataille that as such gives unexpected insight into how Bataille thought about the sacred and the possibilities for sacrificial and ecstatic mystical experience. For this reason, those interested in Bataille and, more broadly, in the religious dimensions of dream may wish to reconsider Bataille's evaluation and activation of dream, attending to what I will describe as his heterological approach to oneiric experience, especially as it culminates in an idiosyncratic and "ferociously religious" version of surrealism—an *extremist* surrealism, in Bataille's words.

Bataille is at once intimate with and opposed to surrealism, displaying a violent ambivalence toward the movement. While recognizing and embracing surrealism's spirit of revolt and its openness to the "disinterested" play of thought and desire,[20] Bataille also considers himself surrealism's "old enemy from within,"[21] situating his efforts "alongside" but also "beyond" surrealism.[22] Operating simultaneously within and beyond surrealism, Bataille's relation to the movement recalls Slavoj Žižek's favored formulation of the Lacanian principle of the inassimilable *das Ding*: "in me more than me." Bataille, as we will see, is in surrealism more than surrealism, and his approach to the dream is at once a realization and radicalization of surrealism's stated but often compromised aims.

Some commentators have unduly simplified Bataille's complex, ambivalent attitude toward surrealism, taking his sometimes disdainful critiques of the movement as a condemnation of the powers of dream and the unconscious.[23] They have interpreted Bataille's efforts to evolve a countersurrealism[24] as indicative of a will to wakeful consciousness in opposition to the surrealists' somnolent reveries and have considered his scatological obsessions[25] and explorations of perverse sexual desire as a critical antipode to the ethereal world of dream—or what Bataille himself once scornfully equated with the "'wonderland' of Poetry."[26]

But reducing Bataille's ambivalence regarding surrealism to a simple condemnation of the dream fails to recognize that by Bataille's account, the aspiration to give "free rein" to fantasy and to actualize the omnipotence of the dream is not realized but *forsaken* by the surrealists. In fact, in the years following surrealism's interwar ascendancy, Bataille seeks to (re)define the movement, insisting on its continuing relevance even as its cultural currency recedes. In his essay "On the Subject of Slumbers," Bataille goes so far as to claim, rather elliptically, that "surrealism is defined by the possibility that I . . . can have of defining it conclusively."[27]

Bataille is thus deeply, if ambivalently, engaged with surrealism; as one commentator has remarked, surrealism provides a "key" to much of his work.[28] This observation thus commends further attention to Bataille's underrecognized fascination with the dream, which had been an object of investigation by surrealism from its inception.

Inspired by their readings of Freud, the surrealists famously sought to release the forces of repressed unconscious desires, thereby achieving a "resolution of . . . dream and reality . . . into a kind of absolute reality, a *surreality*."[29] In his first *Manifesto of Surrealism* (1924), André Breton repeatedly invokes Freud, who "very rightly brought his critical faculties to bear upon the dream" and whose technique of free association helped instigate the surrealist practice of automatic writing, through which the unconscious, freed from censorship, may speak its desires.[30] Breton in fact defines surrealism explicitly in relation to aspects of the unconscious: it is "psychic automatism in its pure state," involving belief in "the superior reality of certain forms of previously neglected associations, in the omnipotence of the dream."[31] With the aim of disrupting a staid and stultifying bourgeois society predicated upon the repression of desire, Breton and company wish to mingle dreaming and waking life, to "live by our fantasies," giving "*free rein to them*."[32]

The desire to dissolve the boundaries that separate the apparently opposed realms of dream and reality, conceiving of them as "communicating vessels," is indicative of a far-reaching synthetic sensibility in Breton— a sensibility that, though present already in the first *Manifesto*, will be stimulated and advanced through his readings of Hegel in conjunction with Alexandre Kojève's influential lectures on the *Phenomenology of Spirit*. Breton's will to synthesis is exemplified in a well-known passage from the first *Manifesto*, where he declares that "everything tends to make us believe that there exists a certain point of the mind at which life and death, the real and the imagined, past and future, the communicable and incommunicable, high and low, cease to be perceived as contradictions."[33] Evident in this early work is an incipient Hegelianism that will characterize Breton's wider oeuvre. As Hal Foster has observed, Breton exhibits an "insistence on resolution, the Hegelian reconciliation of such dualisms as waking and dreaming, life and death."[34]

Breton's thoroughgoing Hegelianism imbues his interpretation of Freud as well; in fact, Breton claims that "Freud is Hegelian in me."[35] This sensibility evinces a certain interpretation of the *Aufhebung*, which Breton reads as the suppression of contradiction through an elevation of opposites into a new synthesis. His eschewal of contradiction is nowhere more clear than in his reading of the Freudian unconscious. Freud observes that whereas rational, conscious thought is governed by the law of noncontradiction, the unconscious not only admits but sustains contradiction. "The way in which dreams treat the category of contraries and contradictions is highly remarkable," Freud writes. Dreams exhibit a "particular preference for combining contraries into a unity."[36] Breton interprets this "unity" of opposites not as a tensive holding-together of contradictory elements but rather as a synthesis that suppresses or dispels contradiction—in other words, a resolution.

Breton's Hegelianization of the unconscious extends, of course, to the dream. Freud famously postulates that dreams are instigated by wishes, with dream content representing the fulfillment of those wishes.[37] The notion of dreams as wish fulfillment is embraced by Breton, for whom dreams, as expressions of the unconscious, not only reconcile contraries but in doing so fulfill desires that had been contradicted in waking life. "The mind of the man who dreams is fully satisfied by what happens to him," he writes in the first *Manifesto*.[38] This satisfaction is doled out in waking life to the extent that a synthesis of the unconscious and consciousness is achieved. In satisfying the individual's wishes, in gratifying desire, the dream underwrites the stability of the ego.

According to Bataille, however, synthetic satisfaction, evident in Breton's thought from surrealism's very origins, marks not the apogee but the abandonment-in-advance of what is essential to surrealism: its vitriolic spirit, its ceaseless interrogations, its channeling of subversive energies into the interruption of everyday life as defined by self-interest, labor, and concern for the lastingness of the individual self. The will to synthesis thus dooms surrealism to failure; its self-betrayal is implicit in the very terms of surrealism's theorization by Breton. In proclaiming his own "extremist" surrealism—a surrealism that, as we will see, remains resolutely hostile to synthetic satisfaction—Bataille notes that surrealism's investigation of the unconscious has "opened up two different paths":

> one led to the establishment of works, and soon [relinquished] any principle to the necessities of works, so accentuating the attraction value of paintings and books. This was the path the surrealists took. The other was an arduous path to the heart of being: here only the slightest attention could be paid to the attraction of works; not that this was trivial, but what was then laid bare—the beauty and ugliness of which no longer mattered—was the essence of things, and it was here that the inquiry into existence in the night began.[39]

The first path that Bataille discerns is, of course, that of the dominant, Bretonian brand of surrealism.

Bataille's critiques of this moderate surrealism reveal (at least) three distinct but interrelated problems upon which the movement devolves. The first avenue of critique has been the object of much critical attention and can thus be dealt with very briefly here.[40] Bataille sees Breton and his cadre of surrealists as indulging in sublimatory tendencies and a concomitant idealism that betray their stated materialist commitments. In early polemical essays like "The Old Mole," Bataille observes that although surrealism seeks to engage the "low values (the unconscious, sexuality, filthy language, etc.), it invests these values with an elevated character by associating them with the most immaterial values."[41] While entreating a synthesis of high and low, the famously coprophobic Breton in fact *suppresses* that which is low, effectively "condemn[ing] the entire earth, the base earth, domain of pure abjection."[42]

Refusing to countenance that which is irrevocably abject and impure, Breton at the same "elevates" them through what Bataille scornfully calls a "game of transpositions."[43] Sexuality, obscenity, and the unconscious itself—all of which Bataille characterizes as "base" forces—are not accepted in their vulgar facticity but are poetically transformed, sublimated. Dreams—a privileged domain of the surrealist "marvelous"—are not exempt from this idealist poeticizing; the base, obscene, and contradictory aspects of dream are elevated, beautified. "The marvelous is always beautiful, anything marvelous is beautiful, in fact only the marvelous is beautiful," Breton writes.[44] The desire to suppress the abject through beautification is a symptom of a synthetic will in which Freudian sublimation and Hegelian sublation coincide: the low is suppressed in being elevated, transformed, purified, idealized.

This play of transpositions opens out onto the second level of critique. The idealism that Bataille sees operating in surrealism is a "*servile* idealism."[45] Under its Hegelian-idealist aspect, surrealism effects not only a sublation and sublimation of the contents of the unconscious; it also reduces them to a servile status. Surrealism, that is, makes a *tool* of the unconscious, thus betraying the touted "omnipotence of dreams." Bataille goes on to observe that surrealists channel dreams into products, goods, mere *things* in the world. Dreams and the unconscious are treated as "no more than a pitiable treasure-trove," a cache of images and affects that are turned into poetic and artistic works that circulate in the market or hang on gallerists' and collectors' walls.[46] In this manner, then, surrealism converts dreams into social and monetary capital.

The alleged omnipotence of dreams is betrayed not only in surrealism's complicity with the market and the production of works; it is also dreams' subjection to *interpretation* that reduces them to things. Whereas the two levels of Bataille's critique discussed above have been treated by other scholars, the problem posed by interpretation has been overlooked by commentators on Bataille. Yet I believe it is above all in Bataille's resistance to the interpretation of dreams that we may discern not only the falsity of claims concerning Bataille's supposed "hostility to the dream" but also begin to elaborate a Bataillean heterology of the dream that reveals the dream under its sacred aspect.

In his book *Communicating Vessels*, the title of which signals a will to synthesis that will animate the text in its entirety, Breton forwards what amounts to a program for dissolving the barriers separating conscious life from the unconscious, waking reality from dream, the material world from the psychic. In doing so, he enacts something of an Oedipal drama, at once extending and critiquing Freud. Breton applies a "Freudian schema" to his dreams, even as he accuses Freud of not carrying his own dream analyses to their conclusions.[47] Freud, claims Breton, censors the seamier elements of his nocturnal visions, thus bowing to bourgeois convention, the desire for self-protection, and the demands of conventional decorum proper to scientific publications. Freud attempts to acquit himself in his correspondence with Breton, where he claims that "timidity in relation to sexual objects" would "rarely," if ever, be the cause of his failure to "pursue the analysis of my own dreams as far as that of others."[48]

If Breton himself, as we have seen, displays a certain censorious chastity in his refusal to acknowledge base reality, there is some irony in the accusations he levels at Freud. But it is not simply a matter of etiquette and censorship that are at stake here; it is, rather, a theoretical issue at the heart of dream interpretation itself. Freud posited what he called the dream "navel," a kernel of uninterpretable material embedded at the heart of a dream. "There is at least one spot in every dream," he writes in *The Interpretation of Dreams*, "at which it is unplumbable—a navel, as it were, that is its point of contact with the unknown."[49] By Freud's account, "even the most thoroughly interpreted dream" contains a "passage" that will remain "obscure." The work of interpretation inevitably arrives at a "tangle of dream-thoughts which cannot be unraveled." This obscure navel, this intense knot, Freud claims, is "the spot where [the dream] reaches down into the unknown."[50]

Though Freud introduces this dream core as an uninterpretable knot, he grants the navel a theoretical double articulation. The navel is not only the blind spot in the dream that effectively banishes the interpretive eye, an unravelable knot of unknowing that announces the *end* of interpretation; it is also conceived of as a generative node in a theoretically limitless *proliferation* of interpretations, an excess of meanings. Shifting his metaphors accordingly, Freud will characterize the nodal point of dream thoughts as "infinitely branching": "the dream thoughts to which we are led by interpretation cannot, from the nature of things, have any definite endings; they are bound to branch out in every direction into the intricate network of our world of thought."[51]

It is the uncanny ambivalence of the dream navel—at once unravelable knot and generative node—that Breton refuses to fathom in his own interpretive endeavors. In contrast to Freud, Breton insists that dreams may be interpreted completely, exhaustively. In *Communicating Vessels*, Breton undertakes to counter the notion that interpretations are in principle "never *complete*": "I insist emphatically on the fact that for me [interpretation] *exhausts* the dream's content and contradicts the diverse allegations that have been made about the 'unknowable' character of the dream, or its incoherence."[52] Breton is here taking aim not only at those who dismiss dreams as meaningless phantasms of no value to waking life, a target he shares with Freud; he is at the same time staking out a position against Freud himself. Though Freud elaborates a theoretical framework that admits the meaningfulness of dreams as well as a method for disclosing that meaning, his positing of the dream navel—irresolvable both in its obscurity and its wild intractability—stands as an obstacle to Breton's synthetic endeavors toward resolution, unity, and ultimately self-identity. For Breton, dreams fulfill personal desire and thereby uphold the individual's ego.

Freud's theorization of the dream suggests that any attempts at ultimate interpretive satisfaction—the arrival at a final, unary, stable meaning—will be doubly confounded by the irreducible ambivalence at the heart of every dream. Breton seeks to neutralize that ambivalence and to domesticate this unruly ambiguity through his own interpretive endeavors in *Communicating Vessels*. But in his very attempt to achieve the interpretive exhaustion of the dream, he undercuts, rather than affirms, the omnipotence of dreams. Though Breton acknowledges the "flight of ideas presented in dreaming" and extols a "delirium of interpretation" proper to the oneiric phantasmagoria, his own dream analyses indicate a will to interpretive closure that grounds the ideational flight and ultimately becalms and concludes the exegetical mania upon which surrealism had staked much of its claim to legitimacy.[53]

Breton does so by reducing dreams to the conditions of a waking life he had sought to disrupt. Though his interpretations comprise remarkable lyrical passages, they do not (only) mingle dream and waking life but convert, through a process of decryption, the former into the latter, in a manner that effectively denounces the omnipotence of the dream. The dream is translated into the terms of conscious life; the insurmountable ambivalence that Freud attributes to "every dream" is thus refuted, domesticated, brought under the control of the analytic framework. Seeking to go *beyond* Freud through exhaustive interpretation, Breton in this instance *moderates* Freud, denying what the latter saw as the dream's irresolvable ambivalence and unmanageable generativity in favor of securing a *final* meaning. Breton's interpretations foreclose meaning and resolve contradictions through the establishment of correspondences between the images of manifest dream content and their sources in waking reality. Doing so at once serves the aims of self-satisfaction and the shoring up of the self.

It should be noted, then, that despite Breton's proclaimed synthetic pretensions, his thought produces a contradiction: on the one hand, he idealizes the material world; on the other hand, he reduces the dream through a process of interpretation that dispels the dream's ambivalence. Breton effectively *rationalizes* the dream, interpreting dreams in a manner that obeys rather than transgresses the law of noncontradiction and capitulates to the telic orientation prevailing in what Bataille identifies as the sphere of the profane. Far from upholding the omnipotence of the dream, Breton's Hegelianism announces the end of the dream.

Toward a Heterology of the Dream: Bataille's Extremist Surrealism

Realizing the dream's omnipotence would entail embracing, rather than resolving, the very ambivalence and excessive polysemy that Breton sought to bring under his interpretive control. Though Bataille leveled no explicit critique of Breton's interpretation of dreams, I want to extrapolate from Bataille in suggesting that there is a hidden, and hitherto unrecognized, critique of this aspect of Bretonian oneiricism in Bataille's writings, a critique that affirms, if not precisely the omnipotence, then the *sovereignty* of the dream—and the dreamer. Bataille, I want to argue, seeks not (or not merely) to interpret dreams but to affirm them in their full heterogeneity. Unlike the Hegelian Breton, who sought to establish a *"conduction wire"*[54] between dream and reality, thus making of them "communicating vessels," the Nietzschean Bataille consecrates and celebrates the dream in its irreducible *difference* from waking life, as a provocation to alter the everyday sphere of the profane. The source of the dream's sovereign and subversive power comes not in an attempted synthesis with waking life but in being *realized*—understood, embraced, and enacted—in its full heterogeneity: contradictory, ambivalent, ambiguous. It is the dream's heterogeneity, its otherness, that transgresses the prohibitions, habits, and attitudes of thought that define the sphere of everyday reality.

Recognizing this ulterior aspect of Bataille's thought gives the lie to the entrenched scholarly perception of Bataille's purported "hostility to the dream," as one commentator has put it.[55] Bataille is not hostile to the dream as such; rather, he is hostile to Breton's rationalization of the dream, his reduction of the dream to a final, stable meaning. Characterizing Bataille as somehow opposed to the dream is symptomatic of the tendency to collapse the dream into Bretonian surrealism—something Bataille himself scrupulously avoided. The erroneous logic that apparently underwrites this move runs something like this: Breton championed the dream; Bataille criticized, and at times openly scorned, Breton; therefore Bataille, being hostile to Breton, must also be hostile to the dream.

Not only is Bataille not hostile to the dream; his writings contain resources that contribute to a revaluation of the dream as an acephalic and "rapturous escape from the self"—a death of the discontinuous self as composed and maintained within the world of rational utility, the sphere of the profane.[56] It is thus refracted through and against Breton's domestication of the dream and its attendant individualizing tendencies that Bataille's own hidden approach to the dream may be revealed. Bataille seeks not exhaustive interpretations of dreams in the interest of shoring up the individual ego but rather to engage in what he will call "heterology," a Dionysian analysis and activation of the "wholly other" forces of the dream in a manner that disrupts the projects and privileging of the individual that define profane life. For Bataille, we will find, the dream is a definitively *sacred* phenomenon—not an object of self-stabilizing interpretation but a mode of and model for sacrificial experience.

In fact, Bataille is, to echo the title of Susan Sontag's famous essay, "against interpretation"—or at least a certain *attitude* of interpretation. Interpretation "presupposes a discrepancy between the clear meaning of the text and the demands of . . . readers. It seeks to resolve that discrepancy" by finding "an equivalent" for the phenomenon in question—a text, a work of art, a dream. To resolve discrepancy, to search in a text for the "true meaning," "is to impoverish, to deplete the world." In terms that recall Bataille's critique of the surrealists as cryptoidealists bent on transposing base realities into ethereal or "high" values, Sontag claims that to interpret is "to turn *the* world into *this* world." Interpretation, Sontag observes, assuages the discomfort, the productive agitation, that attends "real art"—and, I would add, the dream. "By reducing the work of art" or the dream "to its content and the interpreting *that*," Sontag writes, "one tames the work of art. Interpretation makes art manageable, comfortable."[57]

Sontag's critique of interpretation resonates distinctly with Bataille's critique of Bretonian surrealism, with its suppression of base reality—"*the* world" in its full amplitude—and its reduction of the dream to content, tamed through interpretation. Bataille seeks to *experience* the world, and thus the dream, as it is, eschewing conciliatory modes of interpretation and allowing the dream to enact an operation that maintains and even courts contradiction. In renouncing reductive interpretation, Bataille's path into the unconscious diverges dramatically from Breton's.

Bataille's is, rather, the labyrinthine path into the unconscious as the space in which the ambivalent dream navel rebuffs a final, single, unary meaning even as it generates mythic phantasms and chains of associations that undo, rather than integrate, the self. And whereas Freud was Hegelian in Breton, Freud is Nietzschean, even Dionysian, in Bataille; Bataille's is the Freud of warring, contradictory libidinal forces—the forces of life and death in tension with each other, rending the ego, never allowing for a stable sense of self.[58] Bataille's Dionysian Freud is the Freud not of sublimating transpositions but of base materiality. As Bataille says in an essay on materialism, "it is from Freud . . . that a representation of matter"—*base matter*—"must be taken."[59] Bataille goes on to call for a "direct interpretation, *excluding all idealism*, of raw phenomena," an interpretation based on "facts," given experiences in all their ambiguity, rather than thought systems that would guarantee a unary, stable meaning. It is this Dionysian Freud who grants entry to the left-handed path of the unconscious that Bataille follows in developing his extremist surrealism.

These "raw phenomena," or what Bataille elsewhere calls "material facts," are those aspects of material reality that remain stubbornly "insubordinate," exceeding, and often actively expelled from, "the closed systems" advanced by the "reasonable conceptions" that prevail in profane existence.[60] Matter as such "can only be defined as the *nonlogical difference* that represents in relation to the *economy* of the universe what *crime* represents in relation to the law."[61] Matter—raw or base material—is thus transgressive in its very heterogeneity; it is "impossible to assimilate."[62]

As this account reveals, Bataille is not against interpretation as such but against modes of interpretation that fail to contend with the brute and ambiguous facticity of material reality. Bataille proposes the term "heterology" to name his nonreductive "practical and theoretical" interpretation of the "wholly other"—that which exceeds, evades, or is abjected from closed philosophical, scientific, religious, economic, or other systems. As both a theoretical position and a practical attitude, heterology refuses to comprehend otherness, allowing it, rather, to invade and alter the normal course of rational, profane thought, transforming it like a toxin, like an intoxicant. Whereas "homogenous representations of the world" have as their goal "the deprivation of our universe's sources of excitation and the development of a servile human species, fit only for the fabrication, rational consumption, and conservation of products," heterology in its theoretical and practical aspects takes up that "which up until now has been seen as the abortion and shame of human thought."[63]

Dreams, as Freud points out, are one such shameful aspect of human thought for "serious-minded persons" because they evade the pretenses of discursive thought and thus undercut the individual agency, rational explanation, and scientific appropriation that Bataille will identify with the sphere of the profane.[64] And if matter is heterogeneous, inassimilable within a closed system, then reciprocally, that which is inassimilable is aligned with matter. Bataille accordingly considers the unconscious itself in the register of base materiality. "The exclusion of *heterogeneous* elements from the *homogeneous* realm of consciousness formally recalls the exclusion of the elements, described (by psychoanalysis) as *unconscious*," he writes. "The difficulties opposing the revelation of *unconscious* forms of existence are of the same order as those opposing the knowledge of *heterogeneous* forms." Therefore, Bataille concludes, "the *unconscious* must be considered as one of the aspects of the *heterogeneous*."[65]

Bataille explicitly places dreams alongside the sacred in the register of the heterogeneous; as elements of "unproductive expenditure," dreams and the sacred relate to "*homogeneous* society as waste."[66] The "various unconscious processes such as dreams" are in fact decisive instances of the inassimilable: "the knowledge of a *heterogeneous* reality as such is to be found in . . . dreams: it is identical to the structure of the *unconscious*."[67] Most significantly in the present context, Bataille, in elaborating the "principles of a practical heterology," affirms dreams as a form of unproductive *excretion*, while "the analysis of dreams" is indicative of "appropriation as a means of excretion."[68] Unlike Breton, who in attempting to *assimilate* the dream in fact *rejects* the dream in its fully contradictory character, Bataille accepts the dream's heterogeneity, realizing the dream itself as excretion, and the analysis of dreams as an excretory function, part of the process of decay—the decay of rational thought itself.[69]

It should by now be clear that Bataille is not hostile to the dream; rather, he seeks a theoretical and practical approach to the dream that does not attempt to make the dream an element of "servile idealism," nor to treat the dream as yet another *thing* caught up in the all too "reasonable" creation and conservation of products. On the contrary, the approach that he champions sees dreams as evading servile utility and thus remaining *sovereign*, beyond reduction to use. The genuinely sovereign "goes beyond the useful" and is "named the *unconscious*."[70] The unconscious, not confined by "the practice of reason," evokes "risk and caprice" rather "than prudence and the pursuit of usefulness."[71] A far cry from Breton's "pitiable treasure trove," the dream for Bataille exists as provocation, as risk, as something that decays, toxifies, and intoxicates rational and systematic thought. Dream is the toxic excrement of thought and, in this sense, the *sacrifice* of thought.

Dream, intoxication, and sacrifice thus converge in Bataillean heterology, a fact embodied in the contradictory monster of the Acéphale. The heterology of dreams that Bataille's writings augur suggests that much as sacrifice grants access to the sacred by destroying that which is a mere thing in the victim, so too does dream sacrifice rational thought, destroying what has been made a mere thing within the profane sphere of instrumental reason. Though the analysis of dreams is undertaken in a discursive mode, the attitude of thought linked with the sovereign dream is one that is infected by the dream itself; analysis provokes the breakdown of discursive thought in a manner that recalls Bataille's "principle of inner experience: to emerge through project"—that is, with the tools of reason—"from the realm of project"—the sphere of the profane.[72] In Bataille's writings, dreams thus suffer no servility; they are not made into works nor put to work in shoring up the self. Neither are they domesticated under some interpretive regime. Rather, the dream is part of the sovereign counteroperation that Bataille sees as being central to his extremist surrealism, a left-handed religion dedicated to undoing the work of rational, utilitarian thought—the counteroperation of sacrifice.

At the same time, Bataille's writings suggest that dreams themselves must be relentlessly sacrificed lest they become mere objects produced for circulation or subjugated to work. Dreams destroy things, but so too must the thingness of dreams be destroyed. If Breton made things of dreams, Bataille sacrifices what in Breton's hands is domesticated. In doing so, he returns surrealism's dreams to the realm of the sacred that they announce in their very otherness. This, as we will now see, is borne out in Bataille's own dream analyses and in the activation of an oneiric attitude within his mystical practices: a practical heterology.

Sleep Growing Sleepless: Bataille's Dreams

> The spirit farthest removed from the virility necessary for joining violence and consciousness is the spirit of "synthesis."
>
> Georges Bataille, *Theory of Religion*

At the outset of his life as a writer, suffering from "a series of dreary mishaps and failures," Bataille underwent treatment with the unorthodox psychoanalyst Dr. Adrien Borel.[73] Though little is known of his treatment, it is clear that Bataille was not precisely "healed" by analysis, his "virulent" obsessions dispelled. Rather, like the irresolvable but generative dream knot, Bataille's obsessions would now be expressed through writerly expenditures; Bataille becomes prolific.[74] For this reason, Bataille contends that psychoanalysis had a "decisive result," putting an end to his frustrations without reducing his "state of intellectual intensity."[75]

Borel, one may surmise, practiced a left-handed psychoanalysis, by the understanding set out above, for he is said to have gifted Bataille with the photograph of the Chinese torture victim that obsessed the writer for the remainder of his days. Meditating on the horrific image revealed to Bataille the contradictory nature of religious experience, illuminating what he will describe as the religious sensibility—a sensibility characterized by the experience of explosive and contradictory affective discharges: a coincidence, but never a synthesis, of the "perfect contraries, divine ecstasy and its opposite, extreme horror."[76]

This illumination seems also to have been granted in a dream Bataille recorded while undergoing analysis, a fact overlooked in the critical literature on Bataille, which has focused intensely on the use of the torture photo as an object of meditation. In this sense, the dream is a hidden mechanism closely analogous to the highly scrutinized photograph. Like the photograph, meditation on the dream, as we will see, opens onto a mystical agnosia, the anguishing and ecstatic experience of "nonknowledge." Discerning and elaborating this parallel has implications for the study of mysticism. It suggests that dreams, like other violent representations—for example, the torture photo or images of the crucified Christ—might play a role in the "dramatization" of self-directed violence that Bataille believes is essential for stimulating ecstatic experience. And though space constraints prevent a full discussion, broaching dreams in their contradictory violence, as provocations to the risk of self-shattering experience, has ethical ramifications, for it embraces the dream and dream analysis as practices of representation and "direct interpretation" that affirm and provoke psychic woundedness even while avoiding damage to physical bodies.[77]

In the course of his psychoanalytic treatment, Bataille produced at least one dream text, which counts among the very earliest of his known writings.[78] The text begins with a relatively coherent report detailing the fall of an "atrocious darkness" in which are suspended "slimy and bloody fish or dead but menacing rats." From here, what had been a recognizable narrative dissolves into a fragmentary chain of associations that seems to move both within and beyond the frame of the dream account itself; the text evokes a meshwork of early memories as well as other dreams, even as it gestures toward analysis: the "horrible rats and all the terrors of childhood. . . . Dream of the bear with a candlestick. . . . Terrors of childhood spiders etc. linked to the memory of having my pants pulled down on my father's knees. Kind of ambivalence between the most horrible and the most magnificent."[79] Having established this note of ambivalence, Bataille goes on to write of further horrific paternal associations upon waking:

> I associate the horror of rats with the memory of my father correcting me with a blow in the form of a bloody toad into which a vulture (my father) sinks his beak. . . . My father himself . . . since he is blind, he also sees the sun in blinding red. . . . This has the effect of reminding me that my father being young would have wanted to do something atrocious to me with pleasure. . . . My father slaps me and I see the sun.[80]

Much could be (and has been) made of Bataille's evocation of a blind and violent father within a psychoanalytic context. But here we may turn attention to another remarkable feature of this text, namely the manner in which the oneiric mode infects the analytical gestures. Unlike Breton, who will translate dreams into the terms of waking life, Bataille's very mode of analysis extends and exacerbates, rather than forecloses, the dream's ambivalences, making of analysis itself an excretory and disintegrative function, an expression not of a rational framework of interpretation but rather part of the process of the decay of rational thought itself. Neither the dream nor the analysis that Bataille engages in arrives at a "meaning";[81] rather, the dream transgresses the boundaries of codified interpretation, generating a series of lacerating images and thus promoting the decay, rather than integration and shoring up, of the individual self.[82] (Indeed, the dream would seem to provoke or invite castration rather than rebuffing or defending against it).[83]

Bataille does not reduce his dream to the familiar terms of waking life; rather, the analysis propagates associations that extend the oneiric operation. Further, this decay of rational thought moves beyond the strictly clinical context of the analysis, for it is during this same period that Bataille produces among his most hallucinatory and obsessive texts of "mythological anthropology," "The Solar Anus." One finds in this and other works of mythological anthropology not only dreamlike sequences indicating a solar obsession but also various manifestations of the "ambivalence between the most horrible and the most magnificent."

Ambivalence pervades Bataille's writings and characterizes his very attitude of thought.[84] The dream knot theorized by Freud, that point of intractable, interminable ambivalence that Breton sought to abjure, is affirmed and activated by Bataille. Though much has been made of the place of knots in the thought of Bataille's friend Jacques Lacan, Bataille's reading of Freud, including his appropriation and transvaluation of the dream knot, has gone almost entirely overlooked.[85] Bataille appropriates the Freudian dream knot—that point of "contact with the unknown"—as the "blind spot" of "nonknowledge" in which his mystical practices culminate.[86] According to Bataille, nonknowledge—the lived impossibility of Hegelian "absolute knowledge"—is the practical refutation of any possibility of individual completeness or personal enclosure, of any synthetic gratification of desire. It is the wound through which is achieved an experience of continuity with being—being understood not as a closed and static *thing* but rather as immanence, intimacy, continuity: a transpersonal and fluctuating totality. In this ecstatic experience, absence and excess of meaning coincide: an expenditure of meaning in an endlessly ambivalent, ungraspable knot of the unknown.

"NONKNOWLEDGE COMMUNICATES ECSTASY," Bataille writes. "Thus ecstasy only remains possible in the anguish of ecstasy, in this sense, that it cannot be satisfaction, *grasped knowledge.*"[87] It is in the "dazed lucidity" of ecstatic agnosia that one realizes the sacrificial shattering of the self.[88] In a manner that recalls Freud's characterization of dreams, this oneiric mystical experience is "heedless of contradictions"; indeed, it proceeds in and through affective and intellectual contradictions, with "as much disorder as in dreams."[89] This ecstasy is the anti-Hegelian, excessively Nietzschean fomentation of inner experience: the point of extreme "contradiction" in which "*circular, absolute knowledge is definitive non-knowledge.*"[90] Inner experience is the encounter with the dream knot: a "dream of the unknown . . . the refusal to be everything," a loss of self in the night of nonknowledge, which carries the "meaning of dream."[91]

In Bataille's extremist surrealism and its corresponding religious sensibility, bodied forth in the dreaming Dionysus, a left-handed mysticism and oneiricism converge in the experience of nonknowledge. The dream logic that Bataille demonstrates in *Inner Experience* generates an anguishing ecstasy, a loss of self at once dreadful and exalting. In this way, his mystical practice and his writings at once promote and exemplify an "impersonal" mode of thought, that is, an attitude of thought directed beyond the self as defined within the profane sphere of rationality and instrumental reason. Bataille's extremist surrealism thereby overtakes and overturns Bretonian surrealism, with its will to synthetic closure and its individualizing tendencies. Bataille's dreams, his dream analyses, and the oneiricism that underwrites his mystical practice remain sovereign, never reduced to a single meaning, a stable interpretation. In Bataille's dream analyses, the generation of meanings empties out into the experience of ecstatic expenditure. Bataille's sovereign dreams provoke the dreamer to a sacrifice of the self. Ecstasy—a shattering of the self and an intimate communion with others—comes not by the imposition of reason but through the violence of a dream that sacrifices the self: an awakening within sleep.

And sleep, the ancient myths suggest, is the brother of death; as Hesiod tells us, Hypnos and Thanatos are twins. For Bataille, this filial proximity points to a truth dramatically on display throughout his writings. Bataille, who sought to "[formulate] a paradoxical philosophy," finds in sleep and death an impossible coincidence with wakefulness and the exuberance of life.[92] Similarly, he claims that "the condition in which I *would see* would be to die."[93] It is, paradoxically, in the confusions and obscurity of sleep that transgress the boundaries of rational thought that one accedes to the "DIVINE ACCURACY OF THE DREAM"—an extreme point in which lucidity and intoxication converge and clash, each exacerbating the other to the point of explosion.[94] The contradiction here is not merely apparent but *felt*, experienced in its fully shattering capacity. And this is *the* sovereign contradiction of Bataille's dream knot: it holds together sleep and waking, confusion and lucidity, death and life, in a union without unity. From this knot emerges the dreaming Dionysus, that contradictory monster in which birth and death are united in a single eruption: the Acéphale who disturbs sleep.

"Sleep grows sleepless in dreams," writes Bataille's intimate friend Maurice Blanchot.[95] Blanchot makes explicit what is implied everywhere in Bataille's affiliation of sacrificial mysticism and ecstatic oneiricism: that "to dream is to accept [the] invitation to exist almost anonymously, beside oneself, drawn outside of oneself."[96] Dream is within yet beyond sleep, in sleep but more than sleep; it is the awakening of the mind to a sacred world, unconstrained by the instrumental tendencies of the individual in his profane existence. The dream, approached as a heterological phenomenon, enacts a counteroperation, infecting and intoxicating waking life. It upsets the all too rigorous workings of reason. It decays, toxifies, and alters rational thought. To dream sovereignly is thus the invitation and the imperative of Bataille's extremist surrealism. It is to desire to be *sacrificed* unto one's dreams, thereby destroying the thingness of our very selves. It is to accede to a sacrificial identification with the Acéphale, becoming headless, for a time, in a negative ecstasy, an oneiric mysticism.

In *Guilty*, a fragmentary journal recording his wartime mystical pursuits, Bataille remarks that his "dreams are heavy and violent." The Acéphale lives on in these dreams. Bataille's dream accounts recall one of André Masson's renderings of the monster, in which what appears to be an erupting volcano situated in the background of the image appears in the place of the head of the monster, which soars aimlessly amid a stormy sky.[97] A severed head replaced by an erupting, and thus headless, volcano: a double beheading, a doubled ecstasy. Bataille's account, recorded several years after the drawing was executed, first describes, without interpreting, a dream in which he mounts a volcano, on the summit of which he is confronted by "an image of approaching catastrophe." He feels at once "anguish" and the "certainty of death," which give rise to a "lacerating laughter."[98]

This description segues into another dream. Bataille reveals nothing of this dream's content, writing only of its effects, which amount to a practical refutation of any notion of narcissistic wish fulfillment. Rather, the "wish" that this and other dreams represent for Bataille corresponds to the longing for "lost continuity" that he sees as the very "essence" of religion.[99] Such an experience of continuity, as we have seen, is predicated not on shoring up the ego by satisfying desire but on an ecstatic and fearful loss of self. Bataille's dream evinces the anguish of desire for transpersonal continuity, loss of self in a sacred experience of nonknowledge. This is the dream as a provocation, an invitation to risk. Bataille's dream is thus a profession of ungratified desire, a hymn to self-loss. The dream provokes him to "let [himself] go without hindrance":

> What I desired so possessed me, I was swept, raised up on waves of wild eloquence. . . . It was always death (desired and feared at the same time—and essentially consisting of the empty grandeur and unbearable laughter dreams allow), it was always death suggesting the leap, the power to connect up with a totally unknown blackness, which in fact won't ever be really known and whose appeal, not in the least inferior to even the most iridescent colors, consists in what it won't ever have, not the smallest speck of knowledge, since it's the annihilation of the system that had the power of knowing.[100]

Bataille's dreams, at once fearful and sacred, announce a left-handed path into the "unknown blackness" of the unconscious: an extremist surrealism bodied forth in the figure of the monstrous Acéphale. To identify sacrificially with this dreaming Dionysus is to risk a life liberated from servitude. It is to be relinquished unto the sovereign "caprice of dreams" that infects, like a contagion, like a toxin, the rigors of profane life.[101] It is to risk a sacred dream that cannot be owned and to dream unto an experience of the sacred beyond the power of knowing.

Afterword

AMY HOLLYWOOD

For years, I couldn't look at them. In the late eighties, I thought about writing my dissertation on Bataille, but as long as I couldn't look at the photographs—images of a torture victim Bataille describes himself meditating on during the days leading up to and in the midst of World War II—as long as I couldn't look at them, it seemed wrong to pretend to understand anything about Bataille. I thought it would be dishonest to write about him.

Most of the time, I can look at almost anything. But during those years, if I saw something hideous it never quite went away. I'd close my eyes and there it would be—a woman's body dismembered in a car wreck, a severed ear lying on bright green grass, a knife slicing through a man's leg. Movie images, paintings, photographs, but no less real in their effects on my inner eye. One day, a friend and I were crossing Fifty-Eighth Street at University; a pigeon ran under the tire of a moving car; it popped, a bloody burst that followed me for months, mapped onto the veins of my eyelid. (And behind all of this, the excruciatingly painful death of my father; he aged thirty years in a month, his body doubled over and twisted, colorless and gaunt, with one grossly swollen leg hanging off the bed and a mouth and throat covered with thrush.) I constantly read the medieval, modern, and contemporary literature of the grotesque, the horrible, and the abject, from Angela of Foligno to Georges Bataille to Dennis Cooper. But I couldn't look.

There was a paper clip in my copy of Michel Surya's biography of Bataille, holding closed the pages on which the images were reproduced. I had a giant Post-it on the pages of *Tears of Eros* and the *Amok* catalogue in which one of the photographs featured prominently. I wanted to put a Post-it over my brain. But I kept reading, even if I couldn't look.

There were some strange moments. Another, braver, friend described Bataille's meditation practice to a study group at the University of Chicago. People were outraged, as they often are when talking about Bataille. They insisted that it was obscene for him to use the image of a tortured human being as the basis for religious ecstasy. (I have never been convinced that is the best way to describe what he was doing.)

Christ hung, figuratively, and maybe even literally, over our heads. (I don't know if there was a crucifix in the room, but there was definitely a portrait of Paul Tillich hanging unostentatiously in the corner.) That particular torture, as Bataille knew, is barely visible. But what fascinated me, what, frankly, horrified me, was the fascination and glee with which these same men—and they were all men—stared at the photographs. The Surya biography went around the room, one person barely able to pry it away from the person next to him. Hands clutching the book, eyes riveted to the page, and at the same time—"Oh this is horrible, terrible, obscene. How could he stand to look at this?"

But Bataille couldn't stand to look at these photographs. He knew that they were unbearable, horrible beyond belief, obscene in every way imaginable. He tells us this, over and over again—although perhaps not in the same way over the years during which he wrote about the photographs and his relationship to them.

And yes, he looked at them, despite his horror. It was, somehow, essential to him that he do so. My question, when I could finally look at the photographs, and even before, when I couldn't, was why? Why was it so important for Bataille to look, and to see?

The easy answer is that he got off on it. That the shattering, slicing evisceration of another's physical body became the means for him to bring about a shattering of his psyche, one that he experienced as an ecstatic jouissance, a pleasure beyond pleasure because beyond any fixed site of either pleasure or pain, what Bataille's friend, the psychoanalyst Jacques Lacan, would later call a jouissance of the body. An experience, perhaps, but one undergone by a virtual body, one that may be constituted in part by bodily affects but cannot be reduced to them. For Bataille's very use of photographs and of writing to instantiate jouissance point inexorably to the impossibility of the body surviving its own shattering.

The photographs on which Bataille meditates both enact and expose the phantasmatic core of the very idea of a jouissance of the body. (They increasingly suggest to me that Lacan got something very wrong about Bataille.) To survive this shattering—and Bataille was, finally, interested in surviving—it must be one that we imagine, not experience directly in or on our own bodies. He was, in his wartime writings, resoundingly clear about this. If you cut the body apart, there will only be pain or, if you are anaesthetized, nothing. No sensation, no feeling, no suffering, no pleasure, no jouissance. Unlike some of his most avid fans, Bataille knew this. There might be an ecstatic jouissance in the dissolution of the self, but it is only ever phantasmatic and can only occur virtually—for Bataille, first and foremost, in writing.[1] This does not mean that writing and images don't have bodily effects. It does mean that Bataille knew the difference between the effect of torture (or execution, which is what is really going on in the photographs of the Chinese man as well as in the Crucifixion) on those who physically undergo it and those who imagine it.[2] The self-shattering he sought through meditation was, he knew, something very different from the bodily catastrophe undergone by the person in the photographs on which he meditated.

Not only is this experience—the inner experience Bataille sought just before and during World War II—necessarily virtual, it is also not at all clear that it is either erotic or joyful. The wartime writings are too anguished, too distraught, too—I hate to say it—too tortured, to be read in light of some self-shattering nonpleasurable pleasure (even if we try to evade that pleasure by calling it jouissance). Beyond that, like many of the authors of these essays, I think we owe it to Bataille to attend to his desire never to instrumentalize one self or another, his insistence that such instrumentalization is, quite simply, wrong. Could he succeed in this absolute refusal of instrumentalization? Undoubtedly not. But we need at least to read him and to try to think his meditational practice, in all of its complexity, as caught within the contradiction between having a goal, an end, or an object and the demand for a sovereignty—his own and that of others—free from such instrumentalizing agendas. What do you do when your goal is to have no goal? (How can one "live without a why," as Beatrice of Nazareth, Marguerite Porete, Meister Eckhart, and Angelus Silesius all claim that we must?) That is the question Bataille asks throughout the *Atheological Summa* and that haunts his writing both before and after the war.

At stake is—well, everything. And here is why I think Bataille is important and why I think Bataille is right that we should look at photographs like those of the torturous execution on which he meditated—but only if we are horrified by them. Or perhaps better, if we reach the point where nothing has the power to horrify us, to make us feel physically ill, to render us distraught, we are past the possibility of sovereignty, past the possibility of ethics, certainly past the possibility of a meaningful political or religious life.

Which isn't to say that being horrified is enough. This is the central insight of Bataille's short review essay of John Hersey's *Hiroshima*, published in his journal *Critique* in 1947. Dominick LaCapra turns to just this essay to argue that in it Bataille sacralizes trauma, recapitulating it as a transcendental sublime in which violence and sacrifice become the mark of the real, always impossible and inaccessible, yet vital to ethical and political life. For LaCapra, this is to ignore the concrete ethical, social, economic, and political contexts in which we live and in which traumatic events occur; it is to make another's suffering—or our own suffering—the site of what is most real and most valued and thereby to participate in a political defeatism in which only a certain kind of messianic apocalypse—one that will, moreover, never actually arrive—can save us. (LaCapra moves from Bataille to those vaguely in his orbit, like Walter Benjamin, or those who follow, in some way, in his path, among them, on LaCapra's reading, Giorgio Agamben, Jean-François Lyotard, and Jacques Derrida.)[3]

Yet in suggesting that, from one perspective at least, there is little to stand between the horrors of Hiroshima and the death of all of those human beings who have ever lived or will ever live, is Bataille sacralizing death and refusing politics? On the contrary: Bataille is worried about what happens when we move too facilely, too easily, past the horror of Hiroshima and past the horror of our own deaths to ask what we can do to end the atrocity. And for him, the one move entails or prepares us for or is the result of the other; I can't decide which of those logical and temporal terms to use because for Bataille, they *all* apply. In other words, the inability to look death in the face, whether it be our own or the deaths of thousands at Hiroshima and Nagasaki or millions in the Holocaust (about which Bataille does not here speak), is the same inability, the same terror, the same horror, the same fear.

I know it sounds obscene.

But think about it.

For, from one perspective, it is our attempt to deny death, to bring death to an end, that makes it impossible for us to look at death—that of one or of millions—in all of its horror and power. And so, Bataille suggests, our denial of death renders it impossible for us to live.

The sensibility that looks for a way out and enters along the path of politics is always of a cheap quality. It cheats, and it is clear that *in serving* political ends it is no more than a *servile*, or at least a subordinate sensibility. The cheating is quite apparent. If the misfortunes of Hiroshima are faced up to freely from the perspective of a sensibility that is not faked, they cannot be isolated from other misfortunes. . . . One cannot deny the differences in ages and in suffering but origin and intensity change nothing: horror is everywhere the same. The point that, in principle, the one horror is preventable while the other is not is, in the last analysis, a matter of indifference.[4]

If this sounds like a leveling of all particularity, a refusal to recognize that each horror *is* different, if only—but it is not only for this reason—because it is my own, we should note that these sweeping lines are followed by Bataille's injunction that to be sovereign one must look each singular misfortune in the face.[5]

The person of sovereign sensibility, Bataille insists, counter to almost any other conception of sovereignty available in 1947,

no longer immediately says, "At all costs let me do away with it," but first, "Let us live it." Let us lift, in the instant, a form of life to the level of the worst.

But no one, for all that, gives up doing away with what he can.[6]

We must always, Bataille argues, try to do away with what we can, but that work requires that we first acknowledge what it is that we face, and what we face is annihilation. Of ourselves first, of all humanity ultimately, certainly of the planet and the cosmos as we know it. Nothing lasts, and that is how we live. For Bataille, this became visible to him in the body of a man being executed in one of the most excruciating ways imaginable. Or perhaps he simply recognized there something he always knew. The horror remains the same; the injustice of that particular horror can and must be addressed, but not before we recognize the horror.

And still, we die. Death is always political, but it isn't only political. There is an ethics of dying, but no ethics can destroy death. This is probably why religion so often comes to occupy the space around death—the fact of death, the practices associated with death, and our attempts, however feeble, to think about death.[7] Yet if Bataille makes a mistake—or perhaps better, if we make a mistake in reading Bataille—it lies in the attempt to develop from his insights a general theory of religion (or a general theory of anything, for that matter, of economy, of sovereignty, of inner experience), however cogent and interesting that theory might be. For religion doesn't only have to do with death, and an account of religion grounded solely in the thought of death remains, like a politics in which all differences among the dead and dying are leveled, profoundly inadequate to the demands of the living. There is a particular, sharp, and devastating point to all that Bataille did, a particular shadow against the wall of the cave that he desperately wanted to make us see. Bataille was obsessed and obsessive, horrified by what he saw and by his fear that only he could see it. ("I don't know if in this way I express human helplessness—or my own.") What he saw was essential. We need to try to look with him. Yet we can't pretend that it's all that there is to see. Even Bataille, crazy as he was, knew that.

I have other images of death before my eyes—I always have, since I first read Bataille. Other horrors are etched on the inside of my eyelid. People I love who have suffered, gruesomely, and died before me. Sometimes I forget their wracked faces, their twisted bodies, the smell of their decomposing flesh, and the wounded, terrified sounds that emerge from their mouths. And I know that as much as I need to have seen these things, I also need to forget them. We must both remember and forget to live, to live well, to begin to think about what it might mean to live well. Georges Bataille—the man or the man of my imagination, I don't know—but *my* Georges Bataille was one of the bravest human beings to have left a record of his life during the horrible twentieth century, one of the most tortured and the most honest and the most real. There are countless ways in which he has saved me, again and again, even as he's scared the shit out of me. But I also know he probably didn't see everything; he didn't say everything; he wasn't always right. And I don't need him to be, at least not anymore.[8]

Notes

Introduction: Sacred with a Vengeance
Jeremy Biles and Kent L. Brintnall

1. Gill, "Introduction" to *Bataille: Writing the Sacred*, xv. For a detailed study of *Story of the Eye*, see ffrench, *The Cut: Reading Bataille's* Histoire de l'oeil. For divergent readings of the gender politics of the novel, see Hollywood, *Sensible Ecstasy*, 39–54; and Brintnall, *Ecce Homo*, 188–197.

2. Bataille's older brother, Martial, disputes this characterization of their parents. For a detailed biographical account, see Surya, *Georges Bataille: An Intellectual Biography*, 3–13. It is tempting to see the parents—Joseph-Aristide and Marie-Antoinette—as the mad, perverse counterparts of the biblical Joseph and Mary and their son Georges as a sinister reiteration of Christ; Bataille indeed identified with the incarnate word, the carnal god, crucified and crying out.

3. Much of the present biographical account is drawn from Bataille, "Autobiographical Note," collected in *My Mother, Madame Edwarda, The Dead Man*, 215–222.

4. See "Coincidences" in *Story of the Eye*, 94. For a discussion of Bataille's reliability as a narrator of his own life, see Hollywood, *Sensible Ecstasy*, 44–45.

5. Bataille, "Autobiographical Note," 217.

6. See Bataille, *Story of the Eye*, 58–64; see also Leiris, *Mirror of Tauromachy*. Bataille credited Leiris's *Mirror* as central to his own endeavors to unravel the problems of eroticism and its connections to religion. See Bataille, *Erotism*, 9.

7. Bataille, "Autobiographical Note," 218.

8. Bataille speaks of "the open wound that my life is" in a letter to Alexandre Kojève collected in *Guilty*, 123.

9. On Bataille's repetition of Nietzsche, see Abel, "Georges Bataille and the Repetition of Nietzsche." See also Biles, *Ecce Monstrum*, 36–71.

10. Stuart Kendall uses this phrase to describe Bataille's Nietzschean undertakings in the publication *Acéphale*, addressed further below. Kendall, "Editor's Introduction: Unlimited Assemblage," xx.

11. Bataille, *Theory of Religion*, 109.

12. Bataille, *The Tears of Eros*, 206–207. The significance of Bataille's meditations on this photo are testified to by the frequency with which scholars use it as an entry point to their consideration of Bataille. See, for example, Biles, *Ecce Monstrum*, 9–12; Brintnall, *Ecce Homo*, 1–8, 20–24; Buch, *The Pathos of the Real*, 27–39; Connor, *Georges Bataille and the Mysticism of Sin*, 1–7; Hollywood, *Sensible Ecstasy*, 79–94. For critical assessments of Bataille's use of these torture images, see Brook, Bourgon, and Blue, *Death by a Thousand Cuts*, 222–242; and Elkins, "The Very Theory of Transgression: Bataille, *Lingchi*, and Transgression," 5–19.

13. Denis Hollier cites Raymond Queneau's quoting of Bataille in "The Dualist Materialism of Georges Bataille."

14. Bataille, "Autobiographical Note," 218.

15. See André Breton, *Manifestoes of Surrealism*, 119–194.

16. Leiris, "*De la Bataille impossible à l'impossible* 'Documents,'" 689.

17. For further discussion of *Documents*, see Ades and Baker, *Undercover Surrealism*; Falasca-Zamponi, *Rethinking the Political*, 95–103.

18. Bataille, "The Use Value of D. A. F. De Sade," in *Visions of Excess*, 94.

19. Bataille, *On Nietzsche*, 19. On Bataille's understanding of communication and community, see the exchange between Maurice Blanchot and Jean-Luc Nancy: Blanchot, "The Negative Community," in *The Unavowable Community*, 1–26; and Nancy, *The Inoperative Community*, 1–42; see also the essays collected in Mitchell and Winfree, eds., *The Obsessions of Georges Bataille: Community and Communication*.

20. Bataille, "Autobiographical Note," 220.

21. Bataille, "The Sacred Conspiracy," in *Visions of Excess*, 179. Uppercase in the original.

22. Bataille, "The Sacred," in *Visions of Excess*, 242.

23. For the Collège's lectures, see Hollier, ed., *The College of Sociology, 1937–1939*. For intellectual histories of the Collège, see Falasca-Zamponi, *Rethinking the Political*; and Richman, *Sacred Revolutions*.

24. For a discussion of Bataille's sacred politics, see Irwin, *Saints of the Impossible*. See also Surya, *Georges Bataille*, for a detailed account of Bataille's political involvements.

25. Bataille, "Autobiographical Note," 219–220.

26. Bataille himself claims that the secret society "[turned] its back on politics"—a statement that must be read in the context of his wider thought and activity. As Hollywood has argued, the gesture of turning away from politics is, for Bataille, itself a political gesture. See Hollywood, *Sensible Ecstasy*, 60–87.

27. A complete survey of Bataille's religious development would have to take full account of the profound influence exercised upon Bataille's concept of the sacred by Laure. Mostly overlooked or underappreciated in the critical literature

on Bataille, Laure was a key interlocutor for Bataille and a compelling, incisive, and impassioned thinker in her own right. For a detailed treatment of Laure's role in the thought of Bataille and Michel Leiris, see Sweedler, *The Dismembered Community*; see also the notes collected in Stuart Kendall's recent translation of *Guilty*. For Laure's writings, see *Laure: The Collected Writings*.

28. Bataille, "Autobiographical Note," 221.

29. Gemerchak, *The Sunday of the Negative*, 171.

30. On the complex compositional and publication history of *La somme*, see Kendall, "Editor's Introduction."

31. For recent investigations of Bataille's emphasis on consumption over production and the general economy perspective of *The Accursed Share*, see Stoekl, *Bataille's Peak*; Winnubst, ed., *Reading Bataille Now*.

32. Bataille, "Joy in the Face of Death," in *The College of Sociology, 1937–1939*, 325.

33. Bataille, *Erotism*, 16.

34. Bataille, "Autobiographical Note," 222.

35. Bataille, *Erotism*, 19.

36. Referring to Blanchot's notion of "unworking," Jean-Luc Nancy describes Bataillean community as "that which, before or beyond the work, withdraws from the work, and which, no longer having to do either with production or with completion, encounters interruption, fragmentation, suspension." Nancy, *The Inoperative Community*, 31.

37. "Principle of inner experience: to emerge through project from the realm of project. . . . Reason alone has the power to undo its work, to hurl down that which it has built up." Bataille, *Inner Experience*, 46.

38. Bataille, "Autobiographical Note," 222.

39. Michel Surya describes the "little death" of the orgasm as a "negative miracle" Bataille speaks of in discussing sovereignty. Surya, *Bataille: An Intellectual Biography*, 453.

40. To borrow the title of Jürgen Habermas's essay on Bataille, "The French Path to Postmodernity: Bataille Between Eroticism and General Economics."

41. Bataille's formally experimental style has also garnered significant attention. See, for example, Guerlac, *Literary Polemics*; Hill, *Bataille, Klossowski, Blanchot*; Shaviro, *Passion and Excess*; Stoekl, *Politics, Writing, Mutilation*.

42. For representative selections of work by these figures and other leading poststructuralist thinkers, see Boldt-Irons, ed., *On Bataille: Critical Essays*; Botting and Wilson, ed., *Bataille: A Critical Reader*.

43. Bataille, "Formless," in *Visions of Excess*, 31.

44. Bois and Krauss, *Formless: A User's Guide*; Foster, *Compulsive Beauty*. For a slightly different interpretation of Bataille's notion of *informe*, see the introductory essays in Crowley and Hegarty, eds., *Formless: Ways In and Out of Form*.

45. For Biles's prior discussions of Bataille's relation to surrealism, see *Ecce Monstrum*, 72–94. For a selection of Bataille's essays on surrealist themes, see Michael Richardson, ed., *The Absence of Myth: Writings on Surrealism*.

46. For the history of *Tel Quel*, see ffrench, *The Time of Theory*; Kauppi, *The Making of an Avant-Garde*; Marx-Scouras, *The Cultural Politics of* Tel Quel.

47. Kosky, "Georges Bataille's Religion Without Religion," 81.

48. In this way, Lingis extends the work of the first English-language book-length study on Bataille. In *Reading Georges Bataille: Beyond the Gift*, Michèle Richman focuses on Bataille's understanding of the gift and sacrifice and his engagement with—and deviation from—Marcel Mauss to organize her study of the key ideas to be found in Bataille's oeuvre.

49. For other considerations of Bataille's relation to queer theory, see Dean, "The Erotics of Transgression"; Downing and Gillett, "Georges Bataille at the Avant-Garde of Queer Theory? Transgression, Perversion, and the Death Drive"; Irwin, *Saints of the Impossible*, 220–225; Winnubst, "Bataille's Queer Pleasures."

50. Habermas, "The French Path to Postmodernity," 167.

51. Ibid., 168–169.

52. Ibid., 168–169.

53. Ibid., 169.

54. Kosky, "Georges Bataille's Religion Without Religion," 78. For further discussion of the relationship between Bataille and Heidegger, see Gasché, *Georges Bataille: Phenomenology and Phantasmology.*

55. Kosky, "Georges Bataille's Religion Without Religion," 85.

56. For an engagement with these themes and questions, see Mansfield, *The God Who Deconstructs Himself.*

57. Robbins, "Introduction" to Caputo and Vattimo, *After the Death of God*, 13.

58. Kosky, "Georges Bataille's Religion Without Religion," 86.

59. Ibid.

60. Ibid.

61. Ibid., 81.

62. Taylor, *Altarity*, 135–148.

63. For a response to Hollywood's assessment of Bataille's gender politics, see Brintnall, *Ecce Homo*, 171–197.

64. See Connor, *Georges Bataille and the Mysticism of Sin*; Hussey, *The Inner Scar.*

65. Stoekl, *Bataille's Peak.*

66. For a similar project vis-à-vis critical theory, see Plotinsky, *Reconfigurations.*

67. See Mauss, *The Gift.* For the influence of French sociological thought on Bataille's conception of the sacred and its relation to the social, see especially the work of Michèle Richman, *Reading Georges Bataille* and *Sacred Revolutions.*

68. Taylor, *About Religion*, 1.

69. Smith, *Imagining Religion*, xi. The present volume in many ways works against Smith's own rationalistic imagination of religion.

70. David Chidester raises the question of what "counts" as religion throughout his *Authentic Fakes.*

71. Lingis, "Foreword: Why Bataille Now?" in *Reading Bataille Now*, xi.

72. Taylor, *Refiguring the Spiritual*, 199n.h. On the other hand, religious studies scholars are becoming increasingly attuned to the visual and material dimensions of religion and the crucial, if sometimes implicit, ways in which religion animates art. See, for example, Kosky, *Arts of Wonder: Enchanting Secularity*; Morgan, *The Sacred Gaze*; and Plate, *A History of Religion in 5½ Objects*.

Movements of Luxurious Exuberance: Georges Bataille and Fat Politics
Lynne Gerber

1. This chapter was imagined and written in continual conversation with Kent Brintnall, Sarah Quinn, and Susan Stinson. As always, they have my immense gratitude.

2. Seid, *Never Too Thin*; Stearns, *Fat History*.

3. Stearns, *Fat History*, 64.

4. Leslie Blanch, quoted in Fraser, *Losing It!*, 57.

5. Bataille, *Accursed Share*, 2:95.

6. Braziel and Lebesco, "Editor's Introduction," *Bodies Out of Bounds*.

7. Baudrillard, "Figures of the Transpolitical."

8. Stearns, *Fat History*, 64.

9. Farrell, *Fat Shame*, 7.

10. Guthman and Dupuis, "Embodying Neoliberalism," 429.

11. Farrell, *Fat Shame*, 7.

12. Ibid., 137–171; Sobal, "The Size Acceptance Movement and the Social Construction of Body Weight."

13. Braziel and Lebesco, "Editor's Introduction," 1.

14. Lebesco, *Revolting Bodies*, 3.

15. See, for example, Murray, "(Un/Be)Coming Out? Rethinking Fat Politics."

16. Efforts like these belie Lauren Berlant's assertion that "there is nothing promising, heroic or critical" about the alleged "obesity epidemic." Berlant, "Slow Death," 767.

17. "Difficult Seductress!" 14.

18. Bataille, quoted in Biles, *Ecce Monstrum*, 33.

19. Bataille recognizes that scarcity exists in some human locations and that it is a genuine concern. However, he is trying to view the economy from a general perspective rather than a particular one. Bataille, *Accursed Share*, 1:23.

20. Ibid., 1:28.

21. Ibid., 1:21.

22. Bataille, "The Notion of Expenditure," 117.

23. Bataille, *Accursed Share*, 1:55–56.

24. Ibid., 1:59.

25. Ibid., 1:57.

26. "Today the great and free forms of unproductive social expenditure have disappeared. One must not conclude from this, however, that the very principle

of expenditure is no longer the end of the economic system. A certain evolution of wealth, whose symptoms indicate sickness and exhaustion, leads to shame in oneself and petty hypocrisy. Everything that was generous, orgiastic, and excessive has disappeared." Bataille, "The Notion of Expenditure," 124.

27. Bataille, *Accursed Share*, 1:122.

28. Bataille, "The Notion of Expenditure," 125.

29. Bataille, *Accursed Share*, 1:30–31.

30. Stoekl, *Bataille's Peak*, 135.

31. Ibid., 184. Baudrillard's work on obesity can also be seen as a fat-negative reading of fatness and excess grounded, in part, in Bataille's work. See Baudrillard, "Figures of the Transpolitical."

32. On the limitations of dieting as a weight-loss strategy, see Mann et al., "Medicare's Search for Effective Obesity Treatments."

33. Marketdata Enterprises, "U.S. Weight Loss Market."

34. Griffith, *Born Again Bodies*.

35. For parallels between contemporary dieting practices and religion, see Hesse-Biber, *Am I Thin Enough*, chap. 1; Stinson, *Women and Dieting Culture*, chap. 5.

36. Gerber, *Seeking the Straight and Narrow*; Griffith, *Born Again Bodies*, chaps. 4–5.

37. Bataille, *Inner Experience*, 45.

38. Ibid., 21.

39. See, for example, Bataille, *Erotism*, 117–128.

40. Bataille, "The Practice of Joy Before Death."

41. Irwin, *Saints of the Impossible*, 35.

42. Biles, *Ecce Monstrum*, 4.

43. Cited in Moon and Sedgwick, "Divinity," 251.

44. Cited in Stinson, "Fat Girls Need Fiction," 232.

45. "Who Is Fat Girl?" *FaT GiRL* 1 (1994): 41.

46. "Indeed," they write, "it is his absolute refusal of such a move that makes the center of gravity of his inimitably hefty thematics. In a late-capitalist world economy of consumption, the problematics of waste and residue, hitherto economically marginal, tend increasingly to assume an uncanny centrality. . . . If an ecological system includes no 'out there' to which the waste product can, in fantasy, be destined, then it makes sense that the meaning-infused, diachronically right, perhaps inevitably nostalgic chemical, cultural, and material garbage—our own waste—in whose company we are destined to live and die is accruing new forms of interpretive magnetism and new forms, as well, of affective and erotic value." Moon and Sedgwick, "Divinity," 235.

47. This question of the "reality" of these excessive acts echoes some responses to Bataille's work on violence and whether he "really" advocated it or was simply discussing it as metaphor, representation, or the like. This question became especially pressing after World War II made the valorization of real violence nearly impossible for anyone who had lived through it. For a discussion of Ba-

taille and violence in the context of the war, see Chapter 4 of Irwin's *Saints of the Impossible*.

48. Stinson, "Drink."

49. "You Are Cordially Invited to the Join the Kitchen Slut for Dessert," 12–13.

50. Kulik, "Porn."

51. Murray, "(Un/Be)coming Out?"

52. "Oh My God, It's Big Mama! Interview with Max Airborne and Elizabeth Hong Brassil," *FaT GiRL* 1:15.

53. This fat ambivalence became a controversial issue among readers of *FaT GiRL*. In issue 3, in an interview on fat/thin relationships titled "Deva and Laura," Deva expressed her fat ambivalence, saying "So we've all got great fat politics, we know what's up. And fuck that, we all still feel like shit, I don't care what you say. A lot of fat women still feel like shit no matter how much they're up on their politics, and no, they're not 'supposed' to feel like shit, or have fucked up feelings about food, and all that. And I'm sorry, but we still do." (3:31). The next issue contained a letter from a reader responding to Deva's statement by saying "To me, saying you feel like shit only keeps the hatred inside and then the culture wins. It made me sad to read Deva's statements. I've come across similar sentiment in other *FG* stories and interviews. I'm not suggesting we not deal with self-hatred. I'm only suggesting we acknowledge it and push forward to self-love." (4:4). *FaT GiRL*'s willingness to dwell in moments of self-hatred without requiring the concomitant move toward self-love was, in my view, part of its riveting power.

54. My use of death threats is quite different from its traditional usage, which designates threats made on the life of an individual by another individual who intends to carry out the threat personally or to supervise its implementation personally. In my usage, it refers to the generalized, diffuse sense many fat people experience that their life is under continual, often imminent threat. In the case of fatness, this threat is often depicted as self-inflicted (your life is at risk because of your self-evidently dangerous eating/exercising/other personal habits), but it is disseminated widely through a range of social institutions, most prominently in the media and in medicine. The plausibility of those threats is extremely difficult to ascertain and thus extremely difficult to defuse, and thus the threats have a significant impact on people's lives independently of their literal truth.

55. Flegal et al., "Excess Deaths Associated with Underweight, Overweight, and Obesity."

56. For more on the nocebo effect, see Barsky et al., "Nonspecific Medication Side Effects and the Nocebo Phenomenon."

57. LaMendola, "Some Ob-Gyns in South Florida Turn Away Overweight Women."

58. For example, see Fabricatore, Wadden, and Foster, "Bias in Healthcare Settings."

59. On the health debacle that was phen-fen, see Kolata, *Rethinking Thin*, 21–26.

60. On death rates associated with weight-loss surgery see B. I. Omalu et al., "Death Rates and Causes of Death After Bariatric Surgery." Death risks, the article notes, include a quadrupled suicide rate compared to the general population.

61. See Fraser, *Losing It!*, 195.

62. Patterson used the term to describe the strange social status/nonstatus of slaves (*Slavery and Social Death*, 35–76). The term has been taken up by the queer theorist Judith Butler to conceptualize the threats of discursive illegibility and social nonexistence. See Butler, *Antigone's Claim.*

63. Janna Fikkan and Esther Rothblum, "Weight Bias in Employment"; Ernesberger, "Does Social Class Explain the Connection Between Weight and Health?"

64. Prohaska and Gailey, "Fat Women as 'Easy Targets.'"

65. Kolata, "Study Says Obesity Can Be Contagious."

66. Bataille, quoted in Biles, *Ecce Monstrum*, 33.

67. Bataille, *Inner Experience*, 39.

68. Bataille, *Accursed Share*, 2:108–109; Bataille, *Erotism*, 18–19.

69. Bataille, *Inner Experience*, 39.

70. Kinzel, "It Was Supposed to Be Funny."

71. Bersani, "Is the Rectum a Grave?" 29.

72. Bataille, *Accursed Share*, 2:96.

73. Airborne, "The Fat Truth," 49.

74. Bataille shows some recognition of this problem when he writes about extreme poverty and the difference between transgression and hopelessness. He writes: "Extreme poverty releases men from the taboos that make human beings of them, not as transgression does, but in that a sort of hopelessness, not absolute perhaps, gives the animal impulses free rein. Hopelessness is not a return to animal nature. The world of transgression which swallowed up humanity as a whole is essentially different from the animal world, and so is the restricted world of hopelessness." *Erotism*, 135.

75. Hollywood, *Sensible Ecstasy*, 84.

76. Bataille, *Inner Experience*, 3.

77. Bataille, *Accursed Share*, 2:14.

78. "To solve political problems," Bataille writes, "becomes difficult for those who allow anxiety alone to pose them. It is necessary for anxiety to pose them. But their solution demands at a certain point the removal of this anxiety." *Accursed Share*, 1:13–14.

79. Bataille, *Accursed Share*, 1:77.

Sovereignty and Cruelty: Self-Affirmation, Self-Dissolution, and the Bataillean Subject
Stephen S. Bush

1. De Sade "emerged with no revelation, but at least he disputed all the easy answers." De Beauvoir, *Must We Burn Sade?*, 89.

2. Hollywood, *Sensible Ecstasy*, 82–84, 94.

3. Ibid., 84.

4. Brintnall, *Ecce Homo*, 8.

5. "His task as a writer was to communicate a refusal of the logic of power that found its supreme expression in war and to affirm a sovereignty not based on the domination of others, but on the sacrificial calling-into-question of the self." Irwin, *Saints of the Impossible*, 166.

6. Biles, *Ecce Monstrum*, 5.

7. Andolsen, "Agape in Feminist Ethics."

8. Ibid., 74.

9. For example, see Irwin, *Saints of the Impossible*, 147.

10. Shklar, "Liberalism of Fear."

11. Artaud, *The Theater and Its Double*, 41–42, 51.

12. Ibid., 79.

13. Ibid., 122.

14. Ibid., 84–85, 101–103.

15. Blanchot, "Sade's Reason;" Bataille, *Erotism.*

16. Blanchot, "Sade's Reason," 38.

17. For a more extensive comparison of the concept of cruelty in the work of Artaud, Blanchot, and Bataille, see Toal, "Summit of Violence."

18. Bataille, "L'art, exercise de la cruauté," in *Oeuvres completes*, 11:483; Bataille, *Erotism*, 183–184.

19. Bataille, "L'art, exercise de la cruauté," in *Oeuvres completes*, 11:485.

20. Bataille, *Accursed Share* 1:49.

21. Bataille, *Story of the Eye.*

22. Bataille, *Erotism*, 181.

23. Ibid., 187.

24. Bataille, *Inner Experience*, 119.

25. Bataille, *Trial of Gilles de Rais*, 39–40.

26. Bataille, *Erotism*, 22.

27. Bataille, *Inner Experience*, 7.

28. Bataille, *Accursed Share*, 3:197.

29. Ibid., 3:246.

30. Ibid., 3:252.

31. Ibid., 3:254. See also 3:221.

32. Although the loss of self is never total, prior to death. The self is still off there, waiting in the wings, in Bataillean ecstasy. Bataille, *Inner Experience*, 60.

33. Bataille, *Accursed Share* 3:256, 430.

34. Bataille, *Inner Experience*, 60.

35. Bataille, *Erotism*, 189.

36. Ibid., 183.

37. "Ce n'est pas l'apologie des faits horribles. Ce n'est past un appel à leur retour." Bataille, "L'art, exercise de la cruauté," in *Oeuvres completes*, 11:485.

38. Bataille, *Erotism*, 183.

39. Ibid., 183–184. See also Bataille, "Reflections on the Executioner and the Victim," 18.

40. Bataille, *Erotism*, 194.

41. Bataille, *Guilty*, 30.

42. Butler, *Precarious Life*, 25–29.

43. Bataille, *Inner Experience*, 53.

44. Bataille, "Reflections on the Executioner," 19.

45. As Irwin says: "The inner experience of freedom remains the precondition of any meaningful deployment of freedom in the public, political world." Irwin, *Saints of the Impossible*, 163. See also Connor, *Georges Bataille and the Mysticism of Sin*, 151.

46. Bataille, "Reflections on the Executioner," 18.

47. Bataille, *Erotism*, 184; Bataille, "Reflections on the Executioner," 19.

48. Bataille, *Erotism*, 185.

49. Ibid.

50. Bataille, "Reflections on the Executioner," 19.

51. Bush, "Ethics of Ecstasy."

52. I am grateful for helpful feedback on a version of this essay from Fannie Bialek, Jeremy Biles, Kent Brintnall, Joshua Schenkkan, and an anonymous reviewer.

Erotic Ruination: Embracing the "Savage Spirituality" of Barebacking
Kent L. Brintnall

1. Bataille, *Erotism*, 11.

2. Ibid., 31.

3. Bataille, *Theory of Religion*, 57. See Bataille, *Erotism*, 15–16.

4. Bataille, *Erotism*, 17, 18.

5. Ibid., 16.

6. Dean, *Unlimited Intimacy*, 2. Because the term "barebacking" covers a wide range of practices—from drug-induced carelessness to conscientious serosorting between partners—I should clarify that I intend in this essay to apply it solely to the practices of "bug chasing" and "gift-giving"—i.e., male-male, condomless, anal sex intended to transmit the virus that causes AIDS. Dean provides a clear and detailed overview of the various practices that can be included under the umbrella term "barebacking" (*Unlimited Intimacy*, 11–18). Although he insists all types of condomless sex be included when discussing barebacking, given that some forms do not involve intentional encounters with risk and others are consistent with "a desire to contain HIV" (ibid., 12), the various practices comprise remarkably different attitudes, dispositions, and fantasies. They are, in Bataille's terms, profoundly different psychological quests.

7. Dean, *Unlimited Intimacy*, xii, 210.

8. Ibid., 62–69.

9. Ibid., 191.

10. Dean, *Beyond Sexuality*, 165. See also Dean, "Sex and Syncope," 78.

11. Bersani has published "Shame on You" as the second chapter of *Intimacies*, co-authored with the British psychoanalytic critic Adam Phillips, and as a con-

tribution to the anthology *After Sex?*, edited by Janet Halley and Andrew Parker. The essay is identical to the chapter, save for its last two-and-a-half paragraphs. Because I find the concluding paragraphs of the *After Sex?* version helpful for understanding the distinction Bersani seeks to draw between self-shattering masochism and self-dispersing narcissism, I cite the *After Sex?* version of the essay throughout the present pages.

12. Bersani, "Shame on You," 107. Bersani rejects even the psychic death that barebacking as an ethical disposition valorizes (ibid., 108). In a much more interesting critique of barebacking, Dean suggests that it demands too much from sex as a site for reconfiguring the subject's relation to alterity (Dean, *Beyond Sexuality*, 165–173). Insofar as Dean, echoing Bersani, imagines aesthetic—rather than sexual—experience as an alternative site for new relational configurations, Bataille remains a potentially generative conversation partner (see, for example, Bataille, *Erotism*, 24–25; see also Brintnall, *Ecce Homo*, 13–18).

13. Bersani, "Shame on You," 104.

14. Bataille, *Erotism*, 22–23.

15. Bersani, "Shame on You," 108. Bersani recognizes that, for Bataille, sexuality and mysticism can give rise to similar self-shattering experiences ("Rectum," 24–25).

16. Bersani, "Is the Rectum a Grave?" 3.

17. Ibid., 24.

18. Ibid. Although those reading Bersani in relation to queer theory may encounter him first through "Is the Rectum a Grave?" the essay is the culmination of a long exploration of this self-shattering capacity of sexuality. See, for example, Bersani and Dutoit, *The Forms of Violence*; Bersani, *The Freudian Body*. Although he has more recently critiqued psychoanalysis's ability to provide a nonaggressive, nonappropriative relational model and has moved away from his celebration of masochistic jouissance, he continues to repeat these observations about sexuality in his more recent work.

19. Bersani, "Is the Rectum a Grave?" 24–25.

20. Bersani, *The Freudian Body*, 39.

21. Bersani, *The Forms of Violence*, 34.

22. Ibid.; Bersani, *The Freudian Body*, 61–64.

23. Bersani, "Is the Rectum a Grave?" 25. Bersani's characterization of masochism as an "evolutionary conquest" succumbs to just such a risk. On this understanding, the relevant struggle is between self and world, and masochism allows the self to endure long enough to develop the skills needed to master the world.

24. Ibid., 22.

25. Ibid., 30. When he repeats these statements in the prologue to *The Culture of Redemption*, Bersani parenthetically notes that the jouissance he has in mind is figured in Bataille's writing (4). While Dean cites Bersani's analysis with approval in *Beyond Sexuality*, he characterizes it as an attempt to redeem subjectivity, based on a confusion "between a subject founded in the *ego* . . . and a subject founded in—and therefore split by—the *unconscious*" (131). This problem arises, according

to Dean, because Bersani derives "the term *jouissance* from Bataille rather than Lacan" (ibid.). While a full consideration of the relation between Bataille's and Lacan's respective understandings of desire lies outside the scope of this essay, any such comparison, especially as it engages Dean's work, would need to compare Bataille's understanding of the object of desire with Lacan's notion of the *objet petit a.* For a discussion of the former, see Brintnall, *Ecce Homo*, 178–185; for a discussion of the latter, see Dean, *Beyond Sexuality*, 40–50, 195–199, 248–253. Further, given that many scholars have argued that Lacan derived his conception of jouissance from Bataille, it is unclear how great a distinction there is.

26. Bersani, "Is the Rectum a Grave?" 25.

27. Bataille, *Erotism*, 12, 16–17.

28. Ibid., 18.

29. Ibid., 49.

30. See, for example, Bataille, *The Accursed Share*, 1:21.

31. See Bataille, *Erotism*, 102–103; Bataille, *Tears of Eros*, 142–149.

32. Bataille, *Guilty*, 44–45.

33. Bersani, "Shame on You," 108. Mindful of the distinction between masochism serving life by helping the human infant survive and masochism serving life by mobilizing desire over and against the self, it is important to note that Bersani's work has always contained an ambivalence about masochism and an impulse to redeem the self from masochism's most exuberant energies. This ambivalence is also apparent in Bersani's stated concern about the similarity between masochistic jouissance and self-directed, sadistic moral opprobrium. From his earliest articulation of the self-shattering character of sexuality, Bersani has expressed reservations about the violence that inheres in this experience. These concerns are articulated most fully in *Forms of Violence* and *The Freudian Body.* For helpful overviews of the continuities and shifts in Bersani's work, see Bersani, "Conversation"; Dean, "Sex and Syncope"; Dean, "Sex and Aesthetics."

34. Bersani, "Shame on You," 108. Bersani—writing with his frequent collaborator Ulysse Dutoit—complicates the distinction between his conception of masochism and narcissism when he states that the "aesthetic 'violence'" of Assyrian art, which was aligned with masochism in *Forms of Violence*, also illustrates the aesthetic mobility of narcissism outlined in *Arts of Impoverishment* (*Arts of Impoverishment*, 137–140). A similar confusion is produced when he parenthetically notes that Bataille, whom he had aligned with masochistic self-shattering in "Rectum," could have been included in *Art of Impoverishment*'s study of narcissistic self-replication (8). Although I agree that Bataille's novels disperse and disseminate the reader's ego beyond identity, I do not think they allow for its confirmation, replication, or refinding. See Brintnall, *Ecce Homo*, 188–197. For Bersani's most extensive engagement with a Bataillean text, see his analysis of *Blue of Noon* in *Culture of Redemption*, 109–123.

35. Bersani, "Sociality and Sexuality," 118–119. See also "Sociability and Cruising," 55–57, 62. For Bersani's conception of impersonal narcissism, in addition to sources already cited, see Leo Bersani, "Psychoanalysis and the Aesthetic Subject,"

in *Is the Rectum a Grave? and Other Essays*, 139–153; Bersani and Dutoit, *Caravaggio's Secrets*; Bersani and Dutoit, *Forms of Being*, 124–178.

36. Bataille, *Erotism*, 102.

37. Bataille, *Theory of Religion*, 29.

38. See Bataille, *Erotism*, 15. Given that barebacking eroticizes the exchange of bodily fluids, it seems noteworthy that Bataille often relies on images of water to illuminate his understanding of continuity.

39. Bataille, *Theory of Religion*, 50.

40. Ibid., 51. Bataille contends that violence, which he refuses to define (see *Erotism*, 55), should be understood as whatever interferes with the everyday, normal reality of work, labor, goal-oriented, productive activity (*Theory of Religion*, 9).

41. Bataille, *Theory of Religion*, 52.

42. Bataille, *Erotism*, 17.

43. Ibid.,102–103.

44. Bersani, *Homos*, 99.

45. Bersani, "Shame on You," 107.

46. Bersani, "Sociality and Sexuality," 110.

47. Bataille, *Accursed Share*, 2:105–109; *Erotism*, 86–87.

48. Bersani, "Shame on You," 108.

49. Dean, "The Erotics of Transgression," 75. See also Dean, "Bareback Time," 77.

50. Ibid., ix–x, 89–96.

51. Ibid., 48–55, 58.

52. Although I would not accuse Dean of having "suppressed" Bataille to shape his conclusions in a particular fashion, given that *Unlimited Intimacy* is a study of the connections among sex, death, gift giving, intimacy, sacrifice, nonpurposive activity, noninstrumental relations, and ethics—all of which receive significant attention in Bataille's writings—the complete lack of reference to Bataille is, to use Dean's language, "weird" ("Impossible Embrace," 135). In *Beyond Sexuality*, although he does include Bataille in a list of "anti-humanist" thinkers, Dean similarly fails to engage Bataille in his enormously suggestive discussions about the relation between sexuality and aesthetics (172–173, 277–279), even though this connection is given significant attention by Bataille. This elision is even stranger given that Dean cites Catherine Clément's *Syncope*, a Bataillean study of these issues (278n11; see also Dean, "Sex and Syncope," 76–79).

53. Dean, "The Erotics of Transgression," 70.

54. Ibid., 73, 77.

55. Bataille, *Accursed Share*, 1:68–74; Dean, *Unlimited Intimacy*, 77–78.

56. Dean, *Unlimited Intimacy*, 71–72.

57. Insofar as barebacking occurs at parties where several tops have sex with one—or a small number—of bottoms (*Unlimited Intimacy*, 122–144), the prestige accruing to gift givers can be distributed among several people who occupy the position. Bug chasers also secure prestige by exposing themselves to the risk of vi-

ral transmission and other extreme forms of sexual pleasure (50–52). In sum, inasmuch as prestige is conceived in comparative, hierarchical terms, it would be quite difficult to assess who has acquired it in any particular barebacking encounter.

58. Dean, *Unlimited Intimacy*, 53.

59. Ibid., 79.

60. Ibid., 80.

61. Ibid., 94.

62. Ibid., 79–80.

63. Bataille, *Accursed Share*, 1:22–23.

64. See, for example, testimony from Scott O'Hara (*Unlimited Intimacy*, 73–74).

65. See Bataille, *Accursed Share*, 1:28–29.

66. And, insofar as eroticization of viral transmission within the barebacking subculture invigorates and energizes its participants, the virus can be understood as serving life in the same way that masochism does, on the second understanding attributed to Bersani above.

67. Dean, *Unlimited Intimacy*, 79. Emphasis added.

68. Not only does Dean fail to acknowledge Bataille, but the source he cites—Lewis Hyde's *The Gift: Imagination and the Erotic Life of Property*—also fails to credit Bataille.

69. Bataille, *Accursed Share*, 1:23.

70. Ibid., 1:25.

71. Bataille, *Accursed Share*, 2:17.

72. Dean, *Unlimited Intimacy*, 56.

73. Morris, "No Limits," 5. For a slightly different edit of this quotation, see Dean, *Unlimited Intimacy*, 56–57. Bersani also discusses Morris ("Shame on You," 100–101).

74. Dean, *Unlimited Intimacy*, 57–58.

75. Morris, "No Limits," 5–6.

76. Fleshing out his consideration of this "sacrificial ethic," Dean makes an unexpected comparison between Morris's apology for barebacking and Gabriel Rotello's call for greater "responsibility" on the part of gay men. Dean, *Unlimited Intimacy*, 57. Although "Rotello argues that the price of a sustainable gay culture is our sacrifice of certain cherished activities" and "Morris contends that it is preferable to risk lives in order to protect those activities that define the culture," Dean concludes that there is a structural similarity between these arguments: "Morris and Rotello agree we need to sacrifice something in order to preserve gay culture" (58). This comparison fails because of Dean's lack of precision about the difference in the "something" being sacrificed—or, more importantly, saved. Morris wants to save an ethos; Rotello wants to save people. Rotello, like Dean and Bersani, places value on the survival by individual human beings in a manner completely consistent with the logic of the prevailing cultural order; Morris, like Bataille, celebrates a transgressive spirit of risk and danger that flouts the instrumental, future-oriented logic of neoliberal capitalism.

77. Bataille, *Accursed Share*, 1:54–55.

78. Ibid., 1:58.

79. Dean, *Unlimited Intimacy*, 58.

80. Although I am much more sympathetic to—and troubled by—Dean's account of how barebacking practices are connected to a valorization of masculinity as a form of subjectivity that can endure suffering and risk (*Unlimited Intimacy*, 48–55; cf. Bersani, "Is the Rectum a Grave?" 12–15; Bersani, "Shame on You," 102–103), it is subject to a similar critique. While Dean contends that barebacking resignifies suffering, penetration, and submission as masculine, is it possible that the masculine ideal is being radically redefined? If "masculinity" signifies passivity and self-erasure, then does it remain problematic? In other words, is the masculinity that Dean considers politically and ethically troublesome the same as the masculinity being valorized in the barebacking subculture? For a different interpretation of barebacking's relation to phallic masculinity, see Edelman, "Unbecoming." For my account of the complex relation between representations of suffering and masculinity, including Bataille's contribution to thinking through these issues, see *Ecce Homo*, 25–64, 171–197.

81. Dean, *Unlimited Intimacy*, 205.

82. Ibid., 207.

83. Bataille, *Erotism*, 22.

84. Ibid., 102–103.

85. Ibid., 21–22. One similarity between sacrifice and eroticism is a shared dynamic of spectatorship: the witness to sacrifice experiences his own death by viewing the immolation of the victim; the sexual subject experiences her own dissolution by viewing the erotic abandon of her partner. In this way, barebacking is an ideal Bataillean practice. Even if viral transmission and HIV infection occur, the death that results is not instantaneous. Barebacking's risk entails a threat to self that can be witnessed and experienced over time, not unlike the encounter with death figured in sacrifice, eroticism, and the aesthetic.

86. Dean, *Unlimited Intimacy*, 207.

87. Ibid., 205.

88. Dean redescribes the encounter with alterity using the psychoanalytic concept of the unconscious (ibid., 205–212). Although psychoanalysis might provide evidence *that* risk taking is pleasurable, it provides no clear understanding *why* that would be the case, other than those outlined above. Insofar as Dean's recognition of "the pleasure of homeostasis" names the death drive in other terms, self-erasure appears as part of the psychoanalytic understanding of pleasure. With the death drive and masochistic jouissance in mind, Dean's assertion that the self cannot be sacrificed to, or become the slave of, the unconscious seems optimistic (ibid., 207). While the psychoanalytic conception of the unconscious may help us understand that every subject is always already in contact with the other (ibid., 207–208), our cultural order goes to great lengths to deny such an understanding. Barebacking has the capacity to reinforce the psychoanalytic conception Dean commends. The threat barebacking, as a practice, poses to the self does not alter its ability to communicate this message.

89. Ibid., 205.

90. Ibid., 201–211.

91. Bersani, "Sociability and Cruising," 61. Dean acknowledges similarities between his and Bersani's accounts of cruising (*Unlimited Intimacy*, 210n33).

92. Bersani, "Sociability and Cruising," 60–62; Dean, *Unlimited Intimacy*, 210–212.

93. Dean, *Unlimited Intimacy*, 212.

94. Bataille, *Guilty*, 115. See also *Erotism*, 120; and *Theory of Religion*, 33–34, 88.

95. Bataille, *Erotism*, 120–127; *Guilty*, 31; "Notion of Expenditure," 119.

96. Bataille, *Erotism*, 31–32.

97. Bersani, "Sociability and Cruising," 60.

98. Bersani, "Is the Rectum a Grave?" 12.

99. Expressing a similar preference for public spaces as venues that foster the ideal form of cruising, Dean distinguishes online cruising, which often seeks only those strangers who possess very specific traits and particular tastes, from the "ethically exemplary" form he advocates (*Unlimited Intimacy*, 210; see also 191–196). Dean also provides a brief history of the bar scene in the SOMA neighborhood of San Francisco (ibid., 196–204). He mourns the replacement of institutions where men (sometimes) mixed across lines of race and class by upscale, ethnically monolithic drinking holes. Although I share Dean's concern about the increasing homogenization of gay male urban enclaves, I find his account of cruising in working-class leather bars a tad romantic. Regardless of where it occurs, cruising involves selection: it is unlikely that the patrons of the newer SOMA bars would fare well as denizens of the neighborhood's former establishments. It is not only an ethos that has been displaced but also an aesthetic.

100. Dean, *Unlimited Intimacy*, 189–190.

101. Ibid., 190.

102. Ibid., 191.

103. Bersani, "Sociability and Cruising," 59.

104. Ibid., 61.

105. Ibid.

106. Ibid. See also Bersani, "Conversation," 174–175.

107. Dean, *Unlimited Intimacy*, 210. Can we imagine erotic interest that has no particularity? Insofar as gay male desire specifies the gender of the object of desire, can there be any such thing as *aimless* gay cruising?

108. Bataille, *Inner Experience*, 114–122. On Bataille's conception of the erotic object, see Brintnall, *Ecce Homo*, 178–185.

109. Bataille, *Inner Experience*, 6, 46, 54.

110. Ibid., xxxii.

111. Ibid.

112. Ibid., 6–9, 101–102.

113. Bataille, *Inner Experience*, 120.

114. Bersani, "Is the Rectum a Grave?" 30.

Desire, Blood, and Power: Georges Bataille and the Study of Hindu Tantra in Northeastern India
Hugh B. Urban

1. In addition to Bataille's own various writings on religion, such as *Theory of Religion*, see also Hollywood, *Sensible Ecstasy*; Taussig, "Transgression"; Stoekl, *Bataille's Peak*; Hussey, *The Inner Scar*.

2. See Urban, "The Power of the Impure" and *The Power of Tantra*.

3. Hussey, *Inner Scar*, 65. See Bataille, *The Unfinished System of Non-knowledge*, 78.

4. Bataille, "Kali," 55.

5. Bataille, *Tears of Eros*, 206. See also Jean Bruno, "Les techniques d'illumination chez Georges Bataille." Bruno draws many parallels between Bataille's own unique method of meditation and Tantric practice. He suggests that Bataille achieved a "*lucide somnolence*" in 1938 and advanced states of *samadhi* like those described in the Vijnana Bhairava, a *tantra* from the Kashmir region, in which exterior and interior states are interchangeable (716). Hussey likewise argues that there is an "Oriental basis" to Bataille's method in works from this period such as "La pratique de la joie devant la mort": "Bataille here draws upon the cosmology of Tantric literature and in particular borrows from tantric meditative practice which aims at the annihilation of perceived chronological realities" *Inner Scar*, 69.

6. Tantra is notoriously difficult to define and often misunderstood. In simplest terms, Tantra is a complex body of texts and traditions that spread throughout the Hindu, Buddhist, and Jain traditions of Asia since the fourth or fifth century. As Madeleine Biardeau suggests, perhaps the most distinctive feature of Tantra as a religious path is that it attempts to transform desire or *kama*—which is normally a source of bondage—into the supreme path to spiritual liberation. Tantra could thus be defined as a "means of harnessing *kama*—desire (in every sense of the word)—and all of its related values to the service of deliverance" (quoted in Padoux, *Vac*, 40). See also White, *Tantra in Practice*, 9.

7. Various scholars have identified Assam as the "principal center" and "birthplace" of goddess worship in South Asia and as the "tantric country *par excellence*"; see Eliot, *Hinduism and Buddhism*, 278; Eliade, *Yoga*, 305; Sircar, *The Sakta Pithas*.

8. Material for this chapter is drawn from research in northeastern India between 2000 and 2008, using sources in Sanskrit, Assamese, and Bengali. Some of this material has been published in my book *The Power of Tantra*. For other discussions of Tantra in Assam, see Biernacki, *Renowned Goddess of Desire*; Van Kooij, *Worship of the Goddess According to the Kalikapurana*.

9. See McWhorter, "Is There Sexual Difference in the Work of Georges Bataille?" 33–41: "Despite his emphasis on radical, orgiastic sexuality, Bataille pays little if any attention to the presence, the activity and the desire of anyone who is not phallic" (35). See also Suleiman, "Bataille in the Street," 61–79. Suleiman argues that Bataille had an obsession with "virility" conceived in masculine terms that "locked him into values and into a sexual politics that can only be called conformist in his time and ours" (79).

10. Urban, "Matrix of Power."

11. Bataille, *Erotism*, 92.

12. Shastri, *The Kalika Purana*, 39.73.

13. See Urban, "Matrix of Power."

14. White, *Kiss of the Yogini*, 67.

15. Khanna, "The Goddess-Woman Equation in the Tantras," 49. There is a vast literature on menstruation in India; see for example Bhattacharyya, *Indian Puberty Rites*; Wadley, *The Powers of Tamil Women*, 164; Marglin, "Female Sexuality in the Hindu World," 39–60; Caldwell, *Oh Terrifying Mother.*

16. Sarma, *Kamrup Kamakhya* (2002), 23.

17. Sarma, *Kamarupa Kamakhya: Itihasa o Dharmmamulaka* (2001), 108.

18. Bataille, *Erotism*, 121.

19. Shulman, *Tamil Temple Myths*, 29.

20. See Urban, *The Power of Tantra*, chaps. 1–3.

21. On human sacrifice in Assam, see Urban, *The Power of Tantra*, chap. 3.

22. Shastri, *The Kalika Purana*, 55.3–6, 67.3–5. See also Urban, "Matrix of Power"; Kakati, *Mother Goddess Kamakhya*, 65.

23. See Urban, *The Power of Tantra*, chaps. 2 and 3.

24. Biardeau and Malamoud, *Le sacrifice dans l'Inde ancienne*, 146–147.

25. Bataille, *The Accursed Share*, 1:59.

26. See Sanderson, "Purity and Power Among the Brahmins of Kashmir," 190–216; Urban, "The Power of the Impure."

27. Bagchi, *The Kaulajnananirnaya and Some Minor Texts of the School of Matsyendranatha*, 16.7–8, 22.9–11. See White, *Kiss of the Yogini*, 213–215.

28. White, *Kiss of the Yogini*, 17; see Bataille, *Erotism*, 115.

29. The metaphor of sexual union as a sacrifice can be found as early as the *Brhadaranyaka Upanishad*, where the female body is likened to the sacrificial altar with the yoni as the blazing fire, and this metaphor recurs throughout Tantric literature. See Urban, *The Power of Tantra*, chap. 4.

30. *Kaulajnananirnaya*, 18.7–9. See Urban, *The Power of Tantra*, chaps. 4–5.

31. Hindu law books warn repeatedly of the dangers of sexual intercourse during the menstrual period, and Hindu mythological texts contain many examples of the monstrous, demonic, and criminal offspring of such unions. See Urban, *The Power of Tantra*, chaps. 2–3.

32. Schoterman, *Yoni Tantra*, 2.16–26.

33. Schoterman, introduction to *Yoni Tantra*, 30.

34. Bataille, *Erotism*, 65.

35. Ibid., 65, 116.

36. Sanderson, "Purity and Power," 201, 199.

37. See among other texts *Yoni Tantra*, 4.28, 1.8, 4.7, 6.6–7.

38. Bataille, *Erotism*, 115.

39. Bataille, *The Accursed Share*, 2:119. As McWhorter notes, transgression represents for Bataille "moments wherein the self is torn open and exposed to what is other to it. These movements may occur, for example, during religious ecstasy,

extreme physical suffering, or erotic release. In these moments, individuation and identity are threatened and on some sense overcome; the boundaries between self and other tear apart or liquefy, melt away, and communication . . . occurs." McWhorter, "Is There Sexual Difference," 37–38.

40. Bataille, *The Accursed Share*, 2:183–184. See Hussey, *The Inner Scar*, 67.

41. Sanderson, "Purity and Power," 201, 199.

42. See Asrama, *Jnanarnava Tantra*, 22.30–32: "How can there be any impurity in excrement or urine? Undoubtedly, that is a false opinion. The body is born from a woman's menstrual blood. So how can that be impure, when by means of it one attains the highest state?"

43. *Kaulajnananirnaya*, 11.27–9.

44. *Akulavira Tantra*, in Bagchi, *Kaulajnananirnaya*, 24–26.

45. McWhorter, "Is There Sexual Difference," 34. See also McWhorter, "Bataille's Erotic Displacement of Vision."

46. Bataille, *Erotism*, 17.

47. Ibid., 18.

48. McWhorter, "Is There Sexual Difference," 40.

49. *Yoni Tantra*, 7.27.

50. Ibid., 1.6.

51. See Urban, *The Power of Tantra*, chap. 5.

The Religion of Football: Sacrifice, Festival, and Sovereignty at the 2010 FIFA World Cup in South Africa
David Chidester

1. Schechter, "Religion of Football."

2. Durkheim, *Elementary Forms of the Religious Life*, 62.

3. Hobson, "World Cup."

4. Bataille, "Notion of Expenditure," 118.

5. Chidester, *Authentic Fakes*, 119–120; Chidester, "Sacred."

6. Chidester, *Authentic Fakes*, 19; Chidester, "Economy."

7. BBC, "World Cup Stadium 'Cow Sacrifice' Plan Sparks Row."

8. Ibid.

9. Scott, "FIFA in a Stew Over Slaughter of Cows in World Cup Stadiums."

10. Mthembu, "Bull-Killing Ritual to Be Debated in Durban"; Sapa, "Mkhize."

11. BBC, "World Cup Stadium 'Cow Sacrifice' Plan Sparks Row."

12. Regchand, "Bull-Killing Ritual Compared to Communion."

13. Sapa, "Sangomas Sacrifice Ox to Bless the World Cup Stadiums."

14. Reuters, "Cow Slaughtered at World Cup Stadium to Appease Spirits."

15. Sapa, "Sangomas Sacrifice Ox to Bless the World Cup Stadiums."

16. Bataille, *Theory of Religion*, 43.

17. Bataille, *Inner Experience*, 137.

18. Bataille, *Accursed Share*, 1:57.

19. Bataille, *Theory of Religion*, 44.

20. Ibid., 49.
21. Bataille, "The Sacred," 242.
22. Mkiva, *Zolani Mkiva*.
23. Feni, "King's Voice Fulfils Dying Father's Wish."
24. Kaschula, "Praise Poetry."
25. Bataille, *Theory of Religion*, 54.
26. Robins, "World Cup Ritual Worth Every Cent," 13.
27. Devriendt, "Vuvuzelas All Around."
28. Bataille, *Theory of Religion*, 54.
29. Ibid., 55.
30. Fisher, "Unholy Row Over World Cup Trumpet."
31. Maluleke, "South Africa, Christianity, and the World Cup."
32. Pithouse, "On the Path to Crony Capitalism."
33. Bond, *Political Economy of the 2010 World Cup in South Africa*.
34. Bataille, "Notion of Expenditure," 119.
35. Ibid., 121.
36. Ibid.
37. Makhonya.com, "Our Team Visited the Royal African Awards."
38. Sikhakhane, "Shame of Being Colonised by King Sepp."
39. Singh, "World Cup 2010."
40. Tolsi, "FIFA Called the Shots."
41. Williams, *Chieftaincy, the State, and Democracy*, 5–9.
42. Maqhina, "Government to 'Assist' with King's Coronation."
43. Anonymous, "King Xolilizwe [*sic*] Sigcawu Coronation."
44. Makhonya Investments, "Welcome."
45. Jika, "BEE Shock in R3bn Bisho Fleet Contract."
46. Bataille, "Notion of Expenditure," 119.
47. Bataille, *Inner Experience*, 137.
48. Chidester, *Authentic Fakes*; Chidester, "Economy."
49. Bataille, "Notion of Expenditure," 123.
50. Ibid.

Violent Silence: Noise and Bataille's "Method of Meditation"
Paul Hegarty

1. Bataille, *Inner Experience*, 21; Bataille, *Oeuvres complètes*, 5:34.
2. Bataille, *Inner Experience*, 7; Bataille, *Oeuvres complètes*, 5:18.
3. Bataille, *Inner Experience*, 22; Bataille, *Oeuvres complètes*, 5:35.
4. Bataille, "Méthode de meditation," *Oeuvres complètes*, 5:221n.
5. Bataille, *Oeuvres complètes*, 8:189.
6. Bataille, *Inner Experience*, 119; Bataille, *Oeuvres complètes*, 5:139.
7. Bataille, *Inner Experience*, 39; Bataille, *Oeuvres complètes*, 5:52.
8. Bataille, *Guilty*, 18; Bataille, *Oeuvres complètes*, 5:257–258.
9. Bataille, *Guilty*, 17 (translation modified); Bataille, *Oeuvres complètes*, 5:255.

10. Bataille, *Guilty*, 10; Bataille, *Oeuvres complètes*, 5:247.

11. Bataille, *Inner Experience*, 10; Bataille, *Oeuvres complètes*, 5:22.

12. Bataille, *Inner Experience*, 46–47; Bataille, *Oeuvres complètes*, 5:60. Bataille's personal "love" of shame is not a literal necessity for the functioning of his system; we should instead take it as an example of powerful loss of control combined with the residual awareness of the sacred as something wrong.

13. See Bataille, *Oeuvres complètes*, 8:153–154.

14. Bataille, *Inner Experience*, 7; Bataille, *Oeuvres complètes*, 5:18.

15. Bataille, *Inner Experience*, 14; Bataille, *Oeuvres complètes*, 5:27.

16. Bataille, *Inner Experience*, 17; Bataille, *Oeuvres complètes*, 5:30.

17. Bataille, "Méthode de meditation," *Oeuvres complètes*, 5:210.

18. Bataille, *Guilty*, 5; Bataille, *Oeuvres complètes*, 5:242.

19. Bataille, *Guilty*, 35 (translation modified); Bataille, *Oeuvres complètes*, 5:277.

20. Bataille, *Guilty*, 140; Bataille, *Oeuvres complètes*, 5:405.

21. Bataille, *Guilty*, 143; Bataille, *Oeuvres complètes*, 5:408.

22. Bataille, *Guilty*, 149; Bataille, *Oeuvres complètes*, 5:415.

23. Bataille, *Inner Experience*, 13 (translation modified); Bataille, *Oeuvres complètes*, 5:25.

24. Bataille, *Inner Experience*, 17; Bataille, *Oeuvres complètes*, 5:30.

25. Bataille, *Inner Experience*, 74 (translation modified); Bataille, *Oeuvres complètes*, 5:88.

26. Bataille, *Inner Experience*, 127; Bataille, *Oeuvres complètes*, 5:147.

27. Bataille, *Guilty*, 28; Bataille, *Oeuvres complètes*, 5:269.

28. Bataille, *Guilty*, 17 (translation modified); Bataille, *Oeuvres complètes*, 5:256.

29. For more on the history, philosophy, and mutations of music's encounters with noise, see Attali, *Noise*; Goodman, *Sonic Warfare*; Hainge, *Noise Matters*; Hegarty, *Noise/Music*; Kahn, *Noise Water Meat*; Iles, *Noise and Capitalism*; Voegelin, *Listening to Noise and Silence*.

30. Bataille, *Guilty*, 32 (translation modified); Bataille, *Oeuvres complètes*, 5:274.

31. Bataille, *Guilty*, 59 (translation modified); Bataille, *Oeuvres complètes*, 5:307.

32. Bataille, *Guilty*, 92 (translation modified); Bataille, *Oeuvres complètes*, 5:348.

Georges Bataille and the Religion of Capitalism
Jean-Joseph Goux

1. Bataille, *Théorie de la religion*, 59.

2. Mercier, *L'an 2440*, 421n1.

3. Monod, *La querelle de la secularization*, 14–15.

4. See Goux, "General Economics and Postmodern Capitalism"; Goux, *Frivolité de la valeur*.

5. See Löwy, "Le capitalism comme religion."

6. Bataille, *Oeuvres complètes*, 7:209.

7. Ibid., 7:212.

8. Nelson, *Economics as Religion*, 8.

9. Ibid., 132.

10. Goux, "General Economics and Postmodern Capitalism."

11. Nelson, *Economics as Religion*, 148–149.

12. Ibid., 81.

13. Goux, *L'art et l'argent.*

14. Goux, *Frivolité de la valeur.*

15. See Kauder, *History of Marginal Utility Theory.*

16. Bossuet, *Oraisons funébres et panégyriques*, 234.

17. Ibid., 233.

18. Bataille, *Théorie de la religion*, 171.

Sacrifice as Ethics: The Strange Religiosity of Neoliberalism
Shannon Winnubst

1. "Neoliberalism" is arguably one of the most frequently circulating terms in current academic and nonacademic political conversations. Accordingly, it invokes a remarkably elastic set of meanings that run the gamut of political fealties: it can refer, for its advocates, to the enlightened state of a free market that is the essence of democracy, or, for its critics, to the evils of the economic doctrines of globalization, particularly as linked to the IMF and World Bank (Fukuyama, Sachs, Stiglitz, Habermas, Harvey, Brown, J. Dean). As an economic doctrine, neoliberalism argues from two core beliefs: (1) that the freedom of the market is necessary and sufficient to distribute public resources and (2) that the individual is the fundamental unit of sociality and is driven essentially by self-interest. Culturally, these principles came to be associated with Thatcherism and Reaganomics, the first two national administrations to embrace neoliberalism explicitly in the 1980s. But as much scholarship currently argues, neoliberalism has become the standard framework for economics and politics in capitalist-democratic nations (see Harvey, *A Brief History of Neoliberalism*; Ong, *Neoliberalism as Exception*). Scholarship on neoliberalism in the humanities consequently divides into two approaches: (1) the argument that these two core principles are tools of the elite class's ideology (see Harvey, Duggan, Giroux, and Goldberg) and (2) the argument that these two core principles have been so fully internalized by society that they now constitute both the worldview and self-understanding of individuals within neoliberal societies (Foucault, Lemke, Brown, Žižek, Dean). I place my inquiry in this latter view, derived largely from Foucault's lectures.

2. Most scholarship, such as that of David Harvey, Henry Giroux, Joseph Stiglitz, and Lisa Duggan, locates the emergence of neoliberalism primarily in the Chicago School of the 1960s. See especially Ong, *Neoliberalism as Exception*, 10–12, for an overview of these genealogies of neoliberalism.

3. Foucault cites the physiocrats of France, the English economists, and even theorists like Mandeville; see *The Birth of Biopolitics*, 275.

4. Ibid., 271. Foucault locates the emergence of this "subject of interests" in English empiricists such as John Locke and David Hume, thereby locating a split

subjectivity at the heart of modern discourses of the Rights of Man. See ibid., lecture 11.

5. Dean, *Democracy*, 67.

6. Ibid. Dean reads neoliberal subjectivity through Lacanian registers, wherein the force of the Symbolic is effaced and identities are thus reduced to the plane of the Imaginary. Žižek then accentuates this reading as a reduction of subjectivity to the level of the drive, which in turn suggests the possibility of an ethics of the Real. See Dean's *Democracy and Other Neoliberal Fantasies* and "Drive as the Structure of Biopolitics"; and Žižek's *First as Tragedy, Then as Farce*.

7. Bataille, *Accursed Share*, 1:120.

8. Bataille's reading of Luther and Calvin relies on R. H. Tawney's *Religion and the Rise of Capitalism*, which he uses to accentuate the economic shifts at work in Max Weber's reading of the emergence of Protestantism and capitalism. See *Accursed Share*, 1:115–118.

9. Bataille, *Accursed Share*, 1:121, 122.

10. Ibid., 1:121.

11. Ibid., 1:115.

12. Ibid., 1:122.

13. Ibid., 1:123.

14. Ibid., 1:124.

15. Foucault, *Birth of Biopolitics*, 272.

16. See Lacan, *Four Fundamental Concepts*, 167.

17. Bataille, *Theory of Religion*, 53.

18. Ibid., 53–54.

19. See Winnubst, *Queering Freedom*, 140–144, for a discussion of this doubled dynamic of eroticism vis-à-vis animality and sexuality.

20. Both Hollywood, in *Sensible Ecstasy*, and Surya, in *Georges Bataille*, debunk these stereotypical readings. See *Visions of Excess* for examples of these early writings that seem to glorify violent, especially human, sacrifice. This is also echoed in Bataille's discussion of the Aztecs in volume 1 of *The Accursed Share*, but a broader, more general set of concerns frames that discussion.

21. Although both of these were published posthumously, Michel Surya argues that *Theory of Religion* was completed in 1949 (*Georges Bataille*, 415) and *The History of Eroticism* was written roughly during 1951–1957 (ibid., 449), with the research and writing of all three volumes of *The Accursed Share* spanning roughly 1947 onward (ibid., 371).

22. Bataille, *Theory of Religion*, 48.

23. Ibid., 45.

24. Ibid., 49.

25. Bataille, *Visions of Excess*, 180.

26. Ibid., 179.

27. Bataille, *Accursed Share*, 2:202. Emphasis in original.

28. Ibid., 2:203. Uppercase in original.

29. Ibid.

30. For a wide range of examples, see "The Notion of Expenditure," in *Visions of Excess*, as well as volumes 1 and 2 of *The Accursed Share*.

31. Bataille, *Visions of Excess*, 181.

32. This is one reason we might understand Bataille's infamous resistance to the 1960s movements of (alleged) "sexual revolutions." For an analysis of how these dynamics continue to affect our domesticated notions of "sexual freedom," particularly in l/g/b movements, see my "Bataille's Queer Pleasures" in *Reading Bataille Now* and Chapter 4 of *Queering Freedom*.

33. Bataille, *Accursed Share*, 2:29.

34. Ibid., 2:18.

35. The theorists who have influenced my readings of Lacan here are Alenka Zupančič, Tim Dean, and Slavoj Žižek.

36. For accounts of the normalizing effects of this desire-driven subject in the register of sexuality, see Dean, *Beyond Sexuality* and *Unlimited Intimacy*.

37. Hollywood, *Sensible Ecstasy*, 65.

38. Of course, the noumenal concept of freedom also becomes crucial to Kant's system, but that exceeds the parameters of this essay.

39. Zupančič, *Ethics of the Real*, 17.

40. Contra Žižek's critique of Bataille as "premodern" in *Parallax View*, 95.

41. See Zupančič, *Ethics of the Real*, 235–237.

42. See especially Zupančič for full accounts of these kinds of characteristics, as well as Winnubst, "What If the Law Is Written in a Porno Book?"

Bataille's Contestation of Interpretative Anthropology and of the Sociology of Religion
Alphonso Lingis

1. Hubert and Mauss, *Sacrifice*.

2. Bataille, *Erotism*, 91–92.

3. Bataille, "The Solar Anus," 5–9.

4. Ibid., 5.

5. "The subject tries at first to move toward its fellow being. But once it has entered into inner experience, it is in search of an object like itself—reduced to interiority. In addition, the subject, the experience of which is in itself and from the beginning dramatic (is the loss of self), needs to objectify this dramatic character. . . . At each instant of experience, this point can radiate arms, cry out, set itself ablaze." Bataille, *Inner Experience*, 117–118.

6. Ibid., 121.

7. Ibid., 126.

8. Ibid., 127.

9. Bataille, *Visions of Excess*, 134.

10. Bataille, *Inner Experience*, 124–125.

11. Ibid., 123.

12. Bataille, *Accursed Share*, 3:215.

13. Ibid., 3:235.

14. Bataille, *Guilty*, 139.

15. Bataille, *Oeuvres complètes*, 6:79–80; *On Nietzsche*, 64–65. Translation modified.

16. Bataille, *Guilty*, 139.

17. Bataille, *Oeuvres complètes*, 5:222; *The Unfinished System of Nonknowledge*, 97. Translation modified.

18. Lévi-Strauss, *Naked Man*, 639.

19. Geertz, *The Interpretation of Culture*, 100–108.

20. Ibid., 103.

21. Bataille, *Oeuvres complètes*, 8:258; *Accursed Share*, 3:208.

22. Bataille, *Oeuvres complètes*, 8:254–255; *Accursed Share*, 3:204.

23. Deleuze and Guattari see an organism cutting off, segmenting flows of substance and energy. *Anti-Oedipus*, 5–6.

24. Bataille, *Oeuvres complètes*, 5:140.

25. Bataille, *Visions of Excess*, 102n1.

26. Bataille, *Oeuvres complètes*, 2:433–434.

27. Bataille, *Visions of Excess*, 101.

28. Bataille, *Oeuvres complètes*, 5:222.

29. "We must take the values of decline for what they are: judgments formulated by prudence, inspired by fear. We must take from them the prestige that they are given in the opposition of good and bad, in which the good must be done, the bad destroyed. There cannot be positively a morality of the summit. But the critique of the moralities of decline, their reduction to what they are, represent in this sense a negative possibility." Bataille, *Oeuvres complètes*, 6:391–392.

30. Bataille, *Theory of Religion*, 55.

31. Ibid., 77.

32. Ibid., 55.

33. "God rapidly and almost entirely loses his terrifying features, his appearance as a decomposing cadaver, in order to become, at the final stage of degradation, the simple (paternal) sign of universal homogeneity." Bataille, *Visions of Excess*, 96.

34. Ibid., 242.

35. Weber, *The Sociology of Religion*.

36. Bataille, *Oeuvres complètes*, 6:63; *On Nietzsche*, 47. Translation modified.

The Traumatic Secret: Bataille and the Comparative Erotics of Mystical Literature
Jeffrey J. Kripal

1. Bataille, *Erotism*, 32.

2. Ibid., 245.

3. Ibid., 32, 8.

4. Ibid., 7.

5. Ibid., 273.

6. Ibid., 32; cf. 123.

7. Ibid., 34.

8. Ibid., 33.

9. Ibid., 35.

10. Ibid., 34.

11. Ibid., 35.

12. Ibid., 23.

13. Ibid., 118.

14. Ibid., 238, 221, 226.

15. Ibid., 36.

16. Ibid., 254.

17. Ibid., 130.

18. Ibid., 63.

19. Ibid., 62.

20. Ibid., 266.

21. Ibid., 13, 141.

22. Ibid., 17–18.

23. Ibid., 15.

24. Ibid., 18.

25. Ibid., 223–224.

26. Ibid., 225.

27. Ibid., 247.

28. Ibid.

29. Ibid., 22.

30. Ibid., 23.

31. Ibid., 83, 261.

32. Ibid., 124.

33. Ibid., 248.

34. Kripal, *Kali's Child*, 304.

35. Kripal, with Anzali, Jain, and Prophet, *Comparing Religions*, 250–251. For a synopsis and further theorization of the same material, see also Kripal, "Visions of the Impossible."

36. Amatuzio, *Beyond Knowing*, 84–85.

37. Huxley, *The Perennial Philosophy*, v–vi.

38. See "No Aliens Allowed," an ironically entitled chapter on a classic alien abduction experience in Mullis, *Dancing Naked in the Mind Field*. Mullis won the Nobel Prize in chemistry for inventing the polymerase chain reaction process, which led in turn to the human genome project. He is adamant that his alien abduction experience (which occurred before his discovery and right around the same time as Strieber's, in whose account he recognized his own) really happened.

39. Ring, *The Omega Project*, 144.

40. Ibid., 144, 142.

Foucault's Sacred Sociology
Mark D. Jordan

1. Bataille, *Oeuvres complètes*, 1:5. Where they are readily available, published English translations will also be cited for comparison, though in all cases the translations appearing here are my own.

2. This caution applies a fortiori to biographical narratives about Bataille's influence on Foucault, whether in general or in particular. For the former, notoriously, see Miller, *The Passion of Michel Foucault*; for the latter, see Nigro, "Experiences of the Self Between Limit, Transgression, and the Explosion of the Dialectical System," which largely reproduces "Foucault lecteur de Bataille et de Blanchot."

3. Foucault, "Préface à la transgression," *Critique* 195/196 (August–September 1963): 751–769. A corrected and annotated version appears in Foucault, *Dits et écrits*, 1:233–250. I cite the *original* version by page number. There is an English translation by Donald F. Bouchard and Sherry Simon: "Preface to Transgression."

4. I treat Foucault's engagements with religion—and so with Bataille's legacy—much more fully in *Convulsing Bodies*.

5. I am hardly the first reader to point to the importance of Foucault's relation to Bataille—or Bataille, Klossowski, Blanchot—for understanding his writing about or around religion. For example, these relations form a large part of Jeremy R. Carrette's argument in *Foucault and Religion*, especially chaps. 3–4. I disagree with Carrette about where religion is to be found in Foucault and how one should write about it.

6. Foucault, *L'ordre du discours*, 7–8, 81–82. There is an English translation by Rupert Swyer: "Orders of Discourse," reprinted under a different title as an appendix to Foucault, *The Archeology of Knowledge*, 215–237.

7. For useful reminders about the complexity of the term "experience" before and after Foucault's essay, see Jay, "The Limits of Limit-Experience."

8. Foucault, "Préface," 752–753, 760, 762–763, 765, 768–769.

9. I quote from the original preface to the work, reproduced in Foucault, *Dits et écrits* 1:159–167, here at 161, 163. When the book was reissued, Foucault performed the Bataillean gesture of replacing it with another preface in which he disavows prefaces. See Foucault, *Histoire de la folie à l'âge classique*, 9–11. There is an English translation by Jonathan Murphy and Jean Khalfa: *History of Madness*, which includes both prefaces.

10. Bataille, *Oeuvres complètes*, 3:491–494.

11. Ibid., 3:239–251.

12. Foucault, "Préface," 752.

13. Ibid., 754.

14. Ibid., 756, with the reference to A291–292 in the standard pagination of the *Critique*.

15. Foucault, "Préface," 757.

16. Foucault would often link these three names in interviews when he was pressed—as he so annoyingly was—to locate himself in an academic field or an in-

tellectual movement or at least a literary lineage. More interesting are his carefully crafted offerings to these predecessors. For Klossowski, see "La prose d'Actéon" (1964), in Foucault, *Dits et écrits*, 1:326–337; and "Les mots qui saignent" (1964), in *Dits et écrits*, 1:424–427. For Blanchot, "La pensée du dehors" (1966), in *Dits et écrits*, 1:518–539.

17. Foucault, "Préface," 759.

18. Ibid., 765.

19. Ibid., 767.

20. Ibid., 769.

21. Foucault quotes the text of the "new version," in which this passage (among many others) has been revised from its earlier form—perhaps by Bataille, perhaps by the editor-publisher, Alain Gheerbrant, with Bataille's approval. The publication history given in Bataille, *Oeuvres complètes*, 1:643–644, has been variously contested. According to Gheerbrant, the "Seville 1940" edition was printed secretly in Paris in 1945 and was in fact the first to contain the "new version." See Gheerbrant and Aichelbaum, *K éditeur*, 28–29, with the bibliographic notes on 44 (which gives the printing date as 1945), 75–76. The earlier and later versions are printed in Bataille, *Oeuvres complètes*, 1:9–78 and 1:569–608, respectively.

22. Bataille, untitled prefatory note, *Acéphale* no. 1 (June 24, 1936): [3], "des flammes semblables à un sacré-cœur dans sa main droit." I follow the reproduction in *Acéphale: Religion, sociologie, philosophie*. The text is also reprinted in Bataille, *Oeuvres complètes*, 1:442–446, with the quotation at 445.

23. I translate from the French, which carries no citation. For an English version in context, see Hong and Hong, eds., *Søren Kierkegaard's Journals and Papers*, 6:60, entry 6256.

24. Bataille, "Propositions sur le fascisme," *Acéphale* no. 2: 18–20, reprinted in Bataille, *Oeuvres complètes*, 1:467–470.

25. Bataille, "Propositions sur la mort de Dieu," *Acéphale* no. 2: 21, #15, reprinted in Bataille, *Oeuvres complètes*, 1:470–473, here at 473.

26. Unsigned note, "Une 'religion hygiénique et pédagogique': Le néo-paganisme allemand," *Acéphale*, no. 2: 8–9; reprinted in Bataille, *Oeuvres complètes*, 1:458–459.

27. Surya, *Georges Bataille*, 251; Sweedler, *The Dismembered Community*, 89; and so on. It is important to remember that the testimonies to these forest rites are still marked by ironic evasion, comic invention, and simple refusal. Compare, for example, the interviews with Klossowski and Leiris in Henri-Lévy, *Les aventures de la liberté*, at 171–172 (Klossowski contradicting Surya) and 174 (Leiris contradicting Klossowski).

28. "Note sur la fondation d'un Collège de Sociologie," *Acéphale*, nos. 3–4: "Dionysos" (July 1937): 26; reprinted in Hollier, *Collège*, 25–27; and in Bataille, *Oeuvres complètes*, 1:491–492. A footnote in the original explains that the statement had been drafted in March 1937.

29. One testimony to Klossowski's remarkable Latinity can be found in the preface to his much later translation of Virgil's *Aeneid*. Klossowski undertakes to

preserve so far as possible the incantatory force of Virgil's word order, since he reads the poem as a theater in which the poem's words imitate divine actions. See Virgil, *L'Énéide*, trans. Pierre Klossowski, xi–xii.

30. See the interview of Roger Caillois by Jean José Marchand (July 12–13, 1971), "Archives du XXème Siècle."

31. Richman, *Sacred Revolutions*, esp. 1–7.

32. Leiris to Bataille (July 3, 1939), in Hollier, *Collège*, 819–821; compare the mention by Bataille, "Le Collège de Sociologie" (read July 4, 1939), in Hollier, *Collège*, 801.

33. Bataille, "Le Collège de Sociologie," 801–803, 812.

34. Bataille, "Propositions sur la mort de Dieu," 20, #8.

35. Bataille, *Larmes d'Éros*; Bataille, *Oeuvres complètes*, 10:627.

36. Foucault, *Surveiller et punir*, 12, articles 19 and 27, respectively.

37. Foucault, *Les anormaux* (delivered spring 1975), 134 ("la sainteté psychiatrique," "la religion psychiatrique").

38. Bataille, *Oeuvres complètes*, 5:43–76.

39. Foucault, *Surveiller et punir*, 49 ("le théâtre de l'enfer"), 53 ("liturgie des supplices"), 54 ("rituel de la loi armée"), 61 ("de faire éclater rituellement sa réalité de surpouvoir"), and so on.

40. Ibid., 68–70.

41. Ibid., 139 (generalizing monastic techniques), 143 and 145 (monastic cloister and cell), 151 (monastic *horarium*), 163 (asceticism become exercise).

42. Ibid., 293: "'Quel dommage d'avoir à quitter si tôt la colonie.'" Compare 300, "premier saint pénitentiaire."

43. Ibid., 297–299 (trial of the delinquent Béasse), 313–314 (anonymous correspondent).

Bataille and Kristeva on Religion
Zeynep Direk

1. Kristeva, *Powers of Horror*, 56.

2. Kristeva, *Tales of Love*, 365.

3. Beardsworth, *Julia Kristeva*, 1–2.

4. Obviously, this is Kristeva's caricature of Deleuze and Guattari's position. As *A Thousand Plateaus* makes clear, Deleuze and Guattari oppose the full body without organs to the fascist and suicidal body without organs. Deleuze and Guattari, *Thousand Plateaus*, 149–166, 230–231.

5. Bataille, *Theory of Religion*, 19.

6. Ibid., 57.

7. Lévi-Strauss calls the prohibition of incest "a scandalous fact." Lévi-Strauss, *The Elementary Structures of Kinship*, 8. It appears as scandalous only if the validity of the opposition between nature and culture is presumed. The prohibition of incest erases this opposition between nature as governed by universal laws and culture as determined by rules that change from one culture to another, because it is found in one form or another in all cultures. The universal prohibition of incest

is enigmatic for it does not only precede and condition the cultural; it also plays a role in that very distinction between the sacred and the profane. Hence, Bataille is forced to complicate his previous account of religion, for religion should also be signifying in terms of human sexual desire.

8. Bataille, *Accursed Share*, 1:39.

9. Ibid., 1:182.

10. Bataille, *Accursed Share* 2:62.

11. Ibid., 2:63.

12. Ibid., 2:130.

13. Ibid., 2:97.

14. Ibid., 2:81.

15. Bataille, *Erotism*, 67.

16. Ibid., 223.

17. Ibid., 129.

18. Ibid., 35.

19. Kristeva, *In the Beginning Was Love*, 43.

20. Foucault, *Order of Things*, 373–387.

21. Kristeva, *In the Beginning Was Love*, 44.

22. Bataille, *Oeuvres complètes*, 2:217–221.

23. I am not the first to remark the strangeness of Kristeva's reading of Bataille in *Powers of Horror*. Sylvère Lotringer has already questioned Kristeva's abstraction of Bataille's notion of abjection from its political context.

24. Kristeva, *Powers of Horror*, 56.

25. Ibid., 64.

26. Ibid., 64.

27. Ibid., 2.

28. Ibid., 12.

29. Ibid.

30. Ibid., 13.

31. Kristeva, *New Maladies of the Soul*, 115–126.

32. Beardsworth, *Julia Kristeva*, 128.

33. Kristeva, *In the Beginning Was Love*, 40.

34. Bataille, *Ma mère*, 82. Cited in Kristeva, *Tales of Love*, 367.

35. Cited in Kristeva, *Tales of Love*, 366.

36. Ibid.

37. Kristeva, *Sense and Non-Sense of Revolt*.

38. Bataille, *Inner Experience*, 115–116.

39. Bataille, *Erotism*, 24–25; Bataille, *Inner Experience*, 13–14.

40. Kristeva, *Sense and Non-Sense of Revolt*, 43.

41. Ibid., 27. See also Bataille, *Blue of Noon*; Bataille, *Le bleu du ciel*, in *Oeuvres Complètes*, 3:399–487.

42. Kristeva, *Sense and Non-Sense of Revolt*, 27–28.

43. Ibid.

44. Beardsworth, *Julia Kristeva*, 19, 115–142.

45. Kristeva, *Sense and Non-Sense of Revolt*, 49.

46. See, for example, Tauchert, *Against Transgression*, 15–42.

47. Although several authors point out Bataille's heterosexism in thinking erotic experience, I think that his account of erotic experience is open to queer pleasures. See Winnubst, "Bataille's Queer Pleasures."

48. Kristeva, *Revolt She Said*, 20.

49. Ibid.

50. Ibid., 40–41.

Bataille, Teilhard de Chardin, and the Death of God
Allan Stoekl

1. Taylor, *After God*.

2. Altizer, cited in Taylor, *After God*, 201.

3. Ibid., 200.

4. Ibid.

5. It should be stressed that Robespierre was by no means an atheist; he believed in, or wanted the Republic to be under, a God who was not merely reducible to rationality and scientific laws: God, in other words, was to be seen as a higher, ideal, authority. (God was useful in that sense; one senses that Robespierre does not so much "believe" as recognize the practical necessity of positing a God.) Yet at the same time his God authorized the Republic, based as it was on formal and purely reason-based strictures. Sade on the other hand was allied with revolutionaries (for the most part, eliminated by Robespierre) who were openly atheists and who conceived of reason in opposition to all divinity. It was for this allegiance that Sade almost lost his head in 1794 (he was spared because he was improperly identified; he was on a list of those to be executed, a few days before Robespierre himself went to the scaffold). Sade's clearest statements on Nature, God, Law, and the necessity of murder are to be found in his essay "Frenchmen, One More Effort, If You Want to Be Republicans!" in *Philosophy in the Bedroom*.

6. Bataille, *Inner Experience*, 108–111.

7. Ibid., 108.

8. Is this the point where Hegel, for Bataille, morphs into Sade (the Sade who justifies crime through the argument that Nature cannot function—cannot renew "her"self—without omnipresent death)?

9. Ibid., 108.

10. Ibid., 110–111.

11. Ibid., 111.

12. Bataille, *Madame Edwarda*, 12. My translation.

13. Ibid., 21. My translation.

14. Ibid.

15. Bataille plays with the alternation of circle and sphere, two dimensions and three: the Hegelian dialectic is circular, the enucleated eye is spherical, but the two are doubles. One thinks of the film *Avatar*, released in both 2-D and 3-D versions; the two versions complement but also contradict each other.

16. Taylor, *After God*, 310.

17. Ibid., 311.

18. Teilhard, *The Phenomenon of Man*, 268, 270–271.

19. Ibid., 265.

20. Ibid., 73.

21. If the Omega Point is the head of the system, its higher divine consciousness, then it is decapitated, thrown off and reabsorbed as junk (only to be spat out, always again), in Bataille's (non)knowing sphere.

22. Bataille, *Inner Experience*, 52.

23. Snapper, "Language of the Noosphere," 3.

24. Collins, "Is Cybersex Sex?" 121.

Does the Acéphale Dream of Headless Sheep?
Jeremy Biles

1. Bataille, "Nietzschean Chronicle," 206.

2. Bataille, "The Sacred Conspiracy," 181.

3. Ibid., 179, 181.

4. Roudinesco, *Jacques Lacan*, 132. Roudinesco here characterizes Pierre Klossowski's *Acéphale* article "Le monstre," which treats the Marquis de Sade and, by extension, the monstrous Acéphale: "This monstrosity, the negation of the self, proclaimed the absolute power of dream over consciousness, of dispossession over self-possession, of impossibility over possibility."

5. Durkheim, *Elementary Forms*, 52, 53.

6. Hollier, "Dualist Materialism," 65.

7. Bataille, *Theory of Religion*, 27.

8. Bataille, *Erotism*, 18.

9. Ibid., 24.

10. Ibid., 17–18.

11. Bataille, *Theory of Religion*, 43.

12. Bataille, "The Psychological Structure of Fascism," 144.

13. Ibid., 58.

14. Bataille, *Accursed Share*, 3:215.

15. This point is developed at length below.

16. Krauss, "Isotropy," 106.

17. Bataille, *Accursed Share*, 3:215.

18. Hollier remarks on the shared logic of dream and the sacred: "Freud found [in the antithetical meanings of 'primal words'] one of the characteristics of dream logic, which he had shown completely ignored contradiction. As a result of this ambiguity, the sacred can be *high* . . . or *low*. High/low: Freud cites this example just before mentioning the semantic ambiguity of the wor[d] *sacred* itself: 'in Latin, *altus* means both high and deep; *sacer*, holy and damned.'" *Against Architecture*, 132.

19. "Bataille's references to Freud are few and the use he makes of psychoanalysis unorthodox," Bois remarks. "Abattoir," 50. Bataille was, however, "a great

reader of Freud," as Roudinesco emphasizes. *Jacques Lacan*, 131. Whereas much has been written on Bataille's engagements with the likes of Hegel, Nietzsche, and Durkheim, relatively little has been said of the manner in which Freud animates so much of Bataille's thought. One exception is Mansfield's *The God Who Deconstructs Himself*, which offers an account of Bataille's "radical reconsideration of subjectivity in terms of an economics of energy" based on Freud's metapsychology (4). See "Economies of Subjectivity: Bataille After Freud," 9–40. See also Gasché's *Georges Bataille*, especially the chapters "Mythological Representation" and "The Logic of the Phantasm," which together offer a fascinating account of Bataille's "phantasmatology" as it relates to the (Freudian) unconscious.

20. Breton, *Manifestoes of Surrealism*, 26.

21. Bataille, *Absence of Myth*, 49.

22. Bataille, "Method of Meditation," 77.

23. In my book *Ecce Monstrum*, in the context of a discussion of Bataille's formulation of an extremist surrealism that would converge with a hyperchristianity, I, too, place an accent on Bataille's condemnation of Breton's conception of the Freudian unconscious. The present essay should be read in part as an attempt to articulate the other side of the opposition, elaborating a Bataillean reading of the dream as a mechanism for activating the sacred.

24. Suzanne Guerlac describes the journal *Documents* as a "countersurrealist review." "Useless Image," 28. Guerlac does not reduce Bataille's ambivalence but rather reveals how Rosalind Krauss fails to acknowledge the full ambivalence implied in Bataille's notion of "alteration."

25. Breton is widely thought to have characterized Bataille as a "*philosophe-excrément*," or excrement-philosopher, and excoriates Bataille's "pathological" fascination with flies, excrement, impurity, and the like in the "Second Manifesto of Surrealism." *Manifestoes of Surrealism*, 180–186.

26. Bataille, "The 'Lugubrious Game,'" 29.

27. Bataille, *Absence of Myth*, 49.

28. Richardson, "Introduction," 2.

29. Breton, *Manifestoes*, 14.

30. Ibid., 10.

31. Ibid., 26.

32. Ibid., 18.

33. Ibid., 123.

34. Foster, *Compulsive Beauty*, 16.

35. Breton, cited in Foster, *Compulsive Beauty*, 15.

36. Freud, *Interpretation of Dreams*, 353.

37. "What instigates a dream is a wish, and the fulfillment of that wish is the content of the dream." Freud, *Introductory Lectures*, 158.

38. Breton, *Manifestoes*, 13.

39. Bataille, *Absence of Myth*, 50.

40. See, for example, Bois and Krauss, *Formless: A User's Guide*; and Foster, *Compulsive Beauty*.

41. Bataille, "The 'Old Mole' and the Prefix *Sur* in the Words *Surhomme* [Superman] and *Surrealist*," 39. Allan Stoekl places the dating of this essay at 1929–1930. See *Visions of Excess*, 258–259.

42. Bataille, "The 'Old Mole,'" 42.

43. Bataille, "*L'esprit moderne et le jeu des transpositions.*"

44. Breton, *Manifestoes*, 14.

45. Bataille, "The 'Old Mole,'" 41.

46. Ibid., 39. Hollier reveals that in the first version of his early essay on Dali's "The Lugubrious Game," Bataille would seem to condemn the dream on the very grounds that he condemns the surrealist game of transpositions: "The elements of a dream or hallucination are transpositions; the poetic use of dream comes down to a consecration of unconscious censure, that is the consecration of a secret shame and of cowardice." *Against Architecture*, 110. Yet the published version of the article on Dali seems to suggest a rethinking of this stance in the direction elaborated in the present essay. As Hollier suggests, Bataille may not be condemning transposition per se but rather the surrealists' flights of poetic reverie, their "cowardly" fleeing into wishful dreams not so as to "awaken" but further *sublimate* "perverse desire." "The 'play of transpositions' . . . refers to the 'symbolism' discovered by psychoanalysis and exploited by the surrealists. It is a minor form of play because, far from playing the game, far from playing with what plays out in desire, symbolism's only play is to transpose desire and turn it into works. . . . The only way out: a return to perversion in its most naked form, to perversion as play that is a refusal of transposition" and countering of "neurotic cultural sublimation." Ibid., 112. Remarking on the same passage by Bataille on Dali, Bois notes that "against *transposition* . . . Bataille opts for *alteration*, and indeed he valorizes the 'reduction of repression' as an alteration toward the base." "Abattoir," 50. The present essay condones a heterological attitude toward dreams that is consonant with such alteration. For a discussion of the role of symbolism and metaphor within Bataillean mythological representation that complicates Hollier's account of transposition, see Gasché, *Georges Bataille*, chaps. 1 and 2. For a discussion of the place of law and repression in Bataille's thought, see Dean, "Returning to the Scene of the Crime," in *The Self and Its Pleasures*, 221–245. "Repression is the very condition of pleasure," Dean claims (245).

47. Caws, "Introduction," xiii.

48. Freud, *Communicating Vessels*, 151–152. Correspondence between Freud and Breton appears in the appendix to *Communicating Vessels*.

49. Freud, *Interpretation of Dreams*, 143n2.

50. Ibid., 564.

51. Ibid.

52. Breton, *Communicating Vessels*, 45.

53. Ibid., 19.

54. Breton, *Communicating Vessels*, 86.

55. Lomas, *Haunted Self*, 239n160.

56. Bataille, *Visions of Excess*, 181.

57. Sontag, "Against Interpretation," 6–8.

58. "Freud is paradox, or nothing," claims Norman O. Brown. *Life Against Death*, xviii. Brown offers a Dionysian/Bataillean reading of Freud in his lecture "Dionysus in 1990."

59. Bataille, "Materialism," 15–16.

60. Bataille, "The Notion of Expenditure," 128.

61. Ibid., 129.

62. Bataille, "The Psychological Structure of Fascism," 140.

63. Bataille, "The Use Value of D. A. F. de Sade," 97.

64. Freud, *On Dreams*, 2.

65. Bataille, "The Psychological Structure of Fascism," 141.

66. ". . . or as superior transcendent value," the quote continues. Ibid., 142. Bataille here refers to the sacred under its right-handed aspect, thus recognizing the ambivalence of the sacred.

67. Ibid., 143.

68. Bataille, "The Use Value of D. A. F. de Sade," 99.

69. For Bataille, "dreams are soiled," as Fer puts it in a discussion of Bataille's approach to Freud and surrealist painting. "Poussière/peinture," 167.

70. Bataille, *Accursed Share*, 3:226.

71. Ibid., 3:225.

72. Bataille, *Inner Experience*, 46.

73. Bataille, "Autobiographical Note," 218.

74. This is not to suggest that Bataille confines these expenditures to writing; he remained a regular patron of brothels, drank excessively, and gambled profligately, sometimes to the point of financial ruin.

75. Bataille, "Autobiographical Note," 218.

76. Bataille, *Tears of Eros*, 207.

77. For discussions of Bataille and the ethics of representation, see Hollywood, *Sensible Ecstasy*; and Brintnall, *Ecce Homo*.

78. The dream text is collected under the title "[Dream]" in *Visions of Excess*, in which its editor, Allan Stoekl, notes that the dream was "first published in the *Oeuvres Complètes* II, 9–10. The manuscript is marked 'Recorded in 1927, around June.'" *Visions of Excess*, 258.

79. Bataille, "[Dream]," 3.

80. Ibid., 4.

81. We cannot know, of course, whether such a meaning was attempted or arrived at in the clinical situation. What is evident, however, is that whether or not such a meaning was achieved, the dream, like Bataille's analytic treatment on the whole, did not serve to stabilize nor precisely to "heal" but rather furthered his writerly counteroperations. In this connection, what Gasché asserts of Bataille's writings in general might be said about the mode of dream interpretation elaborated in this essay: "Taking into consideration the economy of Bataille's text, which represents an economy of the expenditure of meaning, we must . . . interpret his text in a Nietzschean sense. . . . In accordance with this economy of

expenditure, interpretation can mean only excessive exegesis and following the text in its endless interweaving at the risk of falling prey to its abysmal groundlessness." *Georges Bataille*, 21.

82. Gasche's discussion of the "corroding function" of Bataille's "sequence or chain of images" in *Georges Bataille* has important implications for a Bataillean approach to the dream, 144. See especially the section "The Inclination of the Chain of Images," 141–166.

83. On Bataille's evocations and provocations of castration, see, for example, Denis Hollier, *Against Architecture*.

84. Hollier has noted that dualism defines Bataille's "attitude of thought." "Dualist Materialism," 62.

85. For a discussion of knots in relation to the "real," see Botting, "Relations of the Real in Lacan, Bataille, and Blanchot." Though Botting does not explicitly discuss dream interpretation in relation to Bataille, his treatment of the dream knot or navel is suggestive in the context of the present discussion of Bataille's "nonknowledge," for he articulates a point that resonates with the Bataillean psychoanalytic approach to the dream that I am exploring here. "While the navel is included in the process of dream interpretation as the limit point . . . it offers a glimpse of an unknown territory. It remains an attractive land. There lingers, in Freud's writing, a wish to enter this beyond, a wish to unravel the knot of the navel and, forsaking the meaning that analysis produces when confronted with this limit, become entangled in the expanse of the unknown. This desire on the part of the master of psychoanalysis produces . . . an attempt to chart the unknown beyond. . . . The desire to enter the unknown and complex tangle of dream thoughts remains strong." "Relations of the Real," 36–37.

The implications of Bataille's thought for psychotherapeutic practices has received scant consideration, undoubtedly in part because Bataille is so consistently opposed to notions of "healing" (as a cognate of "salvation") that would seem to be implied in any concept (and the very etymology) of therapy. Yet, counterintuitive though the notion may be, a Bataillean mode of psychoanalytic practice is an implicit concern that pervades the present pages. I agree with Benjamin Noys who, writing on Bataille and psychotherapy, concludes that Bataille "remains as the disturbing reminder of those . . . moments where our limits are transgressed and our boundaries are disrupted. Perhaps these moments are where we might find not only the limits of therapy but also the opening to a new ethics of abjection and a new therapeutic practice." "Shattering the Subject," 135. For a discussion of Bataille's "decentered subject" in relation to psychotherapy, see the sections "Therapy" and "Cure" in Dean, *The Self and Its Pleasures*, 235–245.

86. Roudinesco makes a related point in differentiating Bataille's interpretation of Freud from Breton's: "Having been attracted to Freud through mass psychology and the phenomena of collective identity, [Bataille] saw madness as an extreme experience leading to the void and acephality, and the unconscious as a nonknowledge within consciousness that revealed the conflict inside the individual and the attraction he feels for abjection, ordure, and all that is vile." *Jacques Lacan*, 134.

87. Bataille, *Inner Experience*, 52.

88. Ibid., 27.

89. Ibid., 27, 41.

90. Ibid., 108.

91. Ibid., 28.

92. Bataille, "Autobiographical Note," 217–218.

93. Bataille, cited in Derrida, "From Restricted to General Economy," 252.

94. Bataille, "Nietzschean Chronicle," 207.

95. Blanchot, "Dreaming, Writing," xxviii. Though Blanchot offers this remark in the context of an introduction to a collection of Michel Leiris's dreams, he must also have in mind Bataille, who influenced so much of his thought.

96. Ibid., xxvii.

97. The drawing bears the inscription "Tossa de Mar," the region of Catalonia where Bataille, in the company of Masson, "drew up the first programme of *Acéphale* and the long inaugural text for the journal." Surya, *Georges Bataille*, 234. There is volcanic activity in the Garrotxa Volcanic Zone.

98. Bataille, *Guilty*, 47, 48.

99. Bataille, *Theory of Religion*, 57.

100. Bataille, *Guilty*, 48.

101. Bataille, "The Sorcerer's Apprentice," 226.

Afterword

Amy Hollywood

1. Or in extreme—perhaps we might say queer—sexual practices? I remain unsure. One question, among others, is whether we can identify the extreme (whatever that might mean) with the queer. And despite my general agreement with much of Leo Bersani's work, I am not sure I am ready to associate—no, to identify—gay sexuality with death. I do, however, agree with Jeffrey Kripal, Kent Brintnall, Shannon Winnubst, and others who insist that there is something queer about Bataille. But how do we understand sex in Bataille, given that what we have in the archive under that name are written texts and the occasional visual or photographic image? I am not sure how to relate the explicitly pornographic to the scenes of execution under discussion here. I think that there is a lot we still have to figure out about what Bataille meant by ecstasy, eroticism, sex, death, and their relationship. For Bersani's evocative reading of Bataille, see Bersani, *Culture of Redemption*.

2. Jérôme Bourgon substantiates and offers further evidence for my own earlier claims to this effect. "Bataille's writings of this period depict pain—unadulterated, unambiguous—without ever alluding to anything like 'ecstatic joy' being present in the tortured man's experience. On the contrary, the only expression seen on his face is a grimace, as his body writhes in 'hideous pain.' There is indeed a passing evocation of a trance or a stepping outside of oneself (though this is not an 'ecstasy'), but that experience is Bataille's, not the tortured subject's." Bourgon here cites *Inner Experience* and *Guilty*, going on to quote in full Bataille's insistence in

Inner Experience that the love he felt for the victim of torture was one "*in which the sadistic instinct plays no part.*" See Bourgon, "Bataille et le 'supplicié chinois': erreurs sur la personne." I am citing from the later revised version of this essay, included in a book Bourgon co-wrote with two other scholars. See Brook, Bourgon, and Blue, *Death by a Thousand Cuts*, 234. To this I would add that saying he loved the man and that the man was "beautiful as a wasp" do not entail claims about that man's putative ecstasy. Such a claim only occurs, and there with a question mark, in *The Tears of Eros*, a text the authorship of which Bourgon questions. See below for more on that issue.

3. LaCapra explores these issues in a number of very important essays and books, but Bataille figures most crucially in LaCapra, *History in Transit*, 1–34, 107–194, and 249–270. See also LaCapra, *History and Memory after Auschwitz*, 8–42; LaCapra, *Writing History, Writing Trauma*, 80n55; and LaCapra, *History and Its Limits*, 59–89, 90–122.

4. Bataille, *Oeuvres completes*, 11:180; and Bataille, "Concerning the Accounts Given by the Residents of Hiroshima," 228.

5. We should also note that Bataille, unlike many others who have written about photographs of early twentieth-century Chinese executions by *lingchi*, all taken by Europeans in China in the wake of the Boxer Rebellion, immediately saw that these photographs were of different individuals. "I've found by accident—at Fontenay—another photo of the Chinese torture of a hundred pieces. Completely the same so far as the torture, but it's someone else." Cited in Brook, Bourgon, and Blue, *Death By a Thousand Cuts*, 227.

6. Bataille, *Oeuvres completes*, 11:185; Bataille, "Concerning the Accounts Given by Residents of Hiroshima," 232.

7. Of course Bataille's theory of religion also has to do with community and hence with the living, but I continue to worry that it is an account of community as founded and held together only through the thought of death. Religion also, for Bataille, seeks a kind of fusion between the self and the other in which all boundaries are overcome, itself arguably a simulacrum of death. This might be an accurate, or at least a useful, account of religion, but I am not ready to accede to that claim just yet. I think that much work on the nature of death, sacrifice, and their relationship within various religious traditions and forms of religiosity would be required before we can make this claim—as well as attention to that in religion that arguably does not depend on this particular aspect of human existence.

8. Yet I was unreasonably happy when I first read Jérôme Bourgon's essay, which suggests, quite persuasively, that *Tears of Eros*, putatively Bataille's final book and the one in which he seems to make an explicit link between the Chinese execution by *lingchi* and ecstasy (although even there, with a question mark beside the latter term), might not in fact have been written and the images ordered by Bataille. Letters show that Bataille was upset by the placement of an erotic image "in the midst of images of horrors, of tortures," which, he claimed, "cannot be interrupted in this manner." The French of the passage that accompanies the image of the Chinese execution victim is, uncharacteristically, ungrammatical, suggesting to Bour-

gon that it might have been written by Bataille's Italian collaborator, Joseph Marie Lo Duca. As Bourgon writes, the case cannot be fully decided without access to the full publication dossier for *The Tears of Eros*. Sotheby's sold it to an anonymous buyer in 2002 for 27,000 euros. Who has it? What are they doing with it? The existence of a French horror film, *Martyrs*, based on the idea of a cult of torturers obsessed with Bataille and with the *lingchi* photographs, gives one considerable pause. Not that I think such a cult exists, of course, but it's troubling that the *idea* of such a cult appeals to the imagination.

In other words, I still want Bataille to be right; I still want him to be *my* Bataille, and my Bataille wouldn't condone the fantasy of torturing another in order to hear from her some secret ecstasy lying on the edge of the body's destruction. (In the film, which I haven't seen, although not for any particularly ethical reasons, the tortured woman whispers to her torturer, who then immediately kills herself. As it turns out, that question mark [ecstasy (?)], whether authored by Bataille or not, was there for a reason.)

It should be noted that Brook, Bourgon, and Blue remain critical of Bataille and his disinterest in the particular history of the executed men on whose photographic images he meditated. See Brook, Bourgon, and Blue, *Death by a Thousand Cuts*, 242.

A full examination of the relationship between pain, death, and eroticism in Bataille's late work would require access to the publication dossier for *The Tears of Eros* but also close scrutiny of *Erotism*, the book on Gilles de Rais, and other late works. For the material on *The Tears of Eros*, see Brook, Bourgon, and Blue, *Death by a Thousand Cuts*, 229, 235–236.

Works Cited

Abel, Lionel. "Georges Bataille and the Repetition of Nietzsche." In *On Bataille: Critical Essays*, edited by Leslie Anne Boldt-Irons, 51–59. Albany, N.Y.: SUNY Press, 1995.

Acéphale: Religion, sociologie, philosophie. Edited by Michel Camus. Paris: Éds. Jean-Michel Place, 1995.

Ades, Dawn, and Simon Baker. *Undercover Surrealism: Georges Bataille and* Documents. Cambridge, Mass.: MIT Press, 2006.

Airborne, Max. "The Fat Truth." *FaT GiRL* 2 (1995): 48–49.

Amatuzio, Janis. *Beyond Knowing: Mysteries and Messages of Death and Life from a Forensic Pathologist*. Novato, Calif.: New World Library, 2006.

Andolsen, Barbara Hilkert. "Agape in Feminist Ethics." *Journal of Religious Ethics* 9, no. 1 (Spring 1981): 69–83.

Anonymous. "King Xolilizwe [*sic*] Sigcawu Coronation." *MyPE.co.za* (May 7, 2010), http://www.mype.co.za/modules.php?name=News&file=print&sid=4805.

Arppe, Tiina. "Sorcerer's Apprentices and the 'Will to Figuration': The Ambiguous Heritage of the *Collège de Sociologie*." *Theory, Culture & Society* 26, no. 4 (2009): 117–145.

Artaud, Antonin. *The Theatre and Its Double*. Translated by Mary Caroline Richards. New York: Grove, 1958.

Asrama, Dandisvami Damodara, ed. *Jnanarnava Tantra*. Calcutta: Navabharata, 1982.

Attali, Jacques. *Noise: The Political Economy of Music*. Minneapolis: University of Minnesota Press, 1985.

Bagchi, P. C., ed. *The Kaulajnananirnaya and Some Minor Texts of the School of Matsyendranatha.* Calcutta: Metropolitan Printing and Publishing House, 1934.

Barsky, Arthur, et al. "Nonspecific Medication Side Effects and the Nocebo Phenomenon." *Journal of the American Medical Association* 287, no. 5 (February 2002): 622–627.

Bataille, Georges. *The Accursed Share: An Essay on General Economy.* Vol. 1: *Consumption.* Translated by Robert Hurley. New York: Zone, 1991.

———. *The Accursed Share: An Essay on General Economy.* Vols. 2–3: *The History of Eroticism; Sovereignty.* Translated by Robert Hurley. New York: Zone, 1993.

———. "Autobiographical Note." In *My Mother, Madame Edwarda, The Dead Man,* translated by Austryn Wainhouse, 215–222. London: Marion Boyars, 1995.

———. *Blue of Noon.* Translated by Harry Mathews. New York: Marion Boyars, 2002.

———. "Concerning the Accounts Given by the Residents of Hiroshima." In *Trauma: Explorations in Memory,* edited by Cathy Caruth, translated by Alan Keenan, 221–235. Baltimore, Md.: Johns Hopkins University Press, 1995.

———. "[Dream]." In *Visions of Excess: Selected Writings, 1927–1939,* edited by Allan Stoekl, translated by Allan Stoekl, with Carl R. Lovitt and Donald M. Leslie Jr., 3–4. Minneapolis: University of Minnesota Press, 1985.

———. *Erotism: Death and Sensuality.* Translated by Mary Dalwood. San Francisco: City Lights, 1986.

———. "L'esprit moderne et le jeu des transpositions." In *Documents,* no. 8 (1930).

———. "Formless." In *Visions of Excess: Selected Writings, 1927–1939,* edited by Allan Stoekl, translated by Allan Stoekl, with Carl R. Lovitt and Donald M. Leslie Jr., 31. Minneapolis: University of Minnesota Press, 1985.

———. *Guilty.* Translated by Bruce Boone. Venice, Calif.: Lapis, 1988.

———. *Guilty.* Translated by Stuart Kendall. Albany, N.Y.: SUNY Press, 2011.

———. *Inner Experience.* Translated by Leslie Anne Boldt. Albany, N.Y.: SUNY Press, 1988.

———. "Joy in the Face of Death." In *The College of Sociology, 1937–1939,* edited by Denis Hollier, translated by Betsy Wing, 322–328. Minneapolis: University of Minnesota Press, 1988.

———. "Kali." In *Encyclopaedia Acephalica,* 55–56. London: Atlas, 1995.

———. "The 'Lugubrious Game.'" In *Visions of Excess: Selected Writings, 1927–1939,* edited by Allan Stoekl, translated by Allan Stoekl, with Carl R. Lovitt and Donald M. Leslie Jr., 24–30. Minneapolis: University of Minnesota Press, 1985.

———. *Madame Edwarda,* in *Oeuvres Complètes,* vol. 3. Paris: Gallimard, 1973.

———. *Ma mere.* Paris: 10/18, 1973.

———. "Materialism." In *Visions of Excess: Selected Writings, 1927–1939*, edited by Allan Stoekl, translated by Allan Stoekl, with Carl R. Lovitt and Donald M. Leslie Jr., 15–16. Minneapolis: University of Minnesota Press, 1985.

———. "Method of Meditation." In *The Unfinished System of Nonknowledge*, edited by Stuart Kendall, translated by Michelle Kendall and Stuart Kendall, xi–xliv. Minneapolis: University of Minnesota Press, 2001.

———. "Nietzschean Chronicle." In *Visions of Excess: Selected Writings, 1927–1939*, edited by Allan Stoekl, translated by Allan Stoekl, with Carl R. Lovitt and Donald M. Leslie Jr., 202–212. Minneapolis: University of Minnesota Press, 1985.

———. "The Notion of Expenditure." In *Visions of Excess: Selected Writings, 1927–1939*, edited by Allan Stoekl, translated by Allan Stoekl, with Carl R. Lovitt and Donald M. Leslie Jr., 116–129. Minneapolis: University of Minnesota Press, 1985.

———. "The 'Old Mole' and the Prefix *Sur* in the Words *Surhomme* [Superman] and *Surrealist.*" In *Visions of Excess: Selected Writings, 1927–1939*, edited by Allan Stoekl, translated by Allan Stoekl, with Carl R. Lovitt and Donald M. Leslie Jr., 91–102. Minneapolis: University of Minnesota Press, 1985.

———. *Oeuvres complètes.* 12 vols. Paris: Gallimard, 1970–1988.

———. *On Nietzsche.* Translated by Bruce Boone. New York: Paragon House, 1992.

———. "The Practice of Joy Before Death." In *Visions of Excess: Selected Writings, 1927–1939*, edited by Allan Stoekl, translated by Allan Stoekl, with Carl R. Lovitt and Donald M. Leslie Jr., 235–239. Minneapolis: University of Minnesota Press, 1985.

———. "The Psychological Structure of Fascism." In *Visions of Excess: Selected Writings, 1927–1939*, edited by Allan Stoekl, translated by Allan Stoekl, with Carl R. Lovitt and Donald M. Leslie Jr., 137–160. Minneapolis: University of Minnesota Press, 1985.

———. "Reflections on the Executioner and the Victim." Translated by Elizabeth Rottenberg. *Yale French Studies* 79 (1991): 18.

———. "The Sacred." In *Visions of Excess: Selected Writings, 1927–1939*, edited by Allan Stoekl, translated by Allan Stoekl, with Carl R. Lovitt and Donald M. Leslie Jr., 240–245. Minneapolis: University of Minnesota Press, 1985.

———. "The Sacred Conspiracy." In *Visions of Excess: Selected Writings, 1927–1939*, edited by Allan Stoekl, translated by Allan Stoekl, with Carl R. Lovitt and Donald M. Leslie Jr., 178–181. Minneapolis: University of Minnesota Press, 1985.

———. "The Solar Anus." In *Visions of Excess: Selected Writings, 1927–1939*, edited by Allan Stoekl, translated by Allan Stoekl, with Carl R. Lovitt and Donald M. Leslie Jr., 5–9. Minneapolis: University of Minnesota Press, 1985.

———. "The Sorcerer's Apprentice." In *Visions of Excess: Selected Writings, 1927–1939*, edited by Allan Stoekl, translated by Allan Stoekl, with Carl R. Lovitt and Donald M. Leslie Jr., 223–234. Minneapolis: University of Minnesota Press, 1985.

———. *Story of the Eye.* Translated by Joachim Neugroschel. San Francisco: City Lights, 1987.

———. *The Tears of Eros.* Translated by Peter Connor. San Francisco: City Lights, 1989.

———. *Théorie de la religion.* Paris: Gallimard, 1973.

———. *Theory of Religion.* Translated by Robert Hurley. New York: Zone, 1992.

———. *The Trial of Gilles de Rais.* Translated by Richard Robinson. Los Angeles: Amok, 1991.

———. "The Use Value of D. A. F. de Sade." In *Visions of Excess: Selected Writings, 1927–1939*, edited by Allan Stoekl, translated by Allan Stoekl, with Carl R. Lovitt and Donald M. Leslie Jr., 91–102. Minneapolis: University of Minnesota Press, 1985.

Baudrillard, Jean. "Figures of the Transpolitical." In *Fatal Strategies*, 45–96. New York: Semiotext(e), 1990.

BBC. "World Cup Stadium 'Cow Sacrifice' Plan Sparks Row." *BBC News* (December 1, 2009), http://news.bbc.co.uk/2/hi/Africa/8388001.stm.

Beardsworth, Sara. *Julia Kristeva: Psychoanalysis and Modernity.* Albany, N.Y.: SUNY Press, 2004.

Beauvoir, Simone de. *Must We Burn Sade?* Translated by Annette Michelson. London: Peter Nevill, 1953.

Berlant, Lauren. "Slow Death (Sovereignty, Obesity, Lateral Agency)." *Critical Inquiry* 33 (Summer 2007): 754–780.

Bersani, Leo. "A Conversation with Leo Bersani." In *Is the Rectum a Grave? and Other Essays*, 171–186. Chicago: University of Chicago Press, 2010 [1997].

———. *The Culture of Redemption.* Cambridge, Mass.: Harvard University Press, 1990.

———. *The Freudian Body: Psychoanalysis and Art.* New York: Columbia University Press, 1986.

———. *Homos.* Cambridge, Mass.: Harvard University Press, 1995.

———. "Is the Rectum a Grave?" In *Is the Rectum a Grave? and Other Essays*, 3–30. Chicago: University of Chicago Press, 2010 [1987].

———. "Shame on You." In *After Sex? On Writing Since Queer Theory*, edited by Janet Halley and Andrew Parker, 91–109. Durham, N.C.: Duke University Press, 2011.

———. "Sociability and Cruising." In *Is the Rectum a Grave? and Other Essays*, 45–62. Chicago: University of Chicago Press, 2010 [2002].

———. "Sociality and Sexuality." In *Is the Rectum a Grave? and Other Essays*, 102–119. Chicago: University of Chicago, 2010 [2000].

Bersani, Leo, and Ulysse Dutoit. *Arts of Impoverishment: Beckett, Rothko, Resnais.* Cambridge, Mass.: Harvard University Press, 1993.

———. *Caravaggio's Secrets.* Cambridge, Mass.: MIT Press, 1998.

———. *Forms of Being: Cinema, Aesthetics, Subjectivity.* London: BFI, 2004.

————. *The Forms of Violence: Narrative in Assyrian Art and Modern Culture*. New York: Schocken, 1985.

Bhattacharyya, Narendra Nath. *Indian Puberty Rites*. Delhi: Munshiram Mano-harlal, 1980.

Biardeau, Madeleine, and Charles Malamoud. *Le sacrifice dans l'Inde ancienne*. Paris: PUF, 1976.

Biernacki, Loriliai. *Renowned Goddess of Desire: Women, Sex, and Speech in Tantra*. New York: Oxford University Press, 2007.

Biles, Jeremy. *Ecce Monstrum: Georges Bataille and the Sacrifice of Form*. New York: Fordham University Press, 2007.

Blanchot, Maurice. "Dreaming, Writing." In *Nights as Day, Days as Night*, by Michel Leiris, translated by Richard Sieburth. Hygiene, Colo.: Eridanos, 1987.

————. "The Negative Community." In *The Unavowable Community*, translated by Pierre Joris, 1–26. Barrytown, N.Y.: Station Hill, 1988.

————. "Sade's Reason." In *Lautréamont and Sade*, translated by Stuart Kendall and Michelle Kendall. Stanford, Calif.: Stanford University Press, 2004.

Boldt-Irons, Leslie Anne, ed. *On Bataille: Critical Essays*. Albany, N.Y.: SUNY Press, 1995.

Bois, Yve-Alain. "Abattoir." In *Formless: A User's Guide*, 43–51. New York: Zone, 2000.

Bois, Yve-Alain, and Rosalind E. Krauss. *Formless: A User's Guide*. New York: Zone, 2000.

Bond, Patrick. *A Political Economy of the 2010 World Cup in South Africa, Six Red Cards for FIFA*. Durban: Center for Civil Society, University of KwaZulu Natal, 2010.

Bossuet, Jacques-Bénigne. *Oraisons funèbres et panégyriques*. Paris: Garnier Fréres, 1942.

Botting, Fred. "Relations of the Real in Lacan, Bataille, and Blanchot." *SubStance* 23, no. 1, issue 73 (1994): 24–40.

Botting, Fred, and Scott Wilson, ed. *Bataille: A Critical Reader*. Malden, Mass.: Blackwell, 1998.

Bourgon, Jérôme. "Bataille et le 'supplicié chinois': erreurs sur la personne." In *Le Supplice oriental dans la littérature et les arts*, edited by Dominguez Leiva and Muriel Détrie, 93–115. Dijon: Les Éditions du Murmure, 2005.

Braziel, Jana Evans, and Kathleen LeBesco. "Editor's Introduction." In *Bodies Out of Bounds: Fatness and Transgression*, 1–15. Berkeley: University of California Press, 2001.

Breton, André. *Communicating Vessels*. Translated by Mary Ann Caws and Geoffrey T. Harris. Lincoln: University of Nebraska Press, 1990.

————. *Manifestoes of Surrealism*. Translated by Richard Seaver and Helen R. Lane. Ann Arbor: University of Michigan Press, 1969.

Brintnall, Kent L. *Ecce Homo: The Male-Body-in-Pain as Redemptive Figure*. Chicago: University of Chicago Press, 2011.

Brook, Timothy, Jérôme Bourgon, and Gregory Blue. *Death by a Thousand Cuts.* Cambridge, Mass.: Harvard University Press, 2008.

Brown, Norman O. "Dionysus in 1990." In *Apocalypse And/or Metamorphosis,* 179–200. Berkeley: University of California Press, 1992.

———. *Life Against Death: The Psychoanalytical Meaning of History.* Middletown, Conn.: Wesleyan University Press, 1959.

Bruno, Jean. "Les techniques d'illumination chez Georges Bataille." In *Critique* 195/196 (1963): 706–721.

Buch, Robert. *The Pathos of the Real: On the Aesthetics of Violence in the Twentieth Century.* Baltimore, Md.: Johns Hopkins University Press, 2010.

Bush, Stephen S. "The Ethics of Ecstasy: Georges Bataille and Amy Hollywood on Mysticism, Morality, and Violence." *Journal of Religious Ethics* 39, no. 2 (June 2011): 299–320.

Butler, Judith. *Antigone's Claim: Kinship Between Life and Death.* New York: Columbia University Press, 2000.

———. *Precarious Life: The Powers of Mourning and Violence.* New York: Verso, 2004.

Caldwell, Sarah. *Oh Terrifying Mother: Sexuality, Violence, and Worship of the Goddess Kali.* New York: Oxford University Pres, 1999.

Carrette, Jeremy R. *Foucault and Religion: Spiritual Corporeality and Political Spirituality.* London: Routledge, 2000.

Cassirer, Ernst. *Philosophy of Enlightenment.* Princeton, N.J.: Princeton University Press, 1951.

Caws, Mary Ann. "Introduction: Linkings and Reflections." In *Communicating Vessels,* by André Breton, translated by Mary Ann Caws and Geoffrey T. Harris. Lincoln: University of Nebraska Press, 1990.

Chidester, David. *Authentic Fakes: Religion and American Popular Culture.* Berkeley: University of California Press, 2005.

———. "Economy." In *Keywords for Religion, Media and Culture,* edited by David Morgan, 83–95. London: Routledge, 2008.

———. "Sacred." *Material Religion* 7, no. 1 (2011): 84–91.

Collins, Louise. "Is Cybersex Sex?" In *The Philosophy of Sex: Contemporary Readings,* edited by Alan Soble, 115–131. London: Rowman and Littlefield, 2008.

Connor, Peter Tracey. *Georges Bataille and the Mysticism of Sin.* Baltimore, Md.: Johns Hopkins University Press, 2000.

Crowley, Patrick, and Paul Hegarty. *Formless: Ways In and Out of Form.* New York: Peter Lang, 2005.

Dean, Carolyn J. *The Self and Its Pleasures: Bataille, Lacan, and the History of the Decentered Subject.* Ithaca, N.Y.: Cornell University Press, 1992.

Dean, Jodi. *Democracy and Other Neoliberal Fantasies: Communicative Capitalism and Left Politics.* Durham, N.C.: Duke University Press, 2009.

———. "Drive as the Structure of Biopolitics: Economy, Sovereignty, and Capture." *Krisis* 2 (2010).

Dean, Tim. "Bareback Time." In *Queer Times, Queer Becomings*, edited by E. L. McCallum and Mikko Tuhkanen, 75–100. Albany, N.Y.: SUNY Press, 2011.

———. *Beyond Sexuality.* Chicago: University of Chicago Press, 2000.

———. "The Erotics of Transgression." In *The Cambridge Companions to Gay and Lesbian Writing*, edited by Hugh Stevens, 65–80. New York: Cambridge University Press, 2011.

———. "An Impossible Embrace: Queerness, Futurity, and the Death Drive." In *A Time for the Humanities: Futurity and the Limits of Autonomy*, edited by James J. Bono, Tim Dean, and Ewa Plonowska Ziarek, 122–145. New York: Fordham University Press, 2008.

———. "Sex and Syncope." *Raritan* 15 (1996): 64–86.

———. "Sex and the Aesthetics of Existence." *PMLA* 125, no. 2 (2010): 387–392.

———. *Unlimited Intimacy: Reflections on the Subculture of Barebacking.* Chicago: University of Chicago Press, 2009.

Deleuze, Gilles, and Félix Guattari. *Anti-Oedipus.* Translated by Robert Hurley, Mark Seem, and Helen R. Lane. New York: Viking, 1977.

———. *A Thousand Plateaus: Capitalism and Schizophrenia.* Translated by Brian Massumi. Minneapolis: University of Minnesota Press, 1991.

Derrida, Jacques. "From Restricted to General Economy: A Hegelianism Without Reserve." In *Writing and Difference*, translated by Alan Bass, 251–277. Chicago: University of Chicago Press, 1978.

"Deva and Laura." Interview by Devra. *FaT GiRL* 3 (1995): 30–31.

Devriendt, Tom. "Vuvuzelas All Around." *Africa Is a Country* (July 11, 2010), http://africasacountry.com/2010/07/11/the-vuvuzela.

"Difficult Seductress! Dorothy Allison." Interview by Barbarism. *FaT GiRL* 3 (1995): 10–15.

Downing, Lisa, and Robert Gillett. "Georges Bataille at the Avant-Garde of Queer Theory? Transgression, Perversion, and the Death Drive." *Nottingham French Studies* 50, no. 3 (2011): 88–102.

Duggan, Lisa. *The Twilight of Equality? Neoliberalism, Cultural Politics, and the Attack on Democracy.* Boston: Beacon, 2003.

Durkheim, Émile. *The Elementary Forms of the Religious Life.* Translated by Joseph Ward Swain. New York: Free Press, 1965.

Edelman, Lee. "Unbecoming: Pornography and the Queer Event." In *Post/Porn/Politics: Queer-Feminist Perspective on the Politics of Porn Performance and Sex Work as Cultural Production*, edited by Tim Stüttgen, 194–211. Berlin: b_books, 2010.

Eliade, Mircea. *Yoga: Immortality and Freedom.* Princeton, N.J.: Princeton University Press, 1971.

Eliot, Sir Charles. *Hinduism and Buddhism: An Historical Sketch.* London: Routledge and Kegan Paul, 1921.

Elkins, James. "The Very Theory of Transgression: Bataille, *Lingchi*, and Transgression." *Australian and New Zealand Journal of Art* 5, no. 2 (2004): 5–19.

Ernsberger, Paul. "Does Social Class Explain the Connection Between Weight and Health?" In *The Fat Studies Reader*, edited by Esther Rothblum and Sondra Solovay, 25–26. New York: New York University Press, 2009.

Fabricatore, Anthony N., Thomas A. Wadden, and Gary D. Foster. "Bias in Health Settings." In *Weight Bias: Nature, Consequences, and Remedies*, edited by Kelly D. Brownell, Rebecca M. Puhl, Marlene B. Schwartz, and Leslie Rudd, 29–41. New York: Guilford, 2005.

Falasca-Zamponi, Simonetta. *Rethinking the Political: The Sacred, Aesthetic Politics, and the Collège de Sociologie*. Ithaca, N.Y.: McGill-Queen's University Press, 2011.

Farrell, Amy Erdman. *Fat Shame: Stigma and the Fat Body in American Culture*. New York: NYU Press, 2011.

Feni, Lulamile. "King's Voice Fulfils Dying Father's Wish." *The Herald* (June 14, 2010), http://www.epherald.co.za/article.aspx?id=573036.

Fer, Briony. "*Poussière/Peinture:* Bataille on Painting." In *Bataille: Writing the Sacred*, edited by Carolyn Bailey Gill, 154–171. London: Routledge, 1995.

ffrench, Patrick. *The Cut: Reading Bataille's Historie de l'oeil*. New York: Oxford University Press, 1999.

———. *The Time of Theory: A History of Tel Quel (1960–83)*. New York: Oxford University Press, 1996.

Fikkan, Janna, and Esther Rothblum. "Weight Bias in Employment." In *Weight Bias: Nature, Consequences, and Remedies*, edited by Kelly D. Brownell, Rebecca M. Puhl, Marlene B. Schwartz, and Leslie Rudd, 15–28. New York: Guilford, 2005.

Fisher, Jonah. "Unholy Row Over World Cup Trumpet." *BBC News* (January 16, 2010), http://news.bbc.co.uk/2/hi/8458829.stm.

Flegal, Kathleen, Barry I. Graubaud, David F. Williamson, and Mitchell H. Gail. "Excess Death Associated with Underweight, Overweight, and Obesity." *Journal of the American Medical Association* 292 (April 20, 2005): 1861–1867.

Foster, Hal. *Compulsive Beauty*. Cambridge, Mass.: MIT Press, 1993.

Foucault, Michel. *Abnormal: Lectures at the Collège de France, 1974–1975*. Translated by Graham Burchell. New York: Picador, 2004.

———. *Les anormaux: Cours au Collège de France. 1974–1975*. Edited by Valerio Marchetti and Antoinetta Salomoni under the direction of François Ewald and Alessandro Fontana. Paris: Gallimard and Seuil, 1999.

———. *The Birth of Biopolitics: Lectures at the Collège de France, 1978–1979*. New York: Palgrave MacMillan: 2008.

———. *Discipline and Punish: The Birth of the Prison*. Translated by Alan Sheridan. New York: Pantheon, 1978.

———. *Dits et écrits*. Edited by Daniel Defert and Francois Ewald. 4 volumes. Paris: NRF/Gallimard, 1994.

———. *Histoire de la folie à l'âge classique*. Paris: Gallimard, 1972.

———. *History of Madness*. Translated by Jonathan Murphy and Jean Khalfa. London: Routledge, 2006.

———. *L'ordre du discours.* Paris: Gallimard, 1971.

———. *The Order of Things: An Archaeology of the Human Sciences.* New York: Vintage, 1970.

———. "Orders of Discourse." Translated by Rupert Swyer. *Social Science Information* 10, no. 2 (April 1971): 7–30. Reprinted under a different title as an appendix to Michel Foucault, *The Archeology of Knowledge and the Discourse on Language* (New York: Harper Colophon/Harper and Row, 1976), 215–237.

———. "*Préface à la transgression.*" *Critique* 195–196 (August–September 1963): 751–769.

———. "Preface to Transgression." In *Religion and Culture: Michel Foucault,* edited by Jeremy R. Carrette, translated by Donald F. Bouchard and Sherry Simon (New York: Routledge, 1999), 57–71.

———. *Surveiller et punir: Naissance de la prison.* Paris: Gallimard, 1975.

Fraser, Laura. *Losing It! False Hopes and Fat Profits in the Diet Industry.* New York: Plume, 1997.

Freud, Sigmund. *The Interpretation of Dreams.* Translated by James Strachey. New York: Avon, 1965.

———. *Introductory Lectures on Psycho-Analysis.* Translated by James Strachey. New York: Norton, 1966.

———. *On Dreams.* Translated by M. D. Eder. Mineola, N.Y.: Dover, 2001.

Friedman, Milton, and Rose Friedman. *Free to Choose.* New York: Avon, 1980.

Gasché, Rodolphe. *Georges Bataille: Phenomenology and Phantasmology.* Translated by Roland Vésgő. Stanford, Calif.: Stanford University Press, 2012.

Geertz, Clifford. *The Interpretation of Cultures.* New York: Basic Books, 1973.

Gemerchak, Christopher M. *The Sunday of the Negative: Reading Bataille Reading Hegel.* Albany, N.Y.: SUNY Press, 2003.

Gerber, Lynne. *Seeking the Straight and Narrow: Weight Loss and Sexual Reorientation in Evangelical America.* Chicago: University of Chicago Press, 2011.

Gheerbrant, Alain, and Léon Aichelbaum. *K éditeur.* Cognac: Le Temps qu'il fait, 1991.

Gill, Carolyn Bailey. "Introduction." In *Bataille: Writing the Sacred,* xv–xix. New York: Routledge, 1995.

Giroux, Henry. *Against the Terror of Neoliberalism: Politics Beyond the Age of Greed.* Boulder, Colo.: Paradigm: 2008.

Goodman, Steve. *Sonic Warfare: Sound, Affect, and the Ecology of Fear.* Cambridge, Mass.: MIT Press, 2010.

Goux, Jean-Joseph. *Frivolité de la valeur.* Paris: Blusson, 2000.

———. "General Economics and Postmodern Capitalism." *Yale French Studies* 78 (1990): 206–224.

———. *L'art et l'argent.* Paris: Blusson, 2011.

Griffith, R. Marie. *Born Again Bodies: Flesh and Spirit in American Christianity.* Berkeley: University of California Press, 2004.

Guerlac, Suzanne. *Literary Polemics: Bataille, Sartre, Valéry, Breton.* Stanford, Calif.: Stanford University Press, 1997.

———. "The Useless Image: Bataille, Bergson, Magritte." In *Representations* 97, no. 1 (Winter 2007): 28–56.

Guthman, Julie, and DuPuis, Melanie. "Embodying Neoliberalism: Economy, Culture, and the Politics of Fat." *Environment and Planning D: Society and Space* 24, no. 3 (2006): 427–448.

Habermas, Jürgen. "The French Path to Postmodernity: Bataille Between Eroticism and General Economy." In *Bataille: A Critical Reader*, edited by Fred Botting and Scott Wilson, translated by Frederick Lawrence, 167–190. Malden, Mass.: Blackwell, 1998.

Hainge, Greg. *Noise Matters: Towards an Ontology of Noise*. New York: Bloomsbury, 2013.

Harvey, David. *A Brief History of Neoliberalism*. Oxford: Oxford University Press, 2005.

Hegarty, Paul. *Noise/Music: A History*. New York: Continuum, 2007.

Henry-Lévy, Bernard. *Les aventures de la liberté. Une histoire subjective des intellectuels*. Paris: Bernard Grasset, 1991.

Hesse-Biber, Sharlene. *Am I Thin Enough Yet? The Cult of Thinness and the Commercialization of Identity*. New York: Oxford University Press, 1996.

Hill, Leslie. *Bataille, Klossowski, Blanchot: Writing at the Limit*. New York: Oxford University Press, 2001.

Hobson, Theo. "The World Cup: A Ritual That Works." *Guardian* (June 12, 2010), http://www.guardian.co.uk/commentisfree/belief/2010/un/12/world-cup-ritual-religion.

Hollier, Denis. *Against Architecture: The Writings of Georges Bataille*. Translated by Betsy Wing. Cambridge, Mass.: MIT Press, 1995.

———, ed. *The College of Sociology, 1937–39*. Translated by Betsy Wing. Minneapolis: University of Minnesota Press, 1988.

———, ed. *Le collège de sociologie, 1937–39*. Paris: Gallimard, 1995.

———. "The Dualist Materials of Georges Bataille." In *Bataille: A Critical Reader*, edited by Fred Botting and Scott Wilson, 59–73. Malden, Mass.: Blackwell, 1998.

Hollywood, Amy. *Sensible Ecstasy: Mysticism, Sexual Difference, and the Demands of History*. Chicago: University of Chicago Press, 2002.

Hong, H. V., and E. H. Hong, with Gregor Malantschuk. *Søren Kierkegaard's Journals and Papers*. Bloomington: Indiana University Press, 1967–.

Hubert, Henri, and Marcel Mauss. *Sacrifice: Its Nature and Functions*. Translated by W. D. Halls. Chicago: University of Chicago Press, 1981.

Hussey, Andrew. *The Inner Scar: The Mysticism of Georges Bataille*. Atlanta, Ga.: Rodopi, 2000.

Huxley, Aldous. *The Perennial Philosophy*. Cleveland, Ohio: World, 1962.

Iles, Mattin, and Anthony Iles. *Noise and Capitalism*. San Sebastian: Arteleku Audiolab, 2009.

Irwin, Alexander. *Saints of the Impossible: Bataille, Weil, and the Politics of the Sacred*. Minneapolis: University of Minnesota Press, 2002.

Jay, Martin. "The Limits of Limit-Experience: Bataille and Foucault." *Constellations* 2, no. 2 (1995): 155–174.

Jika, Thanduxolo. "BEE Shock in R3bn Bisho Fleet Contract." *Daily Dispatch* (October 3, 2009), http://www.dispatch.co.za/article.aspx?id=349332.

Jordan, Mark. *Convulsing Bodies: Religion and Resistance in Foucault.* Stanford, Calif.: Stanford University Press, 2014.

Kahn, Douglas. *Noise Water Meat: A History of Sound in the Arts.* Cambridge, Mass.: MIT Press, 1999.

Kakati, Bani Kanta. *Mother Goddess Kamakhya.* Guwahati: Lawyer's Book Stall, 1952.

Kaschula, Russell H. "Praise Poetry: Xhosa Praise Poetry for President Mandela." In *African Folklore: An Encyclopedia*, edited by Phillip M. Peek and Kwesi Yankah, 362–364. London: Routledge, 2004.

Kauder, Emil. *History of Marginal Utility Theory.* Princeton, N.J.: Princeton University Press, 1965.

Kauppi, Niilo. *The Making of an Avant-Garde: Tel Quel.* New York: Mouton de Gruyter, 1994.

Kendall, Stuart. "Editor's Introduction: Unlimited Assemblage." In *The Unfinished System of Nonknowledge*, edited by Stuart Kendall, translated by Michelle Kendall and Stuart Kendall, xi–xliv. Minneapolis: University of Minnesota Press, 2001.

Khanna. "The Goddess-Woman Equation in the Tantras." In *Gendering the Spirit: Women, Religion, and the Post-Colonial Response*, edited by Durre S. Ahmed. New York: Zen, 2002.

Kinzel, Lesley. "It Was Supposed to Be Funny: Death Fat Contextualized." http://blog.twowholecakes.com/2009/06/it-was-supposed-to-be-funny-death-fat-contextualized/.

Kolata, Gina. *Rethinking Thin: The New Science of Weight Loss—and the Myths and Realities of Dieting.* New York: Farrar, Straus and Giroux, 2007.

———. "Study Says Obesity Can be Contagious." *New York Times* (July 7, 2007).

Kosky, Jeffrey. *Arts of Wonder: Enchanting Secularity—Walter de Maria, Diller + Scofidio, James Turrell, Andy Goldsworthy.* Chicago: University of Chicago Press, 2013.

———. "Georges Bataille's Religion Without Religion: A Review of the Possibilities Opened by the Publication of *The Unfinished System of Nonknowledge*." *Journal of Religion* 84, no. 1 (January 2004): 78–87.

Krauss, Rosalind E. "Isotropy." In *Formless: A User's Guide*, edited by Yve-Alain Bois and Rosalind E. Krauss, 103–108. New York: Zone, 2000.

Kripal, Jeffrey J. *Kali's Child: The Mystical and the Erotic in the Life and Teachings of Ramakrisha.* Chicago: University of Chicago Press, 1998.

———. "Visions of the Impossible: How 'Fantastic' Stories Unlock the Nature of Consciousness." *Chronicle of Higher Education* (April 4, 2014).

Kripal, Jeffrey J., with Ata Anzali, Andrea R. Jain, and Erin Prophet. *Comparing Religions: Coming to Terms.* Oxford: Wiley Blackwell, 2014.

Kristeva, Julia. "Bataille, Experience, and Practice." In *On Bataille: Critical Essays*, edited by Leslie Anne Boldt-Irons, 237–264. Albany, N.Y.: SUNY Press, 1995.

———. *In the Beginning Was Love: Psychoanalysis and Faith*. Translated by Arthur Goldhammer. New York: Columbia University Press, 1987.

———. *New Maladies of the Soul*. Translated by Ross Guberman. New York: Columbia University Press, 1995.

———. *Polylogue*. Paris: Seuil, 1977.

———. *Powers of Horror: An Essay on Abjection*. Translated by Leon S. Roudiez. New York: Columbia University Press, 1982.

———. *Revolt She Said: An Interview with Philippe Petit*. Translated by Brian O'Keefe. Edited by Sylvère Lotringer. New York: Semiotext(e), 2002.

———. *Revolution in Poetic Language*. Translated by Margaret Walker. New York: Columbia University Press, 1984.

———. *Sense and Non-Sense of Revolt: The Powers and Limits of Psychoanalysis*. Translated by Jeanine Herman. New York: Columbia University Press, 2000.

———. *Tales of Love*. Translated by Leon S. Roudiez. New York: Columbia University Press, 1987.

Kulik, Don. "Porn." In *Fat: The Anthropology of an Obsession*, edited by Don Kulick and Anne Meneley, 77–92. New York: Tarcher/Penguin, 2005.

Lacan, Jacques. *The Four Fundamental Concepts of Psycho-Analysis*. New York: Norton: 1981.

LaCapra, Dominick. *History and Its Limits: Human, Animal, Violence*. Ithaca, N.Y.: Cornell University Press, 2009.

———. *History and Memory After Auschwitz*. Ithaca, N.Y.: Cornell University Press, 1998.

———. *History in Transit: Experience, Identity, Critical Theory*. Ithaca, N.Y.: Cornell University Press, 2004.

———. *Writing History, Writing Trauma*. Baltimore, Md.: Johns Hopkins University Press, 2001.

LaMendola, Bob. "Some Ob-Gyns in South Florida Turn Away Overweight Women." *Sun Sentinel* (May 16, 2011).

Lawrence, Meridith. "Beyond Self-Hatred." *FaT GiRL* 4 (October 1995): 3–4.

Lebesco, Kathleen. *Revolting Bodies: The Struggle to Redefine Fat Identity*. Amherst: University of Massachusetts Press, 2004.

Leiris, Michel. "*De la Bataille impossible à l'impossible* 'Documents,'" *Critique* 19, nos. 195–196 (1963): 685–693.

———. *Mirror of Tauromachy*. Translated by Paul Hammond. London: Atlas, 2007.

Lévi-Strauss, Claude. *The Elementary Structures of Kinship*. Translated by James Harle Bell and John Richard von Sturmer. Boston: Beacon, 1969.

———. *The Naked Man*. Translated by John and Doreen Weightman. Chicago: University of Chicago Press, 1981.

Lingis, Alphonso. "Foreword: Why Bataille Now?" In *Reading Bataille Now*, edited by Shannon Winnubst, vii–xii. Bloomington: Indiana University Press, 2007.

Lomas, David. *The Haunted Self: Surrealism, Psychoanalysis, Subjectivity.* New Haven, Conn.: Yale University Press, 2000.

Lotringer, Sylvère. "Interview with Julia Kristeva." Translated by Jeanine Herman. http://semiotexte.com/?p=123.

Löwy, Michael. *"Le capitalism comme religion: Walter Benjamin et Max Weber."* *Raisons pratiques* 23 (2006): 203–219.

Makhonya.com. "Our Team Visited the Royal African Awards." *Makhonya.com: Prosperity Through Unity* (2010), http://www.makhonya.com/?page_id=134.

Makhonya Investments. "Welcome: Creating Wealth and Sustainable Growth." *Makhonya Investments* (2010), http://www.makhonyainvestments.co.za.

Maluleke, Tinyiko Sam. "South Africa, Christianity, and the World Cup." *Ekklesia: A New Way of Thinking* (June 5, 2010), http://www.ekklesia.co.uk/node/12326.

Mann, Traci A., Janet Tomiyama, Erika Westling, Ann-Marie Lew, Barbra Samuels, and Jason Chatman. "Medicare's Search for Effective Obesity Treatments: Diets Are Not the Answer." *American Psychologist* 62, no. 3 (April 2007): 220–233.

Mansfield, Nick. *The God Who Deconstructs Himself: Sovereignty and Subjectivity Between Freud, Bataille, and Derrida.* New York: Fordham University Press, 2010.

Maqhina, Mayibongwe. "Government to 'Assist' with King's Coronation." *Daily Dispatch* (May 10, 2010), http://www.dispatch.co.za/article.aspx?id=400264.

Marglin, Frédérique Apffel. "Female Sexuality in the Hindu World." In *Immaculate and Powerful: The Female in Sacred and Social Reality*, edited by C. Atkinson et al., 39–60. Boston: Beacon, 1985.

Marketdata Enterprises. "U.S. Weight Loss Market to Reach $58 Billion in 2007." http://www.prweb.com/releases/2007/04/prweb520127.htm.

Marx-Scouras, Danielle. *The Cultural Politics of* Tel Quel: *Literature and the Left in the Wake of Engagement.* University Park: Pennsylvania State University Press, 1996.

Mauss, Marcel. *The Gift: The Form and Reason for Exchange in Archaic Societies.* Translated by W. D. Halls. New York: Norton, 1990.

McWhorter, Ladelle. "Bataille's Erotic Displacement of Vision: Attempts at a Feminist Reading." In *Panorama: Philosophies of the Visible*, edited by Wilhelm S. Wurzer, 117–127. New York: Continuum, 2002.

———. "Is There Sexual Difference in the Work of Georges Bataille?" *International Studies in Philosophy* 27, no.1 (1995): 33–41.

Mercier, Jean-Sébastian. *L'An 2440, rêve s'il en fut jamais.* Bordeaux: Editions Ducros, 1971.

Miller, James. *The Passion of Michel Foucault.* New York: Simon and Schuster, 1993.

Mitchell, Andrew J., and Jason Kemp Winfree, ed. *The Obsessions of Georges Bataille: Community and Communication*. Albany, N.Y.: SUNY Press, 2009.

Mkiva, Zolani. *Zolani Mkiva: His Royal Heritage, The Poet of Africa* (2010), http://poetofafrica.com.

Monod, Jean-Claude. *La querelle de la secularization de Hegel à Blumenberg*. Paris: Vrin, 2002.

Moon, Michael, and Eve Kosofsky Sedgwick. "Divinity: A Dossier, a Performance Piece, a Little-Understood Emotion." In *Revolting Bodies*, edited by Jana Evans Braziel and Kathleen Lebesco, 292–328. Berkeley: University of California Press, 2001.

Morgan, David. *The Sacred Gaze: Religious Visual Culture in Theory and Practice*. Berkeley: University of California Press, 2005.

Morris, Paul. "No Limits: Necessary Danger in Male Porn." http://www.managingdesire.org/nolimits.html.

Mthembu, Bongani. "Bull-Killing Ritual to be Debated in Durban." *Mail & Guardian* (November 24, 2009), http://www.mg.co.za/article/2009-11-24-bullkilling-ritual-to-be-debated-in-durban.

Mullis, Kary. *Dancing Naked in the Mind Field*. New York: Pantheon, 1998.

Murray, Samantha. "(Un/Be)Coming Out? Rethinking Fat Politics." *Social Semiotics* 15, no. 2 (2005): 152–163.

Nancy, Jean-Luc. "The Inoperative Community." In *The Inoperative Community*, translated by Peter Connor, 1–42. Minneapolis: University of Minnesota Press, 1991.

Nelson, Robert H. *Economics as Religion: From Samuelson to Chicago and Beyond*. University Park: Pennsylvania State University Press, 2001.

Nigro, Roberto. "Experiences of the Self Between Limit, Transgression, and the Explosion of the Dialectical System: Foucault as Reader of Bataille and Blanchot." *Philosophy and Social Criticism* 31, nos. 5–6 (2005): 649–664.

———. "*Foucault lecteur de Bataille et de Blanchot*." In *Michel Foucault, la literature et les arts: Actes du colloque de Cerisy—Juin 2001*, edited by Philippe Artières, 23–45. Paris: Éditions Kimé, 2004.

Noys, Benjamin. "Shattering the Subject: Georges Bataille and the Limits of Therapy." In *European Journal of Psychotherapy, Counselling, and Health* 7, no. 3 (September 2005): 125–136.

"Oh My God, It's Big Mama!" Interview with Marx Airborne and Elizabeth Hong Brassil, by Barbarism. *FaT GiRL* 1 (1994): 14–20.

Omalu, B. I., D. G. Ives, A. M. Buhari, J. L. Linder, P. R. Schauer, C. H. Wecht, and L. H. Kuller. "Death Rates and Causes of Death After Bariatric Surgery for Pennsylvania Residents, 1995 to 2004." *Archives of Surgery* 142, no. 10 (2007): 923–928.

Ong, Aiwha. *Neoliberalism as Exception: Mutations in Citizenship and Sovereignty*. Durham, N.C.: Duke University Press, 2006.

Padoux, André. *Vac: The Concept of the Word in Selected Hindu Tantras*. Albany, N.Y.: SUNY Press, 1990.

Patterson, Orlando. *Slavery and Social Death: A Comparative Study.* Cambridge, Mass.: Harvard University Press, 1982.

Pithouse, Richard. "On the Path to Crony Capitalism." *Daily Dispatch* (September 25, 2010), http://www.dispatch.co.za/article.aspx?id-436143.

Plate, S. Brent. *A History of Religion in 5½ Objects: Bringing the Spiritual to Its Senses.* Boston: Beacon, 2014.

Plotnisky, Arkady. *Reconfigurations: Critical Theory and General Economy.* Gainesville: University of Florida Press, 1993.

Prohaska, Ariane, and Jeannine Gailey. "Fat Women as 'Easy Targets': Achieving Masculinity Through Hogging." In *The Fat Studies Reader*, edited by Esther Rothblum and Sondra Solovay, 158–166. New York: NYU Press, 2009.

Regchand, Sharika. "Bull-Killing Ritual Compared to Communion." *The Star* (December 2, 2009), http://www.thestar.co.za/?fSectionId=&fArticleId=vn20 091202042612982C697058.

Reuters. "Cow Slaughtered at World Cup Stadium to Appease Spirits." *National Post* (May 26, 2010), http://sports.nationalpost.com/2010/05/26/cow -slaughtered-at-world-cup-stadium-to-appease-spirits/#ixzz0pAGwG3dK.

Richardson, Michael, ed. *The Absence of Myth: Writings on Surrealism.* New York: Verso, 1994.

———. "Introduction." In *The Absence of Myth: Writings on Surrealism*, 1–27. New York: Verso, 1994.

Richman, Michèle. *Reading Georges Bataille: Beyond the Gift.* Baltimore, Md.: Johns Hopkins University, 1982.

———. *Sacred Revolutions: Durkheim and the Collège de Sociologie.* Minneapolis: University of Minnesota Press, 2002.

Ring, Kenneth. *The Omega Project: Near-Death Experiences, UFO Encounters, and Mind at Large.* New York: William and Morrow, 1992.

Robins, Steven. "World Cup Ritual Worth Every Cent." *Cape Times* (October 25, 2010): 13.

Robbins, Jeffrey W. "Introduction." In *After the Death of God*, by John D. Caputo and Gianni Vattimo, 1–26. New York: Columbia University Press, 2009.

Roudinesco, Elizabeth. *Jacques Lacan.* Translated by Barbara Bray. New York: Columbia University Press, 1997.

Sade, Marquis de. *Justine, Philosophy in the Bedroom, and Other Writings.* Translated by Richard Seaver and Austryn Wainhouse. New York: Grove, 1965.

Sanderson, Alexis. "Purity and Power Among the Brahmins of Kashmir." In *The Category of the Person: Anthropology, Philosophy, History*, 190–216. Edited by Michael Carrithers, Steven Collins, and Steven Lukes. Cambridge: Cambridge University Press, 1985.

Sapa. "Mkhize: Bull-Killing Ruling Promotes Cultural Tolerance." *Mail & Guardian* (December 4, 2009), http://www.mg.co.za/article/2009-12-04-mkhize -bullkilling-ruling-promotes-cultural-tolerance.

———. "Sangomas Sacrifice Ox to Bless the World Cup Stadiums." *Cape Times* (May 26, 2010), http://www.capetimes.co.za/index.php?fArticleId=5486198.

Sarma, Ganga. *Kamrup Kamakhya*. Guwahati: Visnu Prakasan, 2002.

———. *Kamarupa Kamakhya: Itihasa o Dharmmamulaka*. Guwahati: Visnu Prakasan, 2001.

Schechter, Dave. "The Religion of Football." *CNN Belief Blog* (June 4, 2010), http://religion.blogs.cnn.com/2010/06/04/the-church-of-football.

Schoterman, J. A., ed. *The Yoni Tantra* (Delhi: Manohar, 1980).

Scott, Matt. "FIFA in a Stew Over Ritual Slaughter of Cows in World Cup Stadium." *Guardian* (December 23, 2009), http://www.guardian.co.uk./sport/2009/dec/23/fifa-world-cup-stadium-cow-slaughter.

Shastri, B. N. ed. *The Kalika Purana*. Delhi: Nag, 1991.

Shaviro, Steven. *Passion and Excess: Blanchot, Bataille, and Literary Theory*. Tallahassee: Florida State University Press, 1990.

Shklar, Judith N. "The Liberalism of Fear." In *Liberalism and the Moral Life*, edited by Nancy L. Rosenblum, 21–38. Cambridge, Mass.: Harvard University Press, 1989.

Shulman, David. *Tamil Temple Myths: Sacrifice and Divine Marriage in the South Indian Saiva Tradition*. Princeton, N.J.: Princeton University Press, 1980.

Sikhakhane, Jabulani. "The Shame of Being Colonised by King Sepp." *Sunday Tribune* (May 2, 2010), http://www.highbeam.com/doc/1G1-2253354713.html.

Sircar, D. C. *The Sakta Pithas*. Delhi: Motilal Banarsidas, 1973.

Singh, Nikhil Pal. "World Cup 2010." *Social Text: Periscope* (July 20, 2010), http://www.socialtextjournal.org/periscope/2010/07/introduction-south-africas-world-cup.php.

Smith, Jonathan Z. *Imagining Religion: From Babylon to Jonestown*. Chicago: University of Chicago Press, 1982.

Snapper, Ruth Ginger. "Language of the Noosphere." http://www.nyu.edu/classes/keefer/com/snap1wno.html.

Sobal, Jeffrey. "The Size Acceptance Movement and the Social Construction of Body Weight." In *Weighty Issues: Fatness and Thinness as Social Problems*, edited by Donna Maurer and Jeffrey Sobal, 231–250. New York: Aldine de Gruyter, 1999.

Sontag, Susan. "Against Interpretation." In *Against Interpretation, and Other Essays*. New York: Doubleday, 1986.

Stearns, Peter. *Fat History: Bodies and Beauty in the Modern West*. New York: New York University Press, 2002.

Stiglitz, Joseph. *Globalization and Its Discontents*. New York: Norton, 2003.

Stinson, Kandi. *Women and Dieting Culture: Inside a Commercial Weight Loss Group*. New Brunswick, N.J.: Rutgers University Press, 2001.

Stinson, Susan. "Drink." http://www.susanstinson.net/.

———. "Fat Girls Need Fiction." In *The Fat Studies Reader*, edited by Esther Rothblum and Sondra Solovay, 231–234. New York: New York University Press, 2004.

Stoekl, Allan. *Bataille's Peak: Energy, Religion, and Postsustainability*. Minneapolis: University of Minnesota Press, 2007.

—. *Politics, Writing, Mutilation: The Cases of Bataille, Blanchot, Roussel, Leiris, and Ponge.* Minneapolis: University of Minnesota Press, 1985.

Suleiman, Susan Rubin. "Bataille in the Street: The Search for Virility in the 1930s." In *Critical Inquiry* 21 (1994): 61–79.

Surya, Michel. *Georges Bataille: An Intellectual Biography.* Translated by Krzysztof Fijalkowski and Michael Richardson. London: Verso, 2002.

Sweedler, Milo. *The Dismembered Community: Bataille, Blanchot, Leiris, and the Remains of Laure.* Newark: University of Delaware Press, 2009.

Tauchert, Ashley. *Against Transgression.* Oxford: Wiley-Blackwell, 2008.

Taussig, Michael. "Transgression." In *Critical Terms for Religious Studies*, edited by Mark C. Taylor, 349–364. Chicago: University of Chicago Press, 1998.

Taylor, Mark C. *About Religion: Economies of Faith in Virtual Culture.* Chicago: University of Chicago Press, 1999.

—. *After God.* Chicago: University of Chicago Press, 2007.

—. *Altarity.* Chicago: University of Chicago Press, 1987.

—. *Refiguring the Spiritual: Beuys, Barney, Turrell, Goldsworthy.* New York: Columbia University Press, 2012.

Teilhard de Chardin, Pierre. *The Phenomenon of Man.* New York: Harper and Row, 1965.

Toal, Catherine. "The Summit of Violence: Cruelty in the Work of Artaud, Blanchot, and Bataille." *Paroles Gelées* 18, no. 2 (2000): 64–77.

Tolsi, Niren. "FIFA Called the Shots—And We Have Said 'Yes.'" *Mail & Guardian* (June 4, 2010), http://2010.mg.co.za/article/2010-06-04-fifa-called-the -shots-and-we-said-yes.

Urban, Hugh B. "Matrix of Power: Tantra, Kingship, and Sacrifice in the Worship of Mother Goddess Kamakhya." *South Asia* 31, no. 3 (2008): 500–534.

—. "The Power of the Impure: Transgression, Violence, and Secrecy in Bengali Shakta Tantra and Modern Western Magic." In *Numen* 50, no. 3 (2003): 269–308.

—. *The Power of Tantra: Religion, Sexuality, and the Politics of South Asian Studies.* London: I. B. Tauris, 2010.

Van Kooij, K. R. *Worship of the Goddess According to the Kalikapurana.* Leiden: E. J. Brill, 1972.

Virgil. *L'Énéide.* Translated by Pierre Klossowski. Marseille: André Dimanche, 1989.

Voegelin, Salomé. *Listening to Noise and Silence: Towards a Philosophy of Sound Art.* New York: Continuum, 2010.

Wadley, Susan S. *The Powers of Tamil Women.* New York: Maxwell School of Citizenship and Public Affairs, 1980.

Weber, Max. *The Sociology of Religion.* Translated by Ephraim Fischoff. Boston: Beacon, 1963.

White, David Gordon. *Kiss of the Yogini: Tantric Sex in Its South Asian Contexts.* Chicago: University of Chicago Press, 2003.

————, ed. *Tantra in Practice*. Princeton, N.J.: Princeton University Press, 2000.

"Who Is Fat Girl?" *FaT GiRL* 1 (1994): 41.

Williams, J. Michael. *Chieftancy, the State, and Democracy: Political Legitimacy in Post-Apartheid South Africa*. Bloomington: Indiana University Press, 2010.

Winnubst, Shannon. "Bataille's Queer Pleasures: The Universe as Spider or Spit." In *Reading Bataille Now*, 75–93. Bloomington: Indiana University Press, 2007.

————. *Queering Freedom*. Bloomington: Indiana University Press, 2006.

————, ed. *Reading Bataille Now*. Bloomington: Indiana University Press, 2007.

————. "What If the Law Is Written in a Porno Book? Deterritorializing Lacan, De-Oedipalizing Deleuze and Guattari." In *Gilles Deleuze: The Intensive Reduction*. Edited by Constantin Boundas. New York: Continuum, 2009.

"You Are Cordially Invited to Join the Kitchen Slut for Dessert." *FaT GiRL* 4 (October 1995): 12–13.

Žižek, Slavoj. *First as Tragedy, Then as Farce*. New York: Verso, 2009.

————. *The Parallax View*. Cambridge, Mass.: MIT Press, 1996.

Zupančič, Alenka. *Ethics of the Real: Kant, Lacan*. New York: Verso, 2000.

Contributors

Jeremy Biles is the author of *Ecce Monstrum: Georges Bataille and the Sacrifice of Form* (Fordham, 2007). He teaches courses on religion, philosophy, and art at the School of the Art Institute of Chicago. His writings have appeared in such places as the *Journal of Religion*; *Culture, Theory, and Critique*; and *Performance Research*. A selection of his drawings, some inspired by André Masson's *Acéphale*, appeared in the 2014 group show "Baudy" at the Adds Donna Gallery in Chicago.

Kent L. Brintnall is the Bonnie E. Cone Early-Career Professor in Teaching at the University of North Carolina at Charlotte, where he is affiliated with the Department of Religious Studies and the Women's & Gender Studies Program. He is the author of *Ecce Homo: The Male-Body-in-Pain as Redemptive Figure* (University of Chicago Press, 2011). He is currently working on a monograph, tentatively entitled *Constraining Violence*, that reads Bataille alongside the theorists of antisociality and queer negativity.

Stephen S. Bush is an assistant professor of religious studies at Brown University. His interests broadly are in the theory of religion, philosophy of religion, and religious ethics. He is the author of *Visions of Religion: Experience, Meaning, and Power* (Oxford University Press, 2014) and has published essays in the *Journal of Religion, Journal of Religious Ethics, Religious Studies*, and *Philosophical Review*.

David Chidester is a professor of religious studies and the director of the Institute for Comparative Religion in Southern Africa (ICRSA) at the University of Cape Town in South Africa. He is author or editor of over twenty books in

North American studies, South African studies, and comparative studies in religion. His publications include *Savage Systems: Colonialism and Comparative Religion in Southern Africa* (University of Virginia Press, 1996); *Christianity: A Global History* (Penguin, 2000); *Salvation and Suicide: Jim Jones, the Peoples Temple, and Jonestown* (Indiana University Press, rev. ed. 2003); *Authentic Fakes: Religion and American Popular Culture* (University of California Press, 2005); *Wild Religion: Tracking the Sacred in South Africa* (University of California Press, 2012); and *Empire of Religion: Imperialism and Comparative Religion* (University of Chicago Press, 2014).

Zeynep Direk is a professor of contemporary European philosophy at Koç University, Istanbul, Turkey. She received her Ph.D. from the University of Memphis in 1998. She has published books and edited volumes on contemporary French philosophy and feminism in Turkish. Her essays in English are on Derrida, Bataille, Levinas, and feminism. She is the co-editor of *Derrida: Critical Assessments* (2001) and *A Companion to Derrida* (forthcoming, 2015).

Lynne Gerber studies American religious life in conversation with critical social theory. Her work focuses on the body, sexuality, and the construction of health in contemporary Christianity. She is the author of *Seeking the Straight and Narrow: Weight Loss and Sexual Reorientation in Evangelical America* (University of Chicago Press, 2011), a study of the moral construction of fatness and homosexuality in Christian weight-loss programs, ex-gay ministries, and American culture. Her current research focuses on a queer religious community—the Metropolitan Community Church of San Francisco—and its response to HIV/AIDS from the 1980s to the present. She is the co-chair of the Global Perspectives on Religion and HIV/AIDS seminar at the American Academy of Religion and serves on the steering committee of *Religion Dispatches*. Lynne is a research fellow at the Religion, Politics, and Globalization Program and an occasional lecturer in the Religious Studies Department at UC Berkeley.

Jean-Joseph Goux is Laurence Favrot Professor of French Studies at Rice University (emeritus). He was associated with the *Tel Quel* group in the late 1960s. Between philosophy, economy, psychoanalysis, and aesthetics, his work engages the field of "symbolic economy." He taught at the University of California (San Diego, Berkeley) and at Brown University. He was program director at the College International de Philosophie in Paris and associate director at the École des Hautes Etudes en Sciences Sociales. His books include *Symbolic Economies* (Cornell University Press, 1990), *The Coiners of Languages* (University of Oklahoma Press, 1994), and *Oedipus Philosopher* (Stanford University Press, 1993). He also has published *Frivolité de la valeur* (Blusson, 2000) and most recently *Accrochages, conflits du visuel* (Des femmes, 2007); *L'art et l'argent* (Blusson, 2011); and *Le trésor perdu de la finance folle* (Blusson, 2013).

Paul Hegarty writes on music, sound studies, and visual culture. His book *Rumour and Radiation: Sound in Video Art* is due out from Bloomsbury in late 2014. He teaches philosophy and visual culture in the Department of French, University College Cork, Ireland.

Amy Hollywood is the Elizabeth Monrad Professor of Christian Studies at Harvard Divinity School. She is the author of *The Soul as Virgin Wife: Mechthild of Magdeburg, Marguerite Porete, and Meister Eckhart* (1995); *Sensible Ecstasy: Mysticism, Sexual Difference, and the Demands of History* (2002); and *Acute Melancholia and Other Essays* (forthcoming). She is also the co-editor, with Patricia Z. Beckman, of *The Cambridge Companion to Christian Mysticism* (2012).

Mark D. Jordan teaches at Harvard in the Divinity School and in the Program for Women, Gender, and Sexuality. His most recent book is *Convulsing Bodies: Religion and Resistance in Foucault* (Stanford University Press, 2014).

Jeffrey J. Kripal holds the J. Newton Rayzor Chair in Philosophy and Religious Thought at Rice University and is the associate director of the Center for Theory and Research at Esalen Institute in Big Sur, California. He is the author of seven books, including: *Comparing Religions: Coming to Terms* (Wiley-Blackwell, 2014); *Authors of the Impossible: The Paranormal and the Sacred* (Chicago, 2010); and *Esalen: America and the Religion of No Religion* (Chicago, 2007). Jeff is a historian of religions who specializes in the comparison of extreme religious experiences and anomalous events across space and time.

Alphonso Lingis is professor of philosophy emeritus at Pennsylvania State University. Among his books are *Excesses: Eros and Culture* (1984), *Deathbound Subjectivity* (1989), *The Community of Those Who Have Nothing in Common* (1994), *Abuses* (1994), *Dangerous Emotions* (2000), *Trust* (2004), *Body Transformations: Evolutions and Atavisms in Culture* (2005), *Contact* (2010), and *Violence and Splendor* (2011).

Allan Stoekl is professor of French and comparative literature at Penn State University. He is the author of *Agonies of the Intellectual* and *Bataille's Peak: Energy, Religion, and Postsustainability* and the translator of Bataille's *Visions of Excess: Selected Writings, 1927–1939* (Minnesota, 1985).

Hugh B. Urban is a professor of religious studies in the Department of Comparative Studies at Ohio State University. He is primarily interested in the role of secrecy in religion, particularly in relation to questions of knowledge and power. He is the author of seven books, including *Tantra: Sex, Secrecy, Politics and Power in the Study of Religion* (2003) and *Magia Sexualis: Sex, Magic and Liberation in Modern Western Esotericism* (2006).

Shannon Winnubst is a core faculty member in the Department of Women's, Gender, and Sexuality Studies at Ohio State University. She has published widely in twentieth-century French theory, especially on Bataille, Foucault, and Lacan, as well as on topics in queer theory, race theory, and feminist theory. The author of *Queering Freedom* (2006) and editor of *Reading Bataille Now* (2007), she just completed *Way Too Cool: Neoliberalism, Social Difference, and Ethics.*

Index

abject/abjection, 3, 9, 20, 22, 26, 182, 187, 189–190, 192–194, 274n23
Acéphale (image), 4, 132, 175, 177, 217–218, 237–238
Acéphale (journal), 4, 175–176, 217, 246n10, 281n97
Acéphale (secret society), 4, 128, 175–175, 181, 246n25, 272n27, 281n97
The Accursed Share, 6, 23, 25, 43–45, 59, 95–96, 108, 124, 128, 133, 186–191, 247n30, 267n21
Agamben, Giorgio, 9, 242
Akita, Masam. *See* Merzbow
Altizer, Thomas J. J., 203
Andolsen, Barbara, 40–41, 47, 50
anthropology, 7, 10, 138–152
anxiety, 19–37, 146–147, 190, 252n78
art, 6, 8, 17, 43, 46, 55–56, 96–97, 201, 249n71, 255n12
Artaud, Antonin, 42–43, 185
atheology, 68
Aztecs, 43, 95, 148

barebacking, 15, 51–68, 254n6, 255n12, 257n38, 257n57, 258n66, 259n80, 259n85
Barthes, Roland, 8, 208

Bataille's absence, 11–13
Benjamin, Walter, 113–114, 242
Bersani, Leo, 10–11, 34–35, 52–57, 62–67, 281n1
Biles, Jeremy (*Ecce Monstrum*), 28, 40, 277n23
Blanchot, Maurice, 42–43, 46, 169, 172, 272n16, 281n95
Blue of Noon, 173, 256n34
Borel, Adrien, 3, 233–234
Breton, André, 2, 5, 8, 219, 222, 224–233, 235, 277n23, 277n25
Brintnall, Kent (*Ecce Homo*), 39, 259n80, 256n35, 260n108, 279n77
Buddhism, 69, 99
Butler, Judith, 47–48

Caillois, Roger, 4, 175, 177
Calvin/Calvinism, 115, 125–127, 129–130, 132, 263n8
capitalism, 10, 20–21, 24, 95, 106–122, 250n46
Caputo, John, 11–12
Catholicism, 2, 9–10, 109–110, 119–122, 126, 129–130, 132, 157, 178–179, 202
Chinese torture victim. See *lingchi*

Christianity, 2–3, 5, 63, 68–69, 95, 109–110, 112–113, 161, 183
College of Sociology, 4, 12, 176–177, 246n22
communication, 4–5, 33, 39, 49, 140, 143, 149, 186
community, 9, 150, 176, 180, 246n19, 247n35, 281n7
compassion, 44
Connor, Peter, 13–14
consumption, 14, 21
continuity, 7, 24, 55–56, 158, 186
corpses, 148
crucifixion, 13, 63, 147, 157, 178–79, 234, 240–241
cruising, 62–66, 260n107

Dean, Tim, 10–11, 51–52, 57–66
death, 2, 4, 7, 22–23, 28, 31–33, 34, 36–37, 101, 158–159, 182, 242–243, 251n54, 252n60
death drive, 8, 56
death of God, 2, 6, 9–12, 68, 171–174, 202–216
de Beauvoir, Simone, 13, 38
Deleuze, Gilles, 9, 68, 185, 210, 273n4
Democratic Communist Circle, 5
Derrida, Jacques, 8, 9, 58, 242
dialectic, 2, 171–172
dieting, 19, 26–27, 32–33
Dionysus/Dionysian, 2, 4, 173, 217–218, 238
Discipline and Punish, 177–181
discontinuity, 7, 24, 220
disgust, 19–37. *See also* abject/abjection
Divine (performer), 28–30
Documents, 3, 246n17, 277n24
dramatization, 98, 101
dread. *See* anxiety
dream/dreams, 217–238, 276n18
Durkheim, Émile, 4, 7, 28, 83, 144, 150, 176, 219–221

economics, 6, 10–11, 82–83, 106–107, 111–112. *See also* general economy
ecstasy/ecstatic, 1, 4–7, 13, 39, 44, 48, 51, 98, 140–143, 236–237, 240
ego. *See* self

erotic/eroticism, 1, 5–6, 23, 30–31, 51, 54–55, 61–62, 69, 133–134, 148, 153–154, 158–159, 172, 187, 191, 214–216, 220, 255n15, 259n85, 260n108, 262n29, 274n7
Erotism, 6, 42–43, 46–47, 79, 96, 153–154, 157–158, 161, 171, 186, 190–191
ethics, 38–50, 53–55, 59, 62, 98, 125, 128, 132, 135–137, 242
excess, 1–2, 16, 20–22, 24–25, 102, 188, 249n26
expenditure, 6, 14, 23–26, 82–83, 87–90, 147–148, 188, 220

fascism, 5, 14, 175, 180–181, 193–195
fat, 14–15, 19–37
FaT GiRL, 29–31, 24–25, 251n53
festival, 6, 23, 87–90, 189
football, 81–94
Foucault, Michel, 8–9, 68, 79, 124, 127, 133, 169–181, 266n1, 266n2, 266n4, 271n2, 271n5
Freud, Sigmund, 5, 8, 13, 53, 132, 161, 219, 224, 227–229, 232, 235–236, 276n13, 276n19, 280n86
Friedman, Milton, 116–117
formless. *See informe*
future/futurity, 7, 45. *See also* goal-oriented; project

gambling, 6
Geertz, Clifford, 144–145
gender, 40, 70, 78–80, 245n1, 248n62, 259n80
general economy, 6, 9, 15–17, 59, 188, 247n30, 249n19
gift, 15, 57–59, 248n47, 258n68
Gilder, George, 116–117
goal-oriented, 7, 24. *See also* future/futurity; project
Guilty, 6, 54–55, 96, 98, 237

Habermas, Jürgen, 10
health, 21
Health at Every Size, 21
Hegel, G. W. F., 2, 9, 130, 159, 183–184, 198, 203, 205–207, 224, 275n8
Heidegger, Martin, 10–11, 25, 97, 248n53

heterogeneity, 3, 16, 199
heterology, 230–232
Hinduism, 14, 68–80, 161–163
Hiroshima, 25, 27, 242
History of Sexuality, 170–171
Hocquenghem, Guy, 9
Hollywood, Amy (*Sensible Ecstasy*), 11–13, 36, 39, 68, 135–136, 279n77
Hussey, Andrew, 13–14, 69
Huxley, Aldous, 163–165

impossible, 4–6, 11, 98
individual. *See* self
informe, 8, 97
inner experience, 2, 4, 13, 28, 33–34, 44–45, 66, 96–98, 130, 138, 153–154, 158
Inner Experience, 5–6, 43–44, 65–66, 96–98, 178–179, 236, 281n2
instrumentalization, 7, 11–12, 39, 60–62, 64–66, 241, 247n43
Internet, 213–216
intimacy, 4, 7, 24–25, 30, 33, 38, 55, 61–62, 86–87, 106, 130
Irigaray, Luce, 13, 79
Irwin, Alexander (*Saints of the Impossible*), 12, 14, 28, 39–40, 250n47

James, William, 159, 163
jouissance, 13, 53–55, 137, 240, 255n25

Kali, 69, 161–62
Kamakhya, 69–73, 79–80
Kierkegaard, Søren, 130, 203
Klossowski, Pierre, 4, 169–172, 174–175, 177, 272n16, 272n29, 274n4
Kosky, Jeffrey, 12
Kristeva, Julia, 8–9, 182–201

L'Abbe C, 171, 174
Lacan, Jacques, 12, 127, 134–138, 184, 241, 256n25, 267n6, 268n35
laughter, 1, 6, 105, 188
Laure, 5, 246n26
left-hand sacred, 38, 31, 72–73, 219, 221–222, 238. *See also* sacred
Leiris, Michel, 3–4, 169, 173–174, 176–177, 245n6

limit/limits, 4, 6, 170–171, 185, 210
lingchi, 3, 44, 97, 135–136, 147, 177, 234, 239–243, 246n12, 281n2, 281n5, 281n8
loss of self. *See* self-dissolution
Luther, 126–127, 129, 130, 132, 267n8

Madame Edwarda, 171, 183, 208–210, 215–216
madness, 2
Marion, Jean-Luc, 11
Marshall Plan, 25, 27
Marx/Marxism, 5, 24, 110, 121, 187
Masson, André, 3–4, 132, 175, 237
Mauss, Marcel, 15, 57–58, 139, 176, 187, 248n47
McWhorter, Ladelle, 79–80
meditation, 3, 5, 38, 44, 49, 96–97, 234, 241, 261n5
menstrual blood/menstruation, 69, 71–75, 78, 80, 148, 262n15, 262n31
Merzbow, 97, 102–105
"Method of Meditation," 96
military society, 60–61
monster/monstrosity/monstrous, 3–4, 22–23, 27–29, 217, 262n31
Morris, Paul, 59–61, 258n76
My Mother, 197
mysticism, 2–3, 5–6, 11, 13–14, 28, 53, 68, 96, 138, 142, 153, 156, 158, 160, 255n15

Nancy, Jean-Luc, 9
National Association for the Advancement of Fat Acceptance, 21
negative, negativity, 1–18 *passim*, 183–185, 198, 200, 205–206
negative theology, 11, 158
Nelson, Robert H., 116–118
neoliberalism, 10, 18, 21–22, 123–137, 266n11, 266n2
Nietzsche, Friedrich, 2–5, 10–11, 99, 110, 169, 172–175, 202, 221–222, 246n9
"Nietzsche Dionysus," 217
noise, 15, 99–102
noise music, 8, 97–105
nonknowledge, 211, 214, 236
nudity, 99–100

On Nietzsche, 6

Peignot, Colette. *See* Laure
poetry, 1, 6, 49, 96
politics, 5, 10, 12–14, 17, 22–23, 31, 34–
    37, 47–48, 53, 59, 66–67, 198–201,
    242–243, 246n23, 252n78, 274n23
pornography, 213–216
potlatch, 58, 187
Powers of Horror, 191–195, 274n23
"Preface to Transgression," 8–9, 169–175
prefaces, 171, 271n9
production, 23–24
profane, 1, 4, 7, 18
project, 7, 39, 60–61, 96
Protestantism, 24, 26, 109–110, 115–116,
    120–122, 124–127, 180, 267n8
psychoanalysis, 3–4, 7, 56, 176, 192,
    259n88, 276n19, 280n85

queer/queer theory, 9–11, 34–35, 248n48,
    268n32, 275n47, 281n1

Ramakrishna, Shri, 69, 161–162, 166,
reason, 7, 11, 18, 24, 98, 139, 141–142, 150
religion, 1, 4, 10, 13, 16–17, 19, 51, 81, 95,
    106–107, 112–114, 121, 124–125, 130–
    131, 151–152, 169–170, 175, 179–186,
    188, 190–192, 195–197, 242–244,
    271n4, 271n5, 274n7, 281n7
religious studies, 7, 13, 15–18, 157
revolt/revolution, 199–201
Richman, Michèle, 12
Ring, Kenneth, 166–167
Rotello, Gabriel, 258n76

sacred, 1–5, 7–8, 11, 15, 19, 22, 26–27,
    43–44, 51, 86, 92–95, 130–132, 186,
    189, 219–221. *See also* left-hand sacred
"Sacred Conspiracy," 132
sacrifice, 1, 4, 6–7, 18, 22–24, 38, 43, 60,
    62, 68–69, 72–74, 83–87, 106, 108,
    128–130, 138–139, 142, 150–151, 160,
    220, 259n85, 262n29
de Sade, Marquis D. A. F., 5, 38–39, 42,
    46–47, 98, 172–173, 204–205, 207,
    275n8, 276n4
secular/secularization, 108–111

self, 1, 7, 9, 220
self-affirmation/self-assertion, 41–42,
    45–46, 48, 50, 52, 54, 57, 62, 64–65
self-dissolution/self-loss/self-negation/
    self-shattering, 1, 4–5, 10, 12–15, 24,
    39, 40–41, 43–46, 48, 50–51, 53–56,
    62, 66–67, 70, 77, 96–97, 217, 219,
    236–237, 240–241, 253n32, 255n15,
    262n39
sex/sexuality. *See* erotic/eroticism
silence, 8, 97–101, 172
social, 5, 151
sociology, 4–5, 7, 10, 138–152, 176–177,
    248n66
La somme atheologique, 6, 96, 241, 247n29
Sontag, Susan, 230
South Africa, 81–94
sovereign/sovereignty, 6–7, 44–45,
    48–49, 88–89, 143, 148, 188–189, 220,
    241–243, 247n38
Stinson, Susan, 28–30
Stoekl, Allan, 14, 25–26
Story of the Eye, 1, 43, 174, 206, 208, 245n1
Streiber, Whitley, 166
surrealism, 2–5, 8, 3, 219, 223–226,
    247n44, 277n23

Tantra, 15, 68–80, 97–98, 161–162, 261n5,
    261n6, 262n29
Taussig, Michael, 68
Taylor, Mark C., 13, 202–203, 210–211
Tears of Eros, 3, 6, 97, 171, 240, 281n8
Teilhard de Chardin, Pierre, 12–14,
    153–168, 191, 242
Theory of Religion, 68, 113, 128, 185–186,
    267n21
torture, 3, 38, 44, 49, 97, 135–136,
    177–179
torture photo. See *lingchi*
transgression, 7–8, 13, 16, 18, 23–24, 69,
    70, 75–78, 95, 132–133, 147, 171–172,
    183, 188–189, 262n39
Trial of Gilles de Rais, 44

unconscious, 5, 61, 218–219, 222,
    224–225, 232, 259n88, 277n23
utility, 6, 23–27, 133, 139, 141, 150,
    185–186, 219

On Nietzsche, 6

Peignot, Colette. *See* Laure
poetry, 1, 6, 49, 96
politics, 5, 10, 12–14, 17, 22–23, 31, 34–37, 47–48, 53, 59, 66–67, 198–201, 242–243, 246n23, 252n78, 274n23
pornography, 213–216
potlatch, 58, 187
Powers of Horror, 191–195, 274n23
"Preface to Transgression," 8–9, 169–175
prefaces, 171, 271n9
production, 23–24
profane, 1, 4, 7, 18
project, 7, 39, 60–61, 96
Protestantism, 24, 26, 109–110, 115–116, 120–122, 124–127, 180, 267n8
psychoanalysis, 3–4, 7, 56, 176, 192, 259n88, 276n19, 280n85
queer/queer theory, 9–11, 34–35, 248n48, 268n32, 275n47, 281n1
Ramakrishna, Shri, 69, 161–162, 166,
reason, 7, 11, 18, 24, 98, 139, 141–142, 150
religion, 1, 4, 10, 13, 16–17, 19, 51, 81, 95, 106–107, 112–114, 121, 124–125, 130–131, 151–152, 169–170, 175, 179–186, 188, 190–192, 195–197, 242–244, 271n4, 271n5, 274n7, 281n7
religious studies, 7, 13, 15–18, 157
revolt/revolution, 199–201
Richman, Michèle, 12
Ring, Kenneth, 166–167
Rotello, Gabriel, 258n76
sacred, 1–5, 7–8, 11, 15, 19, 22, 26–27, 43–44, 51, 86, 92–95, 130–132, 186, 189, 219–221. *See also* left-hand sacred
"Sacred Conspiracy," 132
sacrifice, 1, 4, 6–7, 18, 22–24, 38, 43, 60, 62, 68–69, 72–74, 83–87, 106, 108, 128–130, 138–139, 142, 150–151, 160, 220, 259n85, 262n29
de Sade, Marquis D. A. F., 5, 38–39, 42, 46–47, 98, 172–173, 204–205, 207, 275n8, 276n4
secular/secularization, 108–111
self, 1, 7, 9, 220
self-affirmation/self-assertion, 41–42, 45–46, 48, 50, 52, 54, 57, 62, 64–65
self-dissolution/self-loss/self-negation/self-shattering, 1, 4–5, 10, 12–15, 24, 39, 40–41, 43–46, 48, 50–51, 53–56, 62, 66–67, 70, 77, 96–97, 217, 219, 236–237, 240–241, 253n32, 255n15, 262n39
sex/sexuality. *See* erotic/eroticism
silence, 8, 97–101, 172
social, 5, 151
sociology, 4–5, 7, 10, 138–152, 176–177, 248n66
La somme atheologique, 6, 96, 241, 247n29
Sontag, Susan, 230
South Africa, 81–94
sovereign/sovereignty, 6–7, 44–45, 48–49, 88–89, 143, 148, 188–189, 220, 241–243, 247n38
Stinson, Susan, 28–30
Stoekl, Allan, 14, 25–26
Story of the Eye, 1, 43, 174, 206, 208, 245n1
Streiber, Whitley, 166
surrealism, 2–5, 8, 3, 219, 223–226, 247n44, 277n23
Tantra, 15, 68–80, 97–98, 161–162, 261n5, 261n6, 262n29
Taussig, Michael, 68
Taylor, Mark C., 13, 202–203, 210–211
Tears of Eros, 3, 6, 97, 171, 240, 281n8
Teilhard de Chardin, Pierre, 12–14, 153–168, 191, 242
Theory of Religion, 68, 113, 128, 185–186, 267n21
torture, 3, 38, 44, 49, 97, 135–136, 177–179
torture photo. See *lingchi*
transgression, 7–8, 13, 16, 18, 23–24, 69, 70, 75–78, 95, 132–133, 147, 171–172, 183, 188–189, 262n39
Trial of Gilles de Rais, 44
unconscious, 5, 61, 218–219, 222, 224–225, 232, 259n88, 277n23
utility, 6, 23–27, 133, 139, 141, 150, 185–186, 219

violence, 1, 11–12, 14, 23, 38–50, 51, 54, 250n47, 267n20
virtual reality, 10, 211, 213–216

war, 27, 151
Weber, Max, 95, 107, 109, 111, 126, 151, 267n8

Weil, Simone, 14
work. *See* goal-oriented; project; utility
World Cup, 81–94
World War II, 5–6, 12, 14, 96, 241
wound/wounded, 2, 4, 6, 38, 245n8

Perspectives in Continental Philosophy

John D. Caputo, series editor

John D. Caputo, ed., *Deconstruction in a Nutshell: A Conversation with Jacques Derrida.*

Michael Strawser, *Both/And: Reading Kierkegaard—From Irony to Edification.*

Michael D. Barber, *Ethical Hermeneutics: Rationality in Enrique Dussel's Philosophy of Liberation.*

James H. Olthuis, ed., *Knowing Other-wise: Philosophy at the Threshold of Spirituality.*

James Swindal, *Reflection Revisited: Jürgen Habermas's Discursive Theory of Truth.*

Richard Kearney, *Poetics of Imagining: Modern and Postmodern.* Second edition.

Thomas W. Busch, *Circulating Being: From Embodiment to Incorporation—Essays on Late Existentialism.*

Edith Wyschogrod, *Emmanuel Levinas: The Problem of Ethical Metaphysics.* Second edition.

Francis J. Ambrosio, ed., *The Question of Christian Philosophy Today.*

Jeffrey Bloechl, ed., *The Face of the Other and the Trace of God: Essays on the Philosophy of Emmanuel Levinas.*

Ilse N. Bulhof and Laurens ten Kate, eds., *Flight of the Gods: Philosophical Perspectives on Negative Theology.*

Trish Glazebrook, *Heidegger's Philosophy of Science.*

Kevin Hart, *The Trespass of the Sign: Deconstruction, Theology, and Philosophy.*

Mark C. Taylor, *Journeys to Selfhood: Hegel and Kierkegaard.* Second edition.

Dominique Janicaud, Jean-François Courtine, Jean-Louis Chrétien, Michel Henry, Jean-Luc Marion, and Paul Ricoeur, *Phenomenology and the "Theological Turn": The French Debate.*

Karl Jaspers, *The Question of German Guilt*. Introduction by Joseph W. Koterski, S.J.

Jean-Luc Marion, *The Idol and Distance: Five Studies*. Translated with an introduction by Thomas A. Carlson.

Jeffrey Dudiak, *The Intrigue of Ethics: A Reading of the Idea of Discourse in the Thought of Emmanuel Levinas*.

Robyn Horner, *Rethinking God as Gift: Marion, Derrida, and the Limits of Phenomenology*.

Mark Dooley, *The Politics of Exodus: Søren Kierkegaard's Ethics of Responsibility*.

Merold Westphal, *Overcoming Onto-Theology: Toward a Postmodern Christian Faith*.

Edith Wyschogrod, Jean-Joseph Goux, and Eric Boynton, eds., *The Enigma of Gift and Sacrifice*.

Stanislas Breton, *The Word and the Cross*. Translated with an introduction by Jacquelyn Porter.

Jean-Luc Marion, *Prolegomena to Charity*. Translated by Stephen E. Lewis.

Peter H. Spader, *Scheler's Ethical Personalism: Its Logic, Development, and Promise*.

Jean-Louis Chrétien, *The Unforgettable and the Unhoped For*. Translated by Jeffrey Bloechl.

Don Cupitt, *Is Nothing Sacred? The Non-Realist Philosophy of Religion: Selected Essays*.

Jean-Luc Marion, *In Excess: Studies of Saturated Phenomena*. Translated by Robyn Horner and Vincent Berraud.

Phillip Goodchild, *Rethinking Philosophy of Religion: Approaches from Continental Philosophy*.

William J. Richardson, S.J., *Heidegger: Through Phenomenology to Thought*.

Jeffrey Andrew Barash, *Martin Heidegger and the Problem of Historical Meaning*.

Jean-Louis Chrétien, *Hand to Hand: Listening to the Work of Art*. Translated by Stephen E. Lewis.

Jean-Louis Chrétien, *The Call and the Response*. Translated with an introduction by Anne Davenport.

D. C. Schindler, *Han Urs von Balthasar and the Dramatic Structure of Truth: A Philosophical Investigation*.

Julian Wolfreys, ed., *Thinking Difference: Critics in Conversation*.

Allen Scult, *Being Jewish/Reading Heidegger: An Ontological Encounter*.

Richard Kearney, *Debates in Continental Philosophy: Conversations with Contemporary Thinkers*.

Jennifer Anna Gosetti-Ferencei, *Heidegger, Hölderlin, and the Subject of Poetic Language: Toward a New Poetics of Dasein*.

Jolita Pons, *Stealing a Gift: Kierkegaard's Pseudonyms and the Bible*.

Jean-Yves Lacoste, *Experience and the Absolute: Disputed Questions on the Humanity of Man*. Translated by Mark Raftery-Skehan.

Charles P. Bigger, *Between Chora and the Good: Metaphor's Metaphysical Neighborhood*.

Dominique Janicaud, *Phenomenology "Wide Open": After the French Debate.* Translated by Charles N. Cabral.

Ian Leask and Eoin Cassidy, eds., *Givenness and God: Questions of Jean-Luc Marion.*

Jacques Derrida, *Sovereignties in Question: The Poetics of Paul Celan.* Edited by Thomas Dutoit and Outi Pasanen.

William Desmond, *Is There a Sabbath for Thought? Between Religion and Philosophy.*

Bruce Ellis Benson and Norman Wirzba, eds., *The Phenomenology of Prayer.*

S. Clark Buckner and Matthew Statler, eds., *Styles of Piety: Practicing Philosophy after the Death of God.*

Kevin Hart and Barbara Wall, eds., *The Experience of God: A Postmodern Response.*

John Panteleimon Manoussakis, *After God: Richard Kearney and the Religious Turn in Continental Philosophy.*

John Martis, *Philippe Lacoue-Labarthe: Representation and the Loss of the Subject.*

Jean-Luc Nancy, *The Ground of the Image.*

Edith Wyschogrod, *Crossover Queries: Dwelling with Negatives, Embodying Philosophy's Others.*

Gerald Bruns, *On the Anarchy of Poetry and Philosophy: A Guide for the Unruly.*

Brian Treanor, *Aspects of Alterity: Levinas, Marcel, and the Contemporary Debate.*

Simon Morgan Wortham, *Counter-Institutions: Jacques Derrida and the Question of the University.*

Leonard Lawlor, *The Implications of Immanence: Toward a New Concept of Life.*

Clayton Crockett, *Interstices of the Sublime: Theology and Psychoanalytic Theory.*

Bettina Bergo, Joseph Cohen, and Raphael Zagury-Orly, eds., *Judeities: Questions for Jacques Derrida.* Translated by Bettina Bergo and Michael B. Smith.

Jean-Luc Marion, *On the Ego and on God: Further Cartesian Questions.* Translated by Christina M. Gschwandtner.

Jean-Luc Nancy, *Philosophical Chronicles.* Translated by Franson Manjali.

Jean-Luc Nancy, *Dis-Enclosure: The Deconstruction of Christianity.* Translated by Bettina Bergo, Gabriel Malenfant, and Michael B. Smith.

Andrea Hurst, *Derrida Vis-à-vis Lacan: Interweaving Deconstruction and Psychoanalysis.*

Jean-Luc Nancy, *Noli me tangere: On the Raising of the Body.* Translated by Sarah Clift, Pascale-Anne Brault, and Michael Naas.

Jacques Derrida, *The Animal That Therefore I Am.* Edited by Marie-Louise Mallet, translated by David Wills.

Jean-Luc Marion, *The Visible and the Revealed.* Translated by Christina M. Gschwandtner and others.

Michel Henry, *Material Phenomenology.* Translated by Scott Davidson.

Jean-Luc Nancy, *Corpus.* Translated by Richard A. Rand.

Joshua Kates, *Fielding Derrida.*

Michael Naas, *Derrida From Now On.*

Shannon Sullivan and Dennis J. Schmidt, eds., *Difficulties of Ethical Life.*

Catherine Malabou, *What Should We Do with Our Brain?* Translated by Sebastian Rand, Introduction by Marc Jeannerod.

Claude Romano, *Event and World.* Translated by Shane Mackinlay.

Vanessa Lemm, *Nietzsche's Animal Philosophy: Culture, Politics, and the Animality of the Human Being.*

B. Keith Putt, ed., *Gazing Through a Prism Darkly: Reflections on Merold Westphal's Hermeneutical Epistemology.*

Eric Boynton and Martin Kavka, eds., *Saintly Influence: Edith Wyschogrod and the Possibilities of Philosophy of Religion.*

Shane Mackinlay, *Interpreting Excess: Jean-Luc Marion, Saturated Phenomena, and Hermeneutics.*

Kevin Hart and Michael A. Signer, eds., *The Exorbitant: Emmanuel Levinas Between Jews and Christians.*

Bruce Ellis Benson and Norman Wirzba, eds., *Words of Life: New Theological Turns in French Phenomenology.*

William Robert, *Trials: Of Antigone and Jesus.*

Brian Treanor and Henry Isaac Venema, eds., *A Passion for the Possible: Thinking with Paul Ricoeur.*

Kas Saghafi, *Apparitions—Of Derrida's Other.*

Nick Mansfield, *The God Who Deconstructs Himself: Sovereignty and Subjectivity Between Freud, Bataille, and Derrida.*

Don Ihde, *Heidegger's Technologies: Postphenomenological Perspectives.*

Suzi Adams, *Castoriadis's Ontology: Being and Creation.*

Richard Kearney and Kascha Semonovitch, eds., *Phenomenologies of the Stranger: Between Hostility and Hospitality.*

Michael Naas, *Miracle and Machine: Jacques Derrida and the Two Sources of Religion, Science, and the Media.*

Alena Alexandrova, Ignaas Devisch, Laurens ten Kate, and Aukje van Rooden, *Re-treating Religion: Deconstructing Christianity with Jean-Luc Nancy.* Preamble by Jean-Luc Nancy.

Emmanuel Falque, *The Metamorphosis of Finitude: An Essay on Birth and Resurrection.* Translated by George Hughes.

Scott M. Campbell, *The Early Heidegger's Philosophy of Life: Facticity, Being, and Language.*

Françoise Dastur, *How Are We to Confront Death? An Introduction to Philosophy.* Translated by Robert Vallier. Foreword by David Farrell Krell.

Christina M. Gschwandtner, *Postmodern Apologetics? Arguments for God in Contemporary Philosophy.*

Ben Morgan, *On Becoming God: Late Medieval Mysticism and the Modern Western Self.*

Neal DeRoo, *Futurity in Phenomenology: Promise and Method in Husserl, Levinas, and Derrida.*

Sarah LaChance Adams and Caroline R. Lundquist, eds., *Coming to Life: Philosophies of Pregnancy, Childbirth, and Mothering.*

Thomas Claviez, ed., *The Conditions of Hospitality: Ethics, Politics, and Aesthetics on the Threshold of the Possible.*

Roland Faber and Jeremy Fackenthal, eds., *Theopoetic Folds: Philosophizing Multifariousness.*

Jean-Luc Marion, *The Essential Writings.* Edited by Kevin Hart.

Adam S. Miller, *Speculative Grace: Bruno Latour and Object-Oriented Theology.* Foreword by Levi R. Bryant.

Jean-Luc Nancy, *Corpus II: Writings on Sexuality.*

David Nowell Smith, *Sounding/Silence: Martin Heidegger at the Limits of Poetics.*

Gregory C. Stallings, Manuel Asensi, and Carl Good, eds., *Material Spirit: Religion and Literature Intranscendent.*

Claude Romano, *Event and Time.* Translated by Stephen E. Lewis.

Frank Chouraqui, *Ambiguity and the Absolute: Nietzsche and Merleau-Ponty on the Question of Truth.*

Noëlle Vahanian, *The Rebellious No: Variations on a Secular Theology of Language.*

Michael Naas, *The End of the World and Other Teachable Moments: Jacques Derrida's Final Seminar.*

Jean-Louis Chrétien, *Under the Gaze of the Bible.* Translated by John Marson Dunaway.

Edward Baring and Peter E. Gordon, eds., *The Trace of God: Derrida and Religion.*

Vanessa Lemm, ed., *Nietzsche and the Becoming of Life.*

Aaron T. Looney, *Vladimir Jankélévitch: The Time of Forgiveness.*

Robert Mugerauer, *Responding to Loss: Heideggerian Reflections on Literature, Architecture, and Film.*

Tarek R. Dika and W. Chris Hackett, *Quiet Powers of the Possible: Interviews in Contemporary French Phenomenology.* Foreword by Richard Kearney.

Jeremy Biles and Kent L. Brintnall, eds., *Negative Ecstasies: Georges Bataille and the Study of Religion.*

Richard Kearney and Brian Treanor, eds., *Carnal Hermeneutics.*